Group Psychotherapy
Second Edition

Group Psychotherapy

Theory and Practice

Second Edition

Hugh Mullan
and
Max Rosenbaum

THE FREE PRESS
A Division of Macmillan Publishing Co., Inc.
NEW YORK

Collier Macmillan Publishers
LONDON

The Free Press
A Division of Macmillan Publishing Co., Inc.
866 Third Avenue, New York, N.Y. 10022

Collier Macmillan Canada, Ltd.

Library of Congress Catalog Card Number: 78–3208

Printed in the United States of America

printing number

1 2 3 4 5 6 7 8 9 10

Library of Congress Cataloging in Publication Data

Mullan, Hugh.
    Group psychotherapy.

    Bibliography: p.
    Includes index.
    1. Group psychotherapy. I. Rosenbaum, Max
joint author. II. Title.
RC488.M8 1978   616.8'915   78–3208
ISBN 0–02–922080–7

Figures 1 through 7 (Chapter 14) are from *Own Your Own Life* and originally appeared in the McKay and Bantam editions. They are reproduced here with the permission of Dr. Abell and Quicksilver Books, Inc. Copyright © 1976 by Richard G.
Abell, M.D., Ph.D., with Corlis Wilber Abell.

To Barbara, Virginia, Mary, and Eleanor—
companions of my youth, and to Meghan,
Jason, and Caitlin—energizers now and
into the future
   Hugh Mullan

To my wife, Belle
   Max Rosenbaum

Contents

Part III: Alternative Methods of Group Psychotherapy

Preface

THIS BOOK BRINGS together diverse, but related, trends and methods in the expanding field of group psychotherapy. In its overall conception and planning the volume attempts the following: (1) to indicate the significance of the group psychoanalytic approach to patients and (2) to describe not only a psychoanalytic method but also systems and procedures with different emphases and different goals, which are representative of the mushrooming group field today.

This collaboration by two authors and eight contributors defines and describes the therapy group. By combining theory and method, we hope to challenge the reader's customary way of conducting and understandning his treatment approach, and to stimulate him to take a new look at his professional activity. The beginning group therapist is asked to study carefully the methods presented in this synthesis, pick out a sound basis for his current work in the group, and then carefully select a method that is suitable to him and his patients. This book does not propose to offer either a new or a single system of treatment with its own conceptualizations and semantics.

In 1962, upon publication of the first edition of *Group Psychotherapy: Theory and Practice*, we both naively believed that a full account of the practice of group therapy had been rendered. We had offered a book based upon sound principles of individual and group dynamics and of strict clinical observation. Now, sixteen years later, we and our contributors find that treatment methods have been tellingly influenced by the many events that have transpired in our world, the many stimulations and challenges emanating from our professional circle, and our experiences with patients, family, and friends.

As the form and method of group therapy changed during the sixties and early seventies, its use greatly expanded. The overworked mental health specialist, struggling to reduce his/her long waiting lists of patients, found group therapy a most useful tool. Today, group therapy is almost the only psychological method offered to hospitalized patients and to those patients returned to the community. Much of this treatment is inadequate because it is being performed by poorly trained, unsupervised persons. Budget-minded clinical directors and administrators improperly rely upon the group method because of its inexpense. Eight to ten times the number of patients can be seen in groups than in individual sessions. Thus, while keeping the number of therapists constant, the number of therapist-patient hours extends tenfold. These are but two examples of the improper use of the group method. Group psychotherapy practiced without skill, sensitivity, or understanding can do harm to those whom we are supposed to help. Good will is not enough.

Over the years the authors and contributors of this volume have been engaged in training. We all attest to the fact that, as compared with other disciplines, there is in the field of group treatment no generally accepted specific training program. (Couple therapy and family therapy are also neglected.) We are aware that pre-service training in the fields of psychology, psychiatry, and social work do not prepare the student for the role of psychotherapist. Most training in group therapy, therefore, has still to be on an individually determined basis, a make-shift process at best with courses, workshops, and supervision left to the students' decision. Post-degree training schools in group psychotherapy are still few and far between. And where these institutes do exist, there is no requirement that the inexperienced therapist attend.

We fully realize the rapid progress in the field of group psychotherapy. However, our concern for patients mounts because there is no corresponding rapid development of standards in the field. In our view, it is neither old fashioned nor nonscientific to attempt to base the practice of group therapy on an ethical foundation. Where lacking, standards of professional conduct should be established. Without this regulatory device, we are faced with many kinds of deficiencies: poorly trained therapists conduct groups of patients, the least experienced therapists in institutions often treat the sickest patients, and the training needs of students come before the treatment needs of patients. Patients, in some instances behind one-way screens, are exposed to the curious student and to others, who sometimes neither have responsibility nor compassion for the group members. This book suggests that the question of ethics be raised, described, and supported by those of us involved in training. In addition, professional organizations devoted to group psychotherapy should continue their efforts to raise standards and require more rigorous training.

Part I and Part II of this book, "Introduction" and "The Psychoanalytic Method and Innovations," are a revised and broadened version of the previous edition. In Parts I and II, Chapters 2, 3, 7, and 8 are new, while the others have been carefully rewritten indicating that through the contributions of both patients and colleagues we have altered our perspectives and to a degree changed our methods and conclusions. However, in

Parts I and II, we again state our own preference for a group treatment based upon psychoanalytic principles—one that promotes careful personality regression in members followed by their own reconstructive struggle supported and enhanced by a closely knit group where each member and therapist plays his/her part. In this connection, our basic beliefs are still unchanged although our emphasis and the manner in which we elicit the therapeutic experience are now quite different.

Part III of this book, "Alternative Methods of Group Psychotherapy," indicates eight important approaches by the contributors which characterize methods currently practiced today, in addition to the more traditional psychoanalytic method. The significance of these diverse approaches is that each brings about change in the group patient although in each instance a different format, emphasis, technique, and even goal are espoused. Perhaps if the reader pays attention to this fact of *patient change,* he can discover the common ingredient which prevails in all methods.

Part III considers the systems of art therapy, core-Energetic therapy, transactional analysis, Gestalt therapy, encounter therapy, sexual modification treatment, psychodrama, and Existential therapy all as applied to the group and to the individual members in a group. These prevalent schemes with their hypotheses represent the present-day trends and practices within the field of group psychotherapy. The reader will note the similarities which exist among all of these methods and between these and the one described in the first part of the book.

There are both similarities and differences between the analytic method offered in Parts I and II and those offered in Part III. We, along with the contributors, indicate the seriousness of our endeavors, the possible disappointments, the difficulty of the work involved, and the sense of fulfillment when successful. The authors in both sections, some more than others, draw upon a Freudian conceptual frame of reference. All view themselves as psychotherapists and the group member as patient, thus a therapist-patient contract is implied or actual. Each treats the content of sessions as confidential and is committed to modifying the patients' personalities. All practice a prolonged treatment using past experiences while stressing the use of the present (the immediate experience). In these indispensable aspects of a psychotherapy as contrasted to other group procedures, the group approaches described in this volume show an underlying unity.

Dissimilarities between the therapy of Parts I and II and those of Part III are those of differing emphases; format and method vary greatly. However, in marked contrast to the psychoanalytic method, the therapists in Part III for the most part seem alerted very early to the patients' problems—and quickly set in motion a series of events to correct them. In their practice, the therapists' goal for each patient and for the group seems readily discernible, and they immediately produce an appropriate activity to attain each goal. In Parts I and II, interpretative activity follows spontaneous undirected interaction in which all members share responsibility.

The contributors in Part III introduce some new terms. Some of the authors ask that the patients understand the treatment process and some request their cooperation. This is in contrast to the analytic approach where understanding and cooperation must await an intense internal emotional upheaval with a new awareness gained personally by each patient.

The number of different approaches used in group psychotherapy today made it difficult for us to decide what material to include. Nonetheless, our guiding principle in selecting the contributors of Part III was to choose those systems in general use which move toward persistent personality change of group members. But even more important, the selection includes those methods which have profoundly influenced the authors so that they have modified their analytic approach to patients.

HUGH MULLAN
MAX ROSENBAUM

About the Contributors

RICHARD G. ABELL, M.D., was trained as a psychiatrist and later completed his psychoanalytic training at the William Alanson White Institute in New York City. He studied transactional analysis with Robert and Mary Goulding at the Western Institute. He studied Gestalt therapy and incorporated both Gestalt and transactional approaches in his therapy. He is now founder and Director of the Transactional Analysis Institute of New York and Connecticut.

JIM BEBOUT, Ph.D., studied with Carl Rogers at the University of Chicago. He is currently an associate professor in clinical-community and the small group field at the California State University, San Francisco. He is completing a report on his Talent in Interpersonal Exploration Groups Project—a five-year N.I.M.H. study of several hundred intensive small groups—as well as teaching at the Wright Institute, Berkeley, California.

RUTH T. CAPLAN, Ed.D., is a counseling psychologist in private practice. She and her husband, Stanley Caplan, work together in the area of sex therapy and the treatment of sexual dysfunction.

STANLEY W. CAPLAN, Ed.D., is a counseling psychologist in private practice. He has taught in university settings and became interested in the area of human sexuality and the treatment of sexual dysfunction. The Caplans are both associated with the University of New Mexico School of Medicine.

MAGDA DENES-RADOMISLI, Ph.D., is a psychologist who was trained in psychotherapy and psychoanalysis. She is in private practice. She is also adjunct associate professor for the New York University postdoctoral program in psychoanalysis and is a faculty member of the New York Institute for Gestalt Therapy.

ZERKA T. MORENO is the widow of Jacob L. Moreno, the founder of psychodrama. She has worked with him since 1941–42 and is the coauthor with him of many writings. She is President and Director of the Moreno

Institute, which was founded by him. She has conducted workshops and psychodrama demonstrations in the United States and other parts of the world.

HUGH MULLAN, M.D., is a Fellow of the American Psychiatric Association, and a past President of the American Group Psychotherapy Association, the Louisiana Group Psychotherapy Society, and the Association for Physician Analysts. He maintains a private practice in Washington, D.C., and is Staff Psychiatrist at St. Elizabeth's Hospital, National Institute of Mental Health, and a clinical professor of psychiatry at Georgetown University. Dr. Mullan was formerly Chief of Psychiatric Service at the Veterans Administration Hospital in New Orleans and Assistant Director of the Area C Community Mental Health Center in Washington, D.C., as well as being a prime mover in organizing one of the first small group institutes in 1956.

JOHN C. PIERRAKOS, M.D., a psychiatrist in private practice, was formerly the Director of the Institute for Bioenergetic Analysis. He recently founded the Institute for the New Age of Man, which will concentrate on developing new concepts in the healing process. He describes his approach as an integration of Freud's discoveries of the unconscious, Jung's concept of the psyche, the energy concepts of the body by Reich and bioenergetics, the innovations of the humanistic movement, and the work of spiritual and growth centers throughout the world.

MAX ROSENBAUM, Ph.D., is in the private practice of psychoanalysis and of individual, group, and family therapy. He is clinical professor in the Department of Psychiatry, New York University School of Medicine; clinical professor for the Adelphi University postdoctoral program in psychotherapy; and editor of the journal *Group Process*. He serves on the editorial board of or as editorial consultant to five other journals and has participated in radio broadcasts on mental health. He is the author or editor of five books and author of seventy-five articles.

JOAN B. SCOTT, Ph.D., is a psychologist in private practice who in addition to sex therapy specializes in the counseling of adolescents.

INTRODUCTION

1 Group Psychotherapy: Heritage, History, and the Current Scene

Max Rosenbaum

Introduction

THE HISTORICAL REVIEWS of group psychotherapy are far from reaching agreement about its origins (1, 2, 3, 4, 5, 6, 7, 8, 9, 10, 11, 12, 13, 14, 15, 16, 17). There are many incidents in world history that might be interpreted as examples of therapeutic group interaction—Greek drama, medieval plays, Mesmer's hypnotic institute—but the beginning of modern group psychotherapy as we know it is usually credited to Joseph Hersey Pratt, a Boston internist. Group psychotherapy has been called uniquely American, and it certainly is a product of American pragmatism.

Early group psychotherapy was completely empirical. In the early 1900s, Pratt was treating tubercular patients (18, 19, 20). Tuberculosis was both a social and a physical disease during that time, and Pratt's patients were discouraged and disheartened. In the spring of 1905 he "formulated a plan for the treatment of consumption in the homes of poor patients. The organization was called a tuberculosis class" (21). Unable to gain the support of existing organizations, Pratt turned to Dr. Elwood Worcester, rector of the Emmanuel Church in Boston. Worcester advanced five hundred dollars to Pratt, which he used to begin his experiment.

A class consisted of twenty-five patients, although for the greater part of the time there were fifteen to twenty members in a class. Each patient kept a detailed record book in which he entered his temperature, diet, rest periods, and a host of other details. The record book was originally the invention of a North Carolina physician, C. L. Minor. Pratt's class met weekly, and he described this as the most important feature of his system. "The class meeting is a pleasant social hour for the members. . . .

3

Made up as our membership is of widely different races and different sects, they have a common bond in a common disease. A fine spirit of camaraderie has developed. They never discuss their symptoms and are almost invariably in good spirits" (19). During this weekly meeting Pratt would lecture to his patients about the importance of rest periods during the day. His lectures were generally encouraging and supportive.

Pratt had limited contacts with the psychiatrists of his day, who were too busy fighting for recognition of their own medical specialty to be unduly concerned with the problems of one busy internist. After all, it was in 1876 that Beard first publicly proposed his theory that the mind might be the cause of disease, leading to fears on the part of some that psychiatry might become a part of theology. This fear was still active in 1905 (24). Pratt's early work with his tuberculosis class was devoted exclusively to the care and treatment of the patients. His was apparently a strong personality, for at one point, in considering why his method worked with his patients but did not when other physicians organized groups of tubercular patients, he wrote: "Opponents of the class methods have repeatedly stated that our good results have been due to the personality of the medical director, but is it less essential for the physician in charge of a tuberculosis class to have the proper personality than the resident physicians of a sanitarium" (20).

Another problem that later plagued Pratt was the involvement of Dr. Worcester, who had advanced money to help Pratt start his experiment. This minister and another clergyman, Dr. Samuel McComb, founded the Emmanuel Church health classes, known as the Emmanuel Church Movement. Both these clergymen were in turn helped by one of the first American psychoanalysts, Isadore Coriat (24). This movement became the focus of a critical editorial in the journal of the New York State Medical Society. The editorial noted: "The Emmanuel Church Movement in Boston which has resulted in establishing a clinic for the treatment of functional nervous and mental disorders, under the directorship of an able pastor, Dr. Worcester, has assumed such proportions and has been widely exploited" (25). The editorial went on to criticize clergymen who treated nervous and mental disorders. About this time, Pratt was writing about his procedures: "There has been no connection between the class work and the so-called 'Emmanuel Movement,' for the treatment of nervous disorders" (20).

From Pratt's early writings it is evident that he had little understanding of his own impact upon patients when they met in the weekly classes. As time passed, he apparently became more sophisticated. Pratt, in a personal communication (15), denied the influence of the two ministers, Worcester and McComb, on his work. However, since Pratt did acknowledge a debt to Coriat (23), who published a book with the two clergymen, the issue is cloudy.

Many years later, when he was fully convinced of the psychological component in disease, and having worked with groups of patients suffering from psychosomatic disorders, he said he was influenced by the work of Joseph Jules Dejerine, a French physician who pioneered in the treatment of psychoneurosis (23). Pratt's group therapy appears to have developed in line with psychotherapy as conceived by Dejerine—which involved mostly persuasion and reeducation. Pratt complained that Dejerine's contribution was overshadowed by the attention given to Freud's writings. Pratt met Dr. Isadore Coriat in 1913. Coriat had just read Dejerine's book, written with E. Gauckler, *Les Manifestations Fonctionelles des Psychonéuroses; Leur Traitement par la Psychothérapie*. Coriat's praise of the book led Pratt to read it also, and he was profoundly influenced by it. Dejerine's text was published in the United States in 1913, after an English translation by Smith Ely Jeliffe (26); it went almost unnoticed. At a time when psychotherapy was overshadowed by purely physical treatment, Dejerine worked with methods of emotional reeducation and had been doing so for more than fifteen years. Pratt followed Dejerine's basic concepts in his later group therapy techniques: "Psychotherapy depends wholly and exclusively upon the beneficial influence of one person on another" (26).

Before 1917 Pratt had published five papers describing his work with tubercular patients. It is fair to say that only after Pratt had used his class method with these patients for some years did he begin to comprehend the full implications of his work. His later writings, in 1946 and 1953, show much more awareness of psychological dynamics. Pratt may be considered the father of the repressive-inspirational movement in group psychotherapy.

Before World War I several physicians in the United States began using group approaches to patients quite independently. The results of this work were published after World War I and during the early 1930s. In an article published in 1921, Lazell described his group treatment of schizophrenics:

> The advantages of the group method are many; the success is assured by the results obtained. (1) The patient is socialized with reference to the fear of death and the sexual problem, and feels that since there are so many others in the same condition as himself he cannot be so bad. (2) The fear of the analyst as an individual is removed. (3) It was found that many patients apparently absolutely inaccessible heard and retained much of the material even though they sat and phantasied or talked to themselves all the time the lecture was in progress (27).

Lazell's group treatment consisted mainly of lectures to patients (28).

Ten years after the publication of Lazell's article, indicating that he was among the first to use group methods with psychotics, L. Cody Marsh published an article (29) that described in detail his method of group psychotherapy. Earlier, in 1909, Marsh, a former minister who became a psychiatrist, had delivered academic and inspirational lectures to large groups of psychiatric patients at the Worcester State Hospital in Massachusetts. Marsh used almost a religious revival technique, which was very inspirational. Since he began his psychiatric work in the Boston area, he may have been influenced by the work of Worcester and McComb, but this is only speculative. Marsh used everything that he thought might be helpful to the psychological well-being of his patients. He employed techniques such as formal lectures—with patients required to take notes—art classes, and dance classes. A good deal of his work was related to the theory that patients could be supportive of one another (30). When Marsh worked with psychotic patients, he was very active in his use of techniques that contrasted with Lazell's didactic lectures.*

The Americans appear to have had little knowledge of any group psychotherapy work being done in Europe. Freud's new concepts were of interest to some very aware psychologists, for he had been invited in 1909 to lecture at Clark University in Worcester, Massachusetts. Freud's invitation had come from G. Stanley Hall, the great educator and student of human behavior, who at that time was president of Clark University. But none of this related specifically to group therapy. Jones does note in his biography of Freud: "During the voyage the three companions analyzed each other's dreams—the first example of group analysis" (31, p. 55).

Dreikurs (4) has pointed out that in Europe Adler, because of his interest in working-class groups, established guidance centers that used group concepts in treating patients. According to Dreikurs also, German, Austrian, Russian, and Danish psychotherapists were using group methods before 1930. But Pratt did not consider himself primarily a psychotherapist at any time in his professional life. From the outset he had hoped only to overcome the pessimism of his patients, to discourage neurotic secondary gains from illness, and, finally, to encourage self-confidence. He believed that most patients with emotional difficulties could be treated by an internist or a general practitioner.

It is relevant to note that group psychotherapy has a strong relationship to the particular culture in which it is being practiced. The United States was apparently receptive to new techniques. Psychoanalysis stemmed from an environment of the intellectual and financial elite in Vienna. Adler, one of Freud's first students, was also a socialist, and he was interested in the problems of working-class groups. It was because of this interest that he attempted to adapt the techniques of individual psycho-

---

* Freud lectured in Worcester, Massachusetts, at Clark University (September 1909). He then visited the Adirondack Mountain camp of James Jackson Putnam, after he had delivered his lectures. Putnam, who was Professor of Neurology at the Harvard Medical School, was an enthusiastic supporter of psychoanalysis. Freud wrote: ". . . He was an estimable man . . . and the only thing in him that we could regret was his inclination to attach psychoanalysis to a particular philosophical system and to make it the servant of moral aims . . ." (An autobiographical Study, Std. Edn., XX, 51–52). Boston was prepared to listen to new ideas.

therapy so that large groups of people could be reached. In his clinics the services of educators, social workers, and the like were used. It is possible that many traditionally oriented psychoanalysts have expressed opposition and hostility to group psychotherapy because they are bound by their own class and status needs. This appears to agree with the observations of Hollingshead and Redlich (32) in their studies of social class and mental illness. However, Dreikurs, while stressing Adler's contributions to group psychotherapy, does not give a comprehensive or convincing picture of the European contribution to the early history of group psychotherapy.

Jacob L. Moreno claimed that he used group therapy in 1910 (33) and said that he coined the term in 1931 (34). Certainly he used it in an article published in 1932 (35). Moreno came to the United States in 1925 and before then had been actively using group concepts in Vienna. By 1929 he was publicly demonstrating his methods, and in 1932 his techniques were described at a conference held by the American Psychiatric Association. In 1931 Moreno founded the first journal—*Impromptu*—concerned with group therapy. This journal ceased publication, and in 1937 he founded *Sociometry*, which he edited for eighteen years, finally, in 1944, turning it over to the American Sociological Association. It is now primarily a journal devoted to social psychology. During the years that Moreno edited *Sociometry*, many leading psychiatrists and social psychologists served on its editorial board. In 1947 Moreno began to publish another journal, *Sociatry*, whose title he later changed to *Group Psychotherapy*. This publication was edited and issued by Moreno until his death in 1974. His widow, Zerka Moreno edits it now.

Moreno is primarily identified with psychodrama, which he introduced into the United States in 1925. He defines psychodrama as the "science which explores truth by dramatic methods. The psychodramatic method uses mainly five instruments—the stage, the subject or patient, the director, the staff of therapeutic aides or auxiliary egos, and the audience." The stage gives the patient the opportunity to express himself freely, to be himself. He can enact a role, act out a past scene or a present problem. The director serves as the producer, therapist, and analyst. He must keep the actor in rapport with the audience, relate to the patient, and interpret. The auxiliary egos are extensions of the director, portraying the imagined or real persons in the patient's life drama. The audience is a sounding board of public opinion and may well see one of its own collective problems portrayed on the stage (36).

Louis Wender used psychoanalytic concepts when he practiced group therapy with borderline patients in a mental hospital setting. He began his work in 1929 and reported his results in 1937 (37). Wender was quite specific in describing his work as psychoanalytic in nature, differentiating it from the work of others who used what he felt were educational and orientative techniques. At the time he presented his work, he said: "In distinction to the method of extra-mural group analysis described by Trigant Burrow, which is psychoanalytic in technique and carries large sociological and philosophical implications, group psychotherapy is a method confined to the intra-mural treatment of certain types of mild mental disease" (37). He stated that his experience indicated that group psychotherapy was applicable only to disorders in which some degree of affect was present and in which intellectual impairment was absent.

His groups consisted of six to eight patients of the same sex who met two or three times each week for one-hour sessions. Wender encouraged combined treatment, the patient being seen both for individual treatment and in the group setting. He wrote of the transference phenomena that occurred in the group and expressed the view that with the use of group psychotherapy a partial reorganization of the patient's personality would occur. He said that the group could possibly represent the family of the patient, with the therapist as the symbolic parent and the other patients as siblings. Wender's presentation was devoted to treatment of patients within mental hospitals where there were "mild mental patients and psychoneurotics under one roof."

In 1934 Paul Schilder utilized psychoanalytic concepts in an experiment in group psychotherapy. He described his work with fifty patients in the outpatient department of the psychiatric division of Bellevue Hospital in New York City when he reported the study at the annual meeting of the American Psychiatric Association in 1936. The study was published in 1939 (38), but some three years earlier Schilder had reported some of his first observations of group treatment (39).

Since Schilder did not list any bibliography in the 1939 article describing his work, we do not know who influenced it—if, indeed, anyone did. But it is not amiss to recall that in 1922 Freud wrote a theoretical paper on group psychology (40). He observed that emotional ties and currents are the essence of most groups—even leaderless ones in which people are devoted to abstract ideas. Freud also noted that a group is held together by a common identification with a leader. He observed the conflicts and difficulties of group members in handling not only the jealous rivalry, but also the tender feelings they have for one another. It is reasonable to assume that during the 1930s workers in the field of psychoanalytic psychotherapy would have had some knowledge of this monograph by Freud. Freud himself was influenced by Gustav Le Bon, a French sociologist who described the group as a collective entity—a distinct being. Freud's work was highly speculative, but even today it is esteemed by many psychoanalytically oriented group therapists. Freud's observations concerning groups referred primarily to leader-led groups, although he was aware that groups could exist without leaders. But he stressed that the group members relate to one another through their common attachment to the leader. He said, "It is impossible to grasp the nature of a group if the leader is disregarded" (40). Freud described the leader as primarily a representative of the father figure. Other analysts have disputed this conceptualization. Schilder conceived of the group leader as both a mother and a father image (41).

Recently some therapists have advanced the concept of two leaders for a group, a man to represent the father and a woman to represent the mother. This is designed to help the patient experience a "complete and realistic setting to learn new life patterns" (42). To our knowledge, there has been no statement in the literature of the problems the patient may face when the male co-therapist leading a group is not particularly masculine or fatherly and the female co-therapist is not particularly feminine or motherly.

Freud was impressed by the independence and submissiveness the individual displayed in his relation to the leader. He stated that marked dependence on the group was strongly related to the prestige of the group leader. He questioned the differences between the leader-led and leaderless groups and considered the possibility that leaderless groups may be held together by abstract ideas, which serve as a substitute for the leader.

Trigant L. Burrow used the term "group analysis" as early as 1925 (43). Little attention has been paid to Burrow, who was a great and original thinker. Oberndorf, in his book *A History of Psychoanalysis in America* (44), cites Burrow as being among the four most original contributors to the science of psychoanalysis before 1920. Burrow wrote sixty-eight articles and five books that summarized much of his research and concepts. However, his involved style has discouraged many readers. His work has been carried on by his son-in-law Hans Syz, a psychiatrist.*

Burrow obtained his medical degree at the University of Virginia and later his doctorate in the field of psychology at the Johns Hopkins University. He then began to work in the field of psychiatry at the New York State Psychiatric Institute on Ward's Island, under Adolf Meyer. In 1909, while both were attending a performance at Hammerstein's Roof Garden in New York City, A. A. Brill introduced Burrow to two physicians who were in this country to lecture at Clark University. The two physicians were Carl Jung and Sigmund Freud. After this, Burrow was encouraged by Meyer to study psychoanalysis, and he elected to study under Jung in Zurich. Why he chose Jung rather than Freud is not clear, especially since Burrow felt an allegiance to Freud and for twelve years practiced Freudian analysis. On the other hand, since in 1909 Freud and Jung were still close, with no hint of the difficulties that they were later to have with one another, the choice is perhaps not significant. After returning to the United States in 1910, Burrow began to practice psychoanalysis, and in 1911 he was one of the founding members of the American Psychoanalytic Asso-

---

* Burrow's letters have been collected and published. They are readable and comprehensive, revealing the man as well as his work (45).

ciation. He was already a member of the American Psychological Association and the American Psychopathological Association. Burrow was an active and leading figure in the psychoanalytic movement during these early years. In 1913 he planned to have an additional analysis, this time with Freud, but World War I interrupted this plan.

Burrow's work took a new direction after he met Clarence Shields. Shields, an intuitive and somewhat retiring young man, was being analyzed by Burrow in 1918 when he challenged Burrow to reverse the analytic position to test the "honesty" of the relationship—Burrow was to assume the role of the patient and Shields was to become the analyst. Apparently aware of the resistance mechanisms at work, Burrow consented and in so doing became aware of the "authoritarian" attitude inherent in the analytic relationship. Since 1912, Burrow had been dissatisfied with the emphasis psychoanalysis placed on the individual, an emphasis that he felt excluded social forces (46, 47). He believed that behavioral disorders should be traced back to social relatedness and that research should be carried out in a group setting. Burrow and Shields then embarked on a new area of group behavioral exploration, which was in full swing from 1923 to 1932. This research on group behavior, first called group analysis and later called phyloanalysis, estranged Burrow more and more from his psychoanalytic colleagues.

After 1932, Burrow became more and more interested in the biological principles underlying group behavior. His thesis is quite simple: Man is part of a group and the analysis of the individual can never be completed without real study of the group of which he is an essential part. He therefore devised a technique of group analysis, which was his distinctive contribution to psychoanalysis and group psychotherapy. Freud did not support either Burrow's thesis or his work with groups, and Burrow moved away from the psychoanalytic community. In 1927 D. H. Lawrence reviewed Burrow's book *The Social Basis of Consciousness* (48) in *The Bookman*, an English literary magazine. Lawrence was enthusiastic about Burrow's ideas, and the review brought Burrow to the attention of many who were not psychoanalysts. Toward the end of his life, Burrow complained that his contribution to the work of Harry Stack Sullivan had never been acknowledged (45).

During the 1930s Samuel Slavson, originally an engineer who later entered group work and group education, began working with activity group therapy at the Jewish Board of Guardians. His concepts were a blend of group work, progressive education, and psychoanalysis. Activity group therapy emphasizes the acting out of conflicts, impulses, and behavior patterns in the group setting. The therapist is permissive and accepting in the group setting as the patients interact with one another. It is primarily a therapy for children up to about age fifteen. In 1943 Slavson presented his findings based on nine years of work with approximately eight hundred children and sixty-three distinct groups at the annual meeting of the American Orthopsychiatric Association (49). He had also reported his work in a book published that same year (50). In the 1943 paper presented at the meeting, Slavson noted that adults had been treated in groups by Trigant Burrow, Louis Wender, Paul Schilder, James S. Greene, and others, but that his own distinctive contribution was in the field of activity group therapy, treating children between the ages of eight and fifteen. He described his therapy as "situational therapy." At the same symposium other speakers also said that they had been engaged in this kind of work for some years so that apparently quite a few psychotherapists had begun to experiment with group concepts in the treatment of children.

By the end of World War II, group psychotherapy was being used extensively. It had had tremendous growth during the war largely because there was a shortage of trained personnel, while at the same time there was a great need to treat large numbers of psychiatric patients. A strong effort was made to explore newer and briefer treatment methods, and the psychiatric climate generally became more liberal and receptive to methodological innovations in treatment. Every school of analytic technique— Freudian, Horneyan, Sullivanian—was involved in group psychotherapy in 1945. Group psychotherapy ranged from an overtly repressive-inspirational method, in which group psychotherapy was used as a cathartic and supportive device, to the psychoanalytic method in which group psychotherapy was used reconstructively.

Carl Rogers, while not directly interested in group psychotherapy, encouraged students of his "client-centered psychotherapy" to apply his technique to the group (51). In 1942, Rogers presented an extensive picture of his views of counseling and therapy and said: "Group therapy is the name given to the attempt to translate principles of individual treatment into procedures for groups, drawing heavily upon play techniques" (52, p. 440). His view of group therapy at that time, when one reads the references he cited (53, 54), was apparently based on activity group therapy.

After World War II Rogers' students engaged in group psychotherapy with adults. Their effort was directed toward interaction with other group members, rather than toward insight as conceived of by psychoanalysts. The phenomenological and client-centered point of view is essentially devoted to the resolution of situational conflicts on conscious levels. Help is believed to be most useful if first directed toward the problem that causes the individual (or group) concern. An individual is believed to have the capacity to heal himself if he is provided with a secure setting in which he can discuss his problems. Therefore, the therapist is constantly permissive and accepting. Since any relationship that modifies a patient's behavior and enables the client—so-called by the nondirective therapist—to perceive his needs clearly is believed to be therapeutic, no distinction is made between the terms "psychotherapy" and "counseling." The focus is on present behavior, and the client is urged to cope with his present perceptions, which should lead to a clarification of the self-concept, so the client's change of attitude toward himself changes his total personality. The therapeutic approach appears strongly intellectual (55, 56, 57, 58, 59).

The nondirective approach is in marked contrast to the psychoanalytic approach, which stresses the concept of depth in effecting personality change. The psychoanalytically oriented therapist uses the term *psychotherapy* to describe a therapist-patient relationship in which the focus is on personality change. He conceives of *counseling* as a method of treatment for disturbed individuals whose problems are based on situational and reality conflicts. In counseling, no effort is made to explore the intrapsychic. The movement in psychoanalytic psychotherapy is toward the pathology that is believed to be at the root of conflicts and problems. Currently, Rogers and his students support encounter group techniques. Rogers is a very enthusiastic exponent of these techniques and says that "the most important social invention of this century is the encounter group. The demand is utterly beyond belief" (60).

Reports came to the United States after World War II of English psychiatrists who were using group techniques. Bierer (61) organized social club groups among patients, using Adlerian concepts as a theory base for his work. Foulkes, who died in 1976, employed psychoanalytic techniques in his work with groups in England (62, 63). He developed his own theory of group therapy, in which he rejected two hypotheses. The first is the Freudian concept of two basic drives in the individual—Eros (the life instinct) and Thanatos (the death instinct)—which would be expressed in the group as the struggle between constructive and destructive forces. The forces that bring people together to work with one another in a group would be derived from Eros, and the forces that lead to fear and thus to fragmentation of a group structure would be derived from Thanatos.

The second hypothesis Foulkes rejected is that an independent social drive or herd instinct leads to the behavior observed in the group. His basic conviction was that the group is a more fundamental unit than the individual. "*Collectively they constitute the very Norm, from which, individually, they deviated*" (62, p. 29). The group tends to speak and react to a common theme as if it were a living entity, expressing itself in different ways through various mouths (63, p. 219). The concepts of Foulkes have not made an appreciable impact on the practice of group therapy in the United States. There is a great deal of thinking borrowed from Gestalt psychology—the whole is larger than the sum of its parts—in the Foulkes theory. Foulkes was the leading group therapist in England and founded and led an institute which trains group analysts.

In England, J. D. Sutherland (64) and H. Ezriel (65) have been active in group psychotherapy. They have emphasized the "here-and-now" aspects of the transference between the group and the group therapist. Ezriel, in line with his belief that an individual's reactions to the emotion of the group should be analyzed, has attempted to define transference in terms of the group structure. Julius Merry (67) advocated "excitatory group therapy" by deliberately arousing tension, hostility, and anxiety in the meetings of the group. Merry's group consisted of one hundred patients and some nurses. The doctor adopts the leader role in the group situation, and his technique is designed to create emotional excitement with an increase in suggestibility on the part of the patient. This emotionally charged setting leads to flexibility on the patient's part with a consequent change in attitudes.

From his work with therapy groups in England, W. W. Bion set forth a series of rather complex hypotheses concerning the processes he believed to be present in all groups (68, 69, 70, 71, 72, 73, 74, 75). The processes are set up as conscious and rational as well as emotional and irrational. His detailed statement of the processes at work would take us too far afield; his approach, however, may be summarized without too much violence to his theory.

As he observed his patients in the group setting, Bion noticed certain massive emotional reactions in the group. Occasionally, the group would appear to be expressing a need for the group therapist to provide more direction, or the members would show a desire to run away from the group. He developed the theory that a group can be described as a series of emotional states or basic assumption cultures. Affective need was deeply tied in with the work the group was attempting. As the individuals in the group reacted against the cultures or agreed to accept the cultures, they would contribute to the work of the group. The relationship between the individual and the group culture was outlined under a series of "valences." The individual is moving along the valence of pairing, dependency, or "fight-flight." The process of group movement can be seen in a series of shifts from one emotional culture to another, based on the valence. Thus, at all times, the leader is able to ask, "What is the group really doing at this moment? Is it attempting to avoid, or to get to, a problem?" This would be the emotional culture. It is important to note that Bion dealt with his therapy groups in a unique way. He provided the group with no direction or structure, and the patients' reactions to the lack of structure—their anger or confusion—was the material initially used for exploration. Apparently, as soon as Bion became aware of the group's emotional state, he gave an interpretation. The emphasis was on the interpretation of group behavior rather than on individual behavior.

Bion's writings, over the last decade, are more frequently mentioned in the group psychotherapy literature of the United States. For five years Herbert Thelen and his students in the field of group dynamics subjected Bion's hypotheses to systematic research study (76, 77). While these research studies have attracted the interest of sociologists and social psychologists, there has been little attention given to the studies in the group psychotherapy literature.

One further point should be noted in order to understand Bion's approach. He was trained and influenced in his psychoanalytic method by Melanie Klein, and her thinking is an integral part of Bion's view of human behavior (78). Her theories carry great weight among British and South American psychoanalysts. Essentially, Klein has modified the orthodox Freudian depiction of personality. According to her, the ego exists from birth. Bad and good emotions stem from the infant's contact with the mother, who represents the external world to the infant. The infant's ability to love as well as feelings of persecution are directly related to contact with the mother. The contacts are in turn influenced by environment and constitution.

Two major processes appear as the infant's ego develops. These processes are introjection and projection. The people and situations that the infant encounters become part of the inner life of the infant; this is *introjection*. The growing infant attributes different feelings to other people; this is *projection*. The processes of introjection and projection are basic to the infant's development as a person. According to Klein, the ego which exists from birth splits in the early months of life, and objects become divided into bad and good. Following this, anxiety and destructive impulses accompany ego growth; this is called the *paranoid-schizoid* position. What generally occurs from the sixth to the twelfth month of life is a *depressed* period related to the infant's anxiety about destructive impulses as well as accompanying guilt.

There is never a full recovery from the depressed period and this plays a basic part in the child's perception of human relations, which are interpreted in terms of introjection, projection, and *splitting*—where the individual denies bad impulses and accepts good feelings. A therapist who works according to Bion's approach to groups will interpret immediately and move into unconscious material immediately. This is rather unsettling and different for those group therapists who move more slowly and reflect. Many current approaches to group therapy which employ immediate interpretation embody Kleinian orientations. The problem is that the majority of the practitioners who use this approach are unaware of its theoretical origins. There are those who claim that Bion's actual group approach, where he was generally silent, reflected his rather withdrawn personality. The practitioners who follow his approach seem to be far more active. Bion himself has retired from active clinical practice and currently lives in California.*

---

* Bion, following the work of his analyst, Melanie Klein, is concerned with the individual's capacity to integrate "bad" and "good" experiences. Current interest in object-relations theory is based upon the work of Klein, Fairbairn, Winnicott, Guntrip, Kohut,

In 1958 Kraupl-Taylor (79) published an extremely detailed statement of the history of group therapy in Great Britain. He dates much of the work as beginning during World War II, but he does mention that in 1938 Bierer had organized therapeutic social clubs and discussion groups. He states that the majority of group therapists in England have modeled their techniques on psychoanalytic practice. On the European continent, Lebovici and Diatkine in France, Carp and Stokvis in Holland, Haisch and Teirich in Germany, and Waal in Norway have been among the active group therapists since World War II. Their work has had minimal influence on the group therapists in the United States. In 1958 Astrup (80) described group treatment as still in the experimental stage in Scandinavia. Graham in Australia; Gilles and Borowitz in South Africa; Ferschtut in Argentina; Langer in Argentina and Mexico; Carrillo in Mexico; and Blay Neto and de Oliveira in Brazil have all been active in group therapy since World War II, but again there has been little or no awareness of their work in the United States.

In 1949, in the United States, Alexander Wolf published a lengthy paper describing his psychoanalysis of groups (81). He began his work in 1938, stimulated by the work of Louis Wender and Paul Schilder, and by 1940 he was working with five groups of eight to ten patients each. He continued his work with groups during four years of military service and since the war has trained many psychotherapists. Wolf directly applies the principles of individual psychoanalysis to the group setting, using the major tools of the psychoanalytic method: transference, dreams, historical development, and free association. He considers the group a re-creation of the original family.

By 1949, when Wolf reported on his work, many others also were ready to report their experiences with group psychotherapy, and since World War II the literature has grown tremendously. In 1953, one careful researcher was able to unearth twelve hundred papers in the field of group psychotherapy.* At the end of 1955 the group psychotherapy literature consisted of seventeen hundred items. The present annual rate is about two hundred and fifty books, articles, and theses—double the rate of 1950.

After World War II, a psychologist, George Bach, formulated a concept of group psychotherapy based on Kurt Lewin's field theory concepts (82, 83, 84). Bach stated that the "doctor must be group-oriented rather than only patient-oriented. . . . He treats the individual patient by conscientiously creating an atmosphere that stimulates self-treatment" (83). Lewin's great contributions to group dynamics and his own speculations,

---

and Kernberg. Object-relations theory is a way of understanding human behavior in terms of what the individual "gives to, and takes from, the human relationship in any situation. . ." (R. D. Laing et al., *Interpersonal Perception* London: Tavistock Publishers, 1966, p. 40).

* Personal communication from R. J. Corsini.

which evolve from Gestalt theory, are provocative. But in attempting to apply Lewin's concepts—of the group as a dynamic whole operating in a social field—to group psychotherapy, Bach appeared to be "forcing the fit." His most recent work is with "attack therapy" in groups. He believes that "we must all re-learn how to fight to regain our genuineness. Only after this are we ready to share our love" (84, p. 187).

It has not been our intention to present a catalogue of authors but, rather, major points of view that are important in the field of group psychotherapy and that have influenced many current workers. For example, Moreno valued enthusiasm, activity, interaction, role playing, and spontaneity. Slavson's disciplined approach emphasizes the careful selection of patients, adherence to strict methodology, curative processes, and carefully determined goals. To the mixed group of adult patients, Wolf applies orthodox psychoanalytic conceptions, techniques, and aims. These three approaches are to be found in much of current group psychotherapy.

Little attention has been given to the philosophical position that the therapist takes on group treatment. Controversy revolves around the immediate experiencing in the group setting and its value for patients as well as for the group therapist. The question of the total involvement of the therapist has been the interest and concern of such workers as Whitaker and Malone (86), Mullan (87), and Rosenbaum (88). The direction of this concern is toward a humanism in psychotherapy. Van Dusen (89) has given a detailed picture of existential analysis and its impact upon European psychiatry. Hora (90) describes existential group psychotherapy as a living dynamic experience, in which the group represents a microcosm of the world; the loneliness and isolation that patients experience is part of the total anxiety the world experiences. Hill (91) has stressed the importance of the human experience as part of group psychotherapy.

Whitaker and Malone (86) distinguished between a therapy that stresses the patient's intellect and a therapy that emphasizes the patient's feelings. This therapy is called "experiential." Arguments in the field of group psychotherapy often relate to the two opposing points of view—the intellectual and the affective. It is interesting to note that psychoanalysts who adopt an experiential approach to group psychotherapy have much the same feeling for the therapeutic process that Carl Rogers has expressed (92), although the basic themes are quite dissimilar. It is expressly stated in the experiential approach that the therapist has a value system and must be aware that indirectly or directly his value system is expressed in the course of group therapy.

Until some twenty years ago, psychoanalytic psychotherapists avoided treatment of members of the same family; they would even avoid contact with members of the patient's family. Today, there is treatment of families as units. Since Ackerman (93) felt that the patient cannot be understood apart from the family, he treated the patient and the patient's family.

Grotjahn (94) points out that Freud treated Little Hans in 1909 by using the child's father as therapist, so there is a precedent for family therapy. Through the treatment of the entire family, the therapist is believed to gain new perspective on family interaction and on the impact on each member of the family (95). Because Grotjahn predicts radical changes in the family structure, he advocates that the family therapist help in the adjustment to these changes. This new kind of therapist will have to combine the wisdom and experience of the old-time family physician with the knowledge and skills of the psychoanalyst.

One of the major criticisms of family therapy is the therapist's intervention with individuals who are not motivated to seek psychotherapy. While part of the family may welcome or actively seek treatment, other family members may actively resent therapy. The case for family therapy often revolves around the issue of the therapist's active intervention.

At the outset there was great enthusiasm for therapy approaches to the entire family. Many psychotherapists were disenchanted by what they felt were the limitations of the one-to-one approach. Others were discouraged as the person in therapy returned to an obviously disturbed family and became troubled once again. The most sophisticated and aware family therapist who mobilized family interaction and analyzed defenses was Ackerman (96, 97). His approach was clearly in the psychoanalytic tradition, and he stressed both the assets and limitations of his approach. Since his death, his students have formed an institute.

Others were far more definite in stressing family therapy as *the* therapy of choice to the exclusion of others. Satir (98) describes herself as a teacher and expert in communication in her work with families. Bowen (99) retains absolute control of the therapy meeting in his work with families. Minuchin (100), who works with inner-city and lower-class families, gives them "enactive" or "iconic" rather than verbal experiences. Whitaker (112) is the activator and invades the family as a person where his presence is very much felt. Jackson (101) was concerned with maneuvers, strategy, manipulation, and rules, an approach which Haley (102) and his co-workers follow.

There has been little systematic research in the field until recently when Framo (103) brought together family therapists and family researchers. For example, there is very little known about the family structure of the black family and yet practitioners do not seem deterred by this state of affairs as they treat black families. However, the more aware practitioners are now pointing to different family structures in different cultures. Thus, Moses (104) notes the different cultures in Israel when family therapy is used, and Rosenbaum (105) questions the approach to family therapy when the entire concept of the nuclear family is questioned. Zuk (106) has attempted to coordinate and list the different approaches while Boszormenyi-Nagy (107) stresses the substantive theoretical problems involved in the practice of family therapy. The current dialogue is between family therapists who are psychoanalytically oriented and those who stress a systems-oriented family therapy.

The arguments continue between those who stress intensive family therapy and those who advocate supportive family therapy. Beels and Ferber state specifically that family therapy's most distinctive feature is its goal of "changing the family system of interaction, not altering the behavior of individuals" (108). Other practitioners disagree sharply, maintaining that if the family interaction changes, the individual behavior is altered. Alger (109) stresses the advantages of audio-visual techniques in family therapy, such as closed-circuit television where a family can observe patterns of their interaction. Researchers in Canada have pursued the problems of outcome in family therapy as well as the risks to participants (110, 111).

Some therapists report treatment of married couples or groups with the use of co-therapists, or they may call upon a co-therapist at specific times in treating an individual patient or a group of patients (112). The use of more than one therapist at one time in group therapy has been described in different ways—co-therapy, joint therapy, multiple therapy, cooperative psychotherapy. Multiple therapy has been used in the training of therapists, the treatment of families, the treatment of the individual patient, and the treatment of neurotics and psychotics. Spitz and Kopp (113) were able to find thirty-two references to this type of treatment when they surveyed the technique in 1957. More attention has been given to this technique over the past two decades as psychotherapists have become more receptive to innovation. It is still not clear whether the use of more than one therapist results in either a more successful therapeutic outcome or in a briefer period of treatment. Up to now the investigations have not been systematic but, rather, a report on the therapists' experiences (114). (See Chapter 8.)

During the last half of the nineteenth century, hypnosis was used extensively for symptom removal. Direct suggestions were made to the patient by the hypnotist. Freud later used hypnosis to uncover the motivations behind the symptom as well as to encourage a reaction. Later, he ceased using hypnosis because few patients were cooperative subjects. He also felt that when hypnosis was used the transference and resistance mechanisms of the patient were not explored. During and immediately after World War II, psychoanalysis and hypnosis were combined as hypnoanalysis. There has been a strong renewal of interest in the use of hypnosis.

Fox (115) in the United States and Peberdy (116) in England have advocated the use of group hypnotherapy. The trance is induced by Fox in the group setting because "group contagion may be used very effectively to build the belief in the efficacy of reality of the trance." He has found the technique of group hypnotherapy effective in the treatment of alcoholics and drug addicts. Fox has not described the size of his hypnotic group. In England, Peberdy has used the hypnotic approach in a group setting with neurotics who come to an outpatient psychiatric clinic at a general hospital. He treats these patients in groups of six. He reports that he has treated some sixty-five patients, with most of them requiring twenty group meetings. Peberdy has expressed enthusiasm about the use of the group hypnotic method.

Since the advent of the tranquilizing drugs, many psychiatric patients have been discharged from mental hospitals. The consensus at the present time is that the new drug treatments have practically abolished the need for psychosurgery (lobotomies) and have diminished the need for insulin and electroshock therapy. There has been some criticism of the indiscriminate use of psychotropic drugs. Of interest to practitioners of group therapy is a study of Sandison (117), in which he examined the relationship between psychotropic drugs and the environment or human group in which the patient finds himself. His survey of the pertinent studies in psychopharmacology indicates that "patients undergoing long-term drug therapy should be seen in groups." It is possible that these patients will present less dream and fantasy material than patients who are not receiving psychotropic drugs. Many writers have commented on the effects of placebo in the treatment of emotional disturbance. The group of patients with a combined belief in the effect of the drug may be responding to the placebo effect as well as to the drug. It is also pertinent to note that patients who are receiving lysergic acid diethylamide (LSD) treatment may be helped more by group treatment. Patients who experience deep insulin shock treatment may experience the treatment as similar to the feeling of dying. When these patients are concurrently treated in a group setting, the group climate leads to a feeling of rebirth, which is a significant factor in the improvement of these patients. In the most recent statement of his work, Sandison (118) has continued to stress the importance of the group in the psychopharmacological approach to patients.

During the past decade, the influence of humanism has been strongly felt in the fields of group psychotherapy. Whether all of the new approaches are in fact a reaction to what many psychotherapists feel is the static approach of psychoanalysis, is left for the reader to evaluate. Certainly, many psychotherapists are and were unreasonable in their expectations of a dynamic approach to psychotherapy. Perhaps they became impatient with the time that has to be devoted to the practice of psychoanalytic psychotherapy. A close reading of the "new approaches" such as the "encounter movement" * may leave the reader with the reaction that the wheel has been rediscovered. The major new approaches are summarized for the reader.

---

* The encounter movement encompasses many different techniques and theories. But basic to the "encounter" experience is the emphasis on the "here and now"—insight is regarded as secondary. Resistance is to be attacked directly.

Group Psychotherapy and Gestalt Therapy

Frederick S. Perls, a German-born psychiatrist, moved to South Africa where he developed his theory of Gestalt therapy. He stated that while he was in Europe he was trained in psychoanalysis by "outstanding teachers."* He preferred to be called Fritz Perls, and he began to use that name in his writings. He decided to call his approach to psychotherapy Gestalt therapy because of his admiration for Gestalt psychologists, who he believed stressed the wholeness of man (119, 120). His approach is highly flexible, embodies an entire approach to life, and is believed by some to be a theory of personality.

After World War II, Perls and his wife Laura relocated in New York City, where they both practiced psychotherapy and trained others. Perls then began to move about. First he went to Miami, Florida—then to Cleveland, Ohio, and later to Carmel, California, where he stayed at Esalen, the home of the encounter movement. He became unhappy with this setting and the encounter approach, and just before his death he moved on to Vancouver, British Columbia. In each of the places he lived, he practiced and trained others who continued to develop his approach to psychotherapy. His wife remained in the greater New York City area, although she also trained people in Cleveland.

The first comprehensive book that he wrote in the United States was done with the cooperation of a philosopher-commentator, Paul Goodman, and an academic psychologist, Ralph Hefferline, who was particularly interested in learning theory (121). The theory postulated was that the normal individual reacts as a whole organism and not as a disorganized or fragmented person.

Figures and grounds are formed by the organism. A Gestalt is established where a figure (any process that emerges) becomes a foreground which stands out against the background. For people who have no disabling emotional problems, figures emerge from the background and either fade away or are destroyed. In this way, as the need is gratified, a new Gestalt emerges as the old Gestalt is no longer needed. According to Perls, the goal of Gestalt therapy is for the individual to form figures and grounds and to destroy Gestalts in order to utilize aggressive feelings in an appropriate fashion. The terms "aggressive destruction" and "reconstruction" are used in Gestalt therapy, since Perls believed that a person needs healthy aggression in order to survive.

Perls stressed responsibility and "common sense" in his approach to psychotherapy. In the Gestalt practice of group therapy, the "here and now" is stressed. Patients are actively discouraged from asking questions.

* One of his analysts was Wilhelm Reich.

Perls would sit next to an empty chair with a group of patients observing. A patient would volunteer to sit in the empty chair which was called the "hot seat," and the Gestalt group therapist worked with that patient. It is believed that the observing patients are receiving therapy through empathic identification. The posture and speech patterns of the individual in the hot seat are explored. Dreams are explored although there appear to be differences in the way specific Gestalt therapists approach dreams. Generally, a patient will be asked to explore a dream and fantasy with other members of the group watching. Perls believed that each part of the dream represents a different part of the patient. Patients are encouraged to express anger in the group experience, and on occasion they are asked to engage in role playing as a way of evoking emotions.

When Perls practiced Gestalt group therapy, he was in complete control at all times. He discouraged free group interaction and was very specific, even going so far as to tell an interruptive group member to remain silent. He used simple language and was opposed to intellectual inquiry which he described as "mind fucking." He did not approve of an introspective approach. He was extremely intuitive and encouraged patients to experience emotions very fully since he stated that this was the way to change one's personality. This is called the "awareness of the moment."

The introspective or withdrawn patient would not appear to profit from the Gestalt approach since he would not be encouraged to participate in the group. If Perls became impatient with an individual he would simply dismiss him. This is in line with his belief that the patient is responsible for himself—"take care of yourself." The more active individual who wants to become involved will appear to profit from a Gestalt approach, especially if he wants attention. The students of Perls appear to be less critical of their patients and spend more time with them (122). They also encourage more group participation.

Perls introduced his approach in the United States after World War II. Since then, there has been no book written specifically about Gestalt group therapy, although there are writings about Gestalt therapy. The number of Gestalt therapists listed in the 1973 national directory was 210 (123). There are probably closer to five hundred in practice. (See Chapter 15.)

Group Psychotherapy and Transactional Analysis

Eric Berne, a Canadian psychiatrist, moved to New York City where he began training in psychoanalysis. In a series of articles (the first of which was published in 1949) he became concerned with intuition. After this, he wrote about the capacities of the ego and the child ego state (124).

He moved to San Francisco, California, where he continued training as a psychoanalyst, although there is controversy as to whether he completed his training as an analyst.

In California, Berne defined and wrote about his approach to psychotherapy and human behavior. He called his approach *Transactional Analysis*, and organized study groups which met with him from 1958 until his sudden death in 1970 (125).

Berne felt that Freud's approach was too abstract. He postulated three forms of ego function which he called the Parent, the Child, and the Adult. The *Parent ego state* is modeled after parents or those who are parental surrogates. Civilization survives because of the Parent ego state. The *Child ego state* is the behavior of a child. An adult may be in a Child ego state at a party or celebration, or perhaps at an event such as a football game where spectators or participants "let off steam." Otherwise, the behavior is inappropriate. The *Adult ego state* is arbitrary and gathers data. People may behave like adults and actually be in a child state. For example, an excitable and explosive person may attempt to speak in a reasonable manner and act like an adult while actually he is angry and ready to have a temper tantrum.

When a transactional analyst practices group therapy, the patient's behavior is explored as a transaction occurring in the ego states of child, parent, and adult, a transaction that is going on *within* the person. Berne stated that people spend their lives by engaging in games. These games follow a script which is a plan of living. When a patient is in a transactional group the therapist is in control of the group, and works with each group member in turn. Therefore, like Gestalt therapy, psychotherapy occurs *in* the group rather than *with* the group. The therapist explores the script, the games, and the transaction of the patient (126).

The composition of the group is heterogeneous since selection procedures are minimized. The patient is believed to be in a contract with the transactional analyst and agrees that the therapist leads the group. Otherwise, Berne believed, the group therapy session becomes a "party" where irrelevant and time-consuming material is introduced into the session. Berne aimed for total "cure" and hoped to see the time when a patient would be "cured" in one meeting with a therapist.

Although Berne stated that he followed a "no selection" procedure, he did not treat phobic, manic, obsessional, or hysterical patients. Patients who are strongly motivated and verbal and wish a directive psychotherapist, appear to respond to the transactional approach to group therapy. (See Chapter 14.)

In 1976, Goulding (129) stated that there are "four major schools in Transactional Analysis in the Western hemisphere, plus a number of modified and combined training centers in Europe, India, Australia, and the Southwest Pacific. The four schools are roughly categorized as the Eric Berne San Francisco Seminar approach, the Schiff 'Reparenting' approach, the Asklepieion approach, and the 'Redecision' approach using Transactional Analysis and Gestalt as practiced by me and my associates at the Western Institute, and largely by those professionals whom we have trained."

Marathon Groups

In 1963 a sensitivity training group met in California and extended over a weekend. This experience led several group therapists to apply the idea to working with groups, and this accelerated interaction group format became popular (127, 128). The majority of people who first used and presently use the "marathon approach" stress the here-and-now approach. Traditional procedures of therapy are seldom used and the idea is to stimulate intense emotional reactions in a group which meets anywhere from one to three days continuously. There are breaks for rest, sleep, and eating, but the effort is made to confront defense mechanisms immediately and dissolve these defenses through a very emotional and intense experience. There is no desire to encourage either insight or introspection.

While we have used extended meetings in our work with psychotherapy groups, we approach defense mechanisms dynamically and explore the resistances rather than engage in a more abrupt confrontation technique. Patients are often unable to absorb interpretations that the therapist presents "out of the blue." An abrupt confrontation, while salutary at times, may at other times merely strengthen resistances and prolong therapy. (See Chapters 7 and 16.)

Videotape Approaches

The first textbook devoted to videotape approaches to group psychotherapy and individual therapy appeared in 1970 (130). During the group meeting, a videotape is made and the group session may be interrupted at any time while a previous part of the session is played back so that the members may study their own behavior. The videotape approach is used by therapists who are psychoanalytically oriented, as well as by behavior therapists. The use of videotape has been extremely helpful in training psychotherapists. Whether the technique leads to behavior modification or deep-seated change is still debatable.

Bioenergetic Group Therapy

This is basically a physical approach to group psychotherapy. It explores the manner in which feelings are expressed by analyzing body movement, body musculature, body posture, and types of breathing. In the group, members react to and study one another's physical and emotional reactions. Physical contact between patient and patient as well as patient and therapist is encouraged as part of psychotherapy. The bioenergetic approach stems from the original work of Wilhelm Reich (131, 132).

Whether based on Pavlovian concepts, when group therapy is practiced in the Soviet Union (133), or on an effort to capture some of the techniques of the encounter movement (134) in the practice of group psychotherapy, there is clearly an appreciation of the importance of the group in the practice of psychotherapy. There is no longer any question as to the efficacy of group therapy and there is a move away from testimonials toward comprehensive training, more basic research, and careful conceptualization. Indeed, some practitioners appear to rush to the practice of group therapy without careful consideration of the population that is to be treated. The inexperienced group therapist, especially if inadequately trained, will either flounder in the group or tend to dominate it out of his own anxiety. In either case he will not make effective use of the possibilities in working with groups. In the following pages, we present an approach that will enhance his skills and give him a base from which to work.

References

(1) Bach, G. R., and Illing, H. A. Historische Perspective zur Gruppen Psychotherapie. Ztschr. fur Psycho-somatische Medizin (January 1956), 131–47.
(2) Bierer, J. Modern Social and Group Therapy. In Harris, N. G. (ed.), Modern Trends in Psychological Medicine. London: Hoeber, 1948.
(3) Corsini, R. J. Historic Background of Group Psychotherapy. Group Psychotherapy, 8 (1955), 219–55.
(4) Dreikurs, R. Early Experiments with Group Psychotherapy. Am. J. Psychotherapy, 13 (1959), 882–91.
(5) Dreikurs, R. Group Psychotherapy—General Review, First International Congress of Psychiatry (1950). Paris: Hermann, 1952, pp. 223–37.
(6) Hadden, S. B. Historic Background of Group Psychotherapy. Internat. J. Group Psychotherapy, 5 (1955), 162–68.

(7) KLAPMAN, J. W. Group Therapy: Theory and Practice. New York: Grune and Stratton, 1946.

(8) MEIERS, J. I. Origins and Development of Group Psychotherapy. Sociometry, 8 (1945), 499–534.

(9) MORENO, J. L. The First Book on Group Psychotherapy. New York: Beacon House, 1957.

(10) SLAVSON, S. R. Pioneers in Group Therapy. Internat. J. Group Psychotherapy, 1 (1951), 95–99.

(11) TEIRICH, H. R. Gruppentherapie und Dynamische Gruppenpsychotherapie in Deutschland. Heilkunst, 10 (1957), 1–6.

(12) THOMAS, G. W. Group Psychotherapy: A Review of the Recent Literature. Psychosom. Med., 5 (1943), 166–80.

(13) GIFFORD, S., and MACKENZIE, J. A Review of Literature on Group Treatment of Psychoses. Dis. Nerv. System, 9 (1948), 19–23.

(14) DREIKURS, R., and CORSINI, R. J. Twenty Years of Group Psychotherapy. Am. J. Psychiat., 110 (1954), 567–75.

(15) CORSINI, R. J. Historic Background of Group Psychotherapy: A Critique. Group Psychotherapy, 3 (1955), 213–19.

(16) SLAVSON, S. R. Bibliography on Group Psychotherapy. Brochure No. 32, American Group Psychotherapy Association, New York, 1950.

(17) KOTKOV, B. Bibliography of Group Therapy. J. Clin. Psychol., 6 (1950), 77–91.

(18) PRATT, J. H. The "Home Sanatorium" Treatment of Consumption. Boston Medical & Surgical J., 154 (January-June 1906), 210–16.

(19) PRATT, J. H. The Class Method of Treating Consumption in the Homes of the Poor. J.A.M.A., 49 (1907), 755–59.

(20) PRATT, J. H. The Class Method in the Home Treatment of Tuberculosis and What It Has Accomplished. Tr. Am. Climatol. A., 27 (1911), 87–118.

(21) PRATT, J. H. The Tuberculosis Class: An Experiment in Home Treatment. Proceedings, N.Y. Conference, Hosp. Soc. Serv., 4 (1917), 49–68.

(22) PRATT, J. H. The Group Method in the Treatment of Psychosomatic Disorders. Psychodrama Monogr. 19. New York: Beacon House, 1946, pp. 3–10.

(23) PRATT, J. H. The Use of Dejerine's Methods in the Treatment of the Common Neuroses by Group Psychotherapy. Bull. New England Med. Center, 15 (1953), 1–9.

(24) WORCESTER, E., McCOMB, S., and CORIAT, I. H. Religion and Medicine. London: Methuen, 1908.

(25) The Emmanuel Church Movement in Boston (Anonymous Editorial). N.Y. Med. J., 87 (1908), 1047–48.

(26) DEJERINE, J., and GAUCKLER, E. The Psychoneuroses and Their Treatment. Philadelphia: Lippincott, 1913.

(27) LAZELL, E. W. The Group Treatment of Dementia Praecox. Psychoanalyt. Rev., 8 (1921), 168–79.

(28) LAZELL, E. W. The Group Psychic Treatment of Dementia Praecox by

Lectures in Mental Re-education. U.S. Veterans' Bureau Med. Bull., 6 (1930), 733–47.

(29) MARSH, L. C. Group Treatment by the Psychological Equivalent of the Revival. Mental Hyg., 15 (1931), 328–49.

(30) MARSH, L. C. Group Therapy in the Psychiatric Clinic. J. Nerv. & Ment. Dis., 82 (1935), 381–92.

(31) JONES, E. The Life and Work of Sigmund Freud, vol. 2. New York: Basic Books, 1955.

(32) HOLLINGSHEAD, A. B., and REDLICH, F. C. Social Class and Mental Illness. New York: Wiley, 1958.

(33) MORENO, J. L. Die Gottheit als Komediant. Vienna: Anzengruber Verlag, 1911.

(34) MORENO, J. L. Who Shall Survive? New York: Beacon House, 1953.

(35) MORENO, J. L. Application of the Group Method to Classification. National Commission on Prisons and Prison Labor, 1932.

(36) MORENO, J. L. Psychodrama and Group Therapy. Sociometry, 9 (1946), 249–53.

(37) WENDER, L. The Dynamics of Group Psychotherapy and Its Application. J. Nerv. & Ment. Dis., 84 (1936), 54–60.

(38) SCHILDER, P. Results and Problems of Group Psychotherapy in Severe Neurosis. Mental Hyg., 23 (1939), 87–98.

(39) SCHILDER, P. The Analysis of Ideologies as a Psychotherapeutic Method Especially in Group Treatment. Am. J. Psychiat., 93 (1936), 601–17.

(40) FREUD, S. Group Psychology and the Analysis of the Ego. In Complete Works, vol. 18. London: Hogarth Press, 1922.

(41) SCHILDER, P. Introductory Remarks on Groups. J. Social Psychol., 12 (1940), 83–100.

(42) TEICHER, A., and DEMAREST, E. W. Transference in Group Therapy. Psychiatry, 17 (1954), 187–202.

(43) BURROW, T. The Group Method of Analysis. Psychoanalyt. Rev., 14 (1927), 268–80.

(44) OBERNDORF, C. A History of Psychoanalysis in America. New York: Grune and Stratton, 1953.

(45) Editorial Committee, Lifwynn Foundation. A Search For Man's Sanity: The Selected Letters of Trigant Burrow. New York: Oxford University Press, 1958.

(46) BURROW, T. Psychoanalysis and Society. J. Abnorm. Psychol., 7 (1912–13), 340–46.

(47) BURROW, T. The Psychoanalyst and the Community. J.A.M.A., 42 (1914), 1876–78.

(48) BURROW, T. The Social Basis of Consciousness. New York: Harcourt, Brace and World, 1927.

(49) LOWREY, L. et al. Group Therapy (special section meeting). Am. J. Orthopsychiat., 13 (1943), 648–90.

(50) SLAVSON, S. An Introduction to Group Therapy. New York: Commonwealth Fund, 1943.

(51) HOBBS, N. Group-Centered Psychotherapy. In Rogers, C., Client-Centered Therapy. Boston: Houghton Mifflin, 1951.

(52) ROGERS, C. Counseling and Psychotherapy. Boston: Houghton Mifflin, 1942.

(53) SLAVSON, S. R. Group Therapy. Mental Hyg., 24 (1940), 36–49.

(54) DURKIN, H. E. Dr. John Levy's Relationship Therapy Applied to a Play Group. Am. J. Orthopsychiat., 9 (1939), 583–98.

(55) GORLOW, L., HOCH, E. L., and TELSCHOW, E. F. The Nature of Non-directive Group Psychotherapy. New York: Columbia University Press, 1952.

(56) ENDS, E. J., and PAGE, C. W. A Study of Three Types of Group Psychotherapy with Hospitalized Male Inebriates. Quart. J. Stud. Alcohol, 18 (1957), 263–77.

(57) ENDS, E. J., and PAGE, C. W. Group Psychotherapy and Concomitant Psychological Change. Psychol. Monogr., 73, No. 10 (1959), 1–31.

(58) COONS, W. H. Interaction and Insight in Group Psychotherapy. Canad. J. Psychol., 11 (1957), 1–8.

(59) BOCK, J. C. Self-Orientation and Orientation to Others during Non-directive Group Psychotherapy. Med. Svcs. J. Canada, 17 (1961), 111–17.

(60) ROGERS, C. R. The Increasing Involvement of the Psychologist in Social Problems: Some Comments, Positive and Negative. Calif. State Psychol., 9 (1968), 29–31.

(61) BIERER, J. (ed.). Therapeutic Social Clubs. London: Lewis, 1948.

(62) FOULKES, S. H. Introduction to Group-Analytic Psychotherapy. London: Heinemann, 1948.

(63) FOULKES, S. H., and ANTHONY, E. J. Group Psychotherapy. London: Penguin Books, 1957.

(64) SUTHERLAND, J. D. Notes on Psychoanalytic Group Therapy. Psychiatry, 15 (1952), 111–17.

(65) EZRIEL, H. A Psycho-Analytic Approach to the Treatment of Patients in Groups. J. Ment. Sc., 96 (1950), 744–47.

(66) EZRIEL, H. Role of Transference in Psychoanalysis and Other Approaches to Group Treatment. Acta Psychotherapeutica, 7 (suppl.) (1959), 101–16.

(67) MERRY, J. Excitatory Group Therapy. J. Ment. Sc. (1953), 513–20.

(68) BION, W. R. Experiences in Groups, I. Human Relations, 1 (1948), 314–20.

(69) BION, W. R. Experiences in Groups, II. Human Relations, 1 (1948), 487–96.

(70) BION, W. R. Experiences in Groups, III. Human Relations, 2 (1949), 13–22.

(71) BION, W. R. Experiences in Groups, IV. Human Relations, 2 (1949), 295–304.

(72) BION, W. R. Experiences in Groups, V. Human Relations, 3 (1950), 3–14.

(73) BION, W. R. Experiences in Groups, VI. Human Relations, 3 (1950), 395–402.

(74) BION, W. R. Experiences in Groups, VII. Human Relations, 4 (1951), 221–28.

28   Introduction

(75) BION, W. R. Group Dynamics: A Re-View. Internat. J. Psychoanalysis, 33 (1952), 235–47.
(76) STOCK, D., and THELEN, H. Emotional Dynamics and Group Culture. New York: New York University Press, 1952.
(77) THELEN, H. Dynamics of Groups at Work. Chicago: University of Chicago Press, 1954.
(78) KLEIN, M. Contributions to Psychoanalysis 1921–1945. London: Hogarth Press, 1948.
(79) KRAUPL-TAYLOR, F. A History of Group and Administrative Therapy in Great Britain. Brit. J. Med. Psychol., 31 (1958), 153–73.
(80) ASTRUP, C. Group Therapy in a Mental Hospital with Special Regard to Schizophrenics. Acta Psychiat. et Neurol. Scandinav., 33 (1958), 1–20.
(81) WOLF, A. The Psychoanalysis of Groups, Am. J. Psychotherapy, 3 (1949), 16–50; 4 (1950), 525–58.
(82) BACH, G. Intensive Group Psychotherapy. New York: Ronald Press, 1954.
(83) BACH, G. Basic Concepts in Group Psychotherapy: A Field Theoretical View. Ztschr. fur Diagnostiche Psychologie, 5 (1957), 161–66.
(84) BACH, G. Fight with Me in Group Therapy. Chapter (15) in Wolberg, L., and Aronson, M. (eds.), Group Therapy. New York: Stratton Intercontinental, 1974, pp. 186–95.
(85) LEWIN, K. Field Theory in Social Science. New York: Harper and Bros., 1951.
(86) WHITAKER, C. A., and MALONE, T. The Roots of Psychotherapy. New York: Blakiston, 1953.
(87) MULLAN, H. Status Denial in Group Psychoanalysis. J. Nerv. & Ment. Dis., 122 (1955), 345–52.
(88) ROSENBAUM, M. The Challenge of Group Psychoanalysis. Psychoanalysis, 1 (1952), 42–58.
(89) VAN DUSEN, W. The Theory and Practice of Existential Analysis. Am. J. Psychotherapy, 11 (1957), 310–22.
(90) HORA, T. Existential Group Psychotherapy. Am. J. Psychotherapy, 13 (1959), 83–92.
(91) HILL, L. B. On Being Rather Than Doing in Group Psychotherapy. Internat. J. Group Psychotherapy, 8 (1958), 154–60.
(92) ROGERS, C. The Necessary and Sufficient Conditions of Therapeutic Personality Change. J. Consulting Psychol., 21 (1957), 85–103.
(93) ACKERMAN, N. The Psychodynamics of Family Life. New York: Basic Books, 1958.
(94) GROTJAHN, M. Psychonalysis and the Family Neurosis. New York: Norton, 1959.
(95) MIDELFORT, C. F. The Family in Psychotherapy. New York: Blakiston, 1957.
(96) ACKERMAN, N. W. Treating the Troubled Family. New York: Basic Books, 1966.
(97) ACKERMAN, N. W. (ed.). Family Therapy in Transition. Boston: Little, Brown, 1970.

(98) SATIR, V. Conjoint Family Therapy: A Guide to Theory and Technique. Palo Alto, Calif.: Science and Behavior Books, 1964.

(99) BOWEN, M. The Use of Family Therapy in Clinical Practice. Compr. Psychiat., 7 (1966), 345–74.

(100) MINUCHIN, S., MONTALVO, B., GUERNEY, B. C., JR., ROSMAN, B. L., and SHUMER, F. Families of the Slums. New York: Basic Books, 1967.

(101) JACKSON, D. D. The Individual and the Larger Contexts. Family Process, 6 (1967), 139–47.

(102) HALEY, J., and HOFFMAN, L. Techniques of Family Therapy. New York: Basic Books, 1967.

(103) FRAMO, J. L. (ed.). Family Interaction: A Dialogue between Family Researchers and Family Therapists. New York: Springer, 1972.

(104) MOSES, R. Some Comments on Family Therapy in Israel. Israel Annals Psychiat. & Related Disciplines, 9 (1971), 132–37.

(105) ROSENBAUM, M. The Family under Attack in an Era of Family Therapy. Chapter 9 in Wolberg, L., and Aronson, M. (eds.), Group Therapy—1974. New York: Stratton Intercontinental, 1974, pp. 94–109.

(106) ZUK, G. H. Family Therapy during 1964–1970. Psychotherapy: Theory, Research and Practice, 8 (1971), 90–97.

(107) BOSZORMENYI-NAGY, I. Loyalty Implications of the Transference Model of Psychotherapy. Arch. Gen. Psychiatry, 27 (1972), 374–80.

(108) BEELS, C. C., and FERBER, A. Family Therapy: A View. Family Process, 8 (1969), 280–333.

(109) ALGER, I. Audio-visual Technique in Family Therapy. Chapter in Bloch, D. (ed.), Techniques of Family Therapy. New York: Grune and Stratton, 1973.

(110) POSTNER, R. S., GUTTERMAN, H. A., SIGAL, J. J., EPSTEIN, N. B., and RAKOFF, V. M. Process and Outcome in Conjoint Family Therapy. Family Process, 10 (1971), 451–73.

(111) GUTTMAN, H. A. A Contraindication for Family Therapy. Arch. Gen. Psychiatry, 29 (1973), 352–55.

(112) WHITAKER, C. A. Psychotherapy with Couples. Am. J. Psychotherapy, 12 (1958), 18–23.

(113) SPITZ, H., and KOPP, S. B. Multiple Psychotherapy. Psychiat. Quart. Suppl., 31 (1957), 295–311.

(114) ROSENBAUM, M. Co-therapy. Chapter in Kaplan, H. I., and Sadock, B. J. (eds.), Comprehensive Group Psychotherapy. Baltimore: William and Wilkins, 1971, pp. 501–14.

(115) Fox, J. The Systematic Use of Hypnosis in Individual and Group Psychotherapy. Internat. J. Clin. & Exper. Hypnosis, 8 (1960), 109–14.

(116) PEBERDY, G. R. Hypnotic Methods in Group Psychotherapy. J. Ment. Sc., 106 (1960), 1016–20.

(117) SANDISON, R. A. The Role of Psychotropic Drugs in Group Therapy. Bull. World Health Organ., 21 (1959), 505–15.

(118) SANDISON, R. A. Group Therapy and Drug Therapy. Chapter in Rosenbaum, M., and Berger, M. (eds.), Group Psychotherapy and Group Function, rev. ed. New York: Basic Books, 1975.

(119) PERLS, F. Gestalt Therapy Verbatim. Lafayette, Calif.: Real People Press, 1969.

(120) PERLS, F. In and Out of the Garbage Pail. Moab, Utah: Real People Press, 1969.

(121) PERLS, F. S., HEFFERLINE, R. E., and GOODMAN, P. Gestalt Therapy. New York: Julian Press, 1951.

(122) POLSTER, E., and POLSTER, M. Gestalt Therapy Integrated: Contours of Theory and Practice. New York: Brunner-Mazel, 1973.

(123) RAINWATER, J., RESNICK, R., and JONES, P. Directory of Gestalt Therapists, 1973. Gestalt Therapy Institute of Los Angeles, 1973.

(124) BERNE, E. The Nature of Intuition. Psychiat. Quart., 23 (1949), 203–18.

(125) BERNE, E. Games People Play. New York: Grove Press, 1964.

(126) BERNE, E. Principles of Group Treatment. New York: Oxford University Press, 1966.

(127) STOLLER, F. H. Marathon Group Therapy. In Gazda, G. M. (ed.), Innovations to Group Psychotherapy. Springfield, Ill.: Thomas, 1968.

(128) STOLLER, F. H. Accelerated Interaction—a Time Limited Approach Based on the Brief Intensive Group. Internat. J. Group Psychotherapy, 18 (1968), 220–25.

(129) GOULDING, R. L. Four Models of Transactional Analysis. Internat. J. Group Psychotherapy, 26 (1976), 385–92.

(130) BERGER, M. (ed.). Videotape Techniques in Psychiatric Training and Treatment. New York: Brunner-Mazel, 1970. Rev. ed., 1978.

(131) REICH, W. Character Analysis. New York: Orgone Institute Press, 1949.

(132) PIERRAKOS, J. C. Observations and Techniques in Bioenergetic Group Therapy. In Milman, D. S., and Goldman, G. D. (eds.), Group Process Today. Springfield, Ill.: Thomas, 1974.

(133) ZIFERSTEIN, I. Group Psychotherapy in the Soviet Union. Am. J. Psychiat., 129, No. 5 (1972), 595–99.

(134) YALOM, I. The Theory and Practice of Group Psychotherapy. New York: Basic Books, 1970.

2 Toward an Ethic and Philosophy of Group Psychotherapy

Max Rosenbaum

WHEN A THERAPIST practices individual psychotherapy, he often ignores the complexity of the process in which he is engaged. The therapist's belief in what he is doing is so strong and his patient's need is so manifest, that both can obscure the deeper implications of what their search involves. In most cases the psychotherapy becomes a religious quest and, in fact, is a psychological religion, which it should not be. Religion is based on absolute faith. Psychotherapy is earthbound.

When we work together in a group setting there can be no avoidance of the philosophical implications of our task—unless the group is so tyrannized by an omniscient therapist that no member dares question the deeper meaning of why we are all here. Is it to analyze our petty miseries so that we can be prepared for the larger misery of life? Or will awareness and insight into our unconscious needs give us that absolute joy that is promised by so many of the psychological gurus?

Freud chose not to make the philosophical decision. He placed his faith in logical positivism, and toward the end of his life became more and more embittered about a world which he perceived as destructive. His realism was often a pessimism, although he was possibly not as despairing as Thomas Hobbes, the English philosopher who labeled man as "homo homini lupis"—a wolf, a vicious and cruel animal with no compassion for his fellows. Unlike Rousseau and Thoreau, Hobbes believed that man "au natural" would use any method to satisfy his desires and his need for power. Hobbes believed that civilization was the constraining force. Freud remained an agnostic and for the most part presented his clinical observations, although one is led to believe that an agnostic is simply one who cannot make up his mind. It is making up one's mind that is so painful, for history has indicated that man chooses *not* out of a sense of decision, but out of a sense of desperation. The impulsive act becomes a substitute for the considered decision.

The medieval theologians would tell of Buridan's ass, standing between a trough of water and a bale of hay. The animal could not decide which to choose, so it starved to death and died of thirst. It is this dilemma that confronts modern man, and it clearly manifests itself when a group of people come together for psychotherapy. The group therapist avoids confronting this dilemma by embarking on a new set of therapeutic tricks. He becomes excited by what he considers to be new and good. Yet he forgets the rabbinic scholar who noted, when presented with a new theory, that "there is much that is new and much that is good about what you have said. What is good is not new and what is new is not good." While he may have been guilty of some irritation, he was probably annoyed by the lack of thought that led to overeager proselytes.

There is nothing so terrible about the struggle for an ethic and philosophy. It is a lifelong task. Immanuel Kant* wrote his great work in his sixties, and this great work is still a subject of controversy by students who cannot agree with what he said. He attempted to reconcile the rationalist and empiricist points of view. We live in a tortured time, and the world has probably always been tortured. Some psychotherapists simply ignore the time and place. During the early 1940s a labor union produced a musical comedy. The show depicted a form of labor organization and it was titled *Pins and Needles*, which referred to the International Ladies' Garment Workers' Union. One skit was intended to satirize Clifford Odets, the playwright of the 1930s and 1940s who wrote of the workingman's struggle. In this skit the janitor of an apartment house was sitting in his basement apartment eating fruit from a bowl. As he was eating, the tenants from the building gathered around to complain. They said, "The building is a shambles, there is no heat, the garbage is uncollected, the windows are broken, the hallways are filthy, etc.," but the janitor continued to eat as he listened to the complaints. To each tenant he said the same thing: "It's the system. Nothing can be done."

Some group psychotherapists, intent on self-exploration, have decided to remove themselves and their patients from life. The idea of facing life creates too much anxiety, and they have become the "mind fuckers" whom Frederick Perls ridiculed. His impatience with the caricature of inquiry that many psychotherapists engage in led him to some rather extreme positions. But his valid statement was: "Man does not exist to please others, nor do others exist to please him."

Other therapists have decided to reject the complexities of life. These are the therapists who have decided that the unrepressed life is *the* life.

* Kant lived from 1724 to 1804. His great works were published between 1781 and 1790.

Again, they have not done their library reading or homework. As they have rediscovered the wheel, the statement is made that primary pleasure is the solution to all of life's problems. To live in the experience of the *now* will be enough. Yet this is merely another form of behaviorism. It denies the existential anxiety of man as he is caught up in the dilemma of creation. Freud predicted that this would happen in his book, *Group Psychology and the Analysis of the Ego*, as he observed man's passion for authority and his "wishes to be governed by unrestricted force." The unrepressed life approach merely activates the erotic forces that people repress in the unconscious. Thus, individuals come together and pool their collective erotic longings with the endorsement of a leader who is the parent figure, and through this transference phenomena believe that their basic plight in life, the existential dilemma of man's place in creation, is resolved. Perhaps it is, as long as they remain in the "security" of this particular group membership. It is a kind of mutual reinforcement as long as each person reinforces the other in the belief that fulfillment will come from a "primal scream" or touching or hugging. The disenchantment of these people is with a psychoanalysis that proved to be intellectual as it analyzed and talked. There was an understandable void. Somewhere man was searching for a type of experience that would give *him* meaning and some meaning to life, without surrendering himself to the tyranny of a church or theology which insisted on blind faith. But as Martin Buber pointed out, "If you turn dung this way and that way, it still remains dung. And the energy and time that it takes to stir dung, you might be stringing pearls."

The most ambitious inquiry into psychoanalytic psychotherapy became to a large extent devoted to the statistical analysis of results (1). It is almost a paean to rationalistic theory in its failure to distinguish between logic and the facts of life, the fundamental flaw in the rationalistic theory. Perhaps the refuge was to turn to mathematics, so pure a science because it is removed from the facts of life. What the study did not tackle was the complex issues involved in a philosophy of science. It assumed that psychoanalytic psychotherapy can be administered like a drug and ignored the complexity of psychotherapist and patient. More important, it ignored what brings them together. While the study cannot be faulted for its sincerity and its effort to find answers to questions, it, like so many studies, ignored the complexity of man's search for meaning to his life.

What has happened to psychoanalysis is that its supporters have proclaimed it as a new faith. One analyst writes:

> I had four analysts—one before becoming a psychoanalytic candidate, two during training, and one afterwards. Then after some years, I had five years of group analytic therapy and three in the leaderless group. I feel at times hopelessly addicted to therapy, as though treating patients has become a ticket to being a lifelong patient. At other times I suspect myself of pursuing the ideal object and hoping to become an ideal object myself. *Since*

these days, psychotherapy promises perfection and religion does not, I now pursue therapy as I once pursued religion, always hoping to find a theory, individual practitioners, or myself to be perfect (2, p. 458).

A careful reading of Freud does not indicate that his intention was to form a new faith. His effort was to enable the patient to choose, but he never suggested the alternatives to choice. Freud did not take upon himself the burden of prescribing new faiths for mankind. He challenged the existing beliefs. In his own life he was an agnostic; and for him, man became agnostic. However, an agnostic is like Buridan's ass. His despair becomes more intense as he will not move to choice. In this moment of despair, the psychotherapist chooses intellectual inquiry as the new faith. This is his resolution of the agnostic dilemma. This solution is generally the choice of psychotherapists. It is not the choice of the patient who comes to psychotherapy.

What the group psychotherapist believes may or may not work for him, but unless he probes into the meaning of the patient's presence in that meeting, his faith becomes a religion which he fosters. As man has lost faith in the meaning of the world, he is encouraged to turn to psychological inquiry as a new meaning of the world. The therapist, unwilling to give up his own commitment to psychological religion, will not question and certainly does not encourage questioning on the part of his patients. The psychological man that Rieff described is to be "anti-heroic, shrewd, carefully counting his satisfactions and dissatisfactions" (3). This is a parody of man because it makes him little more than an accountant balancing his assets and debits.

It is the quest of man to find meaning to life that has led to more and more psychological gurus. It is the task of therapy to urge man to become more heroic and to face the anxieties of life. It was Job who found that his search for meaning could not be met by ritually following God. The existential meaning of his travail was to find that life itself is anxiety-provoking and that man must face this anxiety. The "comforters" who gathered around him attempted to elicit from him the answer to the question, "Perhaps you, secretly, really didn't believe in God?" They were little more than those therapists who, whenever confronted by the existential dilemma of life, ritualistically turn back to the unconscious. They have distorted the meaning of the unconscious.

There are many versions of what Immanuel Kant meant, but it is not necessary to go into all the arguments. There is common agreement on his *Categorical Imperative*—morality prescribes that all persons shall be treated as ends in themselves and that life shall be organized accordingly. "Each person shall subordinate the pursuit of his own end to the requirements of a harmonious society of such persons" (4, p. 126). As one follower of Kant expressed Kant's ideal, it may be summarized: "The highest good would be attainable if all the conflicting wills fully realized one another" (5, p. 145). Therefore, Kant felt that the harmony of persons is the only ideal that agrees with reason. In his effort to deduce moral imperatives from reason, he ran into a cul-de-sac. This is not too different from the case of those psychotherapists who trace all behavior back to the method of inquiry. What Kant did point out was his ideal of the harmonious society. In this society all people are moral finalities, and this society serves all members who agree to this societal structure. But it is the subordination of one's own ends that is the flaw in Kant's position. For each person can rationalize his own ends as the desirable goal of the society. Kant confused logical universality with social universality. He could not accept the fact that different people will practice different codes of behavior.

Later, we will discuss the overeager patient who masks deep-seated resistance by agreeing quickly to enter a group. We note this as a form of unwillingness to explore the unconscious and a method to enter a group quickly in order to hide. A far deeper problem is the speed with which patients attempt to turn group psychotherapy into a new illusion and to use group psychotherapy as a new religion. Freud viewed religious faith as a remnant of man's infantile need to cling to the parent. But faith can be very much an adult belief, because it is based on man's struggle to be heroic and to confront life and its travails. Man is looking for ideals to live by. Intellectual inquiry is not an ideal. It is a way to an ideal.

The group psychotherapist, as all psychotherapists, all too readily accepts society's need to make him a secular priest. It is because the psychotherapist has not faced his own fears of the life experience that he encourages the new patient to believe that inquiry into the unconscious will solve all of life's tragedies. What we are doing, if we are honest, is to share with the patient the fact that we are all engaged in a struggle to understand and live in the wilderness. The honest therapist accepts the patient's faith (transference) to be used finally to resolve neurotic transference. He does not deny faith but points out that it can be used self-destructively. It is the fundamental premise of our position that the integrity of the group psychotherapist cannot be compromised by the patient's need to believe in him. The therapist must always use this belief to motivate the patient to believe in himself. Of course, the therapist accepts the power that has been granted to him. The neurotic therapist exploits the patient because he ignores or all too willingly accepts the power without the slightest understanding of the deep trust that is expressed. This is why he may carelessly or hurtfully exploit the patient. By both accepting and carelessly exploiting the patient, he does not accept his own fundamental responsibility to the patient. No matter what language he expresses (for example, I am not responsible for what you do), he *is* responsible for the trust that has been placed in him. The religious leader uses that trust because he believes that he has the answer. The ethical psychotherapist realizes that it is his task to encourage the patient to find an answer that is meaningful. This answer may not be meaningful for the therapist. That is irrelevant.

Many psychotherapists recoil from the responsibility of trust. They become wedded to technique in the vague belief that it will make them neutral or objective. This is supposed to be the hallmark of logical positivism. This is what Freud wanted to believe in his concept of the "neutral analyst." But to be objective, for these therapists, means that the therapist and the patient become objects. This is why many psychotherapists take refuge in the belief that skill in technique (translate this as "objectivity") makes them more human in finding their own humanity. It is in essence a denial of the dialogue to which we are committed. In the dialogue we recognize the integrity of the human being who is in psychotherapy. We take no refuge in technique and are prepared to modify technique, not as a new mechanistic method of objectivity, but as a way of establishing a deeper dialogue. All of this dialogue is based upon our recognition of the transference that is at work. The transference is the powerful tool that we use, but we are always aware of its deeper philosophical meaning and its relationship to the patient's search for a belief.

The newly trained group psychotherapist comes to a supervisory session and a meeting with the more experienced therapist in the belief that he will receive directions as to what to do and what not to do. The meeting is often a reinforcement of the older therapist's belief (if he has one) that he really knows the right answers. It is similar to the older teacher who does not really understand education (from the Latin verb *educare*—to lead forth). Secure in the belief that he has the answers, he will *not* listen to the student and does not encourage the student to believe in his own intuition and perceptions. In contrast with this behavior, the great psychotherapists were increasingly humble as they became more and more experienced. It is not mechanistic to look for a *concept* which may help clarify the dialogue. Thus, transference is a concept. It is mechanistic to look for a *technique* (for example, touching patients to clarify the dialogue). The patient, trapped in a world which seems terrifying, turns to the psychotherapist whom he believes can make order out of chaos. He does not meet a human being, but often meets a technocrat. This is clearly seen in behavior modification therapy which cures symptomatology but does not confront the dilemma of man's anxiety.

In 1939, the English translation of Kurt Goldstein's book *The Organism* was published and distributed for American and English readers (6). His aim was to "understand the essential nature of the organism." The book expounded a special philosophy of the biological sciences called "holism." It was this same author (Goldstein) who was to significantly influence Abraham Maslow who, in turn, influenced the human potential movement. About that time (1940), B. F. Skinner reviewed the book and stated that to "understand the essential nature of the organism" (Goldstein's desire) "would be avoided like the plague by most contemporary scientists" (Skinner's comment). Goldstein further stated: "The closer we stand in our relations to a living being, the sooner we may expect to arrive at a correct judgment regarding its essential nature." And further, he said: "Courage, in its final analysis, is nothing but an affirmative answer to the shocks of existence which must be borne for the actualization of one's own nature." Goldstein, in essence, was moving toward phenomenology. Skinner, in his very critical review of the book, could not accept a philosophy of science that did not include careful structure. What Skinner was writing about, to be repeated again in his later research and writings, was a technological view of man. He was astute enough to recognize that the fundamental disagreement was in philosophy. But Skinner is sure in his faith that technological supremacy will solve all problems of life. The psychoanalytic-existential approach does not offer this assurance.

The idea of becoming a person on your own is very frightening. There are patients who move from therapist to therapist, collecting gods. This group of patients is rarely confronted with what their search means. Each therapist becomes trapped into becoming more technically proficient than the last technocrat. The patient reduces the search for life's meaning to simplistic terms. The woman whose husband is unfaithful turns to the group and says, "How can I live through tomorrow night when he visits his girl friend? He does this to me." The group members may be supportive, but somewhere, hopefully, a group member will ask, "What is there about your existence that says you cannot live without him?" The patient is confronted with life's meaning: What am I to myself? Or else he ends up like Kierkegaard's man, who was so perfectly ordered that he woke up one day to find out he was dead. Then there is the charming Hassidic tale of the man who woke up one day and carefully checked his list—his shoes, suit, shirt, tie—he was bathed, shaved, and fed, but he felt that constant gnawing. Where am I? he asked. *He* was not on the list. This is the dilemma of psychotherapy. The list is ordered, but where is the person?

There is a danger that the existential position is distorted. Some group psychotherapists believe that the "encounter" is what therapy is all about. This does not move far from the traditional psychoanalytic view that to uncover or unravel man is the goal of therapy. It is the meaning of the encounter that is to be experienced and clarified. Freud would place faith and reason together. He would question intuition and look toward the unconscious. But this could not give him all the answers he wanted. So reason alone was not the answer. In his famous essay on *Analysis Terminable and Interminable,* Freud recognized that insight divorced from transference would not be effective (7). He referred to the personal qualities of the analyst (called by many "countertransference"), and to the analysts who use psychoanalysis to remain the same. They do not change and that is why he recommended that analysts reenter analysis at five-year intervals. The work with groups forces the group therapist to reexamine himself continually as well as to reexamine life.

As Freud moved into later years, he recognized the enormity of life, but prided himself on being the complete realist. Yet he noted "our anxiety in the face of life's dangers," and was closer to being an existentialist than he admitted (8).

It is the fear of the existential dilemma that pushes psychotherapists to accept a behavioristic position in our culture. Since we live in a Western culture which demands payoff (the *bottom line* is the phrase businessmen use), it is always easier to conceive of human relationships as a push-pull process. The businessman, when confronted with problems in industry, thinks in terms of assigning a larger work force, or devising more complex machinery, or installing a more computerized system. Computer systems will specify areas of criminality but will not get into the basic problem of the motivation toward crime. Sociologists become discouraged and turn to behaviorism (9). The human being is ignored as someone who *discovers*. Skinner dismisses man's inner self and therefore ignores man's search for inner freedom and autonomy. At least Skinner is more honest (10). Human behavior, according to Skinner, is controlled by the chanciness of the environment, aside from genetic factors. He states, "A person does not act upon the world—the world acts upon him" (10, p. 211). He sees the survival of man as the ultimate. For those psychotherapists who are uncomfortable with the thought that survival is the ultimate, there is the alternative offered, to enter into speculations about systems theory (11).

This uneasy compromise is an effort to codify human behavior within the paradigm of Newton's concepts. In a short letter, a theoretical physicist noted:

> The model of explanation in terms of cause, universal law, and movement, does not hold when we describe human actions. Communication—the transfer of pattern or meaning—is the principal relationship between men, while causality—the transmission of energy—suffices to relate things to each other. Human beings respond to meaning, not only to cause. Meanings are established by experience.

Earlier in the same communication, he notes:

> In any psychological or social theory we describe an organism, not a simple, relatively unorganized object like an atom; we have self-movement and evolution. Therefore, the explanation has a different aim from that in physics. (12).

Socrates, on the very day of his death, criticized Anaxagoras, a natural philosopher, for attempting to explain human and natural phenomena with the same principles.

One writer becomes trapped by his own definition of science since he accepts the causal definition. Thus, Chein (13) perceives the psychology of today as divided into neobehaviorism which he calls "scientism" and existential psychoanalysis which he calls "clinicalism." Chein sees the basic difference between these two views as the concept of knowledge and truth. From this he moves into the difference between "truth"* and "verity."† It is not relevant to this chapter to discuss the difference, but Chein bases his arguments as to verities on Newton's theories. Again, he is locked into his paradigm of science.

What all of this leads to is Martin Buber's statement: "All real living is meeting." Much of what passes for meeting is peripheral contact. The encounter group which meets for a series of exercises is not engaged in "meeting." The world of experiencing becomes entirely subjective. It is what Buber called "I-It." It is also, at times, the effort to comprehend and order. The "I-Thou" of Buber is the relationship, the mutualism— whether between men or the world of nature or God.

Martin Heidegger described man's basic fear as anxiety *of* being-in-the-world as well as anxiety *about* being in the world. Soren Kierkegaard viewed man in terms of the story of Adam and Eve, ejected from the Garden of Eden. As man reflected upon himself, "bit the apple," he was ejected from the Garden of Eden. Kierkegaard was rather pessimistic. Buber is the positive existentialist. He reaffirms the "sanctity of man." Man's essence is that "he shares in finitude and he shares in infinity" (14).

Man has this potential and he has the freedom of choice for good and evil. His whole being is part of this existence. To ask "What is man?" is too often to deny the more central questions "Who am I?" and "What is my existence?" The true existential position is acceptance. This has been stated clearly by Buber. It means that the person who comes to therapy is accepted as he is. This acceptance means that he is confirmed—confirmed in his potential to become. This establishes the climate of trust and the transference that ensues. The therapist now confirms the fact of existence and the patient's struggle between the forces of good and evil— the polarities of life—the becoming and the self-destruction.

The goal of therapy is not to reassure the patient that certain learned patterns of behavior will make the world an easier place in which to live. This is the danger of therapeutic techniques which stress manipulation of others. The techniques become the aspirin of life. The techniques ignore the problems of stomach bleeding that may occur, if they are not occurring while the headache is dulled. Our task is to confront the absurdities of life,

---

* "Truth," according to Chein, is "the property that supposedly can be contradicted by data."

† "Verity," according to Chein, is "the property that cannot be so contradicted." Verities are therefore more basic, according to Chein.

to confront its paradoxes, and not to learn how to maneuver to avoid the anxieties of creation. When we can live with the absurdities and accept them as part of the human condition, we have faced life.

References

(1) KERNBERG, O. F., BURSTEIN, E. D., COYNE, L., APPLEBAUM, A., HORO-WITZ, L., and VOTH, H. Psychotherapy and Psychoanalysis. Topeka, Kans.: Menninger Foundation, 1972.

(2) KLINE, F. M. Terminating a Leaderless Group. Internat. J. Group Psychotherapy, 24, No. 4 (October 1974), 452–59.

(3) RIEFF, P. The Triumph of the Therapeutic. New York: Harper and Row, 1966.

(4) PERRY, R. B. Realms of Value. Cambridge, Mass.: Harvard University Press, 1954.

(5) ROYCE, J. The Religious Aspect of Philosophy. Boston: Houghton Mifflin, 1897.

(6) GOLDSTEIN, K. The Organism. New York: American Book, 1939.

(7) FREUD, S. In Strachey, J. (ed.), The Standard Edition of the Complete Psychological Works of Sigmund Freud, vol. 23. London: Hogarth Press, 1964, pp. 216–53.

(8) FREUD, S. The Future of an Illusion (1927). In Strachey, J. (ed.), The Standard Edition of the Complete Psychological Works of Sigmund Freud, vol. 21. London: Hogarth Press, 1961, pp. 3–56.

(9) HOMANS, G. C. The Sociological Relevance of Behaviorism. In Burgess, R. L., and Bushell, D., Jr. (eds.), Behavioral Sociology. New York: Columbia University Press, 1969, pp. 1–24.

(10) SKINNER, B. F. Beyond Freedom and Dignity. New York: Knopf, 1971, p. 211.

(11) RAPAPORT, A. A Philosophical View. In Lipsum, A. (ed.), Positive Feedback: A General Systems Approach to Positive/Negative Feedback in Material Causality. Oxford: Pergamon, 1960, pp. 1–8.

(12) HUTTON, E. H. Letter. Group Analysis, 7. No. 2 (July 1974), 77.

(13) CHEIN, I. The Science of Behavior and the Image of Man. New York: Basic Books, 1972.

(14) BUBER, M. Between Man and Man, trans. by Smith, R. G. Boston: Beacon Press, 1955.

II

THE PSYCHOANALYTIC
METHOD AND INNOVATIONS

3 Psychoanalytic Group Therapy

Max Rosenbaum

THE TREATMENT OF psychiatric patients in groups is now accepted. Shortages in mental health personnel have intensified the search for shorter and more economical means of treatment. In response to this need, group psychotherapy has developed to its present state.

Much of the advance in group therapy is based upon the fruitful participation of mental health disciplines. This cross-fertilization bodes well for the development of group psychotherapy. It brings to the problems of group communication new insights and understandings concerning human nature. It avoids overreliance upon traditional medical points of view and upon psychiatric overconcern with pathological functioning.

The characteristic of flexibility allows the group method to be tried with many kinds of patients, psychotic and neurotic, and in many institutions, both psychiatric and nonpsychiatric. Misconceptions of the method itself, of its potentiality for changing the personality, and of its long-range, reconstructive goals may lead to confusion. Because of the natural desire of people to come together in groups, group formation becomes relatively simple but not necessarily therapeutic.

In 1966, the American Group Psychotherapy Association (AGPA) published the following definition of group psychotherapy:

> Group psychotherapy represents a method within the broader realm of psychotherapy wherein a trained practitioner (usually psychiatrist, clinical psychologist or social worker) utilizes the emotional interaction, in a small, carefully planned group to effect "repair" of personality malfunctioning in individuals specifically selected for this purpose. A clinical orientation, which includes a diagnostic assessment of each group member's problems, is part of this picture. Furthermore, the patients are cognizant of the psychotherapeutic purpose and accept the group as a means to obtain help in modifying their personal mode of functioning.

43

In the following decade, because of the plethora of techniques that came to the surface and that were described by their practitioners as "group psychotherapy," the AGPA was impelled to set up a task force, in 1975, to redefine group psychotherapy and to establish the boundaries of the field. The task force is to study the boundaries of psychotherapy groups and to study the reciprocal interplay between these groups and nonpsychotherapy groups.

In this chapter we focus upon a regressive-reconstructive therapy, suggesting a method that encompasses all ages. The mixed, adolescent discussion group, the activity group of puberty, and the preschool play group are all represented in the interactional portion of adult group psychotherapy. Interaction occurs in a regressive environment in which the men and women emotionally reenact their pasts. In turn, therefore, they are seen to be "adolescent," "child," and "infant." Although it is true that certain techniques must be applied with the younger patient depending upon whether it is play, activity, or discussion, the essential dynamics and their understanding remain unchanged from one age group to another.

Regardless of the therapist's frame of reference, and depending upon the extent of his training, he can interpret behavior in a group as he does in individual psychotherapy. Thus a "Freudian," "Jungian," "Reichian," or "Adlerian" can begin to practice group psychotherapy. However, as he proceeds, he must begin to realize the value of the group as a whole, the means of inducing regressive interaction, and the group techniques that foster and eventually bring about reconstruction of the personalities involved. In all of this, the "group" becomes an essential curative factor.

The Goals of Psychoanalytic Group Therapy

The aim of therapy must always be considered when the efficacy of a certain kind of group treatment is being determined. Slavson states that "while education, suggestion, guidance, and advice may be helpful in dealing with some types of adjustment problems, they should not be confounded with real psychotherapy; the aim of which is to affect within varying degrees changes within the personality structure" (1). This point is consistent with those therapies that are both regressive-reconstructive and repressive-constructive.

The *regressive-reconstructive* approach centers upon the possibility that the patient will become responsible not just for himself, but also for society. The emphasis is on the patient's responsibility as a creator of his culture and as a transmitter of patterns of behavior. In order to achieve this, his personality must continue to change in an evolving way after formal therapy has ended.

In therapies that permit *repression* and *construction,* the patient also develops some responsibility for himself, but at the same time there is an acceptance of the rational authority, which is for the "good of all." Adaptation and adjustment play a more striking role here than in the regressive-reconstructive therapies. The patient's major task in life is considered to be the transmission of culture, but not necessarily the creation of a "new element in his culture."

If one's therapy is regressive-reconstructive, three prominent characteristics emerge in the functioning personality of the patient as he leaves his group:

1. He develops an individual responsibility to choose with risk.
2. He develops a responsibility for others (the group); as he leaves, this becomes both a social and cultural responsibility.
3. He develops an evolving awareness of self and self in relationship to another (or others).

What Is "Cure"?

Cure indicates a total change in the personality by way of sufficient regression followed by reconstruction. This is achieved if there is sufficient interaction in the therapy group with free associative activity.

If group psychotherapy is in the area of repression and construction, patients leave therapy at different levels of growth: at the level of intellectual awareness, at the level of emotional insight, and at the level where moral, ethical, and aesthetic values are quite spontaneously reassessed and reevaluated. These goals are more circumscribed than in the regressive therapies. To be relieved of symptoms, to develop a respect for rational authority, to be adapted and adjusted to one's potential and environment are goals worthy of the efforts of both the patients and the therapist.

Most forms of individual psychotherapy are successful in widening the patient's self-awareness so that he discards attitudes that no longer serve his "best interests." However, often individual therapies fall short by making little effort to advance the patient's necessary relatedness to his fellow man. The major contribution of group psychotherapy to society's mental health is the correction of this fault.

The group meeting must not become an intellectual forum blocking the patient's larger, more total responsibility to relate emotionally. If the therapist is too "analytical," the members are denied the opportunity of, and perhaps are even prevented from, making the final, essential commitments: *love for and reponsible involvement with another.*

Upon entering a therapeutic group, new patients are impressed by the closeness and the frankness of its members. This ability to relate and to reveal establishes an unusual environment. The new patient often feels excluded and finds the interactional process, although conducive to change, very upsetting. The novelty of this reaction indicates that, although the therapeutic group is composed of members of society who fit into the fabric of the culture, it is nonetheless different from all other groups.

This difference between the treatment group and other groups rests in its unconventionality. Sitting in a circle, face to face with other men and women, the members are encouraged to feel and talk freely about themselves, others, the other group members, and the therapist. In this judgment-free climate, a member reveals his likes and dislikes, his past memories and experiences, his present activities, and his hopes for the future. He is encouraged to tell dreams, fantasies, and innermost longings. In this setting rational and irrational bonds are established among all of the interactors, including the therapist.

Schilder (2) indicated that certain basic attitudes held by the "emotionally disoriented patient" had to be uncovered in order for therapy to occur. At any moment in the therapeutic group, the following attitudes are being revealed for one or more patients: (a) the need to love and be loved, (b) the tendency (and the lack of it) to maintain one's own support, (c) the tendency to maintain the integrity of the body, (d) the tendency to eat, drink, and acquire and retain property, (e) the tendency to expel what cannot be used or what is threatening, and (f) the tendency to handle and destroy objects and human beings and to get insights into their structure.

At the first session of a therapy group, there will be a tendency on the part of the members and the therapist to give structure to the meeting. This tendency toward structure is most readily noted in homogeneous groups. These groups, because of their common characteristic regardless of its nature, develop an early quasi-cohesiveness and tend to ignore the therapist, or at best to see him as apart from themselves.

At a later time in the group process a more certain cohesion develops (3). This is based upon the members' realization that it is up to them, that they can no longer incriminate parents or significant adults or the therapist, and that there is an emergency, unique to each one but common to all. Patients at this stage are seen to help each other in two distinct ways:

1. *Accidentally.* Patients who originally found themselves in a group not of their own choosing become aware of their need for this group. This is similar to children being born into a family, also not of their own choice, which they become accustomed to and need. Unlike the patients' own families, the psychoanalytic therapeutic group conveys to them the possibility of, *as well as their responsibility to risk,* new behavior replacing old. The properly organized and conducted group becomes a medium for the members' expression of (a) aggression and hostility toward others, including members and therapist, (b) love and hate, (c) sexual feelings, (d) despair, depression, and anxiety, (e) irrationalities, dreams, fantasies, and intuitions, and (f) gradual renunciation of immediate gratification (4).

2. *Through design.* Patients are placed in a psychoanalytic therapeutic group because it is beneficial to them. Both the proper composition of the

therapeutic group and the individual preparation required before group introduction indicate that the therapist has a plan of treatment. His design is primary, based as it is upon his psychodynamic knowledge and his experience; and his responsibility lies in bringing the group together, conducting it, and finally in terminating it (4). The therapist supplies the original interpretive effort. Soon, however, he finds that he is assisted by seven to nine "co-therapists."

The patients make accurate but untimely interpretations, which do not have the impact usually achieved by the therapist. These responses prepare the member for similar ones given by the therapist at a later time.

The patients make multiple identical interpretations, thus reinforcing the conclusion suggested by the therapist.

The patients give multiple different interpretations, which tend to fill out the therapist's effort to give the member a more total understanding of his problem. The fact that group members come from different backgrounds, cultures, and races insures the overall accuracy of these observations.

In making an objective appraisal of the group, one becomes aware that vastly different kinds of behavior exist from one member to another, because in the continuous group new patients replace the old when they leave therapy. The uniqueness of each person in both healthy and unhealthy personality traits promotes different behavior and different rates of change.

If the therapy is intense there is an increased reverence for self. Prior to group entry, the patient finds that his self-esteem is at a low ebb. Quite soon, in the permissive milieu, so like and yet so unlike one's family, the member becomes aware that he can help and be helped.

There is an acknowledgment of *despair*. After transferences have been activated, and then as they are being undermined, the member feels disheartened, upset, and at times quite helpless and hopeless.

There is a feeling of *being abandoned*. A member is abandoned, not by the group, but by the discovery that values he has long treasured are nonexistent, and he feels abandoned until new values are discovered and made his own through action.

There is an acute *awareness of anxiety*. Anxiety in inherent in life. Patients are required to take risks, to choose, to reflect with action. Anxiety is a necessary part of a regressive-reconstructive group psychotherapy (5).

Resistance to the Small Group in an Institution

Resistance to the therapy group abounds in those institutions that are highly and rigidly structured and in which traditional procedures are prized and psychological, dynamic understandings are thought dangerous (6).

Because this phenomenon of resistance is so general and because, when it is present, it endangers the small-group project, certain precautionary steps should be taken by the group leader. First, the aims, the procedures, and the possible outcomes must be described to the highest levels of both administrative and professional responsibility. The orientation of these persons is best accomplished in a small-group setting so that they can experience for themselves what the group participants will eventually experience. Second, the group leader must make clear, not only to the administrators and others in key positions but also to the small-group personnel themselves, the confidentiality of the small-group productions. The group should meet for a specific number of times, on a set day, at a set time.

During the many meetings—determined by the needs of the participants and the administrative requirement—mixed emotions color the transactions. Colleagues eye one another questioningly, wondering how far they can go in discussing a personal difficulty. There are always a few in search of the security to be found in the well structured staff meeting. Relief from tension can be achieved by the therapist if he fosters goal-directed activities during a difficult time. Here he can bring up a problem that pertains to all, or he can suggest an explanation that relates directly to the immediate group behavior. If self-consciousness prevails or if silence dominates the session, he can lapse back into a "teacher" role. This kind of group activity can be terminated easily, whereas group psychoanalytic psychotherapy requires preparation for discontinuance should this be necessary over a summer vacation period. An intensively involved psychotherapy group *cannot* be terminated casually. Others have noted that "termination is an extremely important aspect of group psychotherapy. . . . Termination in group psychotherapy is related to the institutional ethos, group culture, and therapist attitudes about termination. When genuine termination occurs, it is marked by an explicit plan, group reaction to the plan, and clear implications for the departing member, the group, and the therapist . . . termination in group psychotherapy becomes an extremely powerful and humanizing experience for all concerned" (7).

There are two general results from these "orientation" small-group sessions. If the group leader wants to convey some technical aspect to the group—he will rely heavily upon his leadership role. His group will have little emotional impact but, during the discussion period, it will achieve some of the aims indicated in this section.

If the therapist is interested in broader goals or minimal personality alteration (not so intensive as in psychotherapy), he will allow the agenda to shift with the immediate needs of the members. Sitting down and facing one's problem in open discussion will result quite quickly in serious communication among the members. As the process continues, there is a sharing of responsibility. In general, then, the interpersonal relationships existing among those in the small group are intensified; and the number and amount of the distortions are lessened.

These changes within the personality of each member are reflected in a change in the group structure and climate. As the group itself is modified, the culture of the institution is changed. Martin and Hill state that "the group can proceed and make decisions acceptable to the group without compulsive consensus. The group can now regulate its process to a certain extent and the members feel that they are, to a similar extent, masters of their fate. Thus the group can select their goals and pace themselves in the achievement of them . . . this is an ideal phase . . . and human relations training groups, which are run on quasi-therapy lines, have been observed to operate on this level for periods up to one-half an hour" (8).

Now, let us consider the structure and methodology of the psychoanalytic therapy group, and the basic conceptions that underlie its operation.

The Psychoanalytic Therapeutic Group

STRUCTURE

There should be seven to nine members.

The sessions are once or twice a week or even more often, usually for one and one half hours.

There is no fixed number of sessions. There are at least 200 group meetings (300 hours) or more.

The composition is characterized by psychiatric patients, selected by and prepared by the therapist for a particular environment. Usually the patients do not know one another.

METHODOLOGY

This group is "group-led"—that is, the authority and responsibility are shared.

The therapist is usually nondirective and either experiental or analytic in his approach. To a degree he is nonintellectual and nonrational.

Interaction is fostered to the point of intense expression of emotion.

There is deep and continuous exploration of childhood and of past and immediate interpersonal and intrapsychic problems.

There is promotion of intimate revelations.

Transference relationships are fostered by continuous contact and are reduced toward the end of therapy.

FUNDAMENTAL CONCEPTIONS

Even though a patient has been diagnosed as in need of therapy, he carries within himself forces that impel him toward growth: that is, he desires to change, to relate to others, and to help. These forces are in addition to those which are egocentric and destructive. It follows, then, that a group, which is a microcosm of society, offers a great scope of stimulating momentary and continuing experiences that enhance growth among its members. In this regard the group milieu is distinctly different from the tête-à-tête of the individual therapist and his patient.

A group of seven to nine members is able to capture the dynamic quality of a society and its culture, for not only the group society itself but also its culture are new. This comes about through the interaction of persons from diverse racial, social, religious, educational, and family backgrounds (9).

Two important factors in the maintenance of cohesion in the therapy group are identification and transference. The *identification* of group members, one with another, is based upon similar past and present experiences outside of the group. *Transferences*, on the other hand, are intense neurotic bindings, observed in the group as distorted perceptions when patients expect gratification. These ties hold group members together in fixed relationships.

The group becomes a society because it is composed of a number of persons working toward common goals: the alleviation of symptoms, the formation of better relationships, the desire to live a more productive life, and so forth (10, 11). After the group has been in operation for a time, the binding force of these aims, held to some extent by each member, is reinforced by (a) feelings of kinship, (b) a collective group tradition, (c) a common group membership, and (d) a generally felt need to increase their security (12).

This small society is transformed into a therapeutic group as the following conditions are achieved:

1. Each member's awareness of an ever present emergency. The group brings home to each member his own plight: his society and family have failed him. To achieve happiness and satisfaction, he must alter his, and the group's, condition.
2. Each member's use of his own vernacular. Each person expresses himself through his figures of speech, his feelings, and his actions. Through this unique participation, each member contributes both to the analysis of the others and to the growth of the group.
3. Each member's gradual development from an intellectualization of his feelings to a more concrete expression of them. At first group members ask *why*; later they appreciate the warmth, the attention, the care, and the love that prevails.

4. Each member's gradual self-awareness. Because of the support given by the group, each member risks the anxiety and embarrassment of continuing self-revelation (13).

The group is a "slice of life." Its members represent different racial and cultural origins, different families, and different strata of our society. Upon first entering the group, they are relatively conscious of their status, and are fixed in their roles; with time they become more flexible, and finally they interact together, spontaneously assuming new and different roles. The new member reacts to the others and to the therapist with a contrived role, the one he has been taught to use, which enables him to cope with others with a minimum of anxiety. This "role taking" is discovered in the therapy group and is discouraged. At first, this process arouses anxiety, but eventually it leads to a more realistic attitude on the part of the new member.

The therapy group is a means of dislodging a patient's fixed, neurotic frame of reference. This dislodgment occurs sooner and is thought to be more lasting in group psychoanalytic therapy than in individual therapy. The psychotherapy group exposes each member to the appraisal and criticism of the other members. It is a society that allows a member to participate without overreliance upon a certain status or role. Members begin to behave in authentic ways.

The Concept of the Psychoanalytic Therapeutic Group as a "Family"

Similar to the family, the therapy group is composed of persons in intimate interaction. In many respects, the group duplicates the evolving family. For example, love, support, attention, interest, and care, at first by nurturing and then by preparing the child to depart, are constructive forces to be found not only in the family but also in the therapy group.

A technical advantage of the group is this symbolic resemblance to the family. The formation of group ties that are analogous to intrafamilial relationships is encouraged. The historical past of each member is repeated, being reenacted in the group's presence. Through this the therapist is able to perceive, respond to, and interpret a large portion of the patient's total behavior, past and present. In addition, in conceiving of the group as a family, the therapist applies both psychological concept and understanding to the family-like bindings that spring up between member and member and between member and therapist.

Such terms as "father," "father figure," "mother," and "mother symbol" give the group a generally known, common, semantic-affective system of communication. No other system is as adequate. Further, this feeling of the group as a family readily elicits the past of each member and reawakens childhood events and feelings of dependency and helplessness. These memories and feelings must be uncovered before deep and lasting personality changes can occur.

The interdependence of the group members relieves the therapist of an unrealistic and improperly placed load of responsibility. This is similar to a situation in which a parent allows his children to contribute to his understanding of life and gradually to share with him life's responsibilities. The group psychotherapist relies heavily upon the help that is forthcoming from the group. He permits and to a degree fosters the group's meeting without him (the "alternate session"); he asks the group to aid him (and themselves) through participation; and he calls upon the group to help him more directly at times of emergency. The group psychotherapist is freer to leave his group than is the individual analyst to leave his patient. One therapist, who was treating both individuals and a group, described the following to us:

> Several years ago, upon leaving a mental hygiene clinic, I observed with mixed feelings the reactions of patients whom I had been carrying in individual psychotherapy. Although I was clearly sorry that my leaving caused them obvious distress, I was aware, too, of some slight pleasure because of my importance to these people. This pleasure, however, was denied me when I told the patient-group I had also been conducting; for, although they were obviously displeased that I was leaving, their degree of distress did not appear to approximate that shown by those in individual therapy.

Since many group psychotherapists also practice family therapy, our use of the term "family" may confuse those therapists who believe that the identified patient represents only one part of a larger system of family disturbances; but a study reported in 1970 indicated that there are wide theoretical differences between different practitioners of family therapy (14).

Those who work from a psychoanalytic orientation, concentrate on intrapsychic factors even while acknowledging the influence of the family upon the patient. Others modify the psychoanalytic approach with its concern about ego development and note the family's impact on identity formation (15).

The family therapist who works from a general systems theory approach stresses family interaction. The belief is that when family interaction improves, the patient's personality will change. The family therapists who follow the double-bind theory of Bateson and his co-workers, stress clarification of the multiple signals at work in the family so that the patient is able finally to clarify his thinking and feelings (16). Our approach enables the group therapist to use whatever theoretical structure with which he is most comfortable. It is not doctrinaire.

Group therapeutic effectiveness can be divided into three main categories (17, 18): ,

1. the means
2. the techniques
3. the aims

"The means" of the group psychotherapist is his functioning, or "encountering," personality—the sum of all psychological and physical characteristics. Included are all of his past and present experiences coupled with his evolving personality, and a degree of self-awareness, which has been enhanced through the therapist's personal psychoanalysis and/or his group psychotherapeutic treatment. These last two experiences are of great importance. No other experience will do more to insure the good will of the therapist toward the patients than his having wholeheartedly participated in the treatment that he now suggests and offers to them.

Techniques have to do with whether the therapist *conducts* or *directs* the group. Group composition, duration, and other factors are all related to techniques.

The aims are the results that the therapist and the group members wish to achieve. These goals differ for every therapist and for every patient. Our aim is deep personality change of an evolving nature.

Now let us turn to the fundamental design that shapes the group therapeutic dynamics.

The Design of Group Psychotherapy

The five kinds of forces and elements to be found in the design of group psychotherapy are: (a) group organization, (b) group technique, (c) group leadership, (d) termination, and (e) aims. All of these items, dynamic to a varying degree, are responsible for the effectiveness of group psychotherapy; all are related to the interactional and/or interpretive part of the group method.

The boundaries of group psychotherapy range from *regression and reconstruction* to *repression and construction*. In limited forms of group psychotherapy, relationships remain more or less fixed and the authority remains vested in the leader.

Maximum interaction and the full exploitation of this interaction are to be found in regression and reconstruction (the psychoanalytic group), while minimal interaction and its partial use are found in repression and construction. In regressive-reconstructive therapy, there is minimal imposition of structure, emphasis upon unconscious processes, and heterogeneous grouping. Experiential techniques stress life's paradoxes, the certainty of death, and responsible decision making.

Interaction and its fullest exploitation are two necessities of group psychoanalytic therapy. It is in the successful mixture of these two that the group member is enabled to change. If one is present without the other, therapy is less effective, if not completely prevented. For instance, interaction without careful and continuous interpretation promotes harmful "acting out." Moreno's point of view makes interaction all-important (19). Constant minute analysis of every bit of behavior results in a barren intellectual procedure devoid of meaning and human relatedness.

Corsini and Rosenberg note:

> From this arises the possibility of evaluating any method of group psychotherapy in terms of three factors (intellectual, emotional and actional). For example, it seems that Klapman's textbook on mediative therapy and Dreikurs' group counseling have a high component of the *intellectual* factor; that Rogers' nondirective group counseling and Schilder's analytic group therapy have a relatively high degree of the *emotional* factor, and that Moreno's psychodrama and Slavson's activity group therapy have a large amount of the *actional* factor (20).

Those who practice in an institutional setting, in contrast to those in private practice, probably use a repressive and constructive therapy. But with experience and with administrative sanction, their therapies too may move toward permitting the patients greater regression and reconstruction.

REGRESSION AND RECONSTRUCTION IN THE PSYCHOANALYTIC GROUP

1. *Group organization.* Patients are prepared in individual sessions for an indefinite amount of time, depending upon their needs and the facility of the therapist.

Therapy continues over a prolonged period of time, in excess of 200 sessions (300 hours).

The group is continuous with new members replacing the old.

Groups are totally heterogenous and include persons of both sexes, of the many psychiatric categories, and of a variety of races, cultures, and social classes.

2. *Group technique.* The therapist considers himself to be a full participant, an observer, and a leader. He allows the group members (and himself) to experience whatever life holds in store for them. The therapist emphasizes interaction, the "paradoxical," and the unconscious (dreams and fantasies). He values risk taking—that is, the reaching for something new. He is ever alert to changing relationships and relates behavior to the earlier familial experience.

3. *Group leadership.* The therapist shares leadership with members of the group. He suggests a meeting without him, an "alternate meeting," to further their growth experience.

4. *Termination.* Leaving the group is considered termination of therapy.

The decision is the members's. He is made aware of the full meaning of his decision, which once made is considered final.

5. *Aims.* The therapist desires that each member develop his individual responsibility and autonomy.

TECHNICAL ESSENTIALS OF A REGRESSIVE-RECONSTRUCTIVE (PSYCHOANALYTIC) APPROACH TO A THERAPY GROUP

A therapy that has for its purpose a changing personality of an evolving nature must be regressive and reconstructive. Interaction is promoted, for it allows regression; individual responsibility is fostered to bring about reconstruction. The reconstructed personality is socially aware and creatively involved in his own life.

Affective experiences within the group are permitted and promoted by relying heavily on psychoanalytic, experiential, and existential techniques. This does not include sexual or aggressive acting-out. This results in a breakdown of character defenses so that individual and group anxieties are felt. Affective, interactional behavior is interpreted by the therapist or a group member with either resistance or acceptance by the group members.

Repetitious reenactments of past intrafamilial relationships are permitted and promoted. At first the therapist and later the group members define the transferences, the transferred affects and attitudes. Their incongruity with reality and their lack of appropriateness can be pointed out by the therapist and the group members. Through therapeutic skill and the group's drive toward health, these irrationalities will become unnecessary. The descriptions of dreams, fantasies, bizarre hypnagogic experiences, hallucinations, and delusions are all germane and used in interpreting the transference phenomenon.

The group members, with the therapist, examine immediate interactional behavior—a direct analysis of the "here and now"—and they describe the personality mechanisms used to maintain security, such as immaturity, dependency, overidealized concepts of self, and detachment. The compulsiveness of members' actions is brought home to them.

PSYCHOANALYTIC CONCEPT, THEORY, AND METHOD IN THE PRACTICE OF GROUP THERAPY

Group psychotherapy that is regressive and reconstructive is a logical and inevitable outgrowth of individual psychoanalysis. The technical and behavioral aspects of the group method are most clearly understood in certain Freudian terms.

Freud has stated that "every investigation which recognizes these two facts (transference and resistance) and makes them the starting points of its work may call itself psychoanalysis, even though it leads to other results than my own" (21, p. 939). And, again: "This first is that the genesis of the neurosis always goes back to very early impressions in childhood. . . . That is why it is nonsensical to maintain that psychoanalysis is practiced if these early periods of life are excluded from one's investigation; yet this claim has been made in many quarters" (22, p. 91).

The three requirements suggested by Freud for the proper practice of psychoanalysis—(a) recognition and analysis of the transference, (b) recognition and analysis of resistance, and (c) dynamic use of childhood experiences—are all met in group psychoanalytic psychotherapy. First, transference phenomena are reported in and by the group and the impact of transference reactions in the group between member and member and between member and therapist are constantly observed and felt. Second, the resistance to psychoanalytic interpretations—the breakdown of a defense and rapid construction of another—is observed and felt. Third, childhood memories, including the painful ones, and harmful childhood behavior are reenacted in the group and analyzed.

Wolf (23, 24), along with others (25, 26, 27, 28), has taken a strongly positive position with regard to psychoanalysis of the individual within the group. However, to impose *rigidly* upon the group a psychoanalytic format retards interaction and prevents the patients themselves from developing their inherent abilities to analyze.

Some critics of the group psychoanalytic method may confuse format with transaction (29) when they point out that "free association" does *not* occur in the group. It does not occur in the same way that free association does in individual analysis but free associated behavior—feeling, thinking, and acting—does occur.

Over the past decade, a further source of confusion for the student of group psychoanalytic psychotherapy is the influence of Kleinian psychoanalysis. While we shall make no effort to discuss the merits of the arguments surrounding Melanie Klein's controversial techniques and theories, her influence is to be found not only in the question of suitability for psychotherapy but, more important, in the handling of the transference (30, 31).

The fact is that there is no definite statement as to what is *the* Kleinian psychoanalytic method. An analyst who is influenced by Kleinian theory would be willing to work with all types of patients in the group since he believes all psychic disorders stem from the conflicts between life and death instincts (32).

Klein describes the paranoid-schizoid and the depressive positions (see Chapter 1) as the solution to the individual's conflicts. If these positions are not worked out, mental illness will result (33). The infantile neurosis is the defense against depressive and paranoid feelings. According to her theory, there are no real distinctions to be made between neuroses and psychoses, and the same techniques are to be used in the treatment of these conditions (34, 35). According to Klein, the ego of the infant is formed by a projection of its own aggression. This aggression is projected onto objects that are introjected as the good or bad mother. The ego is identified with the introject of the good mother. The ego exists from birth, and good and bad emotions arise from the infant's contact with the mother who is the external world. The infant's ego develops through introjection and projection. Introjection consists of the people and situations that the infant meets with and takes up in its inner life. Projection consists of the different feelings that the infant attributes to others. In the early months of infancy, the ego splits and objects are divided into good and bad. Healthy development consists of working out the destructive impulses. Klein's theories emphasize psychodynamic object relationships.

The more traditional psychoanalytic approach states that psychic disorders stem from unresolved conflicts between the instinctual drives and the ego, and that psychoanalytic methods may be used if the ego is relatively intact (36, 37). Therefore, interpretations will be made to patients who have an intact ego, while the ego-deficient patient will require a more supportive approach.

If one observes a Kleinian analyst as he works with a group, the Kleinian will make interpretations from the very outset as he attempts to make contact with the unconscious. The more traditional Freudian will offer an interpretation only when the patient's observing ego is able to work with the interpretation and if the therapeutic alliance is strong enough to absorb it. In a group, the Kleinian therapist will interpret transference from the outset. The Kleinian will not be deterred by concern about the patient's anxiety that will arise from new insights. Deep unconscious material is to be made conscious immediately. The Kleinian analyst will interrupt a free association in order to offer an interpretation. Therefore, even the concept of "free association" has a different meaning to the Kleinian therapist who works with a group.

There is some criticism that the Kleinian approach in treatment groups fosters the idea of the all-knowing, omniscient therapist, but this is really a misunderstanding of an entire theory and approach (38). Many of the British and Latin American psychotherapists who work with groups use Kleinian theory and technique, and describe themselves as clearly working with psychoanalytic group therapy.

THE THERAPIST'S PREFERENCE FOR GROUP PSYCHOANALYTIC THERAPY

In stating the advantages of group psychoanalytic therapy the subjective values of the therapist, which in part motivate him to become a group psychotherapist, should not be overlooked. For instance, the established group psychoanalytic therapist generally prefers:

1. "Here and now" emotional interplay—that is, the immediate expression of affect—to the abstracted reporting of past events.
2. Mutual exposure with greater risk to individual exposure with less risk.
3. Mutual analysis of activity to specific, individual, reductive analysis.
4. Multiple, shared, deepening relationships to one-to-one relationships (39).

These preferences, insofar as they exist, bring about the change in the individual therapist that encourages and prompts him to begin the treatment of patients in groups.

Sometimes an unwarranted appreciation of group psychotherapy stems from the therapist's need to see his particular theoretical construct demonstrated and verified in the treatment group. Berne points out that this unwittingly retards our understanding of this method: "(It) is a kind of anaclitic uneasiness which leads to wasteful and often Procrustean efforts at self-justification. The need to lean upon orthodox psychoanalytic theory to explain a whole host of newly observed phenomena encourages an inhibition of independent thinking" (40).

Some psychotherapists, in their desire to conduct therapy groups, may indicate that they are still handicapped with neurotic residuals. The possibility of using the group for exhibitionistic purposes or voyeuristic ones is always a danger.

Although the hazards of unresolved countertransferences sometimes limit the effectiveness of the group psychoanalytic psychotherapist, these difficulties are thought to be less in the group than in individual therapy. The "sounding-board" effect of the group evaluates the behavior of the members and the behavior of the therapist. The therapist's neurotic difficulties, of whatever nature, are easily observed by others, scrutinized by them, and finally described by the most daring member. This reduction of the countertransference of the therapist as he conducts psychotherapy groups is one of the major differences between psychoanalytic group and individual therapy. It has been found that the group psychoanalytic therapist undergoes emotional growth with his maturing groups of long standing.

Suitability for the Psychoanalytic Group Experience

Careful screening of patients is necessary when psychoanalytic psychotherapy is undertaken. There is no guarantee for psychotherapeutic effectiveness even when the "best" selection technique is employed, because a therapy group is more than just a group of individual patients. There are constantly changing configurations in the group, and different patterns of interpersonal relationships occur in each group and, indeed, at each group meeting. If the beginning group therapist carefully researches the literature on selection of patients for group therapy, he is apt to become confused by the contradictory statements concerning criteria for group suitability. Some group therapists stress only personality dynamics, while others use diagnostic classifications. Even diagnostic classifications are misleading. In a study of English, French, and German psychiatrists, it was found that while they had similar concepts of schizophrenia, neurotic illness, personality disorder, and alcoholism, there were marked differences in their concept of affective illness. This was particularly true with reference to manic-depressive disorders. Diagnostic criteria vary from nation to nation, and probably from community to community. Patients were diagnosed as neurotics, depressives, or personality disorders by British psychiatrists and were diagnosed as schizophrenics by American psychiatrists (41, 42).

A good deal of confusion about suitability is related to the different philosophical systems that motivate group psychotherapists. Those therapists who value an intellectual approach to group psychotherapy will be governed accordingly in their selection of patients. The fact that generally their goals are carefully determined influences their patient selection. Therapists who value the affective and human experience in group psychotherapy will not be doctrinaire or specific, and they will take more risks. Since I believe the group therapy experience to be an experience of creative change for the person who is hamstrung by his inner emotional conflicts and by his outer perceptual distortions, and since I believe that beyond man's destructiveness or egocentrism there is a desire to change and a desire to relate to other human beings in the great enterprise of creativity, I express an essential optimism regarding the patient's capacities. I am skeptical of a selection method for group therapy patients which overemphasizes pathology.

The following limited survey of the opinions of therapists on selection of patients for the group experience illustrates the wide differences.

One writer (43) complains about others ignoring the fact that one cannot transpose to group selection the same criteria that one uses in individual therapy. He notes that little attention has been paid to the personality of the group therapist. For example, a strong and directive therapist who leads a group of patients in a basically repressive-inspirational fashion will attract to himself and select relatively dependent patients.

The early group psychotherapists, Pratt, Lazell, and Marsh, in working with specific groups of patients, apparently were concerned about the possibilities of treating groups of patients and spent little time in questioning suitability. When Lazell worked with chronic schizophrenics in a mental hospital, he was so enthusiastic about the use of a group that he simply organized those patients in a group. This practice may still occur. In an institutional framework, patients can be ordered to attend a psychotherapy group.

In 1935 Wender, an early worker in group psychotherapy, stated that his experience indicated

> that group psychotherapy is applicable only to disorders in which intellectual impairment is absent and in which some degree of affect is retained. It is believed that the following groups lend themselves to this type of treatment: (a) early schizophrenics where the delusional trends are not fully systematized and in which hallucinatory phenomena are completely absent; where the splitting of the personality is not marked and there is no blocking; (b) depressions without marked retardation and those who libidinize their ideation—depression *sine* depression; (c) psychoneuroses, with the exception of severe compulsion neuroses of long duration (44).

Slavson, who has been specific in his therapy goals, wrote in 1943:

> Group therapy is not a blanket, universally applicable treatment method. Nor can it substitute for individual treatment where such treatment is indicated. Deep-rooted neurotic anxieties or compulsive manifestations cannot be treated in groups alone, just as many character malformations and habit disorders cannot be affected by individual treatment. The area in which the greatest clarification will be needed is the delineation of problems in personality that are most accessible to one type of treatment as against the other. Some effort in this direction has already been made,* but much more remains to be done in this direction (45).

Some group psychotherapists, as they gained more and more experience, began to question the earlier exclusivity in determining which patients were suitable for groups. Loeser wrote:

> What are the criteria for selection of group patients? At one time we had an elaborate and rather complex set of criteria, based on psychodynamics, character structure and symptom production. In recent years my personal viewpoint has swung over toward a simple and uncomplicated type of reasoning. In general, today, based on considerable experience, I do not think the criteria for selection of patients for group therapy differ at all from selection of patients for individual therapy. Those patients who are good candidates for psychotherapy, who possess reasonable ego strength, are well motivated, etc. will do well in either form of treatment. On the contrary, the refractory patient, the untreatable patient, the difficult patient will remain just that, whatever the mode of therapy. I no longer have any sharp criteria by which one patient is selected for the group, another for individual treatment. The exceptions are those obvious categories referred to above—the psychotic patient, the addict, the retarded, the homosexual, the psycho-

* S. R. Slavson, *An Introduction to Group Therapy* (New York: Commonwealth Fund, 1943), chap. 4; "The Treatment of Aggression through Group Therapy," *Am. J. Orthopsychiat.*, 13 (1943), 419–27 [Slavson's footnote].

path and certain severely ill and demoralized patients who would require adjunct therapy such as drugs, shock therapy or sanitarium care. My conclusion, then, is to the effect that there does not seem to be any sharp criteria by which patients can or must be selected for the group. If they are reasonably good candidates for psychotherapy in general, they will do well in any properly structured group (46).

But what makes a "reasonably good candidate for psychotherapy"? All of the kinds of patients that Loeser would *not* treat in a group have been treated in a group setting by other therapists. Barnett (47) combined group psychotherapy and insulin subcoma with patients who did not respond to other methods. He found that 20 percent of such patients improved markedly and another 50 percent improved moderately. Rosow (48) introduced group therapy at a state prison in California and organized eighty-five groups totaling seven hundred men, about 65 to 70 percent of the prison population. His groups were organized along psychoanalytic lines, and he was quite enthusiastic about the efficacy of the method in a prison facility. He points out that the administration must be supportive of the therapeutic program, a point that we have stressed. He differentiated between groups that are supportive—for patients bordering on psychosis who are unable to tolerate an uncovering type of therapy—and groups in which prisoners were similar in their psychodynamics, their capacity for ego integration was adequate, and there was receptivity for therapy. He also felt that members of these groups should be in the same age category.

The continuing differences between therapists as to which patients are suitable for group psychotherapy appear to be rooted in the therapist's conception of the nature of psychotherapy. Joel and Shapiro noted:

> Diagnostic label per se does not appear to be a very useful index of capacity for social interaction. Group psychotherapy has been conducted with patients of all nosological categories . . . it is safe to state that some patients will respond more quickly or profoundly to group therapy than others, and that these differences are less due to differences in diagnosis than to individual differential capacity for establishing relationships with people. Group therapists, therefore, are beginning to lose interest in diagnostic labels (49).

Yet Slavson noted that therapists should be careful not to impose a treatment of their preference rather than a treatment to suit the needs of the patient (50). He presented an extremely detailed classification for selecting therapy groups composed of children, adolescents, and adults, and noted that "the ideal criterion for grouping of patients is their similarity of psychological syndrome and pathology." This basic view toward homogeneity of a central problem for patients influenced all of his criteria for selection, although there was a later minor modification of his views. He noted:

> With patients in a state of remission, who are in good contact and have tolerably good ego strengths and defenses, quasi-analytic and even analytic

group therapy can be tried. This, however, has to be done with great caution since psychotherapy in which unconscious drives and affect-laden memories and experiences are uncovered is most often not suitable for borderline, latent, or active schizophrenic patients. This rule applies variously according to the defensive resources of a particular patient (51).

He also cautioned: "It is important that not more than one or two borderline patients be included in an analytic group" (51).

Spotnitz, who has had considerable experience with treatment of the borderline schizophrenic, noted in 1957 that "the attitude to group psychotherapy for the severely disturbed patient which is reflected in the current literature is becoming more favorable" (52). He favored a homogeneous group of these patients.

Pinney was optimistic about including such patients in a group but complained that "perhaps the most difficult problem we have encountered in this group stemmed from the poor choice of a patient" (53).

Graham noted:

It has been my practice to treat mainly psychoneurotics in groups. Patients with strong paranoid tendencies, who have little insight into their condition, tend to be too disturbing an element. Some early schizophrenics seem to do well, but I have seen others deteriorate (54).

Wolman stated:

Not all latent schizophrenics can be admitted to psychotherapeutic groups. Two categories should be excluded, namely those who cannot stand the group and those whom the group cannot stand. To the first category belong all those who have been much too hurt in their social relationships and therefore should not be exposed to additional and unpredictable social experiences. . . . The other category consists of patients who tend to act out. The group might not be able to tolerate them or some members of the group might be hurt and drop out (55).

Some group therapists who use a more Freudian approach to work with groups stress a different concept of suitability. Glatzer (56) places basically compulsive personality types in one group and basically hysterical personality types in another group.

Cameron and Freeman (57) chose for group treatment patients suffering from depressive psychoses who had not responded to convulsive therapy. The selection resulted in the presence of patients of different diagnostic categories. So the ostensible diagnosis may be inaccurate.

Klapman related his experiences in treatment of patients in a mental hospital:

Because of prevalent conditions in many mental hospitals . . . it is very difficult to select patients for group psychotherapy and to maintain the selection once the group has started. In the hurdy-gurdy of the large institution practices there is usually a shortage of personnel and often no one available to bring patients to the sessions nor to escort them back to their wards. The list of group therapy patients the therapist may send to the attendants may not be adhered to, and attendants may send chance selections, chosen by criteria known only to themselves. Group therapy membership becoming thus scrambled a therapist in sheer resignation may decide to do what he can with what he actually receives and to see what happens when the chips are allowed to fall where they will (58).

He asked, "Can any therapeutic results flow from such chaotic circumstances?" Klapman concluded that if the therapist employs a structured, leader-led, textbook-mediated approach, with a strong emphasis on lectures by the group therapist and on patients' reading selected material with the group, "from an initially unpromising group of deteriorated appearing patients the group therapy revealed some individuals with residual capacity. Over 25 percent of these patients improved sufficiently to be discharged."

In 1954, Freedman and Sweet (59) presented a detailed statement concerning selection procedures. They researched intensive therapy groups composed of five or six patients. An effort was made to avoid homogeneity with respect to diagnosis. They found that "members of groups uniform with respect to personality structure tend to reinforce each other's defenses" and concluded that the group is not the best therapeutic medium for neurotics with well organized ego structures and for character disorders with strong defenses and good reality orientation. For these patients, individual therapy is the choice of treatment.

They found that the "chaotic and inchoate egos"—patients with strong schizophrenic trends who have experienced emotional deprivation and the lack of good identification figures and who live in a chronic state of agitation, suffering from strong feelings of isolation—are to be placed in a group. For them, the group will serve as the steppingstone to an intensive psychotherapeutic experience to be carried out individually. Freedman and Sweet advised group therapy for "emotional illiterates" who have "little or no familiarity with the language of feeling," rigid personalities who have an inflexible social role and cannot bear any form of dependency, and "belligerently demanding and exceptionally coercive patients." Thus, group therapy is recommended for the "sickest" types of outpatients. Their recommendation runs counter to the general decisions that we have cited.

Frank and his co-workers attempted a different approach (60, 61, 62). They suggested that the patterns exhibited by patients in early meetings of therapeutic groups may be used to diagnose and classify patients rather than the clinical symptoms most therapists use. They identified several behavioral patterns: first, a "help-rejecting complainer," who continually asked the group for help while at the same time either explicitly or implicitly rejecting it; second, a "doctor's assistant," who would attempt to impress all other patients in the group, defend authority, please the group therapist, offer advice to other patients, and hide his own difficulties; third, the "self-righteous moralist," who has a constant need to convince others that he is right and has sacrificed himself because of ethical beliefs.

Frank and his colleagues concluded that the therapist who identifies his patient's behavioral patterns according to these three categories will have a much easier time organizing the group and predicting its movement. In their research, they excluded patients with a diagnosis of organic brain disease, antisocial character disorder, alcoholism, overt psychosis, or mental deficiency. Even more important than diagnosis is the finding that patients who have high expectancies for the helpfulness of treatment are most suitable for all forms of psychotherapy (63, 64).

Neighbor and his co-workers (65), after work in an outpatient mental hygiene clinic, became convinced that group psychotherapy is the "treatment of choice for a substantial percentage of patients whose problems are susceptible to clinic therapy of any type." The patients they describe were seen primarily in groups, and only rarely for individual therapy. The diagnostic groups they treated included a mixture of patients with psychoneurotic, psychophysiologic, and personality disorders, and occasional ambulatory schizophrenics. They excluded from groups patients who displayed tendencies toward overt suicidal, homicidal, or infanticidal acts as well as those who experienced extreme frustration in sharing a therapist with the group, those who experienced extreme anxiety as a result of group participation, and those with an imminent or active psychosis who might deteriorate further because of the material discussed in the group.

The therapist may be overprotective of the group or fail to recognize the flexibility of its members. One therapist notes: "There is, however, an advantage to the borderline patients in being part of a 'healthy' (nonpsychotic) group environment and identifying with healthier patients. . . . But it is essential that the pre-psychotic patient should not be bizarre or so markedly different from the other patients as to make them uncomfortable" (51).

In my experience, when patients have experienced a break with reality within the group setting, other patients in the group have been extremely helpful, warm, and nonrejecting. This has resulted in patients' experiencing and working through a psychotic episode in the group.

SUITABILITY AS A CONCEPT

Since I am risk taking and experiential in the group therapy endeavor and feel essentially optimistic about the patient's capacity for growth, I am not concerned with a particular diagnosis. The concept of the diagnosis moves toward the direction of selection—a more static concept. *Selection* has been defined in biology as any process that results, or tends to result, in preventing individuals or groups of organisms from surviving and propagating, and in allowing others to do so. *Suitability* is defined as that which is suited to one's needs, wishes, or condition. A synonym for "select" would be "choice"; a synonym for "suitable" would be "compatible"—which is more in accord with my concept of group psychoanalytic therapy.

I am concerned with the patient's capacity for relatedness. I look in his background for evidence of an experience in mutuality in relationships with family figures or parent surrogates. I attempt to determine his compatibility with others. Therefore, I see diagnosis as much broader than its usual meaning—as scientific scrutiny rather than symptom assessment. The patient's desire for a mutual experience is a major factor in determining group suitability. A patient who has experienced minimal gratification in early childhood relationships will require extensive individual therapy before he is ready to trust himself to the group. If his life has been composed of a series of power operations, he will attempt to "wheel and deal" in the group. This behavior may evoke such anger or rejection on the part of the other group members that group interaction will cease.

I would agree with Leopold (66) and say that any patient is a potential candidate for group psychoanalytic therapy in private practice or in an outpatient clinic who fulfills the following requirements:

1. He has reality contact.
2. He can be related to interpersonally.
3. He has sufficient flexibility so that he may reduce or heighten intragroup tensions.
4. He can serve at times as a catalyst for the group.

A patient should *not* be placed in a group when:

1. He paralyzes group interaction over an extended period of time.
2. He cannot be reached by other group members because of his constant chaotic behavior, stimulated by his own unconscious feelings.
3. He is constantly in a state of acute anxiety, and his behavior makes him a burden and responsibility to the group.
4. He shows destructive, antisocial behavior, impulse motivated, which evokes reality-based fears in other group members.

A patient who maintains some reality contact, as for example the borderline schizophrenic who has not become completely autistic, may be placed in a group. The group setting permits him to move at his own speed; he can relate to the group and withdraw without pressure. He observes other group members, who often present healthy identifications.

A severely disturbed psychotic patient, unable to follow the verbal pace of a group, or unwilling to face the world of reality, would usually be unsuitable for the group. The anxiety level in the active group exposes more and more unconscious conflictual material in such a patient, and the group participation becomes unbearable. In an institutional setting, the therapy is more directive and leader-led. The psychotic patient obtains relief from the relatedness of the group experience and is gradually able to relate to other group members.

The acutely anxious patient contributes little or nothing to the group experience since he does not move toward any mutualism. He simply looks for relief of anxiety.

The acutely depressed patient may be unable to profit from the group. The tremendous anger, often at the core of the depression, is blocked rather than released by group movement. He becomes more depressed or withdraws from the group. He needs intensive individual therapy before a group experience is contemplated.

Patients who have the capacity to heighten group tension and aid group movement have been labeled *provocateurs*. They are generally helpful and perceptive about other group members and stimulate group movement, but their function is usually limited to their capacity to antagonize since they are unwilling to explore themselves. When the patterns of these patients are attacked by other group members, they are unable to participate any further in a group and quit.

Patients who have never experienced primary gratifying relationships in infancy—oral or dependent or narcissistic or a combination of all three —must first experience a gratifying experience with the parent figure, the therapist. After a prolonged period of individual treatment, these patients may be considered suitable for the group. Some group therapists continue to see such patients in combined therapy—individual and group treatment. The intensity of the group experience is too overwhelming for these patients if they are placed in a group after limited individual therapy. (Such patients include narcotic addicts and alcoholics who are best seen in a homogeneous group where the therapy is less intense. The alcoholic, with his focus on his own desires and their gratification, burdens the psychoanalytic group.) If oral patients have never experienced a gratifying relationship with the therapist, they drop out of the group and often leave therapy. As these patients feel more secure with the therapist and finally enter a group, the presence of other group members becomes educational, and they learn something about social relationships.

The individual who is overtly destructive—actively homicidal, for example—is unsuitable for the group.

Overt psychopaths who develop a relationship with the therapist may become "socialized" enough to enter a group. If they have a long history of antisocial behavior, there is a question of group suitability.

The habitual monopolist who feels compelled to dominate the group should be excluded. These patients defend themselves by compulsive talking. The group members become extremely frustrated, and there is no interaction.

The patient who paralyzes group interaction because he conceives of psychotherapy as relief from pressing environmental problems should be excluded from the group. This patient has no desire to explore or gain insight but merely looks for a speedy solution. Members fall into the trap of giving advice and there is no interaction.

Because there is little to be done for patients who are terminal and dying of an apparently incurable disease and who desire treatment, psychotherapy in a heterogeneous group is not indicated for them. The group becomes discouraged and frustrated because of its inability to help such a patient. Pessimism envelops the group. These patients are often helped in a homogeneous group. If a member develops an incurable disease after being in group therapy, I would permit reentry to the group after hospitalization. The group would then be similar to the family that copes with an ill or dying member.

Patients who are discouraged about living and have ventilated suicidal feelings can be included in a group. The aggression that is often found behind such feelings comes to the surface more quickly within the group framework.

The sadomasochistic patient is difficult to work with in a group. His pattern of constant suffering first traps the group because group members are quite sympathetic. As the group members become aware of the pattern at work, they become enraged by what they consider a ruse and proceed to attack this patient. This feeds the patient's need to suffer, no therapy results, and the entire group comes to a standstill.

The therapist should differentiate between the mentally retarded and the emotionally blocked. A patient of true borderline intelligence will have great difficulty in accommodating a group. A patient who is blocked emotionally and therefore functioning on a minimal intellectual level will generally improve within the group setting.

As the group therapist gains experience, he will become less selective and more concerned with suitability. He will question the appropriateness of the group experience and constantly work with the patient's uniqueness and individuality. He will not be bound by rigid criteria. More and more group therapists are moving toward the broader concept of suitability. Neumann and Gaoni, working in Israel, reported in 1974 that they found analytically oriented group therapy preferable for types of patients who were found by other group therapists to be *unsuitable* for group therapy. The categories they listed include those patients who lack awareness of intrapsychic processes (these patients include those who overemphasize physical symptoms as well as impoverished personalities); overdependent and demanding patients; those with obsessive personality disorders; patients who fear and avoid the dyad in individual therapy; people with difficulties in adjusting and functioning in social settings; people with a life situation of loneliness, dreariness, and lack of stimulation. Many of these patients had discontinued individual therapy or had received minimal benefit from individual therapy (67). There are even reports of some patients who remain with therapists, either in group or individual psychotherapy, when it is clear that the therapist is disinterested (68).

In a study of psychoanalytic group therapy reported in 1971, two British group therapists could find no agreed-upon criteria of suitability, and stated: "When therapy is to be put to the test, we do not think it is appropriate to base patients' suitability on the nature, severity or chronicity of their illness, as these factors are modifiable by therapy and are the object of treatment." They found that patients' "suitability" and "sophistication" were important determinants in evaluating the effectiveness of group therapy. Under the term *suitability* they listed attributes such as patient's age, intelligence, anxiety level, motivation, secondary gain, ego strength, and reality difficulties. *Sophistication* was defined as "the patient's understanding of the psychotherapeutic process brought about by active participation in group psychotherapy" (69).

The most recent evaluations of suitability point to the fact that socioeconomic status is more important as a determinant in judging those who drop out and those who remain in psychotherapy—whether individual or group or family. Indeed, socioeconomic status appears more important than race or ethnic background (70).

The more research is conducted on acceptance of therapy by patients and therapists' judgments of patients' acceptance, the more intriguing are the results. Patients who are not believed to be suitable for group therapy report that they have gained from assignment to a therapy group. Several researchers concluded in 1974: "If these findings stand up on replication, and if they are also found to apply to continued treatment acceptance and effectiveness, then a broader group of outpatient applicants can be managed in group treatment than is probably possible in most clinics at present" (71). Another confusing problem to both the inexperienced and experienced psychotherapist is the difference between psychoanalytic technique based on a Freudian orientation and that based on the theories of Melanie Klein. Kernberg, who has been interested in the borderline psychotic, has been most sympathetic to the Kleinian views in his evaluation of their contributions (72).

Kleinian analysts believe that all patients are suitable for the psychoanalytic approach since they adhere strictly to transference interpretations and will *not* advise, support, or engage in reassurance. Therefore, a psychotic patient *can* be treated with a psychoanalytic approach if the patient is able to "make contact" with a transference interpretation (73). This conviction about suitability is a logical extension of Kleinian theory which relates all emotional conflicts to be the paranoid-schizoid and depressive positions, which exist from birth. Melanie Klein believed that the infantile neurosis is the defense against depressive and paranoid anxieties and that the patient is constantly attempting to work his way through these positions (74). It makes sense, according to this theory, that there are *no* differences between neuroses and psychoses. Furthermore, transference interpretations voiced by a Kleinian may appear confrontational and "far out" to the analyst trained in Freudian theory. After all, Freud stated that psychoanalytic technique is *not* suitable for the prepsychotic and psychotic (1916–17).

To summarize, the group therapist should look for suitability in the patient, based upon the patient's early life experiences and desire to engage in the mutualism of a psychotherapeutic group. This is more important than any effort on the therapist's part to classify the patient in a diagnostic category and then to decide on the wisdom of treating this category in a group.

References

(1) SLAVSON, S. Analytic Group Psychotherapy. New York: Columbia University Press, 1950.

(2) SCHILDER, P. Results and Problems of Group Psychotherapy in Severe Neuroses. Mental Hyg., 23 (1939), 87–98.

(3) VARON, E. Transition into the Therapeutic Phase of Group Therapy. Internat. J. Group Psychotherapy, 10, No. 3 (July 1960), 321–32.

(4) MULLAN, H. The Group Patient as a Therapist. Psychiat. Quart. Suppl., 31, Part 1 (1957), 91–101.

(5) MULLAN, H. Existential Factors in Group Psychotherapy. Internat. J. Group Psychotherapy, 11, No. 4 (October 1961), 449–55.

(6) ROSENBAUM, M. Resistance to Group Psychotherapy in a Community Mental Health Clinic. Internat. J. Social Psychiatry, 9, No. 3 (1963), 1–4.

(7) McGEE, T. F., SCHUMAN, B. N., and RACUSEN, F. Termination in Group Psychotherapy. Am. J. Psychotherapy, 26 (1972), 521–32.

(8) MARTIN, E. A., JR., and HILL, W. F. Toward a Theory of Group Development: Six Phases of Therapy Group Development. Internat. J. Group Psychotherapy, 7, No. 1 (January 1957), 20–30.

(9) LINTON, R. The Cultural Background of Personality. New York: Appleton-Century-Crofts, 1945.

(10) GILLIS, L. S. Group Psychotherapy: An Outline of Some Modern Procedures. Medical Proceedings, Mediese Bydraes, 4 (August 1956), 405–11.

(11) DREIKURS, R., and CORSINI, R. J. Twenty Years of Group Psychotherapy: Purposes, Methods, and Mechanisms. Am. J. Psychiat., 110, No. 8 (1954), 567–75.

(12) MULLAN, H. The Regular-Service Myth. Am. J. Soc., 53, No. 3 (1948), 276–81.

(13) MULLAN, H. The Group Psychotherapeutic Experience (unpublished). President's Address, 14th Annual Conference, American Group Psychotherapy Association, New York, 1957.

(14) Group for the Advancement of Psychiatry. The Field of Family Therapy: Formulated by the Committee on the Family, vol. 7, Report No. 78. New York, March 1970.

(15) WYNNE, L. C. Some Indications and Contraindications for Exploratory Family Therapy. In Boszormenyi-Nagy, L., and Framo, J. L. (eds.), Intensive Family Therapy. New York: Harper and Row, 1965, pp. 289–322.

(16) BATESON, G., JACKSON, D. D., HALEY, J., and WEAKLAND, J. H. Toward a Theory of Schizophrenia Behavior. Science, 1 (1956), 251–64.

(17) MULLAN, H. The Conflict Avoidance in Group Psychotherapy. Internat. J. Group Psychotherapy, 3, No. 3 (1953), 243–53.

(18) MULLAN, H. The Group Analyst's Creative Function. Am. J. Psychotherapy, 9, No. 2 (1955), 320–34.

(19) MORENO, J. L. Transference, Countertransference and Tele: Their Relation to Group Research and Group Psychotherapy. Group Psychotherapy, 7, No. 2 (1954), 107–17.

(20) CORSINI, R. J., and ROSENBERG, B. Mechanisms of Group Psychotherapy; Processes and Dynamics. J. Abnorm. & Social Psychol., 51, No. 3 (1955), 406–11.

(21) FREUD, S. The History of the Psychoanalytic Movement: Basic Writings of Sigmund Freud. New York: Random House, 1938.

(22) FREUD, S. Moses and Monotheism. New York: Vintage Books, 1955.

(23) WOLF, A. The Psychoanalysis of Groups. Am. J. Psychotherapy, 3 (1949), 16–50.

(24) WOLF, A. The Psychoanalysis of Groups. Am. J. Psychotherapy, 4 (1950), 525–58.

(25) FOULKES, S. H., and ANTHONY, E. J. Group Psychotherapy: The Psychoanalytic Approach. London: Penguin Books, 1957.

(26) WOLF, A. et al. Sexual Acting Out in Psychoanalysis of Groups. Internat. J. Group Psychotherapy, 4, No. 4 (1954), 369–80.

(27) ROSE, S. Applications of Karen Horney's Theories to Group Analysis. Internat. J. Group Psychotherapy, 3, No. 3 (1953), 270–79.

(28) ROSENBAUM, M. The Challenge of Group Psychoanalysis. Psychoanalysis, 1, No. 2 (1952), 42–58.

(29) MORENO, J. L. The Significance of the Therapeutic Format and the Place of Acting Out in Psychotherapy. Group Psychotherapy, 8, No. 1 (1955), 7–19.

(30) WAELDER, R. The Problem of the Genesis of Psychical Conflict in Earliest Infancy. Internat. J. Psychoanalysis, 18 (1937), 406–73.

(31) BIBRING, E. The So-Called English School of Psychoanalysis. Psychoanalyt. Quart., 16 (1947), 69–93.

(32) KERNBERG, O. F. A Contribution to the Ego-Psychological Critique of the Kleinian School. Internat. J. Psychoanalysis, 50 (1969), 317–33.

(33) KLEIN, M. Envy and Gratitude. New York: Basic Books, 1957.

(34) SEGAL, H. Introduction to the Work of Melanie Klein. New York: Basic Books, 1964.

(35) SEGAL, H. Melanie Klein's Technique. In Wolman, B. (ed.), Psychoanalytic Techniques: A Handbook for the Practicing Psychoanalyst. New York: Basic Books, 1967.

(36) FENICHEL, O. The Psychoanalytic Theory of Neurosis. New York: Norton, 1945.

(37) FREUD, A. Normality and Pathology in Childhood: Assessments of Development. New York: International Universities Press, 1965.

(38) GREENSON, R. R. Transference: Freud or Klein. Internat. J. Psychoanalysis, 55 (1974), 37–48.

(39) MULLAN, H. The Philosophy of Group Psychotherapy (unpublished). President's Address, 13th Annual Conference, American Group Psychotherapy Association, New York, 1956.

(40) BERNE, E. "Psychoanalytic" versus "Dynamic" Group Therapy. Internat. J. Group Psychotherapy, 10, No. 1 (1960), 98–103.

(41) KENDELL, R. E., COPPER, J. E., GOURLAY, A. J., COPELAND, J. R. M., SHARPE, L., and GURLAND, B. J. Diagnostic Criteria of American and British Psychiatrists. Arch. Gen. Psychiatry, 25 (1971), 123–30.

(42) KENDELL, R. E., PICHOT, P., and VON CRANACH, M. Diagnostic Criteria of English, French and German Psychiatrists. Psychol. Med., 4 (1974), 187–95.

(43) SHASKAN, D. Selection of Patients for Group Psychotherapy. Postgrad. Med., 23 (1958), 174–77.

(44) WENDER, L. The Dynamics of Group Psychotherapy and Its Application. J. Nerv. & Ment. Dis., 84 (1936), 54–60.

(45) SLAVSON, S. R. Values of the Group in Therapy. Newsletter, American Association of Psychiatric Social Workers, 13, No. 3 (Winter 1943–44).

(46) LOESER, L. The Role of Group Therapy in Private Practice. J. Hillside Hosp., 5 (1956), 460–67.

(47) BARNETT, G. J. Group Psychotherapy as an Adjunct to Insulin Subcoma Treatment. Internat. J. Group Psychotherapy, 9 (1959), 62–70.

(48) ROSOW, H. M. Some Observations on Group Therapy with Prison Inmates. Arch. Crim. Psychodynamics, 1 (1955), 866–97.

(49) JOEL, W., and SHAPIRO, D. Some Principles and Procedures for Group Psychotherapy, J. Psychol., 29 (1950), 77–88.

(50) SLAVSON, S. R. Criteria for Selection and Rejection of Patients for Various Types of Group Psychotherapy. Internat. J. Group Psychotherapy, 5 (1955), 3–30.

(51) SLAVSON, S. R. Group Psychotherapy and the Nature of Schizophrenia. Internat. J. Group Psychotherapy, 11 (1961), 3–32.

(52) SPOTNITZ, H. The Borderline Schizophrenic in Group Psychotherapy. Internat. J. Group Psychotherapy, 7 (1957), 155–74.

(53) PINNEY, E. L. Reactions of Outpatient Schizophrenics to Group Psychotherapy. Internat. J. Group Psychotherapy, 6 (1956), 147–51.

(54) GRAHAM, F. W. Observations on Analytic Group Psychotherapy. Internat. J. Group Psychotherapy, 9 (1959), 150–57.

(55) WOLMAN, B. B. Psychotherapy with Schizophrenics. Internat. J. Group Psychotherapy, 10 (1960), 301–12.

(56) GLATZER, H. T. Selection of Members for Group Therapy. Am. J. Orthopsychiat., 17 (1947), 477–83.

(57) CAMERON, J. L., and FREEMAN, T. Group Psychotherapy in Affective Disorders. Internat. J. Group Psychotherapy, 6 (1956), 235–57.

(58) KLAPMAN, J. W. The Unselected Group in Mental Hospitals and Group

Treatment of the Chronic Schizophrenics. Dis. Nerv. System, 20 (January 1959), 17–23.

(59) FREEDMAN, M. B., and SWEET, B. S. Some Specific Features of Group Psychotherapy and Their Implications for Selection of Patients. Internat. J. Group Psychotherapy, 4 (1954), 355–68.

(60) ROSENTHAL, D., FRANK, J. D., and NASH, E. H. The Self-Righteous Moralist in Early Meetings of Therapeutic Groups. Psychiatry, 17 (1954), 215–23.

(61) FRANK, J. D., MARGOLIN, J. B., NASH, E. H., STONE, A. R., VARON, E., and ASCHER, E. Two Behavior Patterns in Therapeutic Groups and Their Apparent Motivation. Human Relations, 5 (1952), 289–317.

(62) FRANK, J. D., ASCHER, E., MARGOLIN, J. B., NASH, H., STONE, A. R., and VARON, E. Behavioral Patterns in Early Meetings of Therapeutic Groups. Am. J. Psychiat., 108 (1952), 771–78.

(63) NASH, E. H., FRANK, J., GLEIDMAN, L. H., IMBER, S., and STONE, A. R. Some Factors Related to Patients Remaining in Group Psychotherapy. Internat. J. Group Psychotherapy, 7 (1957), 264–74.

(64) FRANK, J., GLEIDMAN, L., IMBER, S., STONE, A., and NASH, E. Patients' Expectancies and Relearning as Factors Determining Improvement in Psychotherapy. Am. J. Psychiat., 115 (1959), 961–68.

(65) NEIGHBOR, J., BEACH, M., BROWN, D. T., KEVIN, D., and VISHER, J. S. An Approach to the Selection of Patients for Group Psychotherapy. Mental Hyg., 42 (1958), 243–54.

(66) LEOPOLD, H. Selection of Patients for Group Psychotherapy. Am. J. Psychotherapy, 11 (July 1957), 634–37.

(67) NEUMANN, M., and GAONI, B. Types of Patients Especially Suitable for Analytically Oriented Group Psychotherapy: Some Clinical Examples. Israel Annals Psychiat. & Related Disciplines, 12 (1974), 203–15.

(68) KLINE, F., ADRIAN, A., and SPEVAK, M. Patients Evaluate Therapists. Arch. Gen. Psychiatry, 31 (1974), 113–16.

(69) SETHNA, E. R., and HARRINGTON, J. A. Evaluation of Group Psychotherapy. Brit. J. Psychiat., 118 (1971), 641–58.

(70) SLIPP, S., ELLIS, S., and KRESSEL, K. Factors Associated with Engagement in Family Therapy. Family Process, 13 (1974), 413–27.

(71) HARGREAVES, W. A., SHOWSTACK, J., FLOHR, R., BRADY, C., and HARRIS, S. Treatment Acceptance Following Intake Assignment to Individual Therapy, Group Therapy or Contact Group. Arch. Gen. Psychiat., 31 (1974), 343–49.

(72) KERNBERG, O. F. A Contribution to the Ego-Psychological Critique of the Kleinian School. Internat. J. Psychoanalysis, 50 (1969), 317–33.

(73) ROSENFELD, H. Psychotic States: A Psychoanalytic Approach. New York: International Universities Press, 1965.

(74) KLEIN, M. New Directions in Psychoanalysis. New York: Basic Books, 1961.

4 Administration of the Therapy Group

Hugh Mullan
Max Rosenbaum

General Statement

THE ANALYTIC GROUP brought together for the purpose of producing lasting personality change in its members must necessarily be considered a project which will last two and one half years or longer. The management of this group, then, is more complex than that of a weekend encounter experience or even that of a T-group composed of clinic professionals who meet for twenty sessions during the fall/winter for a half year.

The negotiations related to patient participation in an analytic group are also more numerous, difficult, and time-consuming than those required for individual treatment. In the former, every transaction with each patient has a direct impact on every other person in the group. For example, if the well-meaning therapist reduces the fee of a member who unfortunately lost his job, this fact becomes a part of the group's content and promotes in each member feelings which are then openly expressed. The din caused by such a generous act is hard to imagine and difficult to contend with. Many times accusations of preferential treatment spill out: "I always knew he was your pet!" "You always take his side." "You have never done that for me." "Why do you always excuse him?" and so forth.

The group leader, from the moment he receives a call from a new patient until long after he introduces him to the members of his definitive group, begins and continues a process of administration. At times this responsibility is intensified—for instance, at the start of the group—while at other times, such as very late in therapy, the management factor seems very minor indeed.

In this chapter we will note that much of what we call administration

73

centers around the two patient responsibilities: prompt attendance and prompt payment of fees. These two elements combine to form the first condition of group analytic treatment. It is quite obvious that if patients do not attend sessions they are not treatable. It is less clear, but also true, that if patients do not pay their way they cannot be treated. These outward manifestations of patient commitment are many times overlooked or handled in indirect ways. The fee and attendance are, we believe, to be focused on openly and in the group. Their significance is based upon the fact that the former has to do with time, time's passage, and our finiteness, and the latter has to do with first the therapist's worth and then with the patient's self-evaluation and his own self-esteem.

Group Administration in Private Practice

INTRODUCTION

The administration of the psychotherapeutic group consists of all the practical matters of arrangement that must be established by the therapist and adhered to by each group member. Proper administration quite naturally then depends, on the one hand, upon the requirements established by the therapist in his setting and, on the other hand, upon the patient's cooperation in meeting these requirements.

The setting of the therapy—whether, for example, it is in an institution or in the therapist's private office—is an important factor in the efficiency of group administration. Generally speaking, there are fewer problems of administration in an institution than in individual practice. This statement, however, is true only insofar as the clinic staff, including the chief of service, supports the group therapy program. Should this support be lacking, as is many times the case, not only the administration but the organization and the group process itself are all jeopardized. The administration of therapy groups, therefore, is of crucial importance. This chapter will describe, first, the generalities of group administration, especially as encountered in private practice, and, second, the peculiarities of group psychotherapy administration in institutions. In these two instances the pertinent psychodynamics occurring as a result of group administration will be carefully considered.

THE DIFFERENTIATION BETWEEN ADMINISTRATION AND ORGANIZATION

While group administration is concerned with the myriad of practical and common sense matters of arrangement, organization of the psychotherapeutic group is concerned with the selection and overall resulting composition of the interacting membership. Although both administration and organization are involved in bringing together unrelated persons, the dynamic meaning of organization has more significance than administration. Organization, which has to do with the ultimate composition of the group, determines the quality and quantity of interaction and therefore is considered separately. It is described in detail in Chapter 5.

There has been a tendency in group psychotherapy for the therapist to overlook his administrative duties, not seeing their deeper implications, and to stress his organizational role. Although this emphasis on group composition has been valuable, since many kinds of groups have been tried, it has resulted in considerable confusion as to how one goes about the administering of a group. This bypassing of administration is the natural outcome of the earlier institutional practice of group psychotherapy. In this protective setting, it was taken as a matter of course that the administrative responsibilities were not handled by the therapist but "came down from above" through the chain of command. For example, in a psychiatric hospital the administration of a therapy group is hardly more complex than the arrangements required of the nurse to send seven or eight patients to occupational therapy twice weekly. In this case prompt attendance is no longer the responsibility of the patient and concern and feelings about payment for the session are removed from the province of either patient or therapist. This is quite different from today's practice of private group psychotherapy, in which administrative authority rests directly upon the shoulders of the therapist. In this setting, practical arrangements for bringing a patient into group psychotherapy assume an exceptional significance as the therapist and the patient attempt to find the time to meet twice weekly for two or three years. The therapist, too, must tell the patient in unambiguous terms his fee for individual and group sessions. He must respond with equanimity when the new patient multiplies his group charge by seven, to ten (members) and then confronts him with the total amount. Recently, a very angry patient who had never complained about payment came in to his group clutching a piece of paper covered with figures. When he was able to break into the conversation, he told us that he had a report to make. He then proceeded to describe the income of the therapist derived from individual patients and from groups. He estimated both the monthly and yearly incomes and subtracted income lost through vacations. He estimated office expenses, and finally came up with the yearly income tax. His figures were uncannily accurate causing the therapist to feel very uncomfortable as his personal finances were discussed by all members. It is understandable, then, that some group therapists are able to conduct groups in institutions but find it impossible to administer and, therefore, to conduct a group in their private practice.

DIFFICULTIES IN ADMINISTRATION

The psychotherapist usually finds the administration of the therapy group to be difficult, tedious, and frustrating. This is particularly so during the preparatory phase as he brings patients together, but it remains complex throughout, lessening with the age of the group and with the experience of the therapist. For the beginner, the task is more difficult and taxing. He must work through his own anxiety about organizing and administering his group, while at the same time he must present to the prospective group patients clear and affirmative answers to their many questions about entering, and participating in, the group.

However, even the seasoned leader faces hard-to-accept emotional responses when he changes a "rule" which governs a group. For example, an increase in group fee, although it is expected, causes a flareup of doubt and mistrust; some members question the efficacy of group treatment while others more directly wonder about the intentions and character of their therapist. And, again, a shift in session time will please some patients and irritate others, while a few may even threaten to quit treatment. It is a good idea for the therapist to think through the effects of an administrative change before setting a new course for his group.

The Therapist's Role in Administration

During the individualized preparatory phase and also at the moment of introducing patients into the group, the therapist becomes both active and directive. Because he is burdened with administrative problems at this time, he must assume much responsibility and become somewhat authoritarian. Busy as he may be with the management details, the therapist must also attempt to see their possible unconscious meaning, not only for the prospective group member but for himself as well. Thus, as he deals out administrative rules, such as the need for prompt and regular attendance, he must not sacrifice his interest in, and his empathy for, the troubled patient.

Patients who are already anxious about being in individual sessions find that their anxieties mount when they are asked to join an analytic therapy group and discuss their conflicts with others. Often these persons experience the realities of meeting time and place and the group cost as demands made by the therapist and heatedly resist entering the group. "I couldn't possibly get off from work so as to be here at four o'clock. I can't afford it. You're too expensive! I do have to live and pay rent, don't I?" Hidden behind this outburst are the patient's anxieties at being moved from individual sessions to the unknown group. The forthright, consistent therapist helps to dissipate this understandable fear of exposure. His ability to explain "the group" in an uncomplicated way can be significant in the early establishment of the patient's trust in the group. These explanations give the incoming patient certain obligations and duties to perform, certain expectations to be realized, and thus structure his behavior to some degree. However, it is important to realize that *every explanation* on the part of the therapist and every response by the patient is individual and has its unique psychodynamic.

When the group has been in progress for some months and consists mostly of older members, much of the pressure of administrative duties decreases. This is one of the benefits of the "open group," to which new patients are introduced as older patients leave. The group, then, always consisting of a nucleus of experienced patients, is spontaneously educative, and to a degree self-administrative. As the group gradually becomes "group centered," the members begin to assume the responsibility and authority that was originally the therapist's.

THE IMAGE OF GROUP PSYCHOTHERAPY

The group offers a positive and unique experience for the patient and, therefore, should never be offered as a second-rate or less expensive kind of psychotherapy. Bach describes this attitude as being essential to the group therapist when he states "his [the therapist's] sincere conviction that the group-life experience, more than any other aspect of the therapy, is of crucial importance to the patient's rehabilitation" (1). In the early history of this method the primary aim of group psychotherapy was thought to be the aid of a greater number of patients, possibly at a reduced cost. If this has happened, even partly, it is merely incidental. Group psychotherapy is used because of its effectiveness as a psychotherapy. To use it for any other reason is unscientific, improper, and even destructive. The group therapist should be clear on this point so that he can reveal to the patient, if necessary, that an exceptional therapeutic experience is being provided, which is not second best or less expensive but significantly different from individual psychotherapy.

Today, with the advent of the newer human potential group therapies, those therapists who use an analytic method many times must explain the difference between their approach and that of their colleagues. A clear idea concerning the underlying dynamics, methods, and goals of both approaches is a prerequisite for an explanation which allays fears in the patient and encourages him to enter the analytic group.

THE PHYSICAL SETTING

The group psychotherapist must make arrangements for the setting of the group's meeting. It is advisable for the group to meet in a soundproof, separate room where the chairs are arranged more or less in a circle. It is helpful to have in the center a large table on which to place ashtrays,* handbags, and the like. This table should not be so high as to prevent any

---

* Some therapists discourage or even forbid smoking during sessions. If this is a rule it must be presented as such during the patient's preparation for the group.

patient from seeing the others.* Should pillows be used instead of chairs, no obstructing center table can be used. The arrangement of floor cushions must allow each one the easy observation and inspection of the others. The circle, with members and therapist sitting and facing each other, whether chairs or pillows are used, is the physical format of group psychotherapy. This is vastly different from the format of individual psychoanalysis in which the patient uses the couch and the therapist is out of view. It is also dissimilar to other therapies where patient and therapist sit alone facing each other. Many of the egalitarian and democratic practices in group psychotherapy owe their presence to this arrangement that permits members and therapist to look at each other directly (2, 3).

Because the seating order that patients choose is significant, no seats or floor cushions are assigned. Patients are found to prefer certain definite places. Sometimes they need to sit next to a certain person or in a certain relation to the therapist. The seating arrangement chosen becomes part of the content and dynamic of the group session and is responded to and analyzed.

In order to minimize distractions, it is best not to have a telephone in the room. Although the ringing and the answering of the telephone does give members a chance to express their dissatisfactions and their hostilities, it also tends to lessen group concentration. Further, the group members may feel that there is something disrespectful toward them in using for others the time set aside for them.

It is preferable to have neither nurse nor secretary in the office at the time of group meetings. All involvement in the office is then limited to the therapist and the other group members. In this way, transference between the group members and the group psychotherapist is maintained at a high level of intensity and distortion. Involvement with other office personnel tends to dilute the transference relationship.

THE APPOINTMENT HOUR: DURATION AND FREQUENCY

The therapist must decide the length of time for group meetings. Therapy groups seem to function most effectively when they meet for an hour and a half or for a two-hour period. The frequency should be once or twice a week, though on occasion—that is, in times of emergency— additional sessions are extremely helpful. Many group leaders today use a single two-hour session per week and supplement this with an individual meeting for selected members.

Although the duration (one and one half or two hours) of group psychotherapeutic sessions is arbitrary, there are good reasons for this practice. The group meeting that lasts an hour is generally too short for the group to "warm up"; at the end of one hour the interaction may be

* Some therapists view any center table as a barrier to communication.

at its height, or the members may just be starting to interpret what is transpiring. This difficulty might be overcome if the therapist could meet with the group for an hour three or four times per week. Group sessions that last longer than an hour and a half are wearing for the patients and therapist alike because of the intensity of the emotional involvements (see Chapter 7, "The Extended Session").

In Chapter 6 there is a description and discussion of the "alternate meeting" at which patients get together without the therapist. These alternate sessions often last somewhat longer than the regular sessions. Patients meeting informally without the controlling influence of the therapist appear to be able to accept somewhat longer times together, probably because there is less need to please the therapist and less interpretation.

The group psychotherapist should examine the objections of patients to meeting at a particular time. This is often an expression of resistance to commencing group psychotherapy, and should be carefully delineated and analyzed. Wolf (4) mentions that the resistant candidates for the group make up the majority of patients. We concur in this, but we also see the "curious" and "willing" patient as resisting. Many of the hesitations and concerns that a patient has about entering group therapy at first appear to be caused by such understandable hardships as the frequency and duration of sessions, the distance he must travel, and the expense. Although these difficulties may be real enough, the therapist must realize the importance of his effort—the modification of the personalities of his patients. Therefore, as a general rule, the group psychotherapeutic hours take precedence over all other appointments.

The therapist must set the hour for the meeting of the therapeutic group. He must carefully evaluate possible times, selecting the ones best suited to his own needs and to those of his patients. Evenings after 5:00 P.M. are usually best for an adult group of men and women (5); next, Saturdays and Sundays; and, finally, noontime (lunch hour for most patients) on a weekday.* The reason the therapist selects the hour best suited to him is that it becomes a very difficult task to change the meeting once it is well established. Also, shifts in the appointment time based upon the therapist's requirements seem arbitrary to the patients and signify to them that they are being exploited. Should the therapist change the treatment hour, he can expect the group patients to express considerable resentment, for this means an alteration in their schedules as well.

As the therapist prepares the patient for a particular group, he should be clear about the days and the hours of the group meetings. This forestalls indefiniteness or confusion. When the therapist does not positively designate the hours and days of treatment, patients tend to use his un-

---

* Many patients are able to arrange a longer lunch period twice a week in order to meet with the group.

certainties as a basis for excusing themselves from entering a group, from continuing with a group, and sometimes, more seriously, from continuing with psychotherapy in any form. This decisiveness on the part of the therapist, although authoritarian, is justified. He must take this administrative step because it is basic to the initial group structure. After the group has met for a few sessions, all of the patients' initial objections to particular hours and days lessen.

GROUP RULES

In order to prevent the group from "socializing," the therapist should tell the members during the first sessions his rules—if he has rules. These prohibitions must be generally considered as he commences to administer the group. It is easy for certain groups influenced by certain members to take on a social atmosphere. Because the main purpose of the group is psychotherapy, whatever tendencies the group has toward social activities are incidental, and even retarding, to the therapeutic process.

The therapist should be definite in his prohibitions and restrictions, but they should be kept to a minimum. Generally, it is sufficient to explain that in a therapy group certain activities distract from the purpose of the therapy. The therapist must realize, however, that spontaneous acts are to be expected in the group. For example, Nancy brought a cake with a candle to the group to celebrate Frank's birthday. The entire group was moved, and Frank unashamedly cried with happiness. He had not realized that anyone cared for him.

In the matters of smoking, eating, drinking, playing of instruments, dancing, and the like, the therapist might wait for these to occur before setting down a rule. If any of these actions is believed to be harmful, it can be analyzed immediately and thereby prevented.

GROUP NOTES

The kind and the extent of note taking in group psychotherapy is dependent upon the predilection of each therapist. Some, therefore, take detailed notes, carefully describing all that is going on. Others—and this is believed to be the better practice—limit their note taking to significant behavior and to unconscious material, such as dreams and fantasies.

The habit of detailed note taking probably comes from this practice in individual therapy and, particularly, in psychoanalysis. But to take notes concerning a single patient who is quietly reclining on a couch is vastly different from attempting to record the statements, actions, and feelings of seven to ten group members in heated discussion. It is therefore, impractical, and perhaps impossible, for the therapist to try to take detailed notes at the risk of distracting himself from the group experience as well as ignoring what is truly transpiring in himself.

Notes which pertain to the whole group (group notes) are preferable to individual notes. However, individual notes should be taken during the period of individual sessions leading to group placement, and again at the point of group termination.

It is both advantageous and rewarding for the therapist to have ample free time—a half hour to one hour—before and after each group session. This time may be used for the recalling and reexperiencing of the group session or for careful study of group notes. The more general approach of perusal and recall is probably better. During this time, the therapist connects what happened in the session with what is happening outside the session and integrates the historical and the repetitive behavior in each individual. He also wonders about his own feelings, actions, and reactions toward each patient. Each therapist must discover the most suitable means for bringing the group experience into a meaningful whole so that his interpretations will be most effective.

RECORDING GROUP CONTENT

The use of recording machines in group psychotherapy should be limited to group psychotherapeutic research and, perhaps, to group supervision. This limitation is justified because of the element of exploitation, either real or imaginary, that is felt by the patients upon the introduction of such a device.

If there is a decision to use a recorder, it is wise to begin its use at the first session. The members should be told about it, and their questions concerning its purpose should be answered directly and frankly. It is well to remember (and, incidentally, to tell the group members) that both the immediate and the ultimate use of the recording of a group session is for the benefit of the patients.

If one introduces a recording machine after the group has been in operation for some time, a few sessions should elapse before making use of the record of a group session. This allows for a simmering-down period, and the record will not be biased by the performances of irate group members, self-conscious at the mechanical interruption.

TRANSCRIBERS, OBSERVERS, AND VISITORS

While there can be no hard-and-fast rule concerning the presence of persons other than the patients and therapist(s) in a therapy group, one should be aware of the deep and lasting effect the outsider has. Generally, the overall climate of the group is modified by the presence of a person who does not participate or who plays a fixed, ancillary role. Even though group members appear to ignore the observer or transcriber after the first few sessions, still his presence alters all future group process and content.

Patients in this kind of group are always aware that the therapist has a colleague nearby who is closer to him than they are. They are aware, also, that after the session the therapist and the observer may meet to discuss them. This knowledge must have many psychodynamic implications, different for each member and for each therapist. Certainly there must be a dilution of the transference and possibly, depending upon the sex of the therapist and of the observer, a reawakening of oedipal conflicts and strivings.

Once again, to insure either careful experimentation or training, there are times when a transcriber or an observer is needed. On these bases, and these alone, can such persons enter a therapy group. Patients should be assured that the presence of a transcriber is for their benefit. This peripheral figure, similar to a recording device, should be introduced at the first session. The therapist must answer all questions pertaining to his function and state what is to be done with the transcripts. Also, careful analysis of the patients' feelings as they attempt to discover the observer's relationship to the therapist is desirable.

Visitors to therapeutic groups are quite another matter. There seems to be little advantage in complicating the already intricate interaction by encouraging such interruptions. Should such visits occur spontaneously and without the therapist's sanction, they should be analyzed. The motivation of the member who invited the visitor should be elicited, as well as the many feelings that the other members have concerning this intrusion. The group therapist must determine *himself* whether the visitor is to remain or to be sent away. This choice is his and is not be determined by a consensus of members.

THE USE OF FILMS, PLAYS, AND BOOKS

In analytic group treatment, as contrasted to other forms of groups, the use of material to stimulate and direct the verbal and emotional content of the group sessions is not thought to be necessary. While centering on the theme of a book or the plot of a play has the advantage of immediate interaction on a certain subject, it has the disadvantage of directing the members along a certain path and of being, therefore, goal directed. Since analytic group therapy depends largely upon the establishment of rational and irrational relationships, and their analysis, use of these methods is not advocated.

However, in other group methods, notably those with a behavioristic coloring, film slides, television, and so forth are employed. For example, sexual modification group therapy, because of its reeducative purpose and its goal directiveness, freely uses slides and films to improve member understanding of not only the anatomy and physiology of the reproductive systems, but also to describe sexual activity and to stimulate erotic response.

MEDICAL EXAMINATION OF GROUP PATIENTS

Being a psychological approach to mental and emotional disturbances, group psychotherapy is usually performed by psychotherapists from three different disciplines: the psychiatrist from medicine, the clinical psychologist from psychology, and the psychiatric social worker from the field of social work. Because the group psychotherapist (though he is often a physician) never physically examines his patients, it is important that during the preparation of a patient for entry into a group he be given a complete physical examination.* If at the time the patient applies for therapy he does not have a physician, it is well for the group therapist to have a colleague—a medical practitioner—with a knowledge of psychology and psychotherapy, and particularly of group psychotherapy, to whom such patients can be referred. Periodically—perhaps once a year—throughout the course of group therapy, patients should be encouraged to see their own physicians. Even after a "preliminary medical clearance" (1, 5), a continuing contact between a group member and his physician is necessary. In all therapy groups, in which seven to ten patients are usually being treated simultaneously, there is a chance that certain physical conditions will arise that require diagnosis and immediate treatment. *Medical and surgical conditions come to the attention of the therapist more frequently in group psychotherapeutic practice than in individual therapy because of the greater number of patients involved and their quicker turnover.*

Frequently in the group there is a contagion of physical symptoms from one patient to another. It is well for the therapist to have a base line of physical functioning for each patient determined by a physician prior to the patient's entrance into the group. Physical complaints that a patient brings up early in the preparatory phase can be evaluated by a physician while the patient is still being seen individually. The practice of having patients examined is of value to those who are engaged exclusively in individual psychotherapy as well as to those who primarily do group psychotherapy.

SOCIETY AND FAMILY OBSTRUCTION OF GROUP PSYCHOTHERAPY

Careful and diligent management by the group psychotherapist is sometimes required for the people who are on the periphery of the therapy group. These persons—husbands, wives, fathers, mothers, relatives, employers, and friends of members—often feel themselves threatened, and become upset by the experience of having a person close to them enter a therapy group. They feel that it is bad enough for a person to divulge

---

* Except in unusual circumstances, such as emergencies, we do not advocate that the medically trained group psychotherapist give physical examinations to his patients. Such examinations confuse and further distort the transference.

their confidences to an individual therapist who is professionally trained, but they are overwhelmed by a person close to them disclosing their confidences to a group of strangers. For example, a wife believes that her husband talks in a critical way about her in the group, blaming her for all the squabbles and dissensions. An employer feels that the group sees only one side of him and therefore pictures him as ineffectual and controlling. A close friend will soon become loath to confide in a friend (group patient), realizing that anything revealed between them may be brought up in the group.

Those close to a group member become increasingly curious and anxious as they learn, first, that their relative or friend is having psychotherapy; second, that he is moving toward group psychotherapy; and third, that he is beginning the alternate sessions—a gathering of group members without the therapist. So great may be the fears of these relatives and friends as to lead to the development of certain characteristic tactics to prevent the patient from continuing his therapy. Sometimes these relatives and friends threaten to withhold financial support; sometimes they appeal to the patient's unresolved ethnic and religious biases by stating, for example: "They are not your kind of people." Many times those close to the patient disparage the therapy, the therapist, and the group members by asking, "What can a bunch of neurotics accomplish together?" or "The therapist certainly can't be very interested in you if he sees you with nine others, can he?" or "He makes more money from the group than he does with individual patients." Recently, with the introduction for the first time of an extended session, the wife of a group patient angrily stated, "Don't you see what he does? Whenever Hugh goes on a vacation he has an extended session just to make up for the financial loss!" The therapist must expect these reactions. He will find it best not to argue against them or to defend himself. Later in the therapy the patient will discover the truth for himself and will be strong enough not to comply with the judgments of these relatives and friends.

The therapist should see or communicate with friends and relatives of a patient only with the patient's knowledge. If he receives telephone calls or messages concerning a patient, he should tell the caller of his inability to speak with him unless the patient permits it. At the next group session the group should be told about the call. It is preferable that the patient be aware of all these peripheral contacts, since it is important in maintaining his trust in the therapist and in his group. The therapist should avoid being placed in the position of being an arbitrator rather than a therapist.

When it is thought wise to see an outside person, he or she is included with the patient or couple in a private session.

A couple kept bringing up the possibility of the husband's mother joining us in a couple's session. This was arranged. However, first there had to be the admission by the couple that they were in treatment. At the appointed time, the couple and their six-month-old child arrived along with the mother. After introductions we sat on pillows in the group room, even though the husband wanted to use the more conventional consulting office. We all were uneasy at the start. But wife and husband reported dreams even though the mother viewed dreams as insignificant nonsense.

The wife's dream: Both her mother and mother-in-law were present in a new, partly completed house. Someone was taking construction materials away because they were valuable. The wife's mother was helping in the kitchen while her mother-in-law was helping outside in the garden.

The husband's dream: He was at home too, but in their present house, which was split into two warring factions, the North (wife) and South (mother). He was a part of the South and led the charge with his bayonet up and out. . . . Throughout the session, the mother implied that she saw her son in trouble and would do anything for him, as she always did. The son objected, saying that he did not need this kind of attention, and that he was much more than her *son* with problems. The wife pointed out to her mother-in-law that the constant message they had received was, "You know all that I have is you." Later, the mother said that her two sisters, the ones who were sickly, received an overabundance of attention, loving care, and support from her mother and father just because they were so deserving.

A meeting such as this one is valuable. It required courage and risk for the couple to bring the older woman into the meeting and, once there, to confront her. The early, and to a degree continuing, conflictual relationship between the husband and his mother was clarified. Some slight alteration in behavior was noted among the three of them. In having the patient, outsider, and therapist meet together, the patient(s) is(are) prevented from imagining in a distorted fashion what occurred.

THE FEE AND ITS DYNAMIC IMPLICATIONS

The payment of a fee by the patient to his psychotherapist touches upon the deep emotional ties which unite them. This obligation is both symbolically and realistically a central point for continuing psychotherapy. The patient, beset by feelings of worthlessness, is asked to give not only of himself in psychotherapy, but also of his wealth or current earnings. Patients in individual therapy are sometimes able to avoid the deep meaning that money has for them. But in the group, one or two persons focusing upon payment bring to the attention of all the meaning of this transaction. The therapist should always be deeply involved in this exchange of money. He may attempt to avoid his own conflicts about money by instituting an impersonal billing system, but this may be nothing more than an attempt to avoid his conflict concerning his right (his worth) to charge patients.

Fees are governed somewhat by the community and by the wealth and earning capacity of each patient. In certain clinics and hospitals, groups can meet for therapy without fees. However, in private practice fees are usually charged and may present difficulties for the therapist if they are not handled properly.

The therapist must clarify first for himself and then for the patient the fee that he will ask. In order to work out this decision, therapists must figure what they think the time (one and one half hours, two hours, or an extended session of six or more hours) is worth to them. To illustrate: A therapist who charges forty dollars for an individual session may feel that a two-hour group session is worth eighty to one hundred dollars and charge each member ten or twelve dollars. Some therapists, realizing that a group therapy period is much more difficult and involving, may charge one third to one half of the individual fee. Thus if forty dollars is the hourly fee for an individual patient, twenty dollars would be his group fee. Since a spontaneously interacting group is involved, a session cannot be planned to run exactly one and one half hours or two hours; it may run longer, or a patient may pause to speak with the therapist after the session. Actually, the group therapist should allow at least a half hour over the duration of his group session to reexamine what has taken place, to take notes, and to establish future procedures if this is required.

Thus, the amount of reimbursement for professional services and time becomes an important initial decision for the beginning therapist. This decision becomes a problem on those occasions when patients attack the therapist for being so "handsomely" paid for group sessions. As in individual therapy, the patient is encouraged to divulge all feelings, thoughts, and actions, including his attitudes toward money and paying the therapist. Within the group, supported by his fellow members, the patient often feels free to attack the therapist regarding his supposed wealth, his avarice, and so on. These attacks are expected by the group therapist; they should be analyzed and never be deflected.

A graduated scale of fees is possible. For the beginning group therapist it seems preferable, however, to have a fixed fee. Perhaps at the time of starting one's second group a graduated scale of fees can be considered. A fixed fee for all the members of the first group is thought necessary in order to control or limit some of the objections and rivalries that spring up in the group about this requirement. Although it is true that rivalries and objections about fees and their payment are valuable and pertinent and can be analyzed, the inexperienced group psychotherapist may face more external pressure and inner turmoil than is necessary if he varies his fees. For example, he may be attacked by the group for demanding too much money just at the time that he feels overpaid and is plagued with doubts about his abilities as a therapist.

A more experienced therapist, if he feels equal to the task, may go ahead with a graduated fee system. In addition, realizing how it will complicate matters, he may raise, reduce, or waive fees. He explains to the patients in the preparatory sessions that the group members will be paying various fees based upon their ability to pay. The therapist encourages the patient to discuss openly in the group his feelings about paying and about paying more than (or less than) his fellows. The inexperienced therapist should not waive, raise, or lower the fee while the group is in process unless this problem has been fully explored by the group over a long period of time.

Appointments broken without sufficient warning and unattended sessions should be charged to the patient if an acceptable reason is not given. Statements are generally distributed by the therapist every two weeks or monthly at the end of a group meeting. Some therapists bill weekly. Sometimes the patient can be instructed to leave the payment on the therapist's desk or to give the payment directly to him when leaving the office. The more personal this payment is made, the more effective the therapy. *In any event, the peculiar ways in which patients pay should be analyzed in the group.*

To repeat, the attitudes toward money are a constant ingredient of all therapeutic relationships; group therapy relationships are no exception. Since the group members' attention is often prominently focused on money, it is possible to discover both the collective and the individual meaning that money has for all of us.

Financially, group psychotherapy in private practice is rewarding: in one period of one and one half hours, seven to ten patients are able to pay more than an individual patient. The therapist, however, is not warranted in taking an additional fee unless the therapy is in his hands an effective form of treatment, and unless it forces him to expend a great deal of himself.

Group Administration in Institutions

INTRODUCTION

The characteristics of any institution—to some exent, at least—modify the practices within that institution. There is an essential dovetailing between the housekeeping, or custodial function and the clinical services with which the institution is charged. Consequently, the practice of all psychotherapies, including group psychotherapy, differs in essentials from institution to institution and also between institution and private practice. One has only to recall differences in his own therapeutic experiences as he moved from a training institute to private practice.

Although agency and private group psychotherapeutic practice have an identical aim—that of personality change of the patient—each offers to the patient a different atmosphere, or condition, of change. In the former, the ultimate therapeutic responsibility rests with the administrator and the chief of the professional service; it is they who select the therapist and suggest the mode of therapeutic intervention. In the latter, responsibility rests squarely upon the shoulders of the therapist, who alone is in contact with his patients. In institutional practice, the selection of patients is based upon the needs and characteristics of the community and the policy of the institution, whereas in private practice the therapist is the sole person involved in the selection of his patients.

W. L. Meijering elaborates on these points when he states:

> The theoretical points raised . . . clearly reveal the difficulties that arise at every attempt to describe the mechanism operating in groups in a residential setting. The influence of the total atmosphere is so important, that a study of the group phenomena separately from the hospital phenomena is practically impossible. The hospital climate is in turn intimately linked with local conditions, social customs, and cultural influences, which operate differently in different hospitals. This network of interacting forces presents a complicated picture. Much research is needed to make clear the principles that underlie the manner in which a hospital needs to operate. It is not sufficient just to start a few groups in a hospital. For fruitful group psychotherapy, a revision of the whole hospital plan and operation may be necessary. But when it is done properly, psychotherapy can be very effective indeed (6).

Patients are aware of the rather obvious distinctions between clinic and private therapy and the differences that stem from them. Patients in institutional settings (clinics, hospitals, agencies, and so forth) rarely feel that they are getting the best therapy and envision private psychiatric help as preferable.

What are here suggested as differences between institutional and private practice of group psychotherapy hold for psychotherapy in general. However, because the group constellation has its own characteristics many unique problems arise. These lead, unfortunately, to misunderstandings among staff members and, in some instances, to the abandoning of the group psychotherapeutic program.

A PECULIARITY OF GROUP PSYCHOTHERAPY

To establish group psychotherapy in private practice requires only that the therapist realize the need for it and then that he put his idea into effect. Thus, with or without training or supervision, the therapist decides to establish a group and sets about doing it. The establishment of a therapy group in an institution, however, is another matter. Administrative and professional support, staff acceptance or resistance, and key staff understanding of group psychotherapy are the factors that make the formation and continuation of therapeutic groups possible or impossible. The mere responsibility for a group psychotherapeutic program does not necessarily mean that it will be conceived and executed.

Because of the natural tendency toward cohesiveness, the members of the therapy group develop very close ties with each other and with the therapist. Simultaneously, they question the authority of the institution. Their loyalty is with their group peers and not with the agency staff. They demand of their therapist that he, too, question authority. They discuss critically their relationships with all the professionals and nonprofessionals with whom they come in contact. They attempt to demonstrate that theirs is the *best* therapy and that theirs is the *best* group. Their behavior is viewed by the uninitiated as "bad," "impolite," "unruly," and so forth, and the group members are seen as generally unappreciative. *If this development of cohesiveness in the therapy group is not clearly understood or its significace realized by the general staff of the institution, the group psychotherapeutic program is jeopardized.* Many of the difficulties in establishing a group psychotherapeutic program come from this lack of knowledge, and are made worse by the conscious and unconscious response of staff to the group patients and the group therapists (7).

The Image of Group Psychotherapy in an Institutional Setting

Many times the patient entering a clinic is discouraged unwittingly from entering the group psychotherapeutic program. The intake worker indicates that other forms of therapy are better or that "because we are crowded" and "because we have too few therapists" group psychotherapy might be tried. Rather than this unfortunate approach, it would be better, and certainly more accurate, to assure the patient that he will get the therapy that is preferable for him and his illness. Too often, in institutions, group psychotherapy is offered as an inferior kind of therapy.

Other attitudes held by both the administrators and the chiefs of service handicap the success of the group treatment division. Not realizing the intricacies of group psychotherapy and considering it merely another means for socialization, they assign a relatively untrained person to the task of organizing and conducting the group. For example, they may assign this duty to an untrained social worker, although the success of the treatment could be assured by the experience of either a trained psychiatrist or a psychologist. In many clinics it is the usual practice to give to the group therapist those patients who are the most difficult and those who have been tried unsuccesfully in other methods of therapy. Staff meetings rarely center around the group program and its needs, patients are discharged without an awareness of what it does dynamically to the other group members, and both training and orientation of staff in the field of group psychotherapy are held to a minimum.

Clinics, agencies, and hospitals that ordinarily charge fees for psychiatric treatment should continue this practice with group psychotherapeutic patients, and the same system of determining fee scale should be applicable to these patients as to any others. Patients, however, who have been in individual psychotherapy, and who have then been transferred to a therapeutic group, complain when they have to pay the same amount as formerly. It is suggested that the chief of service, a representative of the group psychotherapy department, and the administrator meet and come to some reasonable determination of fee scale. Here the importance lies not in the actual fixing of payment rate but in the communication that determines a definite point of view, for the outcome of such a meeting will increase understanding and will develop a consistent point of view concerning the patients' responsibility in this matter.

Introduction of Group Psychotherapy in a Nonpsychiatric Institution

A group psychotherapeutic program can be introduced into any institution by administrative order. Thus there are groups to be found in colleges (both teacher and pupil groups), high schools, and grammar schools; in penal institutions, correctional homes, and disciplinary barracks (the armed forces); in industry and labor organizations; in mental hospitals, general hospitals, private hospitals, clinics, agencies, and so forth. *Generally speaking, the more authoritarian the institution, the easier to form the therapy group, but also the less chance for intensive group psychotherapy.* Although they may be either goal directed or limited goal directed, all of these groups have a place in the field of group psychotherapy. It suffices to say here that, if possible, the therapist must explain in detail to the administrative and supervisory staff of the institution the method and the usual results of group psychotherapy.

The Confidentiality of the Patient's Productions in an Institution

In clinics and in hospitals particularly, but also in other institutions, group patients are reluctant to be personal because the therapist takes notes. These patients, being accustomed to the usual hospital chart routines, envision the therapist's notes as a part of the overall chart. A good practice for the therapist is to reassure his patients by explaining to them that group notes are withheld from the chart, are placed in a locked file, and are read only by the authorized psychiatric staff. Naturally, this arrangement must first be established with the administrator. From time to time, if it is required, the therapist can dictate an individual note concerning a patient's progress for the hospital chart. This note need not include the intimate revelations made by the patient during the many sessions of therapy.

The Use of Microphones and One-way Screens

Because the authenticity of the patient-therapist relationship is based upon the good will of the participants, the use of recording devices should be limited. In institutions where training and research occur, it may be essential to use these devices. If it is believed necessary to use either a microphone or a one-way vision screen, the group members and, of course, the therapist should know this. The therapist should tell the patients why these procedures are necessary and attempt to analyze with them their reluctance to have others know what is going on. There must be an assurance, however, that only authorized persons will use these devices and that visitors or nonprofessionals will be prohibited from hearing or viewing the group in session. In all instances these devices are warranted on the basis that they will help, and not hurt, the group member.

Therapeutic Intensity Lessened by Institutional Administration

Although therapy groups form more readily in agencies, clinics, and so forth than in private practice, once formed, the patients' resistance to therapeutic self-question increases. The authority of the institution promotes the easy establishment of the group, yet this same authority in the guise of chief nurses, administrators, or directors often allows the group members either to ignore their inner conflicts or to displace them onto others.

Clinic Staff–Group Member Relationships

In the outpatient department of a hospital, the ties within a therapy group are often reduced by necessary contacts, sometimes of an administrative kind, with clerks, social workers, psychologists, physicians, and personnel of other specialty clinics. For example, one woman projected much of her inner struggle onto her children and then repeatedly demanded to see a social worker about them. Another, at vacation time, sought "concrete" evidence of her progress by asking for a psychological reexamination. In both instances, these patients wanted to bypass their therapy group through the establishment of other contacts, and in this way they ignored their own problems, with which the group would have confronted them. This kind of maneuver is seen less in private practice because the opportunities for extragroup contacts within the office are fewer. However, if the group therapist shares an office, he may expect his patients to view his colleagues in distorted ways and to bring this up in the group.

Extratherapeutic clinic contacts may prove bothersome in another way. Group patients tend to "act out" against the representative of institutional authority. Although expected, this is difficult to handle when, in his antagonism, the patient refuses to come to his group. He may behave deliberately this way in order to manipulate the group therapist into some action against the staff member, who is seen in an authoritative light by the angry patient.

Cancellations are made easy because the patient knows many clinic staff members. Many times he considers cancellations purely an administrative affair and, when actually unwilling to face his conflicts, calls a volunteer, a clerk, or a social worker. But cancellation is more than an administrative affair. A group member's absence completely alters the group's form and its process. Thus cancellations, which should be minimal, should be accepted only by the therapist, who handles the request as well as the resultant absence dynamically, never administratively.

Central not only to group administration, but also to ease or difficulty of group attendance, is the hour of the group sessions. Outpatient clinics that are open from nine to five—the usual workday—tend to limit the kinds of patients treated. Therefore, institutional group psychotherapy sometimes centers about a homogeneous configuration of patients based not upon psychiatric category but upon sex, age, vocation, and so forth. To overcome this limited-selection trend it is suggested, if possible, that group psychotherapy sessions be scheduled after five o'clock in the evening and on Saturdays. It is not necessary for the whole clinic to remain open during these inconvenient hours, just the section devoted to group therapy.

A more realistic appraisal of the clinic's appointment hours will allow many wage earners, both men and women, to participate, whereas now they are unfortunately all but excluded. Also, more convenient hours will reduce the number of cancellations by those who find it difficult to attend either morning or afternoon sessions.

MEDICAL STAFF–GROUP MEMBER RELATIONSHIPS

It has been pointed out that careful and continuing medical evaluation of group members is indicated; yet group patients in either hospitals or clinics or in agencies with a medical department are inclined to demand unnecessarily frequent special physical examinations, special medications and tests. The nonmedical group psychotherapist is many times hard pressed to determine the validity of these requests. Once again a close tie between the group therapist and the medical specialist is crucial. The therapist must analyze these requests as he does all behavior occurring in his group, realizing that somatic complaints will at times be common.

CLINIC PATIENT–GROUP MEMBER RELATIONSHIPS

Group therapy patients are often overly concerned with meeting or being placed in groups with friends, neighbors, and casual acquaintances. This difficulty is prevalent in the small community and in outpatient departments that treat patients from certain areas of the city. Intake staff should be sensitive to this reluctance and suggest to the prospective patient that he take it up with his therapist. Even more support is required if the incoming patient is concerned about a chance meeting with someone he knows in the vicinity of the clinic or hospital.

References

(1) BACH, G. R. Intensive Group Psychotherapy. New York: Ronald Press, 1950.

(2) FOULKES, S. H., and ANTHONY, E. J. Group Psychotherapy: The Psychoanalytic Approach. London: Penguin Books, 1957.

(3) MORENO, J. L. The Significance of a Therapeutic Format and the Place of Acting Out in Psychotherapy. Group Psychotherapy, 8 (April 1955), 7–19.

(4) WOLF, A. The Psychoanalysis of Groups. Am. J. Psychotherapy, 3 (1949), 16–50, and 4 (1950), 525–58.

(5) LOESER, L. H. Group Psychotherapy in Private Practice: A Preliminary Report. Am. J. Psychotherapy, 3 (April 1949), 213–33.

(6) MEIJERING, W. L. The Interrelation of Individual, Group and Hospital Community Psychotherapy. Internat. J. Group Psychotherapy, 10, No. 1 (January 1960), 62.

(7) CLARK, D. H. Principles of Administrative Therapy. Am. J. Psychiat., 117, No. 6 (December 1960), 506–10.

5 Organization of the Group and the First Group Meeting

Max Rosenbaum

The Meeting between Patient and Group Psychoanalytic Therapist

> *Initiation*
>
> Whoever you are, go out into the evening,
> Leaving your room, of which you know each bit;
> Your house is the last before the infinite,
> Whoever you are.
> Then with your eyes that wearily
> Scarce lift themselves from the worn-out door stone
> Slowly you raise a shadowy black tree
> And fix it on the sky; slender, alone.
> And you have made the world (and it shall grow
> And ripen as a word, unspoken, still).
> When you have grasped its meaning with your will,
> Then tenderly your eyes will let it go. . . .
>
> *Rainer Maria Rilke*[*]

THE PERSON WHO COMES to our office does so for many reasons, and is stimulated by many different forces. Sometimes it may be a physician who has observed physical or emotional stress. Or it may be a member of the clergy or an attorney or an educator or even someone locally influential in the community—the owner of the local garage or repair shop. In smaller communities, there are always people who are highly regarded and con-

---

* Rainer Maria Rilke, *Selected Poems*, trans. by C. F. MacIntyre (Berkeley and Los Angeles: University of California Press, 1971). Translation copyright, 1940, by C. F. MacIntyre.

sidered wise. If these people respect the psychotherapist, a referral may come from this source. When referrals come from physicians it is often very difficult for the group psychotherapist since the referral source wants to be part of the therapy and expects to be informed as to what is going on. Ethical attorneys who are consulted when marital tensions reach a peak will often suggest that clients first go for professional consultation. Even the neighborhood pharmacist (and a few still exist even in an era of supermarket drugstores) may make a referral. Probably the most "solid" referral comes from the satisfied ex-patient— someone who has completed treatment and who feels strongly about the advantages of therapy. Or the new patient may be a friend or neighbor of such a person who has observed the progress and feels the desire to undergo a similar improvement.

Occasionally, a judge or district attorney may refer a patient, especially in a time when laws against sale and possession of drugs have become extremely harsh. Or a local attorney may refer someone who has been accused of exposing himself or molesting a minor. This is only a small sample of the vast variety of cases which come to the practitioner's office.

As we move from the more limited private practice, where patients are seen only individually, to the more community-oriented approach to mental health, psychotherapists are increasingly expected to function in a variety of settings (office, clinic, hospital, school, industry, recreational place, prison, court, poverty program, Indian reservation, walk-in drug clinic, and so on). What makes us "professional" is our training and our capacity to function in a variety of settings. Further, we are called upon to function in emergency settings where acute family disturbances erupt, which require the presence of the police.

The patients who are referred to us by others and who come to meet with us voluntarily are people in distress. The general expectation is magical. Indeed, some call psychotherapists the secular priests of the twentieth century. The seed of what begins to grow between patient and therapist from the very first contact, whether by phone or by personal contact, is the *positive transference*. (Transference will be elaborated upon later.) This means that the patient's first reaction, while skeptical, is a search for relief, and the beginning of trust in the therapist. Most of the time the concept of relief is so vague that even the patient who desires relief does not really know what is going on. The first contact gives us a lot of information as to what is at work and what are the secret expectations of the patient.

It is very easy for the psychotherapist to become the guru or the omniscient figure, because the patient or the family is looking for "help," which literally means aid or support. While the therapist offers help, he is looking for something much deeper—"change," which means becoming something different. This involves a much more strenuous task for all concerned—therapist, patient, and any members of the patient's environment who desire to experience change.

For the first time, the patient is brought to an awareness that he is being offered something more than a benign acceptance of him and his problem. Of course, there are many people who feel so relieved by a sympathetic listener that they feel they have been helped. It is part of our task to be sympathetic. If we cannot be empathic, we should not be seeing the person who comes to us. This does not mean that we take on the responsibility for a patient's change. Unlike encounter techniques, which keep insisting that the patient *must* be responsible, we tune into the patient's fear of change as well as the history of trauma which blocked him from growth. It is important to listen to the patient's statement of his problem or the couple's description of their difficulties or the family's presentation.. This may take several visits and the patient(s) may wonder why there is no miraculous relief offered. Yet the sympathy extended as we engage the patient and *listen* is critical to the establishment of a *positive transference*, where the patient feels there is no one sitting in judgment or fitting him or the family into preconceived diagnostic categories. During all this time, we observe the language patterns, the posture, the pauses and lapses in conversation to gain some early clues as to what forces are at work.

What many psychotherapists overlook in the first few meetings is the positive potential in the person who comes for therapy. He comes of his own free will generally, and pays his own way. Most of our ambulatory patients are engaged in work, or go to school, or rear children, or try to work out a marriage. They love, as far as they are able to. They relate sexually—even if sometimes mechanically. They maintain some circle of friendships—however large or small. Therefore, we relate to the whole person and do *not* stress the patient quality. Most people who visit a "shrink" (a pejorative description of the fear in our culture that we will shrink their heads) feel labeled or feel they have failed. The hard-working husband whose wife tells him that he is unsuitable as a sexual companion, and ineffectual as a father, feels crushed and agitated. The mother whose child has been bedwetting, in spite of all of her reading on child rearing, feels defeated. The father and mother who have mortgaged themselves to the hilt to provide a college education for a son or daughter feel genuinely confused and resentful when the child fails courses or refuses to work or "hangs around the house." It takes a good deal of courage to return week after week to listen and to explore one's behavior when the impulse is to run away or to ignore the problem(s).

When the psychotherapist is bewildered or overwhelmed by the enormity of the patient's difficulties, there is a tendency to move to classification as a way of making order out of chaos. It is at this time, in the first meetings, that one must stand firm and continue to feel and experience the patient's confusion.

In all of this quiet listening in the first few visits, we communicate a respect for the person(s) we are with. We are paid for time and not for the interest or concern which we bring to the meeting. If, for reasons which need not concern the new patient, we find that it is difficult to work with him or her, every effort should be made to refer the person carefully to another competent professional who will hopefully accept him or her. There are some psychotherapists who stress "total candor" as a method of "opening up" and reaching the patient during the first few visits. This often masks tactlessness and a brutality which reinforces the patient's distress and distrust. It is not helpful or desirable to brutalize the patient if we see a quality that is repugnant to us. The patient has experienced enough distress.

At the first few meetings, the patient or couple or family will ask many questions which seem quite simple to the therapist. But remember, this is the first time generally for the person(s) asking the questions. At the outset the therapist should familiarize himself with the work schedule and the financial status as well as education of the patient so that there is a frame of reference within which to work.

For example, patients from Brazil may mention spiritism (a modified form of voodoo) as part of a belief. The uninformed therapist may jump to the conclusion that the patient is psychotic, totally ignorant of the fact that many Brazilians believe in spiritism. Or the patient may be devoutly religious. It is important to capture some of the patient's belief in the efficacy of religion. Or the family members, out of need for immediate relief, may make a commitment to therapy which they cannot handle time-wise or financially.

The therapist's time schedule may be simply inappropriate for the family structure. Thus, a family-owned business may require certain working hours which the family is not ready to modify. Perhaps ultimately the wisest thing would be to change the time schedule of the family, but the therapist should be aware of the time necessary for the family to make this transition. There should be no radical intervention (unless an acute situation is present) which serves to agitate the family even more than when they first came to the therapist's office.

During these early visits, very specific instructions are to be given as to how the patient is to pay for therapy, as well as arrangements made for appointments. In one situation, a very manipulative patient began to deluge the therapist with insurance forms from four companies with which she had contracted. It became a tedious experience which required a great deal of time to prepare the forms, and this angered the therapist. The patient had asked in the first two visits, "Do you accept insurance payments?" The therapist quickly answered in the affirmative and ignored the volume of work that this necessitates. Or a parent may ask, "Will you keep in contact with the school that referred me?" Again, this may be very time-consuming, and the therapist should clarify exactly what is being asked of him timewise. This definition of the contract between therapist and patient comes up again and again in the group.

It is in these early visits that treatment often fails. Frequently, the therapist ignores the significance of early questions or comments by the patient, or simply takes too much for granted. Questions as to absences, vacations, illnesses, and contact with other professionals (which may include attorneys when a couple considering a divorce comes to treatment) should all be carefully answered in detail. Obviously, the therapist cannot foresee every exigency, but the patient often has a very unrealistic picture of the therapist's availability. The patient rarely forgets what is considered to be rejection or neglect on the therapist's part, and this frequently relates to an earlier time in the patient's history when a significant figure—generally parent or parent surrogate—has let him down.

The therapist should be very specific as to whether a credit arrangement is acceptable and how much of a debt the patient will be able to accrue in therapy. Some patients use indebtedness to trap the therapist. This maneuver is a test of affection or individual concern. The group therapist will find that this is very contagious in a group and, indeed, unfair to those patients who are prompt in payment of fees. In one situation, a very benign therapist permitted an entire group to accumulate indebtedness. When he asked for payment, most of the group members refused to pay, stating that the therapist had permitted the situation to develop. All of this will eventually "surface out" in a group and should not be concealed or ignored.

The group therapist should be very clear as to place and time of meeting. While much of psychotherapy is practiced by individuals located in urban settings where there are mass transit facilities, there are those who are located in settings where the only accessibility is via automobile. When winter comes and the driving conditions are hazardous, the group therapist, sitting in his office, may not realize the risks involved in driving. Again, there must be a clear statement as to cancellations and reasonable notice. In one case the therapist's office was located at the top of a street which had a very steep incline. Dependent on the town highway department to keep the roads passable, some patients literally could not drive up the hill when there was a heavy snow or when the roads turned icy. The therapist may have to make arrangements for the group or family to meet him in another setting if his own office becomes inaccessible.

All this may seem perfectly logical, but many therapists ignore the patient's dilemma and simply take for granted a certain maneuverability on the patient's part. In another case a therapist stated that he would be available to meet with group members during his vacation. The patients had no idea of the tedious and harrowing trip involved in reaching the therapist, who was staying in a rural, isolated area on top of a mountain.

His simple comment about availability did not present the patient with the reality of what transportation was or was not available.

My policy is to have a trial period of a month to work with a new patient. After a month, both patient and therapist decide if they can work with one another. This has seemed to be very effective over the years. On one occasion, a month passed and the therapist, through oversight, neglected to state specifically that the trial period was over. Another month passed before the patient said, with a good deal of anxiety, "Is the trial over or did you extend it for me?" This oversight on the part of the therapist created a good deal of distress for the patient, and is an example of the type of carelessness against which a therapist should guard.

Through all of the first few meetings, the group therapist who works with families should be aware of the collusive systems that reinforce disturbed patterns of behavior. These systems serve to avoid insight and are in many ways the same systems to be found when a therapist acts as a consultant to any agency or educational setting. There is often a private family language at work which is expressed in either speech or body language, and the group therapist should attempt to tune in to this language.

Sometimes explosiveness is part of the cultural milieu and the group therapist, observing this, may be disconcerted or agitated during the first meetings. When working with many families who come from the Mediterranean area (Italians, Greeks, Spanish, and Portuguese), we often find explosive reactions and threats of violence expressed. However, as quickly as these threats erupt in the therapy setting, they pass away just as quickly. The therapist who stems from a more intellectual or controlled cultural setting may be too quick to pass judgment on this behavior, which is really culturally based. When working with black families, especially in inner-city "ghetto" areas, the tendency of parents to use physical violence to control children and adolescents is to be noted as part of the culture, and not necessarily as an indication of pathology.

When the group therapist meets with a family, they may want to continue meeting together. But there are circumstances where it is advisable to meet with different members of the family or to suggest that family members be placed in different groups. In one family, Sandy, the father, had always been the one who worked hard. Since adolescence he had worked to help support his parents, and after marriage he perceived himself as the workhorse. He was unable to grant himself any pleasures without first making sure that his wife and children were cared for. Underneath all this was a deep-seated rage which reflected itself in hypertension and headaches—a way by which he could keep his wife and children away when he had reached a satiation point. In the family group, he spent most of his time taking care of other family members. He could not "get well" before the rest of the family. While this pattern of his behavior surfaced rather quickly, there was an impasse. He finally agreed to meet with the therapist alone and was placed in a group. For the first time he was able to express his rage as he reacted to other members of the group to whom he transferred as family members.

When the group therapist treats married couples, there is on occasion such bitterness and repressed hatred that the therapy sessions become shouting sessions. If the therapist suggests that the partners meet separately or be placed in different groups, the couple may interpret this as the beginning of a marriage dissolution. Indeed, they may be accurate in this perception, since the only thing that may keep certain marriages together is the desire to fight and engage in vehement quarrels. Such a presentation should be made very carefully since the reaction is usually one of agitation. But a couple may find it easier to get down to the more basic problems when away from the heat of their own intense anger.

There are patients who are referred for group therapy by individual therapists who want to continue seeing them in individual treatment. Some group therapists have found this a feasible approach. This has not worked out well in my experience. Usually, I find that both patient and his individual therapist are locked into a very intense dependency which the individual therapist is often unwilling to dissolve. The individual therapist then becomes part of the group, although the group members do not know this person. A feeling of annoyance arises in group members at the idea of an observer who is not present to react to. The individual therapist becomes a "corridor" out of the group, and a great deal of material is lost to the group because the patient brings it back to another therapist. In clinics or hospitals, where there is close contact between the group therapist and the individual therapist, the idea may be feasible since the effort is made to pool all of the information and the therapists agree to meet and/or share information. More specifically, the patient is encouraged to take material back to the group for discussion and exploration.

The same situation may apply when a patient is being treated psychopharmacologically. There must be close cooperation between the psychiatrist who is administering drug therapy and the group therapist so that there is awareness of any side effects of medication which might crop up in treatment. In hospitals where groups are used largely for social training skills and where there is little effort made or desired to explore intrapsychic material, there is generally little contact between the group leader and the individual therapist or psychiatrist. But the focus is different here, for the major part of the work is often considered to be carried out in individual meetings.

Through all of the first meetings, whether with individuals, couples, or families, the group therapist should assess whether the patients have the capacity to relate in group settings. There is often an eagerness on the part of the beginning group therapist to place *all* patients in a group.

This missionary zeal has nothing to do with the practice of group therapy and makes it a form of religion. It is not true that all patients are suitable for a group. The garrulous, charming "salesman" type of patient may be more interested in joining a group as a way of exercising social maneuvers. The agitated, despairing man who has just been rejected by his wife may be more interested in using the group as a podium to express his tale of woe and anguish. He may require many individual meetings to relieve this distress since his tales of hurt become boring to other group members after the first expression of sympathy.

The group therapist should be listening to himself in all of the first individual meetings. What reactions come to the surface? Does the patient bore him? Does he become easily agitated? Is he intrigued by the stories that are told? Does the meeting with a couple elicit memories of his own relationship with his own marriage partner? Some therapists experience such distress in these first few meetings that they feel a need to speak about themselves. Some practitioners advocate self-disclosure; this is often an unloading of the anxiety that the patients create in the therapist. While it is important for the patients to know that there is an empathic listener who is professionally trained, there is little purpose in expounding upon the therapist's own life style or problems. Much later in therapy, the sharing of such information may advance the progress of group therapy, but this is long after the patient and therapist have become deeply involved.

Is the therapist sexually reactive to the patient? One individual therapist referred a woman for group therapy and in the first phone call described her as a "very beautiful woman." The group therapist overlooked this comment. Later in the conversation the referring therapist suggested that he continue seeing the woman individually after she joined a group. This request was left open for a later decision. The woman's attractiveness was obvious at her first meeting with the group therapist. Her referring therapist, recently divorced, reacted to her as though she were a girlfriend rather than a patient in treatment. He was reluctant to give up his relationship with her because she apparently enlivened his existence. She, in turn, never explored this behavior, and yet she was uncomfortable in some way that she could not understand. She was unconsciously pleased to be with her individual therapist, aware that he found her physically attractive. She presented many excuses as to why group therapy was not for her, although she did feel that she had reached an impasse in individual treatment. Each of the earlier meetings with this woman, Sheila, was followed by a phone call from her individual therapist expressing his interest and concern about her ability to relate to the group therapist. Actually, he was working out his own problem, and it had nothing to do with Sheila. The fact that the group therapist found her attractive sensitized him to the problem of the referring therapist.

The important difference was that the group therapist was happily married and that Sheila did not fill a void in his life. Because of the very special attention that Sheila had received from her individual therapist "quasi-boyfriend," she had a great deal of difficulty in accepting the idea of group therapy. She wanted an enormous amount of individual attention and accurately perceived the group as a place where she would have to share—an experience that was difficult for her. Perhaps this is why she remained in individual treatment so long, in a relationship that was obviously unprofitable aside from reinforcing her neurotic needs.

The pressuring group therapist who pushes the patient to the group may induce a limited change in self-attitude. A climate is set up where the patient in the group models himself or herself after an intrusive, impatient therapist who pushes patients to act in certain ways. Affect is maximized with little cognitive work. This distorted theory of "spontaneity" permits the group therapist to act callously, often brutally and without tact. Narcissism is stressed at the expense of mutualism.

An intrusive and demanding approach on the part of the therapist, especially in the first meetings in psychotherapy, shows the therapist to be the dominant, responsible force. This is clearly seen when structured exercises are used supposedly to enable people to show closeness—exercises such as touching, holding, blindfold touching, and so on. The patient becomes increasingly passive and, while there is some reduction in anxiety level, this appears to be more related to the passivity that ensues as the group leader obviously establishes his dominance. So, in reality, responsibility is not the result, for patients are not encouraged to study and experience their own patterns of response and the *transference* distortions that are involved. The quick ventilation of affect leads to a feeling of euphoria and a "high" which is short lived. The long-term gains are short-circuited and the patient is encouraged from the first few meetings to believe in simplistic answers to living.

The patient's confidence is gained by the nonverbal communication of interest and concern by the therapist. There are occasions where desperate patients want so badly to believe that a therapist is concerned that they will overlook slights and rejection. The culture we live in, with constant mobility on the part of large sections of the population, encourages much loneliness which is seen in many patients who come for group psychotherapy. Often, the attraction to a group experience for patients is to help relieve loneliness rather than to explore what has happened to cause their predicament in the first place. The work that we are engaged in is *not* to serve as a social meeting. The about-to-be-divorced woman, who needs a "halfway house" to help her make the transition to the world of single men and women, needs the group to explore her fears. She does not require a group to establish friendships or arrange dates.

What we are doing in all of these first meetings is to establish trust. This means that the patient(s) begin to experience on a profound level a feeling that we, as psychotherapists, are deeply concerned. But trust means belief—not religious, but human, concern. The culture, with its cynicism, works against the development of trust. The patient may feel, "He only cares about me because I pay him." Here again, the patient is told that we live in a culture which generally asks the patient to pay for the time spent together. But, as noted earlier, we are *never* paid for interest and concern. Like the honest craftsman, the therapist brings interest and concern, things that can never be paid for.

In the first individual visits, the patient may attempt to entertain the group therapist. This may reflect a pattern of family life where there is a need to be liked. Or the patient may attempt to provoke the therapist— again, a pattern of being the unruly child. This provocative behavior can be achieved in many ways. A patient may come into the office on a wet and stormy day, soaking the carpet, although a clothes closet and umbrella stand are readily available in the waiting room. The patient may state, "I was so upset that I didn't notice." Each group therapist has a different life style, and some may not be upset at the idea of mopping up carpeting after the patient leaves. But in a kind, yet firm manner, the patient should be encouraged to hang up the raincoat, or place the umbrella in a stand.

Because of my concern with the hazards of smoking, there are no ashtrays available. On occasion, confirmed smokers become agitated when they want to smoke. A simple statement of concern for health is all that is needed to motivate the patient to spend a therapy session without smoking. The point is that it should not be experienced as a prohibition, but as a statement of concern. A statement such as, "We shall be spending much time together and as we work toward your change, I don't want to see you develop lung cancer," often brings forth a smile.

The consistent behavior of the therapist is important to the development of trust. Most patients have been exposed to erratic behavior on the part of significant people in their developmental years. If the therapist is perceived as erratic or inconsistent, the patient becomes distressed and this distress blocks effective psychotherapy. At the outset, the patient is very much the child and the therapist is very much the parent. But the mature parent, as does the mature therapist, wants the child to grow and encourages growth. He does this by letting the patient know that he (the therapist) is there. The immature therapist maintains the role of the parent and never moves the patient to a peer relationship. The patient's need for adulation of the therapist locks the latter into the role of constantly overprotective parent. While this is consistent behavior, it is not growth-producing.

In our first meetings, I tell patients that I work in many ways—individual therapy, combined therapy, family therapy, and couples therapy. This is not set forth as a sales pitch, but is introduced when relevant to the material brought forth. Thus, an agitated wife may be told, "Sometimes I'd like to see both you and your husband together. How do you think he would react to the idea?" Or, "Perhaps your entire family could meet with me." This type of introduction to other therapy approaches is easily accepted. Most group therapists who are known to the community of professional psychotherapists are known to be group therapists by the patients who come. But some patients are completely unaware of what is involved and become quite agitated when group treatment is mentioned. Their first reaction is invariably one of rejection: "He doesn't care to work with me alone." The exception is the patient who wants to escape into a group as quickly as possible, a move which should be discouraged and explored immediately.

Organization of the Psychoanalytic Group

As the therapist comes closer to the point of practicing psychotherapy with his first group or, for that matter, in commencing any new group, he may begin to experience anxieties that reflect some of his own dilemmas in living. A therapist once asked, "How can you place in the same group a woman from Back Bay Boston and a man from the Lower East Side of New York City?" A psychoanalyst without group therapy experience, who was present at the particular lecture, answered as the experienced group therapist listened. He said, "A little of Boston will rub off on the East Side and a little of the East Side will rub off on Boston." Essentially, this type of question is part of the therapist's need to categorize. It is more comfortable for him to define people than to understand them.

When the therapist is flexible, he is able to meet with persons from various cultures and social levels. However, the therapist stems from a particular setting and he may feel secure only when treating patients who reflect his background. By doing this, however, he hampers the growth of the patients, and his own maturation as well. The more flexible the therapist, the more flexible the group.

The heterogeneous, sexually mixed, and continuous groups offer maximum opportunity for deep and lasting personality change. The success of psychoanalytic groups, organized to be totally heterogeneous, depends in large measure on (a) individualized periods of preparation for each patient and (b) when needed, the use of supplementary individual sessions (combined therapy).

The therapist simultaneously administers and organizes a group. The new patient, however, responds first to the administrative details, and later, after introduction to and placement in the analytic therapy group, he responds to the organization.

The Continuous Psychoanalytic Group

The continuous group introduces newly prepared members as old ones leave. This seems best for the following reasons:

1. It individualizes for each patient the frequency, duration, and kind of preparatory sessions.
2. It individualizes the duration of the group therapy.
3. It permits the group member to experience the entrance birth (entry into the group) and the departure (death and illness) of others.
4. It places the responsibilities more definitely in the hands of the group, as they respond to an old member's leaving and to a new person's arrival. It moves the group from "therapist centered" to "group centered."

The full use of psychoanalytic and existential techniques, especially transference and countertransference, and our awareness and use of emerging new factors in each patient, can be accomplished only by a closely knit group that continues indefinitely, similar to the family and to life itself.

The Size of the Analytic Group

The size of the group should vary between seven and ten members. The minimum of seven is chosen because this number resembles a large family and also provides for any possible absences due to illness, emergencies, and so forth. A group ranging from three to six in number *may* function effectively, but there is usually a decrease in the amount of activity and therefore a lessening in interactional content. Generally, a group that is small in number forces the therapist to become more active in attempting to foster group participation.

In a continuous group of seven members, if one or two leave the group for any reason, it is necessary to introduce one or two additional patients as soon as feasible. The therapist may be preparing two individuals, but it may not be timely to introduce them yet. Therapy can continue for a while with the remaining group of only five members. In a group starting with only five members, if two dropped out only three would remain, and three patients would not be enough for effective therapy.

We place great importance on regular attendance. The lack of concern about regular attendance exhibited by some therapists is a misunderstanding of their role in treatment and, more seriously, a disregard for the patient. If the fee is accepted, and no note is made of the patient's absence, therapy may become a mercantile transaction. Absences are discussed in the group.

HETEROGENEITY

In order to insure maximum interaction, groups should be *heterogeneous*. The group is now organized as a totally heterogeneous combination—that is, of patients with different personality structures and different disorders, coming from all races, cultures, and social strata, of both sexes, of varying ages, of different schooling, and of different physical fitness.* Zilferstein and Grotjahn come to much the same conclusion when they state:

> More recently it has been recognized that homogeneity of symptomatology is not necessarily a valid criterion in group composition. Similarly, it has been concluded, as a result of experience, that homogeneity with respect to sex, age, social or educational level, marital status, or intelligence is not a significant criterion for determining who is suitable for group psychotherapy or which patients should be treated in the same group (1).

The placement of patients with different kinds of personalities and different kinds of disorders in the same group is beneficial, as it forwards the ongoing group process by increasing interaction. Thus, the advantage of the heterogeneous group over the homogeneous one is that it emphasizes the differentness of each patient, acknowledging each as an individual. Stemming from this recognition is the possibility that each patient, through a vastly different life experience, can indefinitely expand the interpretation of another group member's behavior. The fact that one patient can help another is of course one of the bases for group psychotherapy.

The homogeneous group, established as it is around the common denominator of illness—common symptoms (2), diagnosis (3, 4, 5, 6) or personality structure (7, 8)—indicates that the group is organized negatively; that is, solely on the basis of disease. Interaction is thereby lessened, while identifications are easily established and the therapist becomes more directive. There is much less chance for healthy identifications—because of the overall sameness (illness) of the patients (9, 10). Patients in homogeneous groups do seem to relate to each other much more quickly, focusing on the same complaint, experience, and somatic or psychic symptom. In many cases, the members soon tend to compete, using their symptoms as they become aggravated or disappear, in order to get the love of the therapist.

For patients who are specifically excluded from group psychotherapy because of their extreme psychopathology, the homogeneous group does appear helpful. Some therapists, usually in clinics and hospitals, place

---

* I recommend pregroup medical examination and the yearly followup during the course of group therapy to safeguard the patient, not to exclude him from the group. On occasion, patients in the group pick up physical symptoms from one another.

homosexuals, drug addicts, psychopaths, psychotics, and so on in groups with benefit, thus treating seven to ten persons, all of whom have the same general personality structure and symptomatology. In these groups where the membership is based upon the commonality of symptoms or diagnosis, members tend to suppress their memories of unpleasant past events, those which cause them pain or shame. Most, if not all, homogeneous treatment groups appear to be of the *repressive-constructive* variety.

After preparation, the patient is introduced to his definitive group. An exception necessitating delay would be an outcropping of very severe symptoms in the patient or a very rough interactional period facing the group. The patient on entering his group very often loses the presenting symptoms, only to gain others. The group is not described to the patient nor is the patient described to the group before the entry of the new patient. The placement in the group of blacks and whites, the educated and the uneducated, "upper-class" and "lower-class" persons is proper, because it promotes interaction and assists in a more protean interpretation. Parsons, who practices group psychotherapy in Little Rock, Arkansas, stated:

> Nonsegregation by color presents a problem initially with patients who come from the Old South section. If I think of it, I devote some time to preparing them for a nonsegregated group. Generally, I put it on a take it or leave it basis, however. Actually, colored persons in a group are more of an asset than a problem, once the initial reactions are overcome . . . so far the problem has been relatively insignificant (11).

Different educational levels do not, as some maintain, limit the creativity of persons in an analytic therapy group. A graduate of a leading technical university can be in the same group as a grammar school graduate. It is not helpful to compose a "professional group." The mental health professional, along with other professionals, is to be considered a "patient" when seeking psychotherapy, including analytic group therapy. The group therapist's own neurotic residuals, including his anxieties about status, sometimes make it difficult for him to form this kind of group.

In order to increase interaction and its proper analysis, the placement of men and women in the same group is indicated. The advantages of the mixed group are many. It resembles the "family," thus allowing the members to relive their childhoods more easily. Relationships (transferences) similar to those with mother, father, sister, and brother occur more quickly and with more intensity. Long-repressed sexual feelings and fantasies come to the surface in the mixed group. There is also greater chance for therapeutic fulfillment and satisfaction. The therapist in a mixed group finds his task easier because he and the others can more accurately observe and interpret the behavior of the members.

Patients between eighteen and sixty years of age can be placed in the same group. Patients of vastly different ages generally relate well to one another, depending upon their needs and abilities to trust.

Heterogeneity in age supports the development of multiple transferences of both the parent-child and the sibling-sibling variety: for instance, a twenty-five-year-old man was included in a group with a man of fifty-five. Very soon the younger man saw the older one as a controlling, authoritarian father figure. Through this he was eventually able to come to grips with many of his own distortions concerning his father and his family. The older man benefited too. He was finally able to work through his fears and conflicts about being displaced by a younger, more virile man. As their distortions lessened, these two patients could perceive one another as unique and worthwhile persons, without regard for their age differences.

Group psychoanalytic therapy is made more difficult by the inclusion of friends, acquaintances, and relatives in the same group. The increased complexity is centered about a patient's fear of exposure and his difficulty in confiding in a person who knows him outside of the group.

A husband and wife may be placed in the same group. This is not suggested for the beginning and generally anxious group therapist because of the complications that ensue. But for those psychotherapists able to handle and turn to constructive use the extremely provocative material that results, this kind of group composition may be welcome (12, 13, 14). However, the group meeting should never be allowed to become a time of arbitration between husband and wife, with the other members divided and taking sides. A husband and wife in the same group often block each other from discussing past and present sexual experiences, sexual fantasies, transferences, and some dreams.

During a period of "stalemate" for a particular patient in group psychotherapy, some therapists have introduced the husband (or wife) into the group for either a brief or a lengthy period of time. Apparently, this led to movement on the part of the stalemated patient.

Because the procedures of administration and organization of therapeutic groups are basically authoritarian, the therapy is "directive" during this period. The therapist should allow the members ample opportunity to express their feelings concerning the imposition of these procedures. After a while the administration and the organization are seen by the patients to be for their own benefit, and are then accepted by the group.

The First Group Session

Many individual therapists and psychoanalysts may keep the patient and themselves in a kind of collusion. The patient sees the therapist as the powerful, all-knowing expert, and never learns to entrust himself to his peers.

The first session of his first group is challenging to the beginning group psychotherapist. If group organization, preparation of the patient, and overcoming his resistance have been carefully done, the therapist can meet the challenge. After he has been practicing group psychotherapy, especially if he uses the continuous group method, there is never the same challenge as when he contemplates the very first session.

The challenge can be lessened if the therapist considers for the group a nucleus of four or five patients who have been in individual therapy with him for some time. He might then add three new patients whom he has been seeing in group preparation. This is less taxing than preparation of seven to ten new patients at the same time in addition to the individual patients he is already treating. The patients who have been in treatment for some time should also be prepared for the group, but their preparation is easier because of the deep transference already established. Administratively, it is preferable to combine a portion of one's private practice in starting the first group. Hours, days, and fees are easier to determine for the older patients than for the newer ones. This applies to private practice as well as agency and clinic outpatient groups. The group therapist in these settings forms his group from older patients whom he has been treating and new referrals whom he prepares. The group therapist should determine which patients should enter the group and the timing of this introduction.

The therapist has prepared a number of patients in order to place them in a group. He feels deep emotions toward each one and knows them all very well. The patients are aware that they are entering a group. All patients know the therapist, but they do not know each other. They have strong positive feelings for the therapist but none for each other, and they are apprehensive in the extreme (15, 16). Both therapist and patients are very anxious. This anxiety sometimes prevents a therapist who intends to begin group psychotherapy from ever practicing it.

When the therapist meets with the group for the first time, he finds that he is in conflict, being more interested in one person than in the others, and feeling more affection for one than for the others. This makes the first session of the first group very difficult for the therapist. He begins to perceive all his own unconscious countertransference reactions. It is not necessary for him to discuss these reactions with the group, although he may, if questioned, admit they are present. He may find himself over-protecting certain members within the group without ever having been conscious of this need. He may find himself rejecting certain persons, paying more attention to one person or being attracted sexually to one person. His anxiety about all of this may block his effective functioning.

THE FIRST SESSION AND THE THERAPIST

During the first session the therapist should try for a feeling of cohesiveness and togetherness. The less these characteristics are present, the less will be the tendency for the group to interact and the greater the chance for the group to disrupt. The therapist at this time may be didactic and directive. The first session resembles the *repressive-constructive* form of group psychotherapy. The therapist minimizes his analytic function and induces strong positive transferences onto himself during this period. In later group sessions, the analytic function will come to the fore, and the group members will experience more fully. There will be some analysis by a few patients in the first sessions, but the therapist tries to limit *his* analytic interpretations and observations.

During the meeting, in the waiting room, or in the group room, the therapist might introduce his patients to one another. It is wiser to use first names rather than surnames, *if* the therapist is on a "first-name basis" with his patients. Some new members may prefer *not* to use their names and some patients, who have been in the group a while, prefer to introduce themselves. A therapist who uses last names can shift to the use of first names as soon as it feels natural and appropriate. The therapist might say, "I now feel in a first-name relationship with you. Do you mind if I use your first name?" Occasionally, a patient will refuse to identify himself in the first session. This is *not* to be analyzed for some time.

After the introductions, there may be some talking, joking, and the expression of anxious feelings. The therapist should sit back, affectively participating and perhaps joining in. If there is no talking, which often occurs, he may elicit some group cohesion by giving his noncritical reactions to the silence. He should do this warily, because in the long run his major task is to get the group to interact. He should not go to extremes in establishing a social meeting where the members are freed from their anxieties. Humor can easily serve as a diversionary tactic, to avoid conflict on the part of certain members.

In institutional settings (17), there may be a testing of "authority" at the beginning of group psychotherapy, but some (18, 19) find a much warmer climate in the first session.

During the first session, if a patient does not bring up fears about possible "leaks" of information disclosed in the group, the therapist should stress the necessity to keep members' conversations and behavior confidential. There are patients who are deeply concerned about confidentiality and who state they will never be able to divulge anything about themselves. These persons indicate a reluctance to trust others. Only time and positive experiences in the group will help.

The first session is frequently characterized by a reserved attitude, a cautious sparring for position, and intellectualization. The focus is often on the individual members' problems; the group does not function as a team. The spontaneous expression of strong, emotional feelings generally appears later on.

The therapist plays an active role at this time, and usually does this for the first few sessions, depending upon the composition of the group itself (20, 21, 22, 23). A passive group may need more stimulation. He encourages participation and the sharing of dreams. The therapist's activity tends to disappear as group members relate on a deeper level. The intrusive or grandiose therapist precludes group interaction. The therapist suggests that group members talk frankly about themselves, their pasts, and their present relationships (24). The therapist does *not* emphasize presenting symptoms even if patients do. Symptom discussions generally lead to a dead end and discussion of presenting problems is acceptable only when the group members will *not* present reactions of their own. The therapist should try to sense immediate reactions that occur among the patients, or between a patient and himself.

At the outset, the therapist *does* answer *some* questions that patients ask. His answers are general to indicate interest and sympathy, but questioning is discouraged by answering questions slowly and reluctantly. The "question box method" retards therapy since the therapist is perceived as a source of all knowledge. This reinforces dependencies (25), and the group becomes a didactic experience (26).

The therapist may explain basic things to the patients *in simple language* in the first sessions—for example, resistance, transference, or projection (27, 28). He may point out that Jane, a member, is responding to an older woman as though she is Jane's mother. The word "transference" need not be used.

Sometimes a few group members become hostile toward one person. The therapist should try to prevent this scapegoating by becoming more active. He questions the hostility, but he never forbids it.

A major technique that can be used initially is "going around." In this method, one patient describes his reactions to every other patient in the group. Or the group members describe their reactions to one patient. This method of interaction, which allows the group to merge intellectually and emotionally, can be used in the case of a response, dream, fantasy, interpretation, or any other matter. Going around is often used when a patient or the entire group is resisting (27, 28). At the outset, going around should be used to elicit positive feelings, never negative ones. Later, there would be no direction or limitation in the expression of feelings.

The therapist should not stress catharsis so that interaction consists of a series of affective explosions. He encourages ventilation of feelings but is mainly interested in the basic dynamics.

At the beginning the therapist should remind the patients that *all* of their experiences should be brought into the group and *discussed*. He may note the "acting out" * of some patients and ask them to substitute

---

* He should not use the words "acting out."

analysis of the problem for self-destructive acting out. He tells the patients that he will not prohibit or restrict behavior, but he wants to "take their neurosis away from them." He must expect to encounter resistance, even though patients claim to agree.

The therapist should note that the good, concerned parent is not necessarily the permissive one.

During the first sessions, the therapist attempts quite consciously to stay away from any disrupting interpretations that he or others might give. He steps in at times to ward off a hostile interpretation made by a group member. During the first sessions, a correct interpretation made by a patient does not mean too much, because the transferences within the group have not been established. Later, when transferences are established, an interpretation has much more effect.

During the first session, there may be silence and a lag in activity which cause the therapist and patients to become anxious (21, 29). All of this may be due to faulty composition of the group. In underactive groups, there are usually too many dependent and resigned individuals present. The silence can become unbearable and provoke extreme tension. The therapist might then conclude that the group needs a *provocateur*—an aggressive and even annoying patient. The *provocateur* is helpful in early meetings. Later, he becomes difficult to handle since his character structure leads to extreme provocations, and he may have to leave the group. The ideal group requires a mixture of aggressive and nonaggressive persons. The uniform group is often very inactive (30, 31, 32), and little is accomplished.

DREAMS AND FANTASIES

Dreams and fantasies are stressed. In the first session, patients are told that their fantasies, dreams, and free associations are critical if they are to analyze the distortions in their thinking, acting, and feeling. The dreams and fantasies that come up during the first session are talked about and interpreted to a limited extent. The therapist asks the dreamer and the group members to associate to the dream. Although the therapist may know a great deal about the patient and his dream, he gives little interpretation but calls upon the members to help by giving their interpretations as far as they wish and are able. The beginning therapist often feels driven by his anxiety to interpret a patient's dream to avoid the unbearable silence and lack of interaction. But silence and its proper handling can be the real tests of group structure. The therapist should promote interaction in the group; he should not carry on an individual analysis with a patient among the other members. The therapist may help the interaction by expressing his own feelings about the silence. He might say, "This silence makes me feel upset, how about you?" Such comments may help the cohesiveness of the group, as members may identify with the therapist and state that they feel the same way.

References

(1) ZIFERSTEIN, I., and GROTJAHN, M. Psychoanalysis in Group Psychotherapy. In Fromm-Reichmann, F., and Moreno, J. L. (eds.), Progress in Psychotherapy. New York: Grune and Stratton, 1956.

(2) CAMERON, J. L., and FREEMAN, T. Observations on the Treatment of Involutional Depression by Group Psychotherapy. Brit. J. M. Psychol., 28, Part 4 (1955), 224–38.

(3) CANTER, A. H. Observations on Group Psychotherapy with Hospitalized Patients. Am. J. Psychotherapy, 10 (1956), 66–73.

(4) RUBENFELD, S., SHALLOW, R., and WOOD, J. L. Goup Therapy behind Locked Doors. Pub. Health Rep., 71, No. 11 (November 1956), 1075–80.

(5) WOLFF, K. Group Psychotherapy with Geriatric Patients in a Mental Hospital. J. Am. Ger. Soc., 5, No. 1 (January 1957), 13–19.

(6) DE PALMA, N. Group Psychotherapy with High Grade Imbeciles and Low Grade Morons. Delaware M. J., 28 (August 1956), 200–203.

(7) GLEIDMAN, L. J., NASH, H. T., and WEBB, W. L. Group Psychotherapy of Male Alcoholics and Their Wives. Dis. Nerv. System, 17 (1956), 1–4.

(8) HAYS, D., and DANIELI, Y. Intentional Groups with a Specific Problem Orientation Focus. In Rosenbaum, M., and Snadowsky, A. (eds.), The Intensive Group Experience. New York: Free Press, 1976.

(9) KALB, S. W. A Review of Group Therapy in Weight Reduction. Am. J. Gastroenterology, 26 (1956), 75–80.

(10) KLAPMAN, J. W., and MEYER, R. E. The Team Approach in Group Psychotherapy. Dis. Nerv. System, 18, No. 3 (March 1957), 3–7.

(11) PARSONS, E. Some Problems Encountered in the Private Practice of Group Psychotherapy. Internat. J. Group Psychotherapy, 5 (1955), 422–32.

(12) WHITAKER, C. A. Psychotherapy with Couples. Am. J. Psychotherapy, 12 (1958), 18–23.

(13) PERELMAN, J. S. Problems Encountered in Group Psychotherapy of Married Couples. Internat. J. Group Psychotherapy, 10, No. 2 (April 1960), 136–42.

(14) GOTTLIEB, S. Response of Married Couples Included in a Group of Single Patients. Internat. J. Group Psychotherapy, 10, No. 2 (April 1960), 143–59. Also discussion in same issue, pp. 160–73.

(15) LIPSHUTZ, D. M. Group Psychotherapy as an Auxiliary Aid in Psychoanalysis. Internat. J. Group Psychotherapy, 2 (1952), 316–23.

(16) LIPSHUTZ, D. Psychoanalytic Group Therapy. Am. J. Orthopsychiat., 22 (1952), 718–37.

(17) TOWNE, R. D. Group Therapy in a Military Hospital. U.S. Armed Forces Med. J., 5 (1954), 853–59.

(18) Kotkov, B. Experiences in Group Psychotherapy with the Obese. Psychosom. Med., 15 (1953), 245–51.

(19) Stein, A., and Solomon, I. Group Psychotherapy as an Aid to Patients upon Discharge from the Hospital. J. Hillside Hosp., 2 (1953), 72–79.

(20) Hadden, S. B. Group Psychotherapy in General Hospitals. Internat. J. Group Psychotherapy, 1 (1951), 31–36.

(21) Kotkov, B. Analytically Oriented Group Psychotherapy of Psychoneurotic Adults. Psychoanalyt. Rev., 40, No. 4 (October 1953), 333–50.

(22) Fabian, A. A., Crampton, J. E., and Holden, M. A. Parallel Group Treatment of Pre-school Children and Their Mothers. Internat. J. Group Psychotherapy, 1 (1951), 37–50.

(23) Kahn, S. W., and Prestwood, A. R. Group Therapy of Parents of Schizophrenic Patients. Psychiatry, 17 (1954), 177–85.

(24) Byrne, W. A. Group Psychotherapy. Delaware Med. J. (1953), 1–6.

(25) Hill, G., and Armitage, S. G. An Analysis of Combined Therapy—Individual and Group—in Patients with Schizoid, Obsessive-Compulsive, or Aggressive Defenses. J. Nerv. & Ment. Dis., 119 (1954), 113–34.

(26) Klapman, J. W. Some Impressions of Group Psychotherapy. Psychoanalyt. Rev., 31 (1944), 1–7.

(27) Wolf, A. The Psychoanalysis of Groups. Am. J. Psychotherapy, 3 (1949), 16–50.

(28) Wolf, A. The Psychoanalysis of Groups. Am. J. Psychotherapy, 4 (1950), 525–58.

(29) Blau, D., and Zilbach, J. J. The Use of Group Psychotherapy in Post-hospitalization Treatment. Am. J. Psychiat., 3 (1954), 244–57.

(30) Frank, J. D., Margolin, J. B., Nash, E. H., Stone, A. R., Varon, E., and Ascher, E. Two Behavior Patterns in Therapeutic Groups and Their Apparent Motivation. Human Relations, 5 (1952), 289–317.

(31) Frank, J. D., Ascher, E., Margolin, J. B., Nash, H., Stone, A. R., and Varon, E. Behavioral Patterns in Early Meetings of Therapeutic Groups. Am. J. Psychiat., 108 (1952), 771–78.

(32) Bronner, A. Observations on Group Therapy in Private Practice. Am. J. Psychotherapy, 8 (1954), 54–62.

6 The Alternate Session and Extragroup Methods

Hugh Mullan
Max Rosenbaum

Introduction

SHOULD MEMBERS OF A psychoanalytic group be allowed to meet on their own, or should this be forbidden? This question confronts all group psychotherapists. The answers they give divide them into two distinct factions, by defining not only their fundamental conception of group psychotherapy (patient treating patient) but their philosophy of life as well.

A Definition of the Alternate Session

The alternate group meeting is established by the therapist, though he does not attend it, occurring between the regular meetings and held *for the purpose of forwarding the group psychotherapeutic process*. And, although the therapist suggests the meeting, he neither controls it nor prescribes how the patients are to act at these times. The meaning of this session is indicated by the word "alternate," which suggests a process that succeeds by turns, one following upon the heels of the other, and which, further, implies a reciprocation, with one meeting (the alternate) taking the place of the other (the regular) and performing much the same function or duty.

Points of View Concerning the Alternate Session and Extragroup Meetings

This discussion is much more than a polemic over a technical point, for it goes to the heart of the group psychotherapeutic effort—the improvement of human relatedness—by the patients themselves. We contend, along with some (1, 2, 3, 4, 5, 6, 7, 8), that meetings of patients under appropriate conditions, without the therapist, support and increase the necessary interaction, the group interpretive process, and healthy movement; while others (9, 10, 11, 12, 13) just as energetically contend that these meetings are dangerous to the health of group members in that they retard the therapeutic movement.

Kadis, in favor of the alternate session, writes:

> From the foregoing theoretical account it becomes clear that the therapeutic properties of alternate meetings can be described only in terms of the total therapeutic context, not as isolated accounts of happenings at each meeting. In contrasting and comparing patterns of behaviour at alternate and at regular meetings, it is apparent that alternate meetings represent, in general, a phase of testing, exploring and consolidating, wherein the patient learns to separate himself from parental dependency in its various forms. Three aspects of this struggle for separateness can be described: Exploration, vacillation, and incorporation . . . The alternation of hierarchical and peer relations, leading to ever-increasing freedom of expression and ego strength—over-all growth—is seen as a major value in the alternate session (5).

Slavson takes the opposite point of view when he states:

> One of the strategies that favors especially *ex situo* acting out are the so-called "alternate sessions" that some group therapists employ. These are meetings where the patients foregather in the absence of the therapist in addition to those at which he is present. Lacking a person who represents or symbolizes authority, a parental figure, and a central focus of object cathexis for the group members, their hostilities, counter-hostilities, affections and friendships are not canalized and employed therapeutically but run riot. The libidinal cathexis which is ordinarily fixed on the therapist is diffused and is attached to various other members which leads, in mixed groups, to sexual acting out. The abrogation of the rule of social incognito in psychotherapy also results in the patients' confusion as to their role and relationships. Even the conversations at sessions from which the therapist is absent have the characteristics of acting out because they are not directed or focused, and interpretation is lacking. Usually one of the most disturbed and narcissistic patients takes over the leadership of the group and, having no training or insight into the latent content of the productions, confuses his fellow patients.
>
> Such free-for-all sessions, with the attendant amorous consequences, may be very pleasing to patients. They feel unhampered and uncontrolled by the therapist or by impositions inherent in therapy and in society generally. But emotional re-education and intrapsychic changes are never pleasurable; patients must suffer: only in suffering does change lie. Persons who seek change have to bear pain, for suffering is the crucible in which the soul

is purified. Whatever pleasures, peace and happiness accrue are a *result* of psychotherapy. Happiness is not part of the *process* of therapy (12).

Those who allow the group members to meet alone, without the controlling presence of the therapist, see group psychotherapy as different from individual psychotherapy in basic processes, methods, and goals. This is in contrast to those group psychotherapists who minimize the difference (14, 15). Slavson states:

> Actually, the fundamental processes and the dynamics that operate in group psychotherapy are *in every regard* (italics ours) the same as in all good psychotherapy, even though they are modified by the compresence of other persons (15).

The use of the alternate period questions certain traditional psychotherapeutic practices long held sacrosanct: the maintenance of the privacy of the therapeutic session, the strict keeping of confidences, and the retention of the magical aura of the therapist's person. Because of these and other seeming violations of the therapeutic interchange, it is understandable that some individual psychotherapists and psychoanalysts are opposed to alternate sessions. Generally, those group therapists who forbid patients to gather between regular sessions are more traditional in their points of view (10), having been trained in the method of orthodox psychoanalysis. Often they fail to see the unique curative possibilities of the group as a *whole*.

Users of the alternate session see it as a practical means of broadening and intensifying the therapeutic scheme, although they may assign different values to it. Wolf (6), who orginated this technique and gave it its designation (alternate), sees this session as supplementary. Kadis, whose point of view is similar to Wolf's, sees the alternate session as a complement of the individual and regular sessions; she states: "Such alternate meetings represent a mediating bridge, involving a third level of therapeutic development wherein the patient learns to utilize his affective resources independent of the support of an omnipotent parental figure (5)." The alternate session, then, completes the therapeutic scheme: without it, group therapy would not be whole. Others see the alternate session as a testing ground of reality, as a patient's sign of readiness to separate from the therapist, and as an indication of group cohesiveness.

The Importance of the Alternate Session in Group Psychotherapy

The importance of the alternate session stems directly from the results that accrue from its use and from the methodological change it brings about in the psychotherapeutic interchange. Since we have introduced these hours, our patients in group psychotherapy appear to work through their unhealthy parental transferences more quickly, to mature more rapidly, and, consequently, to leave therapy sooner. However, to arrive accurately at this conclusion is difficult, because our goals are extensive—lasting personality change of an evolving nature (16). The results of our psychoanalytic experience can be compared only to those of therapists who have similar therapeutic goals. The more extensive the goals, the longer the person remains in group psychotherapy.

Our experience indicates that group practice is altered in a very rewarding way by the introduction of the alternate hours. The therapist is now able to perceive another dimension in his patients. No longer does his omnipresence mediate either a fixed group response or a "set" individual behavior. A larger Gestalt permits the therapist, with the help of the group members, to make more accurate and timely interpretations. The careful use of the alternate period along with the regular group session adds another quite human element to the therapy, a "being with" the patient at all times even though the therapist is physically absent.

The therapist who uses this additional interactional possibility, the alternate session, is the one who perceives that his patients are *mostly* healthy. He tends to emphasize the constructive or "well" portion of the group members (17). We are indebted to those social psychologists (18, 19, 20), who, through their more general and optimistic appraisal of group dynamics, describe the human being in objective, nonjudgmental terms. In this connection, we have noticed that the members, particularly in the alternate session, conceive of themselves as mostly healthy and responsible.

The therapists who employ the alternate sessions are realists in that they reveal to the group members their need for one another, not only during the time of therapy but always. As group therapy continues, members allow themselves to need other human beings. At first, this newly felt need is restricted to the group. Later, ties with family and friends are deepened. Old superficial friendships are often discarded. There are no psychotherapists who are so shortsighted or so restrictive as to suggest that their patients not meet with *any* other persons during the period of therapy. As a matter of fact, their purpose is always to have patients relate more fully and less egocentrically to all people.* Yet some group therapists forbid group members to be with one another after the regular sessions.

In spite of the psychotherapist's prohibitions regarding what the patient may or may not do, in an attempt to limit harmful "acting out," the patient often does what is forbidden. In individual psychoanalysis, for instance, patients will confide in others the happenings of the therapeutic relationship, although this has been discouraged. More important, they

---

* The patient should be urged to assume a sense of responsibility for his own behavior. The extragroup meeting encourages autonomy.

often repeatedly "act out" infantile behavior, despite the well-intentioned prohibitions of the therapist. We know that the prohibition tends to direct the patient to repeat the action and also increases his gratification. But what is even more destructive is that these patients usually do not report these activities to their therapists, making the activities extremely difficult to analyze and blocking greatly the therapeutic effort.

Before we reached the conclusion that the alternate session was generally beneficial, we found that patients in intensive group psychotherapy would meet one another *even at the risk of dismissal from the group*. It was then that it seemed wiser to use this commonly felt urge to "get together" in a more integrated fashion, attempting to bring it into the treatment plan. Empirically, and at first following the example of Wolf (6), we established the alternate meeting. We have found that whatever occurs there may be brought back to the individual and regular group sessions. Through the use of the alternate session, then, we can observe another phase of our patients' lives, increasing our knowledge of them and making our interpretive efforts more certain.

Originally, it seemed important that patients bring back to the regularly scheduled group feelings, thoughts, or experiences that came about in the alternate session or extragroup meetings. As we matured, it became apparent that trust in the patient's capacity for growth was vitiated by any verbal or nonverbal insistence that what occurred in the alternate meeting must be reported to the regularly scheduled group meeting. Also, we placed less stress upon the alternate meeting following any sequence. We observed that patients continued to have contact with one another after they left the regularly scheduled group meetings, and we encouraged them to use their meetings as part of growth and the effort to leave the group therapist. Patients wanted to meet with one another, and we came to respect the decision of many of them *not* to share the alternate meeting with the group psychotherapist. In the deepest and healthiest sense, the mature parent does *not* know everything that is going on within the child's life experience. Nor should the parent know as the child grows to maturity. We observed that patients would share without prompting. If puzzled or confused, we might state: "I wasn't there. Do you feel like sharing this with me?" Or, "I feel left out. Is this what you have decided?"

Some therapists give permission for the group to meet for *Kaffeeklatsch* immediately after the regular session but forbid them to continue their therapy by any intimate discussion or expression. Others who are generally opposed to the alternate sessions occasionally see *some value* in it. For instance, Lindt and Sherman state: "In other words, we did not establish a prohibition or a rule against sociability among group members. Instead we were guided by the specific needs of individual patients, realizing that to prohibit outside sociability indiscriminately would be as injurious as to tolerate it unquestioningly" (11). There are still other group therapists who prohibit extragroup meetings, making all such contacts clandestine (9, 10).

We can only speculate about the methods of these therapists and their reasons for this point of view, and offer them our experience. We find it impossible to suppose that individuals can meet on the closest of all terms, the therapy group, expressing intense feelings of warmth and love, and then at the end of the hour go their separate ways, with a termination of all feelings and all actions directed by these feelings until the next regularly scheduled group hour. Even if this were possible, it hardly seems desirable, and it would actually, in our opinion, retard therapy. To attempt to terminate the therapeutic process abruptly and then to authorize a social meeting seems farfetched. One group psychotherapist, in correspondence with us, relates that he "allows members to see one another after a group psychotherapy session for coffee and the like, but no close contacts are had, nor do they discuss their therapy at length."

Intrapsychic and interpersonal psychotherapeutic processes in the transactions between persons are certainly not clearly enough known for us to be able to determine when therapy begins and when it ends. For instance, we might ask those therapists who forbid alternate meetings or who allow only a social meeting after the regular session the following questions about when therapy ends: Does it close with the patients' meeting in the waiting room as they put on their wraps? Is the meeting therapeutic only until they arrive at the corner coffee shop, not after they enter? Is nothing therapeutic after the therapy group disbands until the next session? Are there no insights available without the therapist—no moving realizations, no integrating experiences, and no creativity? The answer to these questions is, of course, that there is the possibility of growth and evolvement away from the therapist as well as with him. He is, for the most part, the instigator of the healthy processes in the patient and in the group, and his importance is mostly relegated to the earlier phases of therapy and to times of intense anxiety.

There is an apparent inconsistency in the writings of some therapists who use the activity of their patients yet do not value postgroup sessions. For instance, Slavson describes (21, p. 541) full utilization by the therapist of the "acting out" of patients in activity group psychotherapy. The acting out is encouraged by a highly permissive group climate and the absence of any attempt to control the patients' comings and goings. In group psychotherapy with adults, however, Slavson suggests that the therapist not be permissive—that is, that he not allow the alternate session and that acting out be strictly curbed (12). It is difficult for us to comprehend these admonitions to adult patients, because they seem too authoritarian and too impossible of fulfillment. We question whether the therapists who suggest such restrictive measures have had experience with deeply involved, continuous, adult, heterogeneous groups, remaining together for periods of three to four years.*

There are many reports in the literature of group psychotherapy that indirectly support the use of the alternate meeting. These papers deal with group patients who, in their extragroup life, are inextricably together, such as married couples, members of the same family, students in the same class or school, and residents in the same hospital. There is no denying that the therapies in these cases, by and large, are more complicated but also quite effective (1).

Those who oppose the alternate session give clear reasons, which would seem to justify their stand. For instance, Ziferstein and Grotjahn state:

> Some group psychotherapists have advocated the practice of having alternate group sessions without the therapist. This practice would appear to be of doubtful value. The rationale appears to be that the patients may feel freer in the absence of the therapist. Such reasoning illustrates well the difference between analytic and non-analytic group psychotherapy. A group resistance must be analyzed—and that means interpreted—not managed or avoided (10, p. 254).
>
> Realistic relationships among the patients will obscure the analysis of the transference reactions evoked in the group sessions, encourage acting-out to the detriment of interpretation and insight.
>
> In group psychotherapy, where all of the patients are adjunct therapists, extratherapeutic contact is contraindicated, just as it is between patient and therapist in individual therapy (10).

In this kind of account, there is no distinction made between the alternate session and the ordinary social contact. These authors express a conviction that the group members need the supervision and guidance of the trained professional *always* and give but a single reason for the use of the alternate session, whereas, in fact, there are many reasons. As Kadis states:

> It may, therefore, be assumed that a group climate favoring shifts in perception, more meaningful personal experiences, and tolerance for affective outbursts will be indicative of therapeutic movement. It seems especially desirable to create an atmosphere in which a feeling of "we-ness" can emerge, where participatory leadership exists and where roles can shift easily. *Alternate meetings together with regular psychotherapeutic sessions seem to foster such group organization* (italics ours) (5).

It is not simply that the patients feel freer in the absence of the therapist; nor is this the case in those instances in which certain patients will not,

---

* See D. S. Millman, and G. D. Goldman (eds.), *The Neurosis of Our Time: Acting Out* (Springfield, Ill.: Charles Thomas, 1973). Freud used the German word *agieren* which was translated as acting out. However, another meaning of *agieren* is "action," which can be healthy gratification (see Freud, "Remembering, Repeating, and Working Through," in *Standard Edition* [London; Hogarth Press, 1958], vol. 12, pp. 149–61).

for some time, accept the alternate session. Rather, the alternate session induces in every patient a new behavior which is dependent upon his basic personality. The question of denying realistic relationships between our patients must be an error; the authors must mean that we should not allow transference relationships between our patients, implying that as soon as the patients leave the group session, they perceive each other only in extremely distorted fashion and act only in infantile ways.

These authors, by conducting regular group sessions, emphasize the therapeutic role played by each patient while, at the same time, through denying alternate meetings, they seem to ignore the very existence of such a role. They feel that group patients should not socialize for the same reason that an individual psychotherapist foregoes any relationship, save the therapeutic one, during the course of treatment. Although there is much to say in favor of this argument in terms of a "correct technique," it seems to us that the point taken denies the validity of group therapy— the possibility that persons, through meeting in a group under proper circumstances, can help one another. It does not seem either clarifying or scientific to force the constructs of individual psychoanalysis onto group processes (22, 23, 24). Beukenkamp (25) notes that this practice is unfortunate because it has caused failures in group psychotherapy as well as the spread of skepticism concerning the group method.

We have found that the hesitancy to permit alternate sessions is frequently related not only to the therapist's psychoanalytic indoctrination (22) but also to his psychological makeup (2, 22, 26). In our training of group psychotherapists, we have found that some therapists who are reluctant to start alternate sessions are motivated by needs to dominate and to overprotect. Omniscient and omnipotent strivings are of high order but are usually idealized into "correct" qualities for a therapist to retain. Therapists often treat patients in a manner similar to that of the proper parent protecting his children from harm. In addition, the therapist may, within himself, be coming to grips with certain feelings related to freedom and closeness and be attempting, through the group, to exert control over his own sexual and aggressive impulses.

Although the denial of a purely peer relationship (the alternate session) is well intentioned, it may continue the harmful attitudes of parents and certain significant figures in the patient's past; that is, this tendency may cause a duplication of the environment that first made the patient sick. The group atmosphere may become identical with the original, trauma-laden home environment. The oversolicitous and protecting therapist may negate, as many parents do, the individual's capacity to grow. He may tend to stress the pathology of the person in the same way that the parents stress the "wrongdoing." This results in a strongly fixed group milieu, in which the therapist perceives the group members as all patient— and the members react to this perception. This is similar to the home climate in which the parents perceive their adolescents and young adults as all infant—and the children react to this perception.

It is interesting to note that the parents and relatives of adult group patients are apt to be opposed to individual psychotherapy, even more opposed to group psychotherapy, and most opposed to the introduction of alternate hours. They ask, "How can a group of neurotics help one another? Aren't they all uncontrollable? Won't they get into all kinds of (sexual) trouble?" Friends, acquaintances, and fellow workers also wonder about group psychotherapy; they understand the highly structured group, approving of the assignment of definite statuses and the playing of fixed roles—for example, the teacher-student group. But when the patient tells them about the group and attempts to explain the alternate meetings, they want to know, "What is it for? What can be accomplished? Don't you need the Doctor?"

Patients, feeling that they require control and supervision, value first, individual hours; then, regular group sessions; and, lastly, alternate periods. Thus, they have the parent's, society's, and in some instances, the therapist's belief that they are irresponsible, inadequate, and helpless. Unfortunately, *because they seek psychiatric help and admit to needing it, they are not trusted nor do they trust themselves.* This self-derogation is undermined in a most helpful and dramatic way by the introduction and the use of the alternate sessions.

Practical Considerations in the Adoption of the Alternate Sesssion

Much of the disfavor expressed concerning the alternate session is probably the result of its haphazard introduction and its incomplete use by some therapists. Certainly these factors increase the tendency—so detrimental to therapy—for members to act out destructively.

To a newly organized group we introduce the idea of the alternate meeting only after the group has been meeting for at least four months. This is an arbitrary time, empirically arrived at. We wonder if those who oppose the alternate session so vehemently would accept, at least in theory, an alternate meeting *just prior to the termination of group therapy.* In other words, we can understand and appreciate the criticism that suggests that our alternate session may be introduced *too early,* but not that it is of doubtful therapeutic value.

Both in individual and group sessions certain indications give the therapist the cue to commence alternate periods. For example, meetings may be arranged between two or more members of the group, usually as they are leaving the regular session, which are reported to the therapist or are noticed by him. Sometimes the excluded patients are hurt and bring this up, wondering about it. There may be an obvious attempt to prolong the regular sessions, or there may be early gatherings prior to the session in the waiting room or the group room. A patient may suggest that the group meet more often or when the therapist goes on his vacation. (If the group has well-established alternate hours, therapy continues during the therapist's absence.) An anxious person may state that it would have been wonderful had the group met yesterday when he was so upset. The therapist becomes aware of an increasing frankness and directness in the way that most of the group members discuss themselves.

Before announcing the alternate sessions, the therapist is wise to wait for the group to go through its first "explosive situation" during a regular session and to return unscathed for a few weeks afterward. Because hostility and aggression have come to the surface and are uncensored during this outburst, the members are reassured, for the group (family) has not suffered a falling apart. Thus, the therapist and patients become aware of strong empathic forces binding their group together. This awareness is not spoken of but is keenly felt. At this time, the group becomes clearly delineated from all other societal groups that also claim the therapist and each group patient as members.

Perhaps one or two group members will bring up the possibility of meeting alone without the therapist; they may have heard that other groups are meeting alone. As these indications for the introduction of an alternate meeting come up, they are carefully analyzed. The patients' wish to meet without the parent figure is not neurotic—far from it. Rather, it is an indication of growth, an adult requirement to separate from the parent, to seek an existence apart, and to be creative in a peer relationship. To be sure, some patients are exhibiting neurotic trends because they actually desire to overthrow the authority of the analyst and even to take the group over themselves. But this very desire, in its full expression and in its analysis, benefits the group process.

The therapist then brings up the alternate session. He states that it would be helpful for the entire group to meet on their own and that the meeting is for the continuation of psychotherapy and not for social purposes. He mentions at this time, as he has in the past, that, rather than acting upon their feelings for one another, the patients should talk about them. He indicates in this fashion that he cares for the group members.

This suggestion to the group that they meet alone is not greeted with enthusiasm, as some writers who oppose the alternate session imply. Among group members there is a great deal of questioning as to its propriety and its practicality. Sometimes the group spends many fruitful hours on the mechanics of establishing an alternate session. There are certainly as many patients who are opposed or indifferent to the idea at first as there are those who are wholeheartedly for it. Again, all of these responses, both the pros and the cons, are used in furthering the therapist's understanding of the psychodynamics of the individual patients and their transferences.

The therapist continues by describing to the group the value of this part of group therapy. He mentions that they will all feel and act differently away from him. He emphasizes again the importance of analyzing these dynamics.

The time, whereabouts, and content of these meetings are worked out by the group. In some instances, when members come from widely dispersed areas, we have allowed them to use our own offices for this session. This practice has the possible advantage of structuring the alternate meeting along regular group lines and also of discouraging socializing. But still this is not a good idea. The very "group centeredness" that we are attempting to foster—that is, a cohesion without the authority of the parent-therapist—we inadvertently obstruct if we permit them to use our office.

Usually, one member offers to hold the meeting in his own home or suggests a restaurant on a certain evening. This suggestion is then gone into by all the others; the discussion may take place in front of the analyst or in his absence. Generally speaking the majority attend this first meeting. *There is, of course, no fee connected with the alternate meeting.* Those who are reluctant to go are not forced to attend; the therapist should realize that they are actually fearful of attending. He must seek the motivations for this resistant behavior in the personality of a disturbed person. The continued inability to attend alternate sessions is in itself an indication of psychopathology, as is the inability of the patient to consider group psychotherapy when confronted with the idea. Many times this reluctance, if extreme, is an expression of pre-Oedipal disturbance in which the mother and father have not been sufficiently or clearly separated in the patient's perceptions and conceptions.

Ralph, an adult, had great difficulty remaining alone with his father. They were hostile and hardly spoke to each other. With his mother, however, Ralph enjoyed security and a dominant position similar to that of a very spoiled child. He liked being with his mother, playing bridge with her women friends, and going away on visits without the father.

Ralph perceived the whole group as the father-figure, and the therapist, although a man, as the mother-figure. He found that he could come for individual sessions (with his "mother") and to the regular group sessions (with his "mother" and "father") but that he could not make the alternate sessions (with his hated "father" alone). The one time he tried it, he got out of hand. He found himself drinking and disrobing in front of the group—the very same behavior that he practiced before his father. The group would not tolerate it. It was as if he wanted to show "father" what a big boy he was.

A new patient entering a continuous, involved psychotherapeutic group is usually invited to attend the alternate session. The invitation is extended by the members and not by the therapist. The therapist may have mentioned the alternate hours in the individual orientation of the new patient during the preparatory phase, but often he does not. This poses a question as to the proper timing of the entrance of the new group patient into the alternate meeting. Should it not be different for each person? We feel that ideally it might be different for each one but that actually it is worked out in two general ways. First, there is the insistence of certain members to immediately include the newcomer or, less explicitly, exclude him for a while. Second, the new patient feels his way and may not want to attend the extra sessions for many reasons, some being rationalizations (delaying devices) and others being real, such as other commitments. In other words, these pulls and tugs individualize the time that the new patient enters the alternate session.

The therapist does not insist that the new patient attend this session. He continues to explain its importance to the newcomer. Later on, if the patient still cannot make his way to the alternate meeting, his reluctance is analyzed and related to his past life experience with the members of his family. In this way all of our patients experience the group session away from the therapist-parent.

The Use of the Alternate Session

The alternate session, properly integrated into the therapy scheme, helps fulfill the first necessity of group psychotherapy—interaction. Here, as in the individual session and the regular group session, the interaction is both psychological and somatic-affective.

We can be sure that the alternate session, with its different composition, structure, and goals, modifies the behavior of each member in a most telling fashion. The highly structured psychotherapeutic group, with many of its polarities quite rigidly fixed through transferences to the leader, suddenly changes. The leader's absence requires of the members different relatedness patterns, shifts in responsibilities, a search for new values and goals, and mutual efforts toward the solving of problems.

Bach states that there are four processes of particular clinical interest, which can be observed:

(1) the therapeutic reinforcement of insight gained in the work session of the group, (2) the preparation to deal with difficult and resistance-evoking

material through the development of social alliances, (3) the opportunity to release pent-up tensions that were instigated but remained unreleased in the clinical work session, and (4) the provision of experiential data on neurotic set-up (acted-out transference) behavior for later analysis (1, p. 107).

We would list the following gains from the use of these sessions away from the therapist:

1. Increase in the creativity potential of each member and of the group.
2. Ego-building for each member and the development of true cohesiveness in the group.
3. Development of the co-therapeutic function in each member and the therapeutic function in the group.
4. Test of the individual's need to act out and of his control and, also, of the group's control.
5. Relocation of all ties (transference-countertransference).
6. New appraisals of (a) the therapist (parents), (b) the group (human beings), and (c) self.
7. Denial of leader role with resultant heightened "group-centeredness" and individual sense of responsibility.

These constructive gains from the use of the alternate session are strikingly illustrated in the following unusual happenings:

Recently, a group psychotherapist died suddenly. The members, on learning of this, called each other and arranged for an alternate session. Later they attempted to continue their therapy, *as a group and not as individuals.* In another instance, one of us had to notify members of a colleague's group after he had suffered a heart attack. Although all the members were quite upset, none asked for individual hours and three called the others to arrange alternate sessions until their therapist came back.

In general, the group members should be confronted with the differences in the ways that they *behave* in the individual session, in the regular group session, and in the alternate session. The therapist should also note the different productions (content) in these three sessions. The therapist and the individual patient are responsible for confronting themselves with the differences between the individual and the clinical group hours, while the group patients are responsible for describing the differences between the alternate and the regular group meetings. However, the therapist must stress the importance of these comparisons if the patients are to do their share. In all ways possible, then, the therapist should contrast these shifts in the behavior and in the verbal and emotional content occurring in the individual, group, and alternate sessions.

The shifts and the modifications in the transference-countertransference polarity assume major importance in group psychotherapy. The therapist continuously contrasts this transference behavior in the three media—individual, regular group and alternate sessions—by referring it to past and present transference figures and by pointing out the distorted fantasies of self and of others who are involved.

In the individual session and, to a lesser extent, in the regular group session, the members insist that the leader *actively lead*. This dependency, similar to that of a helpless child with his parent, is not to be supported by the therapist's assuming the role of the leader. Rather, this need for a leader is to be seen as a regressive phenomenon, a cover-up for both the patient's anxiety and as well, his symptoms. The alternate session disrupts the tie with the therapist and demands that the group members realign themselves in a more mature fashion, seeking the necessary resources in themselves. The following is fairly typical of the use of the alternate session:

Mary had had a very rigid background, and in both individual and regular group sessions she evaded all of her difficulties, particularly those in the sexual area. She remained distant from her therapist and controlled all emotion. (She had been unsuccessfully treated in individual therapy by three different analysts.)

She remained blocked until the introduction of the alternate hours.

After Mary entered the alternate session, there was a marked change in her behavior, which became much more spontaneous with a new ability to give affective historical material. After some time, she was encouraged to reveal to her peers, *but only in the session where the therapist was absent*, that she had developed a very strong sexual feeling for her therapist (transference), whom she saw as both her father and her lover. These sexual thoughts, which had caused her to leave her previous analysts, overwhelmed her, and the guilt they engendered in her was almost unbearable.

The group reassurance, as well as the expression of their own not too dissimilar reactions, did much to clarify this patient's feelings. The material was brought back to the regular session, responded to, and analyzed. The alternate session proved to be a basic factor in her successful completion of therapy.

If a patient reports a change in himself or in another member during his own private hour, he is listened to and responded to. The therapist then suggests that the patient bring this up in the regular session. If the patient cannot do this, the therapist analyzes with him what it is that blocks him, who holds him back, and who this person is like (the transference figure). This relationship is further examined in the regular hour until its components become clearer and the relationship itself is modified. The therapist should point out that whatever happened that makes everyone so silent, so excited, or so anxious can be brought up for the benefit of all. The therapist who has shown his interest and his liking for the group members and who, in addition, has been noncondemning and nonjudgmental is likely to be the most successful in gaining this alternate material.

We heartily concur with, and can add little to, Kadis' remarks about the efficacy of the alternate session (5, pp. 268, 274), but we also see the alternate session as serving the human need to communicate and participate in *responsible* fashion in one's community with one's peers. The successful outcome in the use of the alternate session would mean that the patients renounce infantile incestuous contact, *even* in the face of incestuous bindings activated in the group meetings without the therapist (parent).

In group psychotherapy, the therapist maintains an anonymity and a privacy about himself and his extragroup life. This is not to be construed as denying the members his affective and human side, for this should always be present to some extent. (*The deeper the ties in the group, the more the therapist can express his actual feelings without fear of unduly disturbing the patients.*) Although the therapist may be invited to an alternate session, he never goes.

Extratherapeutic Contacts in Emergencies

There are certain extenuating circumstances in which the nature of the emergency and the humanness of the situation demand that the therapist urge the members to convene either with him or without him outside of the regular time and place. Some examples are (a) sickness of a member, (b) death of a member, (c) suicide of a member (27) and (d) marriage of a member. These sessions are neither alternate nor regular sessions, and their purpose is to be with the group as it goes through an emergency life situation. They are also for the purpose of mutually experiencing the inevitable. Even in these cases, the therapist maintains a certain reserve. For instance, in the marriage ceremony, the wedding is attended but generally not the reception. The therapist must be alert to the fact that his patients may wish to involve him in social relationships. We adhere, except for the above and similar situations, to the traditional psychoanalytic practice that prohibits the therapist from having social contacts with group members.

Pregroup and Postgroup Sessions

Group psychotherapists describe, in addition to alternate sessions, both pregroup and postgroup meetings. The pregroup gathering, without the therapist but usually in his office, has for its purpose the mutual stimulation of the patients toward therapeutic interaction. When the regular session commences a half hour or so later, the members have already divested themselves of certain role-playing behavior required by society but not by the therapy group. They have, in a sense, been through a warmup period, and are now ready for therapeutic interaction with their therapist.

The postgroup session, occurring directly after the regular session, usually in the therapist's office or in some nearby meeting place, is much less structured than the pregroup session. It comes about quite naturally through the patients leaving together and discussing what has just transpired in their therapy session. The behavior in this meeting is extremely important. It is suggested that if this kind of meeting is allowed, it should be made more formal *and, in fact, it should become an alternate session.* If the therapist cannot see his way clear to bring this get-together into the plan of therapy, then it should be discouraged and stopped.

The dynamics of pregroup and postgroup sessions are similar to alternate sessions. The therapist can use his patients' desire and need to meet profitably if he will refer to these meetings and suggest that the patients bring in the content of these meetings and if he then treats this material with thoroughness as he does that of the usual alternate meetings.

The Interdiction against the Alternate Session

Although it is believed that the careful use of the alternate session in group psychotherapy, employing the safeguards suggested, is beneficial, there are two general situations where it should not be used: (a) in institutional settings in which either the therapist is inexperienced or the administrator or head of psychotherapeutic services is opposed to the inclusion of this kind of meeting, and (b) in certain groups with homogeneous symptoms in which destructive acting out is a constant threat not only to therapy but also to the lives of the group members.

In the first instance, it is understandable that the device of the alternate session might cause more harm than good if the institution, which after all has the ultimate responsibility, opposes such a plan. As has been pointed out throughout this volume, there are difficulties enough in introducing the group method into institutions without further threatening the entire group program with what is thought to be so unorthodox. It should go without saying that if the therapist is inexperienced in group therapy, he should not attempt to use the alternate meeting.

In the second instance, the alternate session cannot be used, because the patients involved do not have sufficient control of their impulsive behavior. To suggest meetings without the therapist means abandoning them and leaving them to their own devices. Many such groups come to mind, such as (a) psychopaths, (b) drug addicts, (c) alcoholics, (d) psychotic patients in remission, (e) prisoners and parolees, and (f) certain groups of adolescents in which there is a great deal of delinquent behavior. The introduction of alternate sessions with alcoholics during a vacation period is a case in point. It was observed that either of two kinds of behavior detrimental to therapy occurred. First, in some instances there was extreme acting out with increased drinking, telephone calls, home visits, and so forth. Here the element of contagion was seen to operate in a negative and harmful way. Second, in a few instances the groups seemed to become merely a refuge for the members. They no longer discussed their deeper problems but instead reestablished their group around quasi-cohesive elements of unhealthy dependency. Their therapy was not enhanced, because they returned to a more morbid form of interaction (28, 29).

References

(1) BACH, G. R. Intensive Group Psychotherapy. New York: Ronald Press, 1954.

(2) MULLAN, H. Transference and Countertransference: New Horizons. Internat. J. Group Psychotherapy, 5, No. 2 (April 1955), 169–80.

(3) ROSENBAUM, M. The Challenge of Group Psychoanalysis. Psychoanalysis, 1 (Fall 1952), 42–58.

(4) GOLDFARB, W. Principles of Group Psychotherapy. Am. J. Psychotherapy, 3, No. 3 (July 1953), 418–32.

(5) KADIS, A. L. The Alternate Meeting in Group Psychotherapy. Am. J. Psychotherapy, 10, No. 2 (April 1956), 275–91.

(6) WOLF, A. The Psychoanalysis of Groups. Am. J. Psychotherapy, 3, No. 4 (October 1949), 525–58; and 4, No. 1 (1950), 16–50.

(7) BROSS, RACHEL. The "Deserter" in Group Therapy. Internat. J. Group Psychotherapy, 6, No. 4 (October 1956), 393–404.

(8) WOLF, A. et al. Sexual Acting Out in the Psychoanalysis of Groups. Internat. J. Group Psychotherapy, 4, No. 4 (October 1954), 369–80.

(9) SPOTNITZ, H., and GABRIEL, BETTY. Resistance in Analytic Group Therapy: A Study of Group Therapeutic Process in Children and Mothers. Quart. J. Child Behavior, 2, No. 1 (January 1950), 71–85.

(10) ZIFERSTEIN, I., and GROTJAHN, M. Psychoanalysis and Group Psychotherapy. In Fromm-Reichmann, F., and Moreno, J. L. (eds.), Progress in Psychotherapy: I. New York: Grune and Stratton, 1956.

(11) SHERMAN, M., and LINDT, H. Social Incognito in Analytically Oriented Group Psychotherapy. Internat. J. Group Psychotherapy, 2, No. 3 (July 1952), 209–20.

(12) SLAVSON, S. The Nature and Treatment of Acting Out in Group Psychotherapy. Internat. J. Group Psychotherapy, 6, No. 1 (January 1956), 3–26.

(13) McCormick, C. Group Dynamics: Homeopathic Treatment. Internat. J. Group Psychotherapy, 7, No. 1 (January 1957), 103–12.

(14) Ackerman, N. Some Structural Problems in the Relations of Psychoanalysis and Group Psychotherapy. Internat. J. Group Psychotherapy, 4, No. 2 (April 1954), 131–45.

(15) Slavson, S. Current Trends in Group Psychotherapy. Internat. J. Group Psychotherapy, 1, No. 1 (April 1951), 7–15.

(16) Mullan, H. Conflict Avoidance in Group Psychotherapy. Internat. J. Group Psychotherapy, 3, No. 3 (July 1953), 243–53.

(17) Horney, K. Neurosis and Human Growth. New York: Norton, 1951.

(18) Cattell, R. New Concepts for Measuring Leadership in Terms of Group Syntality. Human Relations, 4 (1951), 161–84.

(19) Schachter, S., Ellertson, N., McBride, D., and Gregory, D. An Experimental Study of Cohesiveness and Productivity. Human Relations, 4 (1951), 229–38.

(20) Cartwright, D., and Zander, A. Group Dynamics: Research and Theory. Evanston, Ill.: Row, Peterson, 1953.

(21) Slavson, S. An Introduction to Group Therapy. New York: Commonwealth Fund, 1943.

(22) Folkes, S. H. Leadership in Group-Analytic Therapy. Internat. J. Group Psychotherapy, 1, No. 4 (November 1951), 319–29.

(23) Peck, H. B. Group Psychotherapy and Mental Health. Internat. J. Group Psychotherapy, 1, No. 4 (November, 1951), 301–10.

(24) Syz, H. An Experiment in Inclusive Psychotherapy. In Experimental Psychopathology. New York: Grune and Stratton, 1957.

(25) Beukenkamp, C. The Multi-dimensional Orientations in Analytic Group Therapy. Am. J. Psychotherapy, 9, No. 3 (July 1955), 477–83.

(26) Wolf, A. et al. The Psychoanalysis of Groups: The Analyst's Objections. Internat. J. Group Psychotherapy, 2, No. 3 (July 1952), 221–31.

(27) Bowers, M. K., Mullan, H., and Berkowitz, B. Observations on Suicide Occurring During Group Psychotherapy. Am. J. Psychotherapy, 13, No. 1 (January 1959), 93–106.

(28) Mullan, H., and Sanguiliano, I. Group Psychotherapy and The Alcoholic: Early Psychotherapeutic Moves. Presented, in part, at World Congress of Psychiatry, Montreal, Canada, June 4–10, 1961.

(29) Mullan, H., and Sangiuliano, I. Group Psychotherapy and The Alcoholic: II. The Phenomenology of Group Interaction with "Alcoholics." Presented, in part, at Fifth International Congress for Psychotherapy, Vienna, Austria, August 21–26, 1961.

7 The Extended Session in Analytic Group Therapy

Hugh Mullan

> A work of art can be seen as significant to the
> extent that it tends to change basically the
> consciousness of man (1).
> —Michael Kirby

Definition

A SUCCESSFUL CROSS-FERTILIZATION has occurred between the standard analytic group psychotherapy of the fifties, on the one hand, and the newer, exotic group encounters of the present, on the other. This fruitful merger is perhaps best seen in the *extended* session, used in the course of psychoanalytic group therapy, which blends analytic understandings, methods, and aims with the conceptions, techniques, and goals of the encounter movement.

The extended session bears some similarity to both the regular group session and the alternate session because all three are prescribed by the therapist and all three are a part of the system of analytic group treatment. The extended session differs from the regular in that the therapist's observation, response, and interpretation is directed at the members and their continuing behavior over a prolonged time, usually ten hours or more. In addition, a part of the therapist's function is diagnostic and prognostic as he evaluates each patient. The extended session differs from the alternate in that in the former the therapist, and perhaps a co-therapist is *always* present, whereas in the latter the therapist(s) is (are) *always* absent.

The encounter movement has directly influenced analytic group treat-

133

ment in two ways: First, leaders of traditional groups, when called upon to conduct encounter and sensitivity sessions, return home optimistic, enthusiastic, and sensitized with new insights. And, second, group patients sometimes experience a weekend marathon. Each one returns to his group usually to find its routines seemingly meaningless and laborious, the therapist to be stodgy and unimaginative, and the other members fainthearted and repetitious. The patient, impregnated with this new experience, seems freer and much more aware of time's passage. For example, therapist change was noted when I shifted from a group room rigidly fitted with ten identical chairs to a room overflowing with pillows of all sizes, colors, and shapes. This dramatic replacement of furniture, which undoubtedly reflects a more subtle change in my approach to patients, came about after I conducted a two-day marathon in a western city. And, again, a usually nonassertive woman irritably demanded that her group and particularly its leader change direction and method, institute much more activity, role playing, and expression of feelings after she had returned from a significant weekend devoted to sensitivity training.

It is hard to understand the intransigence of some analytic group therapists who have remained unaffected through the 1960s and even up until today, while around them burst forth the encounter group phenomenon. This uncompromising attitude, maintained by some, is perplexing because for the last fifteen years group therapists in general have been called upon to experience different kinds of groups in different settings and with different goals. When a group therapist leaves his office to meet with community mental health workers in a neighborhood center, he must put aside his therapist-patient treatment model. Again, when he is asked to conduct a discussion group in the psychology department of a university, he must not *treat* these graduate students as "sick." And, again, when the therapist responds to the demand of therapists-in-training to conduct a weekend encounter process, he must realize that the group members are not seeking psychotherapy. In short, the group therapist is required to "don another hat," to perceive these new tasks as separate from the usual treatment method, to use or adopt from others a new, dynamic system of meeting with these persons and, most important, to refrain from categorizing the participants of these groups as patients.

When the sensitivity and encounter methods have had no effect upon the practice of the group therapist we are confronted with a strange manifestation in the therapist; he presents a much-too-rigid doctrinaire attitude and suffers from an "ivory tower" syndrome. We would suspect that at the root of his irreconcilable attitude is not his stated fear of the limitations of an approach which mixes two therapies but, rather, his personality structure which refuses to permit him to budge. A confined, nonrisking, "afraid-of-his-shadow" group therapist will produce a treatment group constricted in its behavior, in its language, and, in all probability, in its results.

Purposes

The extended session, repeated as often as every three or four months, is one part of an overall treatment plan. It is a seven-hour or more period grafted onto a continuous system of weekly or twice-weekly group meetings. During this drawn-out session the treatment contract is still upheld; the patients remain *patients* and the therapist(s) remain *therapist(s)*. As this prolonged session is an integral part of the analytic group therapy method, its goals cannot be separated from the aims of the entire therapeutic effort. The reader may recall that the goal of analytic group psychotherapy does not differ from that of individual therapy. It is personality change of an evolving and constructive nature.

The scope of the extended session, as compared to the closely related weekend encounter, seems to embrace a somewhat larger "slice of life." Schutz (2), in describing the process of the encounter, fails to describe an existential matrix which includes a basic core of continuing "responsible give and take," an unbroken search for ethical conduct, and the evolvement of a self which is aware of its finiteness. For example, Schutz omits one's responsibility to the other and also any need to determine ethical conduct when he points out that

> the underlying philosophy behind the human-potential thrust is that of openness and honesty. A man must be willing to let himself be known to himself and to others. He must express and explore his feelings and open up areas long dormant and possibly painful, with the faith that in the long run the pain will give way to a release of vast potential for creativity and joy. This is an exhilarating and frightening prospect, one which is often accompanied by agony, but which usually leads to ecstasy.

Because we focus upon the unfolding individual—that is, his total personality change—I do not agree with Rogers when he emphasizes as socially beneficial the global learning impact of encounter group sessions. Here he mixes the two distinct processes of therapy and living for the good of society. In the following two quotations there is, too, an air of manipulation of weekend members, making them over to the leader's image and sending them out to alter the community: "Over the years orientation toward personal and therapeutic growth has become merged with the focus of training in human relations skills, and the two combined form the core of the trend which is spreading so rapidly throughout the country today" (3). And, again, Rogers in very practical terms indicates desirable changes in encounter weekenders when he states, "With this greater freedom and improved communication, new ideas, new concepts, new directions emerge. Innovation can become a desirable rather than a threatening possibility. These learnings in the group experience tend to carry over, temporarily or more permanently, into the relationships with spouse, children, students, subordinates, peers, and even superiors following the group experience" (3).

The extended session is a prolonged meeting of persons known to each other, with one exception, the co-therapist, who is usually a stranger in their midst. The members and therapist have shared a joint treatment experience, developed a sense of responsibility for self and other(s), and intend to remain together after the extended session for an indefinite period, regardless of what happens. The extended session, therefore, cannot be considered an exercise or a temporary drill in the mechanics of relating. At the end of the lengthened session neither the members nor the therapist depart for distant cities. Next week, on schedule, they gather face to face in their circle to continue their questioning and conflictual lives together as long as needed.

Under these favorable circumstances where continuity and responsibility are encouraged, the analytic group member can focus upon his human condition, his finiteness, his requirement to risk, to face the paradoxes of life, and to be anxious. In the extended session I do not necessarily seek a peak experience; rather, I find the lengthened period of interaction to be a time when the inherent tragedy in the members' lives can be sought and expressed. To make the nature of this personal tragedy clear to old members, I present a written evaluation of each patient to be read to the group at the start of an extended session. For example:

Richard's early excitement about "getting going" in group therapy has now given way to a kind of presence in his group in which he describes his difficult plight of not having a daughter, while at the same time he expresses his feelings for the others and offers them aid. Richard does not realize that the same satisfactions that he gets from group members *are his entitlement* outside of the group from his friends, family and wife. After three years of careful psychoanalysis (before coming to us) we must all begin to see that analysis without decision, action and choice is empty intellectualization. Do we, as does Richard, indulge in this too? The only way to make a daughter is to *fuck*—group therapy, compliance, and ass-kissing are to no advantage in getting a girl baby!

Thus this patient is confronted with his life's theme while at the same time he is encouraged by the support of his peers whose knowledge of him, interest, and care over a period of time prove to be beneficial. This most significant element of human experience—facing one's central conflict while receiving support—seems to be lacking in many human potential meetings where strangers meet for only a day or two.

The value of the extended session rests in the session itself as a "happening"; when compared to the encounter method, it is less dependent upon the leader's techniques and games and his much-heralded idiosyncratic behavior. Howard (4), in directly quoting a prominent trainer who leads laboratories (sensitivity groups), states, "You have to learn oblique intervention, too, and develop a repertoire of fantasies, analogies and games to provide people with ways to experience directly things that aren't intellectual." And Howard, in the same vein, describes the singular importance of the way the leader is perceived: "The styles of trainers and leaders are as distinctive as those of mezzosopranos, abstract painters or skiers. Some are so restrained as to seem almost stuffy, venturing little, and in the judgment of their rivals, not gaining much either. But some prefer top-volume noise, primary colors and maximum risk." As this protracted session unfolds, we must realize that it is a "real life" struggle and that not only members but the therapist(s), too, is (are) engaged in it. There is a shared responsibility in the outcome of this event. To the degree that a member "digs in" by telling of embarrassing facts(usually of a sexual nature) and by openly expressing love and hate, he gains immeasurably. The subjective feelings which follow—those of increased worth, closeness, warmth, and affection—are crystallized in the ensuing weeks through attendance at the regular sessions.

To summarize, the extended session of seven or more hours is an event in therapy offered to patients, which consists of a new experience because of the presence of a co-therapist and other distinct characteristics. While it is both evaluative and diagnostic, its main purpose is to move the patients further (than the regular session permits), to consolidate gains already achieved, and to offer an intense and prolonged meeting so as to reduce the remaining resistances and defenses.

Theoretical Considerations

Solely on the basis of an increase in interactional time, the extended session allows the stubbornly held resistances of some patients to lessen and the tenaciously held defenses of some to be undercut. Fatigue plays a part here as does peer influence or group contagion; the former fosters the breakdown of inhibitions with the appearance of hidden emotions and feelings, while the latter, contagion, encourages hesitant members to follow the example of a "trail blazer" and let "everything hang out."

During the once- or twice-weekly regular session the very restrained member is many times able "to hide" for the entire one and a half or two hours in the sense that he participates only when confronted with direct questions. Others, perhaps less opposed to the process, join in, but make their contribution so late in the period, when the group is disbanding, that no psychologically adequate exploration and response is possible. But during the lengthened session members and therapist alike have ample opportunity to confront the silent one and to tell him how displeased they are with him. Once again, calling upon the preextended session evaluation for an example of this kind of confrontation, the therapist sets the stage for the expected change in Sally's behavior when he openly states to all the group as they take their places on the comfortably arranged pillows:

"Sally, my patience has worn thin but this is not allowed because I must act as the therapist and you, Sally, as the patient. What is there about any of us that prevents Sally from telling us who she is, where she is in life, where she is in her work, with her family, and so forth? What prevents her from considering herself young and attractive, and from talking about it? She comes across to me as a scared, stubborn, little girl. But this is not really Sally. Recently she has changed and has begun to talk to us. However, we need her emotions, her fantasies, her fears, her doubts, and her sexuality. I for one don't want and mustn't have her silence any more."

Members, too, who have "sticky" problems, one with the other—that is, unexplained hates, fears, and anxieties and also those dealing with sexual feelings—can be encouraged to express them through the use of direct confrontation and fantasy. Thus, there is an opportunity for the patient to come to grips directly with the conflict, and abundant time to resolve it.

In considering what transpires in the extended session, the vicissitudes of the relationship between each member and the therapist become a central focus. From the preparatory period at the start of analytic group treatment until two or three years later, when the patient departs from therapy, he is offered a series of experiences which at first activate in him excessive feelings for the therapist (and for other group members), and later he is exposed to treatment situations which reduce these feelings, making them much more appropriate. The introduction of an extended session into the analytic group effort is a method which allows the patients more quickly to reduce these transferred feelings onto the person of the therapist (and others). This is especially so when the co-therapist is of the opposite sex from the therapist.*

Right from the start the presence of an unknown co-therapist of the opposite sex tends to shift the form of the extended session away from the regular weekly one. The members and the original therapist must accommodate a new authority figure whose presence disrupts all previous factual and fantasized ties, ways of achieving satisfaction and gratification, and methods for controlling anxiety. Seen in this way, the extended session is

---

* For the remainder of this chapter the co-therapist in the extended sessions will be considered to be female. In cases where the co-therapist is male, this will be appropriately indicated.

an *un*structuring of the regular meeting. For example, each member must now contend not only with the others for the therapist's attention, love, and expert counsel, but also must contend with the co-therapist. This new tension, which permeates the group, is reflected in the members' many questions concerning who the intruder is, her relationship to me, and her purpose in the group. The patient's struggle is reflected in these paraphrased questions. "Why is she with us?" "What is her purpose?" "Who wants her here?" "Weren't we doing all right without her?" "What is she to the therapist?" "Do they love?" "Do they have intercourse?" And so forth.

In a male-led group, the members initially attempt to exclude the co-therapist and to pretend she is not present. (I suspect that in a female-led group attempting to accommodate a new male therapist, somewhat the same process would occur, but that naturally the transference patterns would be the opposite.) The exclusion has for its purpose an attempt by the members to keep their relationship, especially to the therapist, intact; to play their usual roles; and to risk no new behavior. Without question, in group therapy, patients after a while seek or drift into positions free from anxiety. Naturally, a part of the therapist's function during regular meetings, as well as in the extended session, is to dislodge these members from their fixed postures and to intervene in their role playing, asking them to be or to become themselves.

In the extended session with a co-therapist, it is more difficult for Jane to continue to amuse us, for John to intrigue and titillate us with his extramarital excursions, for Robert to extol the celibate life, and for Jim to defeat us with his pessimism: "I can't make it," "It will always be the same," and "It will never be any better." The patients must hurriedly put aside their play acting and face the immediate business at hand: "What is Virginia (the co-therapist) doing in our group?" "What is she to *my* therapist?"

A kind of new reality, a fresh awarenesss of what actually *is*, impinges upon the members, who must now with difficulty give up two central notions that each has privately kept up to this point: (1) This is my and Hugh's group; (2) I am Hugh's favorite (because I amuse, intrigue, titillate, and so on). The strain and tension caused by this intrusion must be maintained by the therapist while the newcomer seeks and finds her way into the group: he focuses upon *his* co-therapist's presence and the specific meaning that her presence has for each one.

Practical Points: The Extended Session Is Costly

Today many group therapists offer prolonged sessions to their patients in a variety of ways and perhaps, too, for a variety of reasons. In this chapter a standard method which is consistent with other activities and goals in an analytic group psychotherapy regimen is described. However, different forms, frequencies, duration, and techniques that can be used in this adjunctive session seem both plausible and worthy of continued investigation.

Although a single group of seven to ten members with a co-therapist of the opposite sex is thought to be the preferred extended session form, there are others: two groups (same practice) with or without a co-therapist, two groups (different practices) with co-therapists from each group, and others. When two groups unknown to each other are combined, even though known by the original therapist, patients must adjust not only to an unknown co-therapist, but to seven to ten others as well. For an extended session of ten hours or less, the attention and energy required is too great to adapt, not only to the unknown authority (co-therapist), but also to the seven to ten new members.

The ambience of the extended session is somewhat similar to that of a weekend encounter. Should two groups unknown to one another be used, this similarity is increased in that now there is necessarily an emphasis on group process over individual, with interpretations directed toward the "here-and-now" behavior of members. This is because the total complement of unknown persons resembles an unselected marathon group. Another element which makes the atmosphere of the extended session resemble that of the weekend encounter is its lack of formality. Extended sessions which use the group therapist's office should perhaps meet in a different room, and use pillows and the floor instead of chairs arranged in a circle. An extended session that meets at a resort hotel where old routines are broken is rewarded by new, emerging behaviors. Patients schooled in the analytic group process, however, even with this degree of informality, which may include some pre- and postgroup socializing, still do not act out sexually.

Usually, also, meals are informal. The therapist, we believe, should be responsible for the buying, the arrangement, the preparation, and the serving of food, including the cleaning up. The group members may volunteer, but they should not *be expected* by the therapists to do anything in relation to the meal. This practice is similar to the serving of food in activity group therapy where teenage boys or girls, regardless of their behavior, are always given a wholesome and bountiful meal toward the end of a three-hour activity session.

It is desirable, but not essential, to have a co-therapist from another city. A visiting therapist makes an excellent choice, one who neither knows the mores of the community nor the patients themselves. But the co-therapist should know the therapist, having co-led groups before under other circumstances. The problems inherent in the two therapists working together are brought up in a later section of this chapter.

Extended sessions should occur every three or four months. An excellent time to have a prolonged meeting is just prior to a recognized vacation period, or just after the group and leader return from a vacation. An extended session prior to a holiday gives the members an experience to hold on to, a rewarding event of long duration and intimacy. Those patients offered an extended session after vacation look forward to this meeting throughout, for example, the month of August. Patients should expect these sessions and realize that it is their responsibility to attend. It should be a part of their unwritten "contract" as they enter regular group sessions. It is difficult to introduce these periods when patients have not expected them. At first they seem to want to be together for the many hours required. Later, when they are offered quarterly, many become upset at the additional commitment needed and the increased cost of treatment. Group psychotherapists, as pointed out, charge different fees, depending upon many factors. Usually, fees per hour for the extended session are about one half those charged for a regular group session.*

The length of this session is arbitrarily fixed (from four hours to an entire weekend). In my practice, I began with a sixteen-hour period, over two days, with a sleep break in between. Further modification has led to a seven- or eight-hour period, followed on another day by a three-hour evaluation of the total group and each patient. This latter activity gives the therapists a chance privately to review the patients' behavior, to visualize group dynamics, and to focus upon each member's life theme. These notes are then typed up and distributed to each member as soon as possible after the session, usually at the next regular group session.

It is required that all patients attend each extended session. The dates of these meetings must be announced well in advance. Those who are reluctant to attend must be encouraged by a careful and deliberate analysis of their resistance. Resistance to a shift in the form of treatment indicates the nature of the patient's personality defect, his degree of reliance upon a certain form of treatment and time span, and his degree of commitment to the therapist and the process of therapy (see example below). It has been found that the occasional group member who does not come to the prolonged period is unable to continue in his regular group sessions as well. His premeditated absence suggests that he is neither responsible for himself nor for the others. He denies that his presence in the regular group session (in life as well) plays any part in what transpires in the two hours of heated interaction, and in the resultant mood and consciousness alteration of members and therapist as they leave the group room. Other group therapists may disagree but the intentional absence from this special treatment period is an indication that this patient has achieved all that he

---

* A hardship is created in groups where some patients are insured and others are not. For the insured patients, however, it is difficult to explain to the third-party agents what the extended session is all about. Insurance companies somewhat arbitrarily determine what they will allow or not. Group therapists, as well as individual therapists, more and more are unfortunately modifying their practices to accommodate to the rigidities in insurance companies' policies.

will in treatment, and that his character structure is such that further exposure to his group will be of no benefit to him or to the members.

The therapist gave Tom, along with the other members of his group, a typed notice which listed practical suggestions concerning insurance payments, holiday dates, vacations, and so forth. On this announcement the date of the next extended session was included. Tom had left the last extended session two hours before its termination, giving extreme fatigue and a very long drive home as his reasons.

During the regular weekly sessions which followed and as the next extended session time approached, Tom began to complain about the fee. The members pointed out to him that he alone in the group was receiving money from his parents, and that therefore this could not be the real problem. Also, it was suggested to him that he could use his own income, as he was employed full time. His withdrawal from the last extended session was tied up with his all-too-frequent tendency to doze in the regular group and his general detachment from all the others.

Tom stated that he was not going to come to the next extended session, that his parents would not pay for it. One or two members remonstrated with him again, telling him that they wanted him present. The other members tended to ignore him. Tom dropped out of treatment (regular sessions), saying nothing. A letter sent to this patient indicates both the anger and vexation felt by the therapist and reflected to some extent, but not totally, by the group members:

Dear Tom,

I was very surprised that you decided to leave your group in such a precipitous fashion. As far as I know you did not discuss it, and your actual reasons for leaving treatment are not clear to me.

It would seem to me by this time that you would realize that your treatment is more important than other activities in your life, and that you would center the other activities around your getting well. I think too, that at another level to leave people who are very much involved with you and your welfare, and not to tell them good-bye nor to make any explanation is something that you should personally investigate.

I suggest most strongly that you continue your treatment indefinitely.

Sincerely,

Tom's reply:

My leaving the group precipitously is just in the same fashion as my job came upon me—precipitously. I did not have time to consult the group because the job immediately conflicted. However, I am continuing treatment but it will no longer be in your group or under your tutelage. As for the importance of treatment, I consider all activities I do to be going toward my improvement. My sitting in a therapy group at all times would not do me any good, nor would exclusive work nor exclusive play. I try to find a happy medium and yours is not it. Thank you, Sir.

Tom's reply suggests a flight from treatment because of extreme anxiety. His refusal to be present during an extended session suggests his inability to risk, which would lead to inevitable change.

Methodology

INTRODUCTION

"Therapy is life but life is not *therapy*." This gnomic statement simply means that patients in groups, along with the therapists, are very much in life but that life outside of the (therapy) group is not treatment. The group experience is decidedly different from everyday life; it is a highly emotional meeting where a more veridical behavior is required and where a more authentic awareness of self and others is developed. A patient pointed this out clearly as he debated entering a therapy group. He stated that he could get away with it outside of the group and even in individual sessions. Then he said, "The group really is the place for me just because of the reasons that I don't want to go into the group. They [the group members] would make me different."

I take the position that the way (the form) in which a person experiences himself and others in the group is the way in which he experiences his life; they cannot be separated. As a corollary to this, we might suggest that the longer a person is in the group, the more his outside behavior resembles his changing group behavior.

It is essential, then, that in order to bring about change, the extended session must continue the task undertaken in the other treatment hours which preceded it, while at the same time it must offer a different experience of greater emotional intensity. During the prolonged session each person is to find out more about himself and the other(s) and to risk behaving in a way that deviates from the old, a way more in keeping with his human condition.

A patient comes to therapy after having experienced a life bounded by fears, hurts, and misunderstandings. A circumscribed set of experiences, particularly in his family, has limited his capacity to grow. The patient on entering his original treatment group and now even more so, on starting the extended session, must find a new and variegated atmosphere which is hopeful and at the same time anxiety producing. It is in this manner that the therapist(s) intends to set aside each patient's rigid cast so that he may experience himself, the others, and life differently.

METHODS FOR INCREASING TENSION

The term "extended" merely describes the single characteristic of this treatment session which is easily observable—the unusually long meeting time, seven hours or more. However, in addition to this, there must be an increase of tension in the group which alters the field of interaction and stimulation. All activities entertained by the therapist(s), of whatever nature, should have for their purpose the shift in both interaction and stimulation. And because, in the group, each person is a part of each other person's personal-social environment, the therapist and each member must behave differently.

The therapist, then, must set the stage if the experience of the extended session is to be different. He must, we believe, do two primary things: first, offer a new dimension of *his self*—his unconscious functioning; and, second, set aside his usual degree of authority. Behaving in this manner, the leader employs no new techniques, no games, and no exercises. His actions are solely in the service of increased authenticity—nothing more.

Although the physical environment of the extended session differs from the regular by virtue of its greater informality, length, and so forth we are, in this section, mostly concerned with the psychological environment. The therapist quite deliberately initiates a shift in the psychological atmosphere which requires that the new co-therapist and the patients participate in a distinctly different fashion.

The therapist, in selecting a co-leader of the opposite sex, admits *his* incompleteness, his need of help, and his aloneness. This decision, on being announced to the persons in the group, immediately causes all manner of anxious questions, doubts about themselves, and concerns about their relationships with the therapist. Also, and of equal significance, the therapist has set aside his usual degree of authority when he accepts another to co-treat with him.

The fact that the intruding co-therapist, selected by *their* therapist, is of the opposite sex beneficially disrupts the sexually energized transferences. Their therapist, who seeks the aid of a woman (therapist), no longer operates in "the realm of the asexual." During an extended session, ideally, women patients should acknowledge the following: "My therapist is neither asexual nor a virgin, and yet he is not and never will be *with* me." Yet, this is not achieved easily. For example, toward the end of an extended session a woman patient spoke directly to the co-therapist with obvious difficulty, "I like you now but I didn't at first. I like what you have done here with us. You are very sensitive and 'right on target' with your observations. But I hate to admit that the real reason I like you is that you pose no threat to me sexually. I'm still preferred by Hugh (the therapist)."

Responses to the co-therapist intruder, always present but sometimes denied, vary according to the personality structure of the patient and to his or her point in treatment. No reaction whatsoever is seen to be a very strong response of denial. Some women patients attempt to exclude their rival and behave as before, apparently forgetting her presence. Others, still hopeful of union with the therapist, attempt to ingratiate themselves with the new leader, using obvious measures to include her, to fill her in, and to suggest that she is really wanted. Still others, more mature perhaps and more ready to leave treatment, accept the co-leader, relate to her, and attempt to find out who she is, while at the same time they seek from her some validation as to their emotional health.

In a male-led group with a female co-therapist, male patients respond in various ways. They tend generally to see the co-therapist as an ideal "mother" or as an ideal sexual object. More specifically, however, they respond to the sexually tinged atmosphere in ways which portray their fear of sex. For example, a homosexual became very upset when the group discussion centered upon male therapists having intercourse with their female patients. He hotly denied that this ever happened, and then went on to say that if it ever did occur it was only because the woman wanted it and tricked the therapist. Another man, dominated by his intense anger, seemed to warn not only the other men in the group but also the male therapist when he blurted out, "I love to fuck but I keep my feelings of affection to myself!"

In sum, then, the psychological environment is altered by the introduction of a second therapist: the first therapist more fully describes himself and, as well, he lessens his authority by sharing it with another.

The Use of the Therapist's Dream

The psychological environment of the interactors can be altered in still another important way. For groups of long standing where ties have been tested over a period of months, the therapist not only suggests that group members dream before an extended session, but that *he himself dream and report this dream early in the session.* This dream to be used must be recent and the therapist, as he contemplates telling it, and as he later does tell it, should be anxious. As the dream is revealing, there is no reason for the therapist *not* to be anxious. It must be remembered that the extended session is to be a different period, not alone for the patients but for the therapist(s) too, with both the course and outcome uncertain.

In suggesting that the therapist reveal his dream to the group in the extended session, we do not state that he should analyze it himself or ask the others to do so. The dream is given, as pointed out, to insure a greater degree of authenticity in this session *than ever before*. A new dimension of the therapist, his unconscious life known only to himself, is shared with the others. The co-therapist and members are to do what they will with his dream—ignore it, respond to it, analyze it, and so forth. The therapist's dream and its telling, which serves as a model for the others to follow, is to be responded to simply as new behavior on the therapist's part. The following is an example of a dream, the manner in which it is brought up in the group, and the response.

"My dream seems remote from all of you. It is not difficult to bring in and to share it with you, except that it seems very intrusive.

"This is a long dream which I had early today. During the dream I felt frustrated mostly, and that I was in the midst of a struggle. Also in it I am strangely unrelated to others, attempting to take care of my basic needs. It was a prep school situation. I am not sure whether I was a student or a teacher, but probably the latter. We lived in one area and had to travel to another for classes and to give lectures. I found it very difficult to go from where we lived to where we worked; to go one had to go through endless corridors, wards, and so forth. Not cluttered with people, however; it was long and arduous and never-ending, like going through the coaches of a train. A sick boy was in one ward. I thought he was pretending sickness, but it really didn't matter.

"Finally, I came to the end of my trip. I was on the other side of town, it was raining hard, and I got very wet getting to the classroom building. Someone told me that the school authorities (teachers) had told the people who lived in the area of the school that they had taken care of the school so that it would not be a danger to the neighborhood, but that they had overlooked the internal needs of the school. They had sacrificed the latter for the former. I was angry because all that was needed was a gravel road where we lived to where the class was.

"I had left my car at the place I lived and had called a taxi driver to deliver it to the other side of town. However, I didn't tell him where to bring it or to put it. So I thought I would have to search for it. However, as it is yellow I thought this might help. I was angry and very upset.

"The main part of the dream is still to come. There were two rooms: one a lecture hall, and one a 'primitive' room next to it. I don't know whether I was to lecture or to be a part of the group. I went through the lecture room to get my clothes dry in the other room. I busied myself trying to get my socks, shoes, and pants dry. The room changed and there were little fires all around like small campfires. We were now outside in a very desolate area. Fires were small and kindled with wood scraps from a carpenter's leavings, not wood from the forest.

"I jokingly told others I wanted a fire for myself, one that had been left. The room became the side of a great and steep hill—dangerous. There were now two kinds of beings: primitives with potbellies, and others like me. While trying to get my fire going and moving around I found myself in a very tight spot. I couldn't turn in a narrow trail to go back. The steps were narrow, with a wall of rock on one side and nothing on the other. I put my left hand out to a passerby and asked him to hold me. I could not see him but he was dressed. He took my hand but failed to really hold it, failed to give me needed support to prevent me from slipping and falling. He did not seem to know that I needed him. I awoke very frightened. This was early this morning. . . ."

The entire group listened to this dream with rapt attention. The members seemed to gather closer to the therapist after the telling, suggesting that he did not have to take care of everything himself. Members pointed out the paradoxicality of the therapist's position; student and teacher, related to others and unrelated, lecture hall and "primitive" room, personal basic needs and the needs of others, intellect (lecturing) and instinct (food, fire, warmth), and so forth. Group cohesion and intensity of interaction seemed to result from this statement. The scenario seemed right for an extended session of struggle, danger, and risk. Following the therapist's lead, the others could and did follow.

THE CO-THERAPIST'S ROLE

The co-therapist's position, as she approaches the extended session, is equally as difficult as the therapist's. This is particularly true if it is the co-therapist's first prolonged session with the therapist. Some therapists privately fill their co-therapist in, giving her all the details pertinent to the history, symptoms, and current behavior of members before the session starts. I have up until recently refrained from doing this, preferring that the co-therapist enter the group room, relate to the patients and contribute her perceptions unhindered by bias or prejudice, which might result if the therapist had already described each patient. However, now we have found it advantageous to compromise in that, at the outset of the long meeting with everyone present, the therapist gives to the group and to the co-therapist a brief report which describes each patient's present life's theme and where he is at the moment. Although my earlier position of not telling the co-therapist anything reassured the patients, suggesting to them that we (the therapist and co-therapist) had no secrets and had not been discussing them, it had the disadvantage of making it very difficult for the co-therapist to come into the group and relate to the members.

Two evaluations are listed below. The reader will gain an idea of the depth of these sessions and the degree of emotionality from these reports which, unfortunately, are out of context.

Roberta:

Preextended Impression: Finally Roberta is trying to save herself. She does not want to go over the falls. For years she has been mostly "cunt"—"cunt" in her presentation of herself to others, mostly men; "cunt" in her realization that she could seduce anyone; "cunt" in her realization that she would never be lonely, and never need a man. (She has never been able to understand what Sarah's problem with men is all about.) By centering her needs on her "cunt," Roberta has not needed anyone really. Greg *is one person that she needs and with Greg,* at this time, she is not sexually attuned. Why?

Jake:

Preextended Impression: All Jake has to do is to "cut his hair" and get his doctorate! I wonder about his feelings in having Gail leave without seeing him or being with him. A greater and greater responsibility is falling upon Jake, requiring that he grow up. It has nothing to do with demands coming from authorities. It has to do with his own age and the urgency which results from seeing his father grow old. As he changes he pushes me out of the picture. As he changes (matures) he *kills* his father. He would like his father to play his new violin forever! Jake's anger must be encouraged!

This sizing up of patients as the extended session starts is to describe the member "in flight," caught, as it were, at a given moment. It is descriptive rather than analytical and emotional, and judgmental rather than detached and indifferent. Focusing upon the "here-and-now" aspects of the patient's behavior, its message is clear: Do something with your precious life now before it is too late. In this it is exhortatory. This evaluation tells the patient in no uncertain terms that his previous and present mode of behavior is destructive, neither helpful to him nor to the others. He is to be persuaded that a new way of life is essential (see following section).

The method of interpretation also vitalizes and modifies the psychological environment of the extended session. Sangiuliano and Mullan, in describing the conditions and dynamics of the experiential interpretation, suggest the following:

> Such interpretative activity is distinguished by four basic conditions which ideally should pervade all therapeutic responses: (a) The therapist in his search for meaning responds totally to the patient's *latent* life theme. (b) The therapist through his response heightens the possibility of choice and evolvement. (c) The therapist responds of and to the moment. (d)

The therapist addresses himself primarily to the experiential rather than to the explanation of the patient (5, p. 140).

It is beyond the scope of this chapter to examine the makeup of the interpretation in any detail. However, it is well to point out that in analytic group therapy, and especially in the extended session with seasoned, involved, and committed patients, the nonintellectual experiential interpretation uses in part the therapist's fantasies and allegories and in part both the paradox and the absurd. Occasionally, too, when called for and when it is appropriate, blasphemy is spontaneously employed. In all instances the therapists refrain from psychologisms and use instead the colorful and emotionally tinged language of the group members.

The purpose of the experiential interpretation is similar to Kierkegaard's *indirect communication* and his *communication by means of reflection*. "It endeavors to bring someone up to the threshold of knowledge, so as to permit him to cross over it by himself. In addition to polemic, the instruments of the moral teacher are, thus, irony, satire, comedy and allegory. By shocking or by poking fun at or attacking a position, these forms achieve what speculative argumentation cannot; they bring men to the point where they must choose" (6, pp. 159–60).

The therapist operates in the belief that patients should be moved by the events of the extended session itself—that is, by the emotional forces inherent in the prolonged meeting. Growth possibilities outside of the session, including reality testing, may have their place, but this is not the concern of the leader. As the happenings in the group are of prime importance, the therapist is required to directly probe, push, undercut, and so forth. The preextended evaluation, which often shocks as it confronts each person, is the starting point. Each patient's characteristic behavior is identified; highlighted are themes to be explored, qualities to be eradicated, artificialities which must go, fictitious relationships which must be corrected, and so forth.

All group therapies break with the artificialities of psychoanalysis, where the patient's and the analyst's roles are prescribed and different. And again, in the extended session, when the form that this treatment course takes is unknown, the orthodox analytic position seems highly conventional and contrived. When seven to ten persons live together for seven hours or more, as their anxieties mount and decline, under the circumstances described in this chapter, their relationship to each other and to the therapist(s) undergoes constant subtle alterations. The ambience of this prolonged meeting is created to a large extent by the members themselves and by the risks that the therapists take, and not by preconceived concepts and techniques. Along with the members' fatigue, their eating, occasional naps, visits to the bathroom, confinement in a few rooms, and so forth, the extended session becomes a still greater "slice of life" than the individual or regular group session. Patients, on arriving at the extended session, have an expectation that *it* will be different. There is a greater tendency toward gratification through voyeurism, and this probably accounts for a heightened feeling of excitement. All in all, the extended session is much more naturalistic than individual treatment, especially psychoanalysis. Thus the two therapists have a much larger range of patient behavior to observe, respond to, and interpret.

EXISTENTIAL PARAMETERS

In the extended session the therapists, especially the original leader of the group, undercut the usual manner that patients have for relating to one another and to the therapist. The therapist calls upon his unconscious and theirs; he indicates the absurdity of their life unless they change. Directly, in his interpretations and generally in his responses, he emphasizes the three events in all lives: birth, intercourse, and death.

Spontaneous groups meeting freely, with little imposed structure, are seen as moments in the lives of both patients and therapists. This is particularly true of the extended session, where rules and conceptions give way to the exigencies of the emerging behavior of the participants. The patients and the therapists expend themselves (their lives) during these many hours together. *Their existence then is primary.* Artificialities such as role playing, and the use of techniques and games, are not only superfluous but are contraindicated. If the therapist attempts to determine before the extended session the techniques to be used, he will soon find that he is using the wrong procedure.

The fact that the group experience is not an exercise is dramatically shown when unexpected physical behavior erupts: when members scream, yell, strike themselves, or suddenly strike out at one another. In one session, some time ago, a member caught in an epileptic seizure immediately led to the drastic alteration of each person's previous behavior as all came to the aid of the stricken patient. These untoward acts, although not sought, leave no doubt that the extended encounter is real.

The point of view expressed above is easily entertained by the therapist who has been personally challenged by existential inquiry:

> Existentialism in one's individual quest to find meaning in life while at the same time one becomes aware of his human condition, experiences and accepts it. For the psychotherapist it must be emphasized that these two activities, i.e., search for meaning and acceptance of one's plight, continue unabated, not only in personal pursuits but in professional as well. The human condition must be seen for what it is, a condition of transitoriness between birth and death where sadness and pain are as significant as joy and well-being. The endeavor of one bent on the experience of his existence

is serious and continuous. For the therapist it must take place during treat-ment hours with patients as well as at other times.

The therapist with an existential philosophy may or may not be known as such to either himself or to others. However, in common with other existentialists he will be deeply involved with himself and with his destiny. His responsibility will be of a high order although it will center mostly on himself and his relations with others. This therapist, confronted by the major dichotomy of life, that of *being alive today and dead tomorrow*, attempts to avoid the usual defensive measures of resignation, denial and mastery as he contends with his fear of death. This single paradox, however, more than any other, alters this therapist's behavior with patients (7).

The therapist with this kind of concern is not neutral. Whatever his tendencies toward an objective neutral approach to patients have been, they are dispensed with as he sits on a pillow in a room circled by ten others, all with unique strengths and needs. Neutrality under these circum-stances gives way to a special form of therapeutic presence; he exerts his power and influence in the unconscious area, in the areas of affect and anxiety.

Goals: Consciousness

The patient's acceptance of therapy, perhaps not originally, but later, becomes a *mandate to change him*. Each upsetting interpretation which causes him anxiety and which also reduces his perceptual distortions, and which does not cause him to leave treatment is an indication that he de-sires change. While this is not true in treatments which are either brief or episodic, it is quite true when we consider the intensive system of analytic group psychotherapy over a two- or three-year period.

The patients' injunction to the therapist—"Change me"—does not sug-gest the method nor does it limit the scope of the alteration. When group members over a period of years anxiously attend and participate in a series of extended sessions their consciousness of themselves, others, and life markedly increases. The goals in the extended session are reorientation of the personalities of the members, with constructive changes in their be-havior (thinking, feeling, and acting). Michael Kirby writes about changes in the consciousness of man. "The important changes are those more or less permanent ones in a state and organization of consciousness." He goes on to state: "Some types of experience, on the other hand, can cause a com-plete change in the structure and efficiency of consciousness itself." And, finally, he suggests activity and engagement. "We are concerned here with those basic changes that occur when consciousness is formed against the things of this world, so to speak, rather than withdrawn from them" (1, pp. 51, 52).

For Kirby, the significance of art is that it has the possibility of permanently expanding the consciousness of those who experience it. The extended session does just this, both while participating in it and afterwards.

References

(1) KIRBY, M. The Art of Time. New York: Dutton, 1969.
(2) SCHUTZ, C. Joy—Expanding Human Awareness. New York: Ballantine Books, 1973.
(3) ROGERS, C. On Encounter Groups. New York: Harper and Row, Harrow Books, 1973.
(4) HOWARD, JANE. Please Touch: A Guided Tour of the Human Potential Movement. New York: Dell, 1970.
(5) JANIK, A., and TOULMIN, S. Wittgenstein's Vienna. New York: Simon and Schuster, Touchstone Book, 1973.
(6) MULLAN, H., and SANGUILIANO, I. The Therapist's Contribution to the Treatment Process: His Person, Transactions, and Treatment Methods. Springfield, Ill.: Thomas, 1964.
(7) MULLAN, H. The Psychotherapist Is Challenged by Existentialism. Pilgrimage, 3, No. 1 (Fall 1974).

8 The Co-therapeutic Method in the Psychoanalytic Group

Max Rosenbaum

MOST THERAPISTS experience anxiety as they begin to work with group therapy. In order to dispel the anxiety, there is an understandable desire to search for techniques that may ease the burden of group psychotherapy. Therapists assume that if they share the load the tensions will be eased and they will function more effectively. Co-therapy seems to be the answer. Co-therapy is the use of more than one therapist at one time in group, individual, or family psychotherapy. Co-therapy has been called dual leadership, role-divided, three-cornered therapy, multiple therapy, three-cornered interviews, cooperative psychotherapy, conjoint therapy, and joint interview. Clinical examples have been presented of as many as two to ten therapists with one patient. An entire group of therapists has joined a group of patients.

Co-therapy has been practiced in many varieties during the history of dynamic psychotherapy. Freud used a co-therapist when he treated Little Hans by collaborating with Hans' father. Adler (1) and his students at the Vienna Child Guidance Clinics used different forms of co-therapy. Moreno (2) used a "trained auxiliary ego" to play the role of the patient, and used others as aides in his psychodrama. Dreikurs (3), trained by Adler, used associates to side with and expound the patient's logic, while at the very same time another therapist would argue with the therapist who played the role of the patient. The actual patient would observe what was occurring. This approach seems to work with psychotic patients, since it validates the therapist as a helpful, feeling person.

In group therapy, every group member is a co-therapist, which seems to explain why members appear to be more responsive to the idea of another therapist joining the group. In some settings individual therapists

153

are invited to visit groups. The pattern of "visiting" is harmful to the group, and the reasons for this will be described a little later on. If an individual therapist comes to a group, he should be a recorder for the group, or an observer or trainee. Ultimately, he should become a co-therapist for the group. The use of co-therapy enhances group process because it often increases interaction. The group member is more apt to accept two interpretations that are in accord. Indeed, the group therapist, as he works with a co-therapist and enjoys the experience, welcomes the help for family therapy sessions or an individual session. The presence of another therapist often helps to work through an impasse. Neurotic problems may exist for any therapist, and these may be problems which obstruct therapy and may be dissolved by the presence of a co-therapist.

When a co-therapist is present, there is another person upon whom the patient may transfer. This causes a change in the traditional transference response of patient-therapist, which up to this point has been modified by the presence of other group members. Now there is more movement in the group, and members move to greater depth. Blockages are dissolved. One therapist may undermine, and his co-therapist may support, the patient's defenses. A therapist may take more risks in interpretation since his co-therapist can balance him. When we treat psychotic or near psychotic patients, there is an anxiety that surfaces about one's own psychic balance. The co-therapist helps with this anxiety.

The co-therapist who joins another therapist out of his own anxiety may find himself agreeing with certain clinical judgments out of fear of alienating his colleagues. As a result the co-therapists never differentiate themselves from one another and are often perceived by the patients as one. This type of fusion is to be seen in the practice of many co-therapists who stress a "here and now" approach. When one reads the protocols of this approach and the stress on the immediate present, there seems to be little note of overt disagreement. The borderline psychotic or acutely psychotic patient has enough difficulty in sorting out the "fused" people of the world. A clear statement as to difference between co-therapists, while potentially anxiety-provoking, is related to real life. Since we stress the importance of transference, we always note the therapist's need to avoid analysis of countertransferential behavior.

Max, the co-therapist, began to confront Steve, a group member, with Steve's murderous rage toward women and his hostility toward his wife, based on the deep sense of rejection he experienced from his mother when he was a child. Steve became visibly agitated and began to experience difficulty in breathing. Gloria, the co-therapist, became very upset about Steve's behavior. She became protective and blocked any further inquiry. Since her work history included the practice of internal medicine before she became a psychiatrist, Max became anxious and "backed off." Gloria then became the "good mother" and Max sensed that he was becoming angry. He deferred to Gloria's medical judgment although he felt that Steve was repeating a pattern of childhood in an effort to block further exploration. Later in the session another group member, Irwin, began to attack Gloria (the co-therapist) for being a smothering mother and Max found himself encouraging Irwin's anger. Max decided to share his original anger with the group. This precipitated many memories amongst group members of mother and father intervening out of their anxiety.

Co-therapy seems to have arisen via serendipity. Hadden (4) one of the first group psychotherapists in the Pennsylvania area, asked interns and psychiatric residents to observe didactic group therapy with neurotics. The interns and psychiatric residents became part of the group discussions and Hadden encouraged them to take part as group leaders. Gradually a more defined approach arose. Most psychotherapists did not know that others were using co-therapy or multiple therapy. Whitaker (5) stated that for the previous six years he had used multiple therapy to train physicians who were confronted with patients having emotional difficulties. From varied sources, with clinicians using a trial-and-error approach, co-therapy and multiple therapy began to become more structured and theoretical.

MacLennan (6) noted that in some settings co-therapy is used routinely, with the dynamic implications and consequences ignored. The administrative advisability of co-therapy is often not accompanied by consideration of the theoretical problems (7). Some advise co-therapy in order to treat larger groups. Intimacy, a problem for many patients, is obscured. Both patients and therapists join to conceal this problem with the use of large groups. The use of larger groups implies that the therapist will understand the dynamics of this expanded group and, by inference, endows the therapist with strengths and skills he may not possess.

Some advise co-therapy to give the therapist flexibility with reference to his vacations or illness, and other professional concerns. This viewpoint overlooks the patient, who does not express feelings but usually feels rejected when the therapist is casual about his own attendance at group meetings and seems minimally committed. The double message is at work, since the therapists who complain about the absence of patients from group meetings may be the same therapists who tend to overlook their own absences.

When Gloria (co-therapist) went on vacation, the group felt very rejected. Both therapists agreed to encourage responses and reactions to Gloria's vacation. Most of the group fantasied that Gloria would take them along. Max (co-therapist) was aware that Gloria had made her vacation plans without considering Max's feelings. She had told

Max, "I'm sure you can handle it." Max, out of his own overprotective-ness toward the group, had ignored Gloria's earlier suggestions as to a mutual vacation time that would fit both their schedules. He experi-enced some of the group members as so disturbed that at least one therapist would have to be on hand. He wondered out loud as to his need to "outmother" Gloria, who also wondered out loud as to how grateful Max might be if she left him alone as the benign father. Gloria's competition with Max came to the surface, as well as her feeling that the group sessions should have been canceled in the two weeks she was on vacation. This experience was very helpful because it made the co-therapists aware of their rivalry, which had to be worked out in the group lest the group members become left out of the process.

After Gloria left on vacation a lot of anger surfaced toward Max for not having been more forceful. Much of this was related to his-torical feelings about the passive father who would not confront the mother with her patterns of absence. Max became aware that much material had not been worked out before Gloria left and felt angry that he was "holding the bag."

There is a difference between a co-therapist who is active and responsible in the group and an observer who does not take responsibility (8). How-ever, the observer is a person to whom the patient reacts and transfers. While the interactional is important, the intrapsychic cannot be ignored. The patient reacts, although he may not share his thoughts and feelings with the observer-therapist or more active co-therapists. Certain patient populations may be helped when therapists of a different sex head a group. Often juvenile delinquents have not known a man and a woman who live together in a stable marriage where there are healthy differences. This new experience leads to a "working through" of distortions of the male-female relationship, and of the oedipal problems. Therapists who treat adolescents have observed that young people profit from observing the surrogate parent figures (male and female co-therapists) disagreeing with each other and yet communicating with each other.

Ross has summarized the interplay of gerontology and group therapy (9). Groups of aged patients may be very stimulated when working with female and male co-therapists. The experience seems to awaken hetero-sexual drives. Therapists may become troubled by their own enthusiasms.

A therapist described to me an experience in which he served as a psychiatric consultant to a home for the aged. He decided to use group therapy at the home and worked with a co-therapist. His plan seemed good because he experienced the group members as too wearing in their demands. The members of the group improved and found a renewed interest in heterosexuality. Some began to formulate plans to remarry and leave the home. This resulted in marked protests from the children of these aged people. They were upset because they had no intention of encouraging their parents to remarry. They had placed their parents in a home for the aged, and the setting was intended to provide for the remaining years of these aged people. The children were angry. The patients were depressed and the co-therapists were discouraged. The executive board members of the home were bitter that endowments that they had counted upon from the children of the aged failed to materialize. The members of the aged group were consoling to the co-therapists. Their life experiences had strengthened them enough so they could live with disappointments.

If co-therapists serve as ego models, they must not compete for the attention and affection of members of the group. They should be clear as to their goals. Co-therapists are helpful in dealing with intense negative transference reactions that the patient experiences. These intense reactions are very upsetting to the therapist and this often results in a strong attack on the therapist who, through projection, is accused of being hostile. On occasion, the therapist does express hostility after prolonged attacks. In this case the co-therapists provide a "splitting," where one therapist is seen as the good parent and the other is seen as the bad parent. There are group therapists who do not work with a co-therapist but introduce a colleague to the group for several sessions in order to work through an impasse when the patient's rage blocks group interaction. MacLennan (6) has noted that poorly formed groups of disturbed children need co-therapists. In this type of group one therapist interacts while the other watches the children and/or acts like a policeman.

I served as a consultant to a mental health clinic in the "inner city" of an urban area. A group was formed of adolescent girls who came from an impoverished setting. The group therapist was a female psychiatrist who had no children, but she felt an enormous desire to be a mother. She was effective and accepted the orality expressed by the girls. She was unable to set limits since she feared the anger of the teenagers, and feared losing their love. A co-therapist was introduced to set some "limits." The first group therapist would not accept another woman as a co-therapist, since she perceived this as a move to take away her children. A male co-therapist was effective as a disciplinarian, but he reinforced for several of the adolescents a distortion of the father as punitive and uncaring. This, in turn, blocked heterosexual development. The therapy became distorted.

The idea of co-therapy appeals to some therapists who are anxious about their skills. Patients often notice this anxiety and wonder about the anxieties of the co-therapists, who are not ready to lead the group. This is different from work with a group of psychotic patients, where the group leader wants the balance of a co-therapist. When co-therapists work with a married couples group, a therapist may serve as a balance for his co-worker, particularly when unresolved problems of the therapist come to the surface. Co-therapists should not join one another's neurotic behavior or attack one another. Co-therapists serve as a balance to one another in family therapy and help pick up distorted patterns of communication in the family. The primary focus in this approach is on interaction and unconscious conflicts or transference phenomena are not dealt with.

One individual who uses co-therapy in his work writes: "It is important that the group have a set of unwritten rules, or norms, that encourage behavior that will ultimately prove therapeutic. The leader shapes these norms both explicitly and implicitly" (10, p. 608). If such an approach is used, it is vital that the co-therapists decide on the norms to be established. A therapist who pays attention to historical material will have great difficulty with a co-therapist who stresses the here and now; the feelings of the members toward one another in the immediate present.

One therapist described a group meeting where Mike's relationship with his boss was important and difficult for him and "material for the group. However, the members do not know the boss, what he is like, what he is thinking and feeling—and thus are limited in offering help. . . . They can often give valuable feedback about feelings and reactions that occur between them rather than trying to guess what the boss may be thinking. . . . Thus, examining relationships within the group clarifies relations outside the group" (here and now approach) (10, p. 609).

Contrast this with another group where Stanley began to discuss his reactions to the chairman of the board at the hospital he directed. He accused the board chairman of being a "promoter and a crook." As he talked, his rage became more and more apparent. He stated that he could not be in the same room with the board chairman. The co-therapists and group members encouraged Stanley to "feel" whom the chairman reminded him of (transference). It became more and more apparent that Stanley felt impotent with his own rage. He became agitated by the intensity of his anger and said that it reminded him of his mother, who had been described as crazy when she became enraged and who had received intensive shock therapy during a brief period of institutionalization. Stanley was fearful that this would happen to him (historical approach).

Group therapy is used a great deal in private practice, clinics, and hospitals. Because of this, some administrators push the quick training of group therapists. This on-the-job training ignores rivalries that may arise. The more experienced therapist really runs the group and the trainee never develops skills but "sits at the feet of the teacher." The trainee eventually becomes a co-therapist and in the future trains others (11). He has never had the experience of leading a group independently.

The Relationship between the Co-therapists

Some therapists have a need to join one another and lead groups. Here co-therapy is used as therapy for the group leaders at the patient's expense. Some therapists support co-therapy but ignore their own loneliness, as they recruit male or female therapists to work with them. There are some therapists who become intrigued with marathon therapy as a means of relieving loneliness.

Co-therapy is not a simple technique; it requires maturity and sensitivity on the part of both leaders. It should be used carefully in specific situations and with therapists who are experienced. Patients are exploited when co-therapy is used routinely for training novice therapists who receive minimal supervision. This approach to training obscures the complexity of group therapy, the manifold relationships and the intricate transference problems.

The idea of a co-therapy relationship engenders anxiety even for people who have been practicing individual or group psychotherapy, because they are faced with many of their own unresolved problems as they practice co-therapy. From the beginning, and possibly throughout the entire co-therapist relationship, strain will exist as unresolved transference phenomena surface. However, anxiety does serve as a stimulus for change and the tension between co-therapists generally furthers therapeutic change. Most therapists find it hard to conceive of their impact upon a group. Videotape techniques may capture some of the dimensions. When another therapist joins a therapist in a group, many unresolved feelings become obvious. Rosenbaum has discussed this in some detail (12). The therapist who has "successfully" masked his omniscience as he leads a group, or his need to be seductive, or his need to avoid anger, or his need to foster aggression, will have all of this exposed when a co-therapist joins him. The therapist who is "omniscient" generally selects as a co-therapist someone who is passive.

Group therapists generally avoid facing their own countertransference problems in the group, and the co-therapist who perceives the problem usually is seen as a threat. A novice co-therapist may be reluctant to confront his mentor, or he may have a need to confront and humiliate the senior therapist. A therapist who experiences difficulty in conducting groups may turn to a co-therapist for help with the pressures and anxieties that arise.

Diane, a therapist-in-training, was invited by Herb to join him as a co-therapist for a limited time. She was very pleased with the invitation. Herb complained that the group was at an impasse. Herb is a very soft-spoken, benign figure who does not like to deal with anger or angry feelings. He is so "kind" that patients simply feel guilty when they become enraged, since this indicates that they are "clearly irrational." When Diane entered the group she became the focus of much attack. Herb justified her participation in the group as an effort to dissolve the impasse. In fact, the impasse was one that he had created. He did not want to explore negative transference and used Diane to deflect the hostility that was really intended for him. Diane, who looked up to Herb as a senior therapist, was "floored" by the attack. She felt betrayed and used but was unable to confront Herb. She became very upset with group psychotherapy and described her experience as "being crucified." No one in the group could risk confronting Herb. The group began to dissolve and Herb was none the wiser.

The therapist who leads a group takes on certain responsibilities. He enters a contract with the patient, which becomes modified when a co-therapist joins the group. The patients may become confused and upset unless there is a statement of the areas of responsibility. What can the patient reasonably expect from both group leaders? This should be worked out by the co-therapists before they agree to lead the group together. Often the resistances of patients entering group therapy are mirrored in the resistances of co-therapists to confronting their own problems in interaction.

Shirley, a co-therapist, went through a difficult divorce proceeding. She decided to leave the Greater New York area and move to California. She sold her practice to John, and he agreed to work with her for several months so that she could "turn over the group." The group members, ostensibly accepting of Shirley's decision, spent much time attacking John (co-therapist). Shirley had never really faced her contract with the group members and they experienced rejection and rage. John, a young therapist, anxious to purchase what he believed to be an established practice, was "sucked into" Shirley's unresolved problem. It was Shirley's responsibility to work out her contract with the group before inviting John to lead the group with her. Out of unresolved transference feelings, group members had not exercised their option to discontinue therapy with Shirley and work with someone else. Shirley rationalized her own behavior by telling group members who questioned *her* behavior that they were resistant.

Choice of a Co-therapist

The selection of a co-therapist is more of an art, but experience indicates that certain individuals are more effective as co-therapists than as sole leader of a group. A female-male pairing is effective for a co-therapy team, but the subtleties must be faced. On occasion the male therapist is quite feminine and the female is masculine, and the patient becomes quite confused.

Equal clinical experience is helpful for a co-therapist team. This precludes the possibility of "one-upsmanship" and establishes for the patient that therapists of established competency are working *with* rather than *for* one another. Compatibility of temperament, comfort with intimacy, and the ability to accept individual differences in "style" are important. Experienced therapists establish a style and co-therapists *must* respect the style of each therapist as the team meshes together. An experienced team of co-therapists has its own style. Trust must be present since there are occasions when a therapist interprets or reacts in a way which makes little or no sense to the co-therapist. There must be respect for one another. Sometimes co-therapists vie for the patients' affections or engage in ploys or techniques which, while exciting at the beginning, later prove to be obstructive.

My experience has indicated that spontaneous-choice pairing will not survive the hostility when it comes to the surface between co-therapists. Haley describes complementary and symmetrical behavior in co-therapy (13). *Complementary* behavior occurs when two persons exchange different types of behavior which complement or fit the other person's behavior. This happens when one person teaches and the other is the student. Or one person leads and the other follows. *Symmetrical* behavior occurs when two people exchange the same type of behavior. The behavior is both competitive and equalitarian and the interaction is on a peer level where both are equals. Both complementary and symmetrical behavior exist in co-therapy. Experienced co-therapists work in a symmetrical pattern. Some co-therapists work in a complementary pattern, but their goals seem limited because one dominates the other. When an experienced and inexperienced co-therapist work together there is at first a complementary pattern. As the team meshes and matures they will move to a symmetrical pattern. Some co-therapists remain in a complementary pattern. Some co-therapists state that the patient can react to the group as a second family, which is a healthier model than the original family. In this type of group the patient is helped by one therapist to face unresolved problems toward the feared parent or dominating sibling. A patient may be able to face a feared parent (one therapist) because he feels that there is another therapist to support him.

Even experienced psychotherapists learn from the practice of co-therapy. Research questions may be answered. Some have observed that transference reactions intensify in groups led by co-therapists. This has not been my experience. Possibly, unresolved Oedipal feelings may surface more quickly if the patient faces both a male and female therapist. As I noted earlier, some patients may successfully manipulate co-therapists so that rivalry erupts between them.

Bill began to share with the group his feelings about Mary, a woman with whom he was living. He was very attracted to her and yet found himself brutalizing her. While he could not face the closeness, he was also trying to provoke Gloria (co-therapist) as he described occasions when he would "beat up" on Mary. Gloria kept cautioning Bill as to his brutality and the possible implications (criminal violations) of his conduct. Max (co-therapist), who experienced Mary (from Bill's description) as a passive masochistic individual, felt irritated by Gloria's intervention. He voiced the feeling that if Mary didn't find Bill, she (Mary) would find someone else to "beat up" on her. Gloria became very angry with Max and attacked him for being insensitive. Both therapists became aware that Bill was smiling with obvious enjoyment as he watched them argue.

Groups led by a man and a woman therapist seem to be valuable when a patient experiences and works through multiple transferences, and when sexual transferences are activated. The patient reenacts his early expectations of a male and female figure—his father and mother. But the possibility exists of a woman co-therapist who is perceived as masculine and a male therapist who is perceived as the mother. In this case, the patients become confused.

Bonnie, an active athlete and expert skier, is a very aggressive therapist. She invited Seymour to join her in leading a group. He is a rather effeminate man and enjoys reading and music. Jimmy, a group member, felt very content with this type of co-therapist experience. Andy, another group member, who felt ashamed of his father's passivity, reacted to Seymour as a father figure and became very confused. Andy's wife, who complained bitterly about Andy's passivity, was told by Andy that Seymour was the model with whom he felt comfortable. He confused Seymour's behavior and cultural style to justify his own isolated behavior.

A rationale for co-therapy presented by some postulates that the original family situation is replicated in the group, but that the patient is identified with a therapist who is of the same sex, and clarifies problems with a therapist who is of the opposite sex (14). The use of co-therapy in this case is restricted to a special goal or problem.

In co-therapy, both therapists are able to supplement and complement each other's skills. Therefore, they must accept one another emotionally, understand each other's methods, and share common therapy goals of treatment. Prime requisites are emotional acceptance and mutual respect; neither should feel the need to mold the other, to become defensive, or to use the group as a forum for rivalry.

Much of the literature of group psychotherapy describes co-therapy, but never states this as such. An example of this is the report of Elmore and Fowler, who used group therapy to treat unwed mothers in an institutional setting (15). They used phrases such as "we opened the sessions," but there is never a specific reference to the fact that co-therapists led the group.

The earliest detailed description of co-therapy, reported by Demarest and Teicher (16), was based on a group of five hospitalized schizophrenic patients in intensive psychotherapy for a period of one and a half years. The authors stated that "the goal of therapy is to enable people to effect changes in life patterns and that transference is the enabling instrument, the working tool, which allows therapy to accomplish this goal."

They observed that, in the group they led, transference occurred on many levels, "patient-patient, patient-therapist, patient-group, and therapist-group. *Where there are co-therapists* (italics ours), it also occurs on the therapist-therapist level." Transference was defined as "the process in which a person projects a pattern of adaptation which was learned, developed and adopted in a previous significant life situation to a current life situation; he then displaces the affect of the previous situation from that situation to the present situation." The use of co-therapists of the opposite sex in the group led by Demarest and Teicher (16) brought to the foreground the intensity of transferences that occur in a group. Earlier, Trigant Burrow, one of the pioneer American psychoanalysts, described *all* behavior in the group setting as transference (17).

Some therapists *stress* the use of co-therapists as a way of recreating a family setting. Dreikurs (3), an Adlerian, found this valuable, as did Lundin and Aronov in work with psychotics (18). Hulse (19) stated that when co-therapists were of different sexes, it would "stimulate the creation of a milieu that repeats family and society." Demarest and Teicher were more specific. Their group of five patients, hospitalized and in a VA setting, met twice a week for one and three quarter hours. The experimenters tried to establish a careful balance and match patients, using as criteria verbal ability, presenting problems, education, background, and motivation for therapy. There were too many external variables, so that the matching failed. They concluded that the presence of a male and female therapist helped the patients structure a family group. This led to the acting out of family conflicts. Family constellations emerged, and soon sibling rivalry and mother-son and father-son power struggles erupted and were worked through.

The authors noted that the co-therapist encouraged the patients to work out their problems with the opposite sex. When the female therapist took a vacation, there were transference responses expressed in the group. She was seen as the mother deserting her children. Aggression was displaced to the male therapist who was present. "The absence of one therapist became a valuable device with which to precipitate feelings and fantasies on the therapist-group transference level that could not be expressed or experienced in the presence of both therapists."

Transference is present in a group and when co-therapy is used, there is a more objective evaluation of the different levels of transference. One therapist can check the other. It is advisable that supervisors be involved when a co-therapist discerns a very obvious countertransference problem at work with his partner. The objectivity of the supervisor should avoid any possibility of squabbling. Co-therapists may become so possessive of group leadership that an observation by a co-therapist will be interpreted as an attack.

There was no clear presentation of the method of co-therapy until 1952 (18), when Lundin and Aronov reported on their work with psychotics at Chicago State Hospital. They believed that co-therapists helped re-create the family structure because "by the presence of two authority figures, the child must learn to adjust to a reality determined by the presence of two adult figures . . . our experiences to date indicate that the two therapists need not be of opposite sexes. As might be expected, the physical characteristics of the therapists become less important than the subtle psychological difference which schizophrenic patients can easily detect and respond to. One therapist will be seen as more aggressive and masculine, the other as more protective and feminine; one will be reacted to with more or less fear and guilt; one will be closer to the idealized image of the patient. . . . The co-therapist method by its very nature is a potentially powerful stimulus." Similar to my experience, they noted that if patients are to identify with healthy models in contrast with the original disturbed parent figures who helped traumatize them, there must be a healthy respect between the co-therapists. If the schizophrenic patient experiences the type of bickering between co-therapists that influenced his formative years, his neurotic defense mechanisms might become reinforced, rather than changed.

The co-therapists must have a peer relationship. If they don't, the patient may sense this and put one therapist against another. Therapists who have an honest relationship can express a disagreement and patients will accept different viewpoints.

Mintz considers male and female co-therapists as mother and father figures and models for the patient (20). As a result, psychotherapy becomes a corrective learning experience. Some practitioners of conjoint therapy, where a patient is in individual therapy with one therapist and in group therapy with another, maintain that this approach helps the patient work through unresolved intrapsychic conflicts to one or both parents. The idea is to use therapists of different sexes and thereby to elicit Oedipal and pre-Oedipal problems.

The Problems That May Occur in Co-therapy

Among the problems that may occur in co-therapy is the group member who ventilates all his anger toward one therapist rather than risk alienation of the preferred therapist. He thereby denies his ambivalent feelings.

Some practitioners state that the use of co-therapists of the opposite sex makes easier the development of transference reactions, but other co-therapists stress that what is at work is not sex, but personality differences. I would agree. Patients respond in terms of transference rather than in terms of the apparent reality. Gans (21), who advocates co-therapy, notes that psychotherapy training is built upon a core of transference and countertransference responses.

Bardon observed that male and female co-therapists are responded to as father and mother figures (22). As a result, there is speedier working through of transference responses toward mother and father figures than occurred in individual treatment. His therapy groups were composed of six to eight university students, equally distributed in terms of men and women. His approach was psychodynamic and reconstructive. In his work, he observed that the group members had strong feelings about the relationship that they believed existed between co-therapists. The group members, because of their transference responses, expected the co-therapists to have the same problems as the patients' parents. The transference seemed to be to each therapist and to their joint presence and interaction. Bardon's experience seemed to confirm that using co-therapists of the opposite sex is not necessarily valuable. He found a competition and rivalry between the co-therapists along aggressive/gentle or active/passive dimensions.

The most recent report of what occurs when co-therapists are replaced is that of a long-term continuous group of patients who were convicted pedophiles (sex offenders) on probation (23). A co-therapist who had led the group for three years accepted a position in another city. The other co-therapist, a third-year psychiatric resident, had led the group for one year. When the leader was changed, transference reactions became very strong among group members and co-therapists. The original article by Rosenthal

(24) on change of a group leader summarized her experience with the groups led by Paul Schilder, one of the pioneers in group psychotherapy.

> The writer participated for many consecutive months in the group psychotherapy sessions conducted by Dr. Schilder before his death. It thus developed upon her to help adjust these abandoned patients to the death of the father-figure, a task beyond the psychological means at her disposal.

It is a task which is still difficult since the therapist must face the patient's rage at feeling rejected by the death or absence of the co-therapist.

Exhibitionists were sent for mandatory group therapy (25), and male and female co-therapists led the group in order to simulate a family far different from the families in which most of the patients had grown up. The male co-therapist was organizer of the program, and he was the leader without being overbearing or harsh. The female co-therapist was relatively passive, but understanding and kind. She was not seductive or susceptible to seduction. She encouraged the patients to practice being masculine without reprimanding or rejecting them. The group leaders felt that the patients' past relationships with women had provoked constant anxiety and a need to prove masculinity. In this type of group, the female co-therapist must be mature and secure in her own femininity.

The co-therapists adopted constant roles. The male co-therapist confronted the group members with their overt behavior and the impact upon their lives. The female therapist interpreted the psychodynamics, and her interpretations were rarely accepted during the first months of therapy. Later on, interpretations began to be made by other group members. In another group of exhibitionists, the use of co-therapy was hampering (26). The majority of the men in the group apparently reacted to women as powerful and dangerous. They appeared to be willing to talk about sexual problems when a woman therapist was present.

J. D. Teicher (27) organized groups of disturbed adolescents from poverty areas. The groups had eight patients who met with therapists of different sexes. The emphasis was on role modeling. Teicher stated:

> The therapist has many roles thrust upon him. He represents reality, authority, educator. . . . The male therapist should be dominant in the group. Most of the girls in the groups here discussed had no father at home or in some Negro families the mother was very strongly dominant.

The literature on psychotherapy suggests that black clients prefer to work with black counselors rather than with white counselors. How is a "white" therapist to be defined? As a Catholic, Protestant, or Jew? German, Italian, Greek, Dane, or Swede? Easterner or Westerner, Northerner or Southerner? Is it helpful to pair therapists of different races, religions, or cultural levels? In some settings, co-therapists of different races are used to "reach" the black community. Transference reactions are ignored.

While some suggest that more positive results will accrue when therapist and patient are of the same race, the theory is vague. Active feminists state that many male therapists are chauvinists. They have compiled referral lists of "sympathetic" therapists. It is a replay of the 1930s and 1940s when political leftists "screened" psychotherapists who did not support the capitalist system. Psychiatrists had to pass political "tests." If I accept this (and I do not), why not specify class differences as a criterion? It has as much validity as religious, racial, or ethnic differences. When too much attention is paid to the manifest material, we ignore the psychological reality; the patient responds from his unconscious.

Private practitioners should clarify the question of fees before a person enters a group led by co-therapists. Rules regarding payment vary for co-therapists. Each team of co-therapists works differently. Some divide the fee equally after payment to one therapist. Others are paid directly by the patient. If a group member requests an individual session with one of the co-therapists, the therapists should be aware of this and must agree. Otherwise, co-therapists are locked into the patient's resistance maneuvers.

My experience indicates that the *interaction* emphasis in co-therapy is not as constructive as the *intrapsychic* approach. The premise that male and female figures serve as father and mother ignores the clinical reality. Acutely disturbed patients perceive therapists of the *same sex* as father and mother. Also, transferences are not "diluted."

Much occurs in a deeply involved group. While I stress the transference-countertransference model as a framework for psychotherapy, learning theory approaches may become more relevant since a co-therapist serves as a check upon the other therapist.

Indeed, there are therapists who believe that the majority of patients need models to emulate, since the culture appears to be so chaotic. Cooper (28) has attempted to bring together systems theory and a psychoanalytic point of view to explain the benefits of co-therapy. He believes the transference model to be too limiting and bases his psychoanalytic views on the work of the group therapists from the Tavistock Clinic in London, England, where there has been considerable research on group therapy but no specific research on co-therapy (29, 30). The Tavistock approach emphasizes the group rather than the individual. Cooper notes that "therapists who assume a relatively distant and group process role for the sake of consistency and simplicity might want to stay within this mode for their own communication to each other in the group" (28, p. 493). The importance of a model for co-therapists cannot be overemphasized, since problems arise when co-therapists are using different models of therapy. If the group is perceived as a social system, interpretation is a fundamental approach, since group members would be encouraged to explore how their social roles are related to intrapsychic forces (31).

There are therapists who believe that co-therapists can work out differences in front of the therapy group and that patients who observe co-therapists clarifying issues will learn healthy models (32). I do not support this approach because I believe the group members to be troubled enough without adding this additional burden. I believe that, when possible, differences should be worked out when the therapists are *not* meeting with the group.

Co-therapy should help in assessing psychotherapy. The research may answer a major question in co-therapy: Is the amount of time spent by two therapists warranted? (Is treatment time shortened? Are there more successful results?)

Co-therapists can work together before they organize a group. If possible, *both* therapists should interview and screen possible candidates for the group. The patient is then prepared for co-therapy from the beginning. The most detailed and recent group psychotherapy research (30) has pointed up that unsuccessful results will come from the indiscriminate use of group psychotherapy. It must be applied with care. Central to the research findings are recommendations that patients should be carefully selected for group treatment. (I prefer the term "suitability" and have discussed this in the chapter, "Psychoanalytic Group Therapy.") Also, patients should be carefully prepared through individual sessions, and attention should be given to the process of termination. These are all recommendations that I would agree with strongly and, indeed, these points have been made in the original edition of this book and elsewhere in the current volume. The research findings appear to confirm our earlier and present writings (33 and this volume). Co-therapists can, from the initial interview, serve as a balance upon one another in preventing possible overeagerness to place patients in a group. There are patients who desire and require a supportive approach and who are not suitable for a reconstructive approach. The overzealous group therapist may become more of a missionary than a professional. Co-therapy should help dispel missionary zeal and the need to proselytize. The patient will react at times in transference from the first contact with the co-therapy team. There is a type of co-therapy for every patient who enters psychotherapy, since the person who contacts a clinic or hospital or receptionist establishes some kind of relationship with the first figure contacted at the clinic, hospital, or office. In private practice, I find that the patient who calls for an appointment will react to the answering service, nurse, or secretary.

Co-therapists are carefully observed by patients in the group, who later compare reactions while the therapists are not present. Co-therapists should note their own reactions to patients meeting on their own after the regularly scheduled group meeting; meeting before the scheduled group time; arriving together or separately; or leaving together or separately. Some co-therapists meet socially outside of the group, and this affects their work in the group. The administrative structure of the institution affects the co-therapists and the group. I noted earlier that trainees may use co-therapy as a vehicle to attack teachers while both are leading the group. The attack may be verbal or nonverbal. There are also trainees who fear reacting spontaneously in the group, since they perceive the co-therapist as a superior, possessing some intellectual or administrative power. For example, a second-year psychiatric resident may believe that he will not be appointed to a third year if his neurotic behavior is observed in the group. There are senior therapists who have great difficulty in accepting the contributions of the younger member of the co-therapy team. The patients observe this and may or may not comment upon the dynamics.

In most institutional settings co-therapists are not carefully selected. Attention is paid to the training needs, and very little attention is paid to the anxieties and problems of the novice co-therapists. The novice co-therapist should be prepared through assigned reading of the pertinent literature. A supervisor should be assigned at the outset, not after co-therapy has begun. Intake workers at a clinic or hospital should tell patients that co-therapy may be used. In this way, the patient does not barrage the novice co-therapist if he believes that co-therapy is not for him.

Careful note should be made of the personality characteristics of therapists who will join one another in a co-therapy team. While this is sometimes done in private practice, co-therapists are generally paired because of personal friendship. A husband and wife who practice psychotherapy may plan to practice co-therapy as a convenience. For some it is the creation of the ideal family, with the husband and wife the ideal parents (34). In one instance a couple who had been previously married were unconsciously attracted to the idea of co-therapy. They were acting as a model for patients who had experienced unsuccessful marriages. The message was "We (the co-therapists) can make it in a second marraige, and you can too." This is a "modeling" type of therapy and is actually supportive. Unfortunately, the therapists were not aware of what they were doing. Their model was inappropriate for many patients.

If co-therapists treat acutely disturbed patients, they must be compatible because the pressure is intense (35). Kraus (36) noted that in group therapy of chronic schizophrenics "each member, including the therapists, was considered to be a participant of equal value." The co-therapists joined in group fantasy. This appears related to the earlier practices of Whitaker and Malone (37). Because of pressures on co-therapists, they should not choose one another because of friendship. The friendship may not survive when mutual fantasies and intense transferences come to the foreground. Friendship may ignore or avoid significant issues. Honesty must exist between co-therapists; in this way personality differences can be resolved. The interaction is a healthy model for patients. When differences are masked or denied, the group begins to stagnate and may come to an end. I feel that differences in approach between co-therapists should be aired before the first group session, but of course all issues will not be clarified at the outset. I have observed that the group led by co-therapists which functions best generally mirrors an openness that exists between the co-therapists. However, neurotic conflicts between co-therapists should not be worked out in the group.

When co-therapy is practiced, the personal preference of the therapist will become obvious. Some therapists unconsciously continue patients in individual treatment because they resent sharing patients with a co-therapist. Some patients make efforts to separate the co-therapists by "emergencies." When this happens, both therapists should meet with the patient in an individual session. (There is often a patient's need to separate the mother and father figures in the person of the co-therapists.)

When family therapy is practiced, the co-therapists generally serve as a model. If the co-therapists are unclear about their attitudes toward men and women, the therapy is blocked. In one instance, a very dominating female, who practices co-therapy, had chosen a passive male as a partner. In another setting an experienced, but rather omniscient, male therapist chooses attractive and seductive women as co-therapists. In this way he tells the patients of his "machismo." The patients and the psychiatric residents he trained rarely challenged this behavior. I have treated patients who have left therapy with him. These patients have confused marriage with harem-type living. The practice of family therapy brings to the fore many unresolved countertransference problems, since co-therapists have to work within an established family system. The history of each co-therapist is intertwined with his own family system and values that he took for granted. Suddenly, he is compelled to work in a value system that is unrelated to anything that he experienced before. The value systems of each co-therapist, heretofore obscured, may impact upon one another in a healthy or destructive fashion.

In some hospitals a female nurse will be chosen as co-therapist. She generally ranks low in the hierarchy of a hospital setting and may be supportive and convey feelings of inadequacy and submissiveness to the women members of the group.

Supervision of Co-therapists

The supervisor should not establish patterns of favoritism or approve one therapist and demean the other. This may be done unconsciously. Supervisory meetings should not take place unless both therapists are present. Supervisors may observe for the first time that they prefer one of the co-therapists. The supervisor must stress mutualism.

As one practices co-therapy, unreal and overidealized expectations come to the surface (38, 39). Experienced therapists will have difficulty coping. One competent therapist plus another competent therapist do not add up to better therapy. The new team of co-therapists may become too easily disenchanted. It is hoped that they will "stick it out" and help one another. Problems of sibling rivalry, status, and power needs at the expense of each other can be handled with competent supervision. But the therapists are not there to treat one another. Their primary responsibility is to the patient. There will be many tests of maturity, but the rewards and challenges of co-therapy are great. If the therapists are authentic, both patients and therapists will benefit.

References

(1) ADLER, A. Guiding the Child. New York: Greenberg, 1930.

(2) MORENO, J. L. (ed.). Group Psychotherapy: A Symposium. New York: Beacon House, 1954.

(3) DREIKURS, R. Techniques and Dynamics of Multiple Psychotherapy. Psychiat. Quart., 24 (1950), 788–99.

(4) HADDEN, S. B. The Utilization of a Therapy Group in Teaching Psychotherapy. Am. J. Psychiat., 103 (1947), 644–49.

(5) WHITAKER, C. A. Teaching the Practicing Physician to Do Psychotherapy. So. Med. J., 42 (1949), 809–903.

(6) MacLENNAN, B. Co-Therapy. Internat. J. Group Psychotherapy, 15 (1965), 154–65.

(7) FRIEDMAN, B. Co-Therapy: A Behavioral and Attitudinal Survey of Third Year Psychiatric Residents. Internat. J. Group Psychotherapy, 23 (1973), 228–34.

(8) STONE, W. N. Dynamics of the Recorder-Observer in Group Psychotherapy. Compr. Psychiat., 16 (January/February 1975), 49–54.

(9) Ross, M. Community Geriatric Group Therapies: A Comprehensive Review. Chap. 39 in Rosenbaum, M., and Berger, M. M. (eds.), Group Psychotherapy and Group Function, rev. ed. New York: Basic Books, 1975.

(10) YALOM, I. D. Theory and Practice of Group Psychotherapy, 2nd ed. New York: Basic Books, 1975.

(11) KAYE, H., and KEW, C. E. Reactions of an Ongoing Therapy Group to the Temporary Introduction of a Co-Therapist. Dynamic Psychiat. 21 (1973), 231–37.

(12) ROSENBAUM, M. Group Psychotherapy and Psychodrama. Chapter in Handbook of Clinical Psychology. New York: McGraw-Hill, 1965.

(13) HALEY, J. Strategies of Psychotherapy. New York: Grune and Stratton, 1963.

(14) SCHONBAR, R. A. Group Co-Therapist and Sex-Role Identification. Am. J. Psychotherapy, 27 (1973), 539–47.

(15) ELMORE, J. L., and FOWLER, D. R. Brief Group Psychotherapy with Unwed Mothers. J. of Med. Soc. of N.J., 67 (January 1970), 19–23.

(16) DEMAREST, E., and TEICHER, A. Transference in Group Therapy: Its Use by Co-Therapists of Opposite Sexes. Psychiatry, 17 (1954), 187–202.

(17) Burrow, T. The Problem of Transference. Brit. J. Med. Psychol., 7 (1927), 193–203.

(18) Lundin, W. H., and Aronov, B. M. Use of Co-Therapists in Group Psychotherapy. J. Consulting Psychol., 16 (1952), 77–80.

(19) Hulse, W. The Social Meaning of Current Methods of Group Psychotherapy. Group Psychotherapy, 3 (1950), 56–57.

(20) Mintz, E. Male-Female Co-Therapists. Am. J. Psychotherapy, 19 (April 1965), 293–301.

(21) Gans, R. W. The Use of Group Co-Therapists in the Teaching of Psychotherapy. Am. J. Psychotherapy, 9 (1957), 618–25.

(22) Bardon, E. J. Transference Reactions to the Relationship between Male and Female Co-Therapists in Group Psychotherapy. J. Am. Coll. Health Assoc., 14 (April 1966), 4.

(23) Sadoff, R. L., Resnik, H. L. P., and Peters, J. J. On Changing Group Therapists. Psychiat. Quart. Suppl., 42 (1968), 156–66.

(24) Rosenthal, P. The Death of the Leader in Group Psychotherapy. Am. J. Orthopsychiat., 17 (1947), 266–77.

(25) Mathis, J. L., and Collins, M. Mandatory Group Therapy for Exhibitionists. Am. J. Psychiat., 126 (February 1970), 1162–67.

(26) Witzig, J. S. The Group Treatment of Male Exhibitionists. Am. J. Psychiat., 125 (1968), 179–85.

(27) Teicher, J. D. Group Psychotherapy with Adolescents. Calif. Med., 105 (July 1966), 18–21.

(28) Cooper, L. Co-Therapy Relationships in Groups. Small Group Behavior, 7 (1976), 473–98).

(29) Heath, E. S., and Bacal, H. A. A Method of Group Psychotherapy at the Tavistock Clinic. In Sager, C. J., and Kaplan, H. S. (eds.), Progress in Group and Family Therapy, pp. 33–42. New York: Brunner-Mazel, 1972.

(30) Malan, D. H., Balfour, F. H. G., Hood, V. G., and Shooter, A. M. N. Group Psychotherapy—A Long-Term Follow Up Study. Arch. Gen. Psychiatry, 33 (1976), 1303–15.

(31) Foulkes, S. H. Group Dynamics and Group Analysis—A TransAtlantic View. J. Group Psychoanalysis and Process, 1 (1968), 47–75.

(32) Benjamin, S. E. Co-Therapy: A Growth Experience for Therapists. Internat. J. Group Psychotherapy, 22 (1972), 199–209.

(33) Mullan, H., and Rosenbaum, M. Group Psychotherapy. New York: Free Press, 1962.

(34) Low, P., and Low, M. Treatment of Married Couples in a Group Run by a Husband and Wife. Internat. J. Group Psychotherapy, 25 (1975), 54–66.

(35) Seeman, M. V. Focus on Co-Therapy in a Rehabilitation Programme for Advanced Schizophrenia. Canad. Mental Health, 24 (1976), 13–14.

(36) Kraus, R. F. The Use of Symbolic Technique in the Group Psychotherapy of Chronic Schizophrenics. Psychiat. Quart., 44 (January 1970), 143–57.

(37) Whitaker, C., and Malone, T. The Roots of Psychotherapy. New York: Blakiston, 1953.

(38) MITCHELL, C. The Uses and Abuses of Co-Therapy as a Technique in Family Unit Therapy. Bull. Family Ment. Health Clinic Jewish Family Service, 1 (Spring 1969), 4–6.

(39) MITCHELL, C., and SZALITA, A. Further Explorations in Co-Therapy. Bull. Family Ment. Health Clinic Jewish Family Service, 2 (Spring 1970), 4–5, 18.

9 Transference and Countertransference

Hugh Mullan
Max Rosenbaum

Transference and Countertransference as Basic
to Analytic Group Therapy

THE ONE CONCEPT *above all others* which compels our attention is that of transference and countertransference. *Transference* exists in the persons whom we see for therapy; it motivates them to seek help, and encourages them to remain in treatment and to accept the various arrangements and the upsetting interpretations. Without transference, analytic psychotherapy could not be practiced.

The patient is usually in a morass and distorts relationships focusing upon the early relationships: for example, his original, intense ties to mother and father. The therapist can begin to understand what is at work. The earlier entanglement with a parent which was appropriate for infancy and childhood continues to operate in therapy. It is now the relationship between the patient and his therapist. The transference relationship is basically the analogue of this earlier bond.

Because the patient transfers onto the therapist, it allows him to form an intensive relationship of dependence, and it reflects the degree of his immaturity or the amount of psychopathology present. The group therapist should use the transference constructively. It exists, even if he doesn't use it or is unaware of it. The presence and *recognition* of transference establishes analytic group psychotherapy as distinct from the encounter and humanistic psychology movements.

In most analytic therapy groups, meetings occur over a period of months *without a single member being absent*. Alternate sessions, once well established, also have a fairly good record in this respect. Attendance

174

at the regular sessions is consistently 90 percent or more, and attendance at the alternate sessions is 80 percent or more.

The devotion to the psychotherapy group can be viewed psychodynamically. The constructs of transference and countertransference, although modified when applied to the group, help to explain the need of the members for consistent attendance in their group.

Regressive and reconstructive (analytic) group therapy is differentiated from all other group psychotherapies by the presence and recognition of *activated* transferences on the part of the members. The therapist desires these activated transferences, uses them, and works them through before a patient leaves the group. Transference and countertransference are the hallmarks of psychoanalysis. Group psychoanalytic therapy transference is observed, utilized, and analyzed (1, 2). Transference and countertransference differ in the group from that in individual sessions, but the definitions given by Freud still hold:

> It is therefore entirely normal and comprehensible that the libidocathexes, expectant and in readiness as they are in those who have not adequate gratification, should be turned also toward the person of the physician (3, p. 313) . . . but the transference is not bound to this prototype (father imago); it can also proceed from the mother or brother imago and so on (3, p. 314).

Freud was just as definite about countertransference. In 1910 he stated:

> We have begun to consider the "countertransference," which arises in the physician as a result of the patient's influence on his unconscious feelings, and have nearly come to the point of requiring the physician to recognize and overcome this countertransference in himself (4, p. 289).

Later, in 1912, he proposed that analysis for the therapist be made a formal requirement:

> Such analysis of a person who is for all practical purposes healthy will naturally remain uncompleted. Whosoever knows how to appreciate the high value of self-knowledge and increase in self-control so acquired, will afterwards continue the analytic examination of his own personality by a self-analysis, and willingly recognize that, in himself, as in others, he must always expect to find something new (5, p. 329).

Because of transference (and countertransference) the perception, sensation, cognition, or conception of another individual is distorted (6, 7). Transference makes the other person appear *to be* what he is not.

Transference makes the perceived one appear to be another in the present or in the past. The distortion clothes the object (the perceived one) with attitudes, abilities, purposes, judgments, and affections that he does not have. It emphasizes or deemphasizes these traits out of all proportion. *Transference* can exist within the therapist or the patient, based upon the individual's need to distort because of his residual neurosis. The term *countertransference* is not reserved for the therapist alone; it is used to mean the irrational response to another's transference behavior, which results in compounding the irrationality.

The psychotherapist is in a "set" with his patient prior to his patient's original consultation, because there is a "pretherapeutic transference" in our culture, which labels the person coming to us as "patient" and us as "therapist" (8). This condition is the cultural analogue of transference-countertransference, and it is contiguous with the same phenomena that we observe in the group therapy process. The therapist's adherence to his status and his nonacceptance of his own emotional problems is considered to be countertransference behavior, compounding the distortion already held by the patient that this therapist is the "magic helper."

Our culture establishes the therapist (the mother or father figure) as the healer. The culture has decreed that certain persons (but only when they are in therapeutic session) are patients. The patient reinforces our status and simultaneously becomes more deeply entrenched in his own.

KINDS OF BEHAVIOR

The behavior (thinking, feeling, and acting) of one, as opposed to the behavior of another (patient, therapist, and group as a whole) can be of the following varieties: (a) rational-rational, (b) rational-transference, (c) transference-transference, and (d) transference-countertransference. The rational-rational (a) behavior is the ideal, for here each person perceives the other(s) as he (they) actually is (are), and neither distorts the others to control his own anxiety nor to maintain his own self-image. The transference-countertransference (d) behavior is the most detrimental, for here one person is responding irrationally to the already irrational behavior of the others.

All four kinds of behavior exist in group therapy. It is to be hoped that the therapist's responses to a member are rational-transference (b). Between two patients there is often transference-transference (c) and transference-countertransference (d). It is an error to consider transferences as taking place only within the patient and countertransference only within the therapist; it is factually not so. This error comes strikingly to light in deeply involved therapy groups, and in multiple therapy (9, 10) in which it is possible to observe the rational responses of the patients and the irrational ones of the therapist. Countertransference for either patient or therapist is more noxious than transference, for when it is unknowingly in operation, it precludes the possibility of a response that would lessen the distortion already clouding the interaction. A group member said, "You are much tougher on women in this group than on men. With men you take more pains and are sympathetic. With women you are short, direct, and caustic." Some of the others concurred. (The therapist thought, *I wonder if in some way the women in the group were replicas of my sisters and if my response to them, both quantitatively and qualitatively, was in error. I became anxious and upset. . . . Without describing to the group the reason for my distorted behavior, I shall have to watch myself more carefully.*)

Success in group psychotherapy depends largely upon lessening transference and countertransference. The interactional and interpretive portions of the group process encourage particular kinds of transference behavior. But the overall patterns of transference differ from those of individual therapy because the group is both a small culture and a society.

TRANSFERENCE AND INTERACTIONS AND INTERPRETATION

Group interaction is composed of the spontaneous "here-and-now" responses among the members and with the therapist. It is the first necessity of group psychotherapy. Without it, there is no effort by members to risk becoming different. If there is no interaction, there is no opportunity to discover the meaning of the interaction through interpretation. Although spontaneous behavior is important, we would disagree with Moreno, who states that "the principal hypothesis in all cases (all kinds of psychotherapy) is that the interaction produces the therapeutic results" (11), since interactional behavior is always identified by an overabundance of irrationality. This irrationality at specific times demands the intervention of the therapist's and patients' interpretations. The newcomer to the established therapy group meets the irrational element. He is greeted mostly with reactions of the transference-countertransference (d) or transference-transference (c) variety. He is not aware that underlying these outbursts there is still a conventionality, which can be called upon by the therapist or another member at any moment to control the nonrationality. The newcomer invariably becomes somewhat anxious. One patient said, "I have no idea what anyone is talking about. I seem to be in a dream; nothing makes any sense to me." The form of group psychoanalytic therapy—a circle of members and therapist, sitting upright and facing each other—does *not* preclude intense emotional transactions between the participants. The patient continues his distorting tendencies whether sitting up or lying on the psychoanalyst's couch.

To place such importance upon transference and countertransference acknowledges the very early intrafamilial genesis of psychic disturbance and of unconscious motivation and process. Group psychoanalytic therapy is quite removed from didactic, inspirational, and dramatic (role-playing) methods, which appear to repress certain drives while changing the personality only superficially. The customs and mores of our culture have the same effect.

Early in group therapy, after a certain amount of regression has been encouraged and accomplished, the ties between members are mostly of the transference-countertransference variety (d). Later, as reconstructive tendencies come to the fore, the relationships become more honest, resulting in behavior that is mostly transference-transference (c), and then rational-transference (b). At termination, the group bindings are largely rational-rational (a), particularly between the most mature members and the therapist.

Therefore, the early relatedness patterns in the group are those of maximal distortions; later, just before termination, these patterns are based on a more real foundation, the departing members tending to see themselves as they actually are. In some respects, this process is similar to that described by Horney (12), Goldstein (13), and Fromm (14) as self-actualization and self-realization.

During the early sessions patients are increasingly made aware of their relationships with family members and other influential figures. It is pointed out to the members how frequently they respond to another group member or the leader as though he were a significant person in either the present or past. There is a tendency for each patient to see the group in terms of his own family and others with authority.

There is an obvious attempt to establish the group as a societal one, similar to a classroom, with instructor and students. Toward the end of therapy, as the person is about to leave, there is generally a much more real (actual) meeting.

The Use of the Interaction

The therapist imposes a purpose onto the interactional behavior of the group. He might limit it or even prevent it to control "acting out," and to lessen the group's anxieties. A search is made, through reductive analysis, for the past reasons to be found for the present behavior: an attempt to remember rather than to repeat (15). This is the interpretive portion, which the therapist does first alone, and later with the others when they develop co-therapeutic ability (16).

This part of the group analytic work stops transference behavior that is archaic and blatant (but not the transference tie itself). It ushers in a more deliberate and essential activity. Many of the members, in attempting to copy the therapist's treatment design, become compulsively competitive in an effort to unseat the others in the therapist's affections.

Transference Behavior in Psychoanalytic Groups

Freud referred to transference as "an almost inexhaustible subject" (3). The analysis of transference in group psychotherapy reemphasizes the truth of this statement. The patients' modes of relating in the therapy group are similar to those they use outside of treatment. Demarest and Teicher have noted that transference is "the process in which a person projects a pattern of adaptation which was learned, developed, and adopted in a previous life situation to a current life situation; he then displaces the affect from that situation to the present situation" (17).

In the same way in which the positive transference feelings that a patient has for his analyst are both a tool and an indication of psychopathology, so too is the transference pattern of the group. This same level of transference becomes a tool in the hands of the group therapist, because it enables him to bring the group together and then allows him, with the help of the group members, to analyze the absurdity and the incongruity of certain behavior.

The therapist should be sensitive to the need of patients to impose societal patterns on the therapy group in order to obscure intensive therapy. In a clinic group, the patients often come to talk about their children's problems and to seek advice from the "expert." They project their psychic difficulties away from themselves and seek the solutions in an authority rather than in themselves.

As noted earlier, if the group is organized according to the homogeneous nature of the members' complaints, the members will meet only to discuss an impairment, hoping to get some relief from it while at the same time getting the attention of the group and the therapist. When the group stresses the status of the therapist, making him their leader, they become his followers and avoid analysis of transference. Worse still, if the therapist sees himself as leader *and the group members as merely his followers,* analysis of transference-countertransference is avoided. This is a faulty approach and a primary defense used by the group and the therapist against a more fundamental, immediate experiencing, although some therapists see a value in it. The repressive-constructive therapies maintain a rather fixed reciprocation between the therapist and the group members. The members' veneration of their leader remains unexamined and unaltered throughout the therapy.

The "dilution of the transference" in group therapy, reported by some to occur (18, 19), appears to be the result of the imposition of a social structure onto the group or of the therapist's tendency to enhance his status before the group. The therapist may remain the leader throughout the life of the group, constantly being directive. The group never becomes "member centered," always remaining "leader-led" and "leader centered."

In the early stages of the therapy group, the group may move itself and the therapist toward a more directive and didactic form of therapy. The group does this by repressing and quite consciously suppressing thoughts and feelings. Group members then avoid anxiety and establish the therapist as the "leader."

The following schema, divided into four sections, is an attempt to give

(a) the polarity of the transference, (b) the usual distortion, and (c) some hypothetical examples relating to the kind of transference.

1. *Polarity*	*Distortion*
Group-Therapist Therapist-Group	Members consider themselves helpless and ineffectual. They follow the leader. "We all have problems. We're in the same boat. Our therapist will save us." The therapist is directive and controlling.

GROUP–THERAPIST

The therapist is the "boss," the teacher. "Where is Johnny today?" is a question asked of the therapist, not of the group, and all eyes are focused upon the therapist. When the therapist does not answer, tension mounts.

THERAPIST–GROUP

The therapist knows what is best. He believes that the patients can not make it without him. He must tell them what to do and not do.

2. *Polarity*	*Distortion*
Patient-Group Group-Patient	The patient feels the group is the opposite parent to the therapist. Most members feel certain patients are egos, ego ideals, ids (uncontrollable), and, most common, superegos (conscience).

PATIENT-GROUP

An early reaction that is expressed later comes from the patient who sees the group as composed of sick persons who are beneath him. This is part of the negative transference, splintered from the therapist and often worked through without the therapist's being subjected to the extremes of hate of which the patient is capable. This is usually a misdirection of the negative transference. The therapist should redirect it from the group members to himself, where it belongs. (Here the patient sees the therapist as the good parent and the rest of the group as the bad parent.)

GROUP–PATIENT   G → P

The group as a whole perceives single patients as epitomizing the characteristics of ego, id, and superego, without even knowing these terms. Sharpe (20) has pointed out that this possibility of topographical transference occurs in the psychoanalysis of individuals. Experience with groups clearly bears this out. For instance, a common response to a group member will be that he is the brightest, the most wonderful, the most social, the strongest, the fairest, and the like (ego and ego ideal). This is "the seeking of unwarranted gratifications" in the distorted relationship of transference. Or the group will see one person as the most irrational and the craziest (id). Finally, and most often, the group will see one person as the conscience and will be relieved when he does not show up. They will state openly that he controls them and that he makes them feel uneasy and guilty (superego) (21). Often, many of the members have difficulty in talking about intimate sexual matters until the forbidding individual is absent.

3. *Polarity*	*Distortion*
Patient-Therapist	The usual primary transference, child-parent.
Therapist-Patient	The usual omnipotent and omniscient "counter-transferences," parent-child.

PATIENT–THERAPIST   P ⟶ T

This is the usual transference level that is considered. It is the primary polarity, as described by Beukenkamp (22), of the patient relating to the therapist as the parent, either mother or father. It is easily seen when the patient wants undivided attention, love, and forgiveness. It manifests itself in many different forms. A young attractive patient, new to the group, was asked if she had had a dream. After she had reported her dream, a much older group member who had been in treatment three and a half years became visibly upset and said to the therapist, "You've never asked me yet for a dream." This accusation was manifestly untrue.

THERAPIST–PATIENT   T ⟶ P

This level is the traditional countertransference of the therapist onto an individual patient. The therapist responds to the patient as though he is a parent or one in authority. This occurs in group psychotherapy, but because it is observed and commented upon by the group members, it is lessened throughout therapy.

4. *Polarity*	*Distortion*
Patient-Patient	The usual secondary transference of child-
Patient-Patient	child, brother-sister, or friend-friend. Also tertiary polarity of Beukenkamp (23).

PATIENT–PATIENT   P ⟶ P

Among the commonly noted transferences in the group are the sibling relationships. Patients usually see each other as brothers and sisters—less frequently as other relatives and friends. Much of the interaction is made up of these distortions and the behavior that is a direct outcome of them.

Intensification of Transference

In the psychoanalytic group, there is an overall intensification of transferences (17, 24). Foulkes and Anthony noted: "Although the intensity of
the transference on any one individual is reduced, the total emotional
feeling is multiplied and intensified by the group situation" (25). In deeply
involved groups of long standing, there is a more comprehensive form of
transference behavior, which Beukenkamp (23) called "transference life"
interaction that is mostly irrational, consisting of both transference and
countertransference components. But there is a degree of rational behavior.

Peculiar Manifestations of Transference in Groups

The group is composed of many interacting persons and the nature of
each transference is different from that in individual psychoanalysis. In
individual therapy there tends to be a single kind of transference overtly
exhibited at any one time. This does not occur in the therapy group, because the format is not so rigid. There are changes in group membership,
and there are different growth processes for different patients.

The patient-therapist and patient-patient transferences have four characteristics much of the time: they are multiple, variable, fragmented, and
labile. Several examples follow.

Multiple
A fifty-two-year-old man, older than the therapist, responds to him with
very warm feelings, calling him "Pop" with tears of love and gratitude. He
has much the same feelings toward another man in the group, although
with less intensity. He has multiple father transferences for he is protective
of a young woman in the group who reminds him of his daughter; but, at
the same time, he has overt sexual feelings for this woman. He also relates
with anger and fear to another woman who reminds him of his mother.

Variable
A patient can relate to one woman as though she were his mother when
he was nine years of age, expecting from her the gratifications that might
be appropriate for that age. Simultaneously, he might react to another
woman who appears to him to be his mother when he was twenty, seeking
gratifications appropriate to this time of life.

Fragmented
A male patient transferred onto one man in the group the hateful
characteristics of his father. At the same time, he transferred onto the
therapist all of his father's loving and protective qualities.

There is a mistaken idea that psychoanalytic group therapy is primarily interested in the interpersonal processes rather than the intrapsychic ones. It has been suggested that because the approach is molar rather than molecular, it is not sensitive to the latent activity of each individual. But in practice we see in the transference behavior of every person clues that identify the underlying dynamic personality.

DREAMS AND TRANSFERENCE

Dreams are used to elicit and work through transference. The following two dreams describe the dreamers, much of their personalities, their major defenses, their points of fixation, and their real relatedness patterns in the groups as compared to their stated reasons for being in the group.

Dream 1

I was out in the country, I don't know where. I was with a teenage boy, in bed with him. He fondled my breast and I liked it. Later I was before my mother and the boy's mother. I was telling them, "See, he likes me."

This twenty-five-year-old woman was attempting desperately to separate from home. Her mother was irately against it, demanding, through the family physician, that she stop therapy. Although she had only been in the group for one month, there was a sense of tentative belonging, based upon her need to "seduce" the immature men in the group. Already, this patient had given up any purely social reason for being with us. There is no indication in the dream of her transference to the therapist, except that the woman is the powerful figure in her life. Certain competitive strivings also come to the fore, as she omits the women group members from her dreams.

Dream 2

I was in the Marines. My brother was there also, and he complained to me that he wanted to be in the artillery rather than the infantry. I went up to the sergeant and tried to fix it up for my brother. The sergeant hazed me, but I knew he did not mean to harm me. He threw me around and I did not resist. He finally pinned me down and I got frightened. He took out his bayonet and stuck it in my mouth, back to my throat. I knew he would not harm me on purpose—he might make a mistake, or worse yet, I might make a false move and drive the very sharp point into my throat. I was very upset.

If one regards this dream as the reality of the group situation at the time, this is the dreamer's latent knowledge of and true feeling for the therapist and for the others, "his brother." Here, we can easily see how compliant this man actually is, how ruled he is by authority, and how powerless he feels himself to be. His transference to the therapist (sergeant) was positive at the time but, without stretching one's imagination too much, negative elements might soon come to the fore. The punishment in the dream, in a sense, was deserved, for he was estranged from his father and filled with incestuous thoughts toward his sister.

These dreams can be used to refer to familial figures—father, mother, siblings—attempting, through reductive analysis, to seek causes in the past. This is done routinely, but it is more important to use the dreams to delineate ties in the group so that the latent meaning of the group's interaction gradually becomes more obvious to all. In the first dream, the dreamer is to realize that she is in the group for seductive reasons—to prove to her mother that she is lovable, that her brother loves her more than her mother, and so on. In the second, the dreamer does not come to the group for treatment, but, rather, to be an enlisted man with a tough, all-responsible sergeant over him; perhaps he also comes so that he can be punished.

The latent meanings for the patient's presence in the group are to be found in the transferences, which must be discovered and clarified. Conscious reasons for group participation, such as "I come for psychotherapy," serve as camouflage, preventing the immediate experience. Group members need to overcome interpersonal isolation and intrapsychic alienation by biological (total) togetherness, regardless of the form that the physical contact takes. They must realize this and take responsibility.

Simone Weil has said:

> To be rooted is perhaps the most important and least recognized need of the human soul. It is one of the hardest to define. A human being has roots by virtue of his real, active, and natural participation in the life of the community, which preserves in living shape certain particular treasures of the past and certain particular expectations of the future. This participation is a natural one, in the sense that it is automatically brought about by place, conditions of birth, profession, and social surroundings. *Every human being needs to have multiple roots.* It is necessary for him to draw well-nigh the whole of his moral, intellectual, and spiritual life by way of the environment of which he forms a natural part (italics ours) (26).

Transference and Countertransference in the Individual, Group, Extended, and Alternate Sessions

All nonveridical or distorting behavior, then, can be seen in the concept of transference-countertransference. Faulty perceptions may be analyzed as due to the member's need to maintain an idealized concept of himself and the need to prevent the awareness of conflicts with the accompanying anxiety. In all instances of defensive and resistive maneuver, the member's relationships are affected. Transferences can be observed, clarified, and reduced, with a resulting fundamental change in the personality of the patient. Analysis of the transference is basically existential, since it forces the person to exist without his parents. When he joins the alternate session (without the therapist), the patient assumes responsibility and participates in group-centered activity. During the extended session, the patient realizes that he is no longer central and that his therapist is quite human.

Preparatory sessions lead to the establishment of a strong, positive transference in the patient. This is developed by the patient partly because of his psychopathology and partly in response to the therapist's persuasive techniques, authentic affect and empathy, and development of countertransference. Countertransference, the *therapist's* remaining psychopathology, is always present in group psychotherapy. It is actively dealt with by those therapists who rely upon existential techniques and goals.

The illness of the patient becomes more manifest, but not greater, as he desires even more to be with the therapist. Simultaneously, and in direct proportion to the patient's increasing dependency, the therapist becomes more sure of himself. *The development of the transference neurosis in the patient is responded to by omniscient and omnipotent feelings, fantasies, and strivings in the therapist—the countertransference neurosis.*

In a bilateral transaction, if transference occurs in one person, a similar but opposite phenomenon—countertransference—occurs in the other person. In group psychotherapy, two members are seen to have reciprocal ties, binding them to one another. It appears easy for the group psychotherapist to objectify the therapist-patient transaction, to look at himself with his patient, and to see the development of an irrational tie. But this is not always so. Loeser has noted: "The present emphasis on techniques and practices (in group psychotherapy) represents in some way a tacit, collective resistance towards examination of factors involving countertransference" (27). However, the nature of group psychotherapy (the spoken perceptions of the patient) encourages the therapist to admit to difficulty, to investigate problems through continuing formal analysis or self-analysis (5), and to face this through the experience and example of "sick" patients. If disturbed group members admit to transference faults, perhaps the "well" therapist can also do this. *When there is successful reduction of the patient's transference, there is also a lessening in the therapist's countertransference. One does not occur without the other.*

The development, recognition, and proper use of the countertransference dynamic can benefit the therapeutic process. If the countertransference dynamic is denied, not recognized, and not used, it retards therapy indefinitely. In the extended session, if there is a co-therapist, he is able to observe the other therapist's countertransference and to confront him.

THE INDIVIDUAL SESSION

After some individual sessions with the patient, the group therapist usually begins to feel hopeful and thinks that he can help him. This is the time when the countertransference is developing. Later on, his optimistic feelings may be rudely jolted. This may occur when he considers placing the patient in the group or when he suggests alternate sessions for the first time. Should the patient resist these moves the therapist may lose his complacency and become uncertain. Fearful, he may delay certain steps until he feels more secure. The beginning group therapist may experience such anxiety, in an extreme case, that he gives up the practice of group psychotherapy.

The reluctance of psychotherapists to consider the practice of group psychotherapy, as valid or to under go a personal group experience is usually rationalized. It appears to be based upon countertransference problems of which they are but dimly aware. Because of this, group psychoanalytic treatment is advised for those who want to practice group psychotherapy (28). Problems of the therapist are more easily hidden in individual therapy, particularly if the patient is *required* to use the couch. In the group setting, everyone *sees* everyone else. Group psychotherapy patients, supported and protected by each other, "analyze" their therapist.

The patient generally objects to entry into the group. The threads of negativism in the transference appear, although the tie is still positive. The patient and the therapist move *together* toward the first group session.

Unless the group is "directed," group members, unlike the situation in individual therapy, question the intimacy and the bond between the new patient and the therapist, comparing it to their own relationship with him. Certain questions are asked: "Why is he bringing him in now?" "We told him that we wanted a man, and he brings in a woman. Why?" "Is she more attractive than I am?" "Will he keep her in individual sessions also?"

It is possible that in some cases the individual therapist overlooks group psychoanalytic therapy because he fears exposure of his neurotic ties with his individual patients. The group therapist who has a fixed number of preparatory sessions and a directive approach, may do this to cover up certain feelings that might develop.

THE GROUP SESSION

The moment the therapist and patient enter the group from the individual sessions, both countertransference and transference are reduced. Dynamically, entry into the group is seen as a desire on the part of the therapist to come to grips with his countertransference and to lessen the patient's transference. The therapist, through insistence on group therapy, *indicates that he alone cannot help his patient and that he needs the group to assist him.*

The group therapist, unlike the individual therapist, goes against his fantasy that he is the sole healer, and recognizes the capacity of all people to help one another. Group members are accepted as "co-therapist." This enhances each member's feeling of worth.

The therapist cares for his patients (29) and at the same time becomes more human, and permits an experience that is replete with different kinds of transference.

In regular group sessions, transference is focused upon by referring back into the group all of the reported outside happenings. If a patient complains of how mean her boss is, other group members and the therapist may point out that she is talking about her boss but also about the leader of the group. They explore her need to be preferred. This is referred back to significant persons in the past. The transference in the present with an extragroup figure is brought back into the group and also into the patient's past. This is not done systematically but as the information unfolds and as feelings are reenacted in the group, as past, present, and future coalesce into a whole—the ongoing group process.

It is helpful to focus attention on the late or absent member, and to overlook facile excuses and stress feelings. The therapist might ask, "How does everyone feel about John not being here?" Encouraged to go into their fantasies, group members will imagine that John has been killed or that his wife finally decided he could no longer come to the group, and so on. The fantasies reveal the underlying interpersonal and intragroup dynamics, the transferences, the interaction, and open up new areas. If the therapist is satisfied by the *rational* excuse—for example, "John had to work late"—much content will be lost.

Vacations of the therapist often bring out feelings of helplessness in patients. These feelings are explored because many death fantasies about group members and about the therapist are revealed. The mode of travel is gone into in some detail. Travel by plane brings forth many fantasies about death. The difference between the alternate and the regular sessions is now seen as related to the patient's intense bonds with the therapist. Funerals and illness are subjects which arise at times of departure of either therapist or a group member.

More archaic transferences surface when there is analysis of body functioning. For example, a person may mention that he has diarrhea. If no one else responds, the therapist should and may wonder that no one says anything about it. Early bowel habits and early punishments and restrictions are then discussed. This kind of regression and analysis is promoted far more easily in a nonjudgmental group climate.

The beginning group therapist is loath to admit that he prefers one patient in his group to another. It is *not* the *rational* preference but the *blind* preference for a patient that must be investigated. If the group brings this to the therapist's attention, he must question it, and may admit it if it is true. He should *not* give the reasons behind this irrationality.

(There are some therapists who do this and by seeking this kind of thera-peutic aid exploit the group.)

A group psychotherapist may have preferences that are free from countertransference but that relate to the truly human in the person. A therapist may prefer the person who risks a new behavior when earlier this patient had clung to the status quo. This is usually acceptable to the entire group.

The Extended Session and the Co-therapist

The alternate session suggests to the patients that they can lead life away from the group leader. The extended session (see Chapter 7) pro-poses to the group members that they can exist with a much more human leader who has faults and who is not an expert.

This extended session, meeting for a prolonged period, forces a new awareness of who the leader is, and a new sense of who the member is. The patient may learn through *the presence* of a co-therapist (see Chapter 8) that his therapist prefers another to himself. He begins to realize that he can still function effectively without the special imagined tie to the thera-pist. When the co-therapist, introduced solely for the extended period, is a woman and the therapist is a man, each woman patient is confronted with the fact that her efforts to please, seduce, and be lovable have been to no avail. She must face the fact that there can be no lasting union with the therapist. Patients learn—although they were somewhat aware before—that their therapist has a life outside of the group.

Each patient feels the presence of the co-therapist and responds to her or him in ways which are unique. Patients are presented with a new set of circumstances, which demands a marked shift in their behavior. Later, there is a search for the reasons for their anxieties and disquiet.

The fact that the therapist requires the help of a colleague is an eye-opener to most patients. If the co-therapeutic form has not been used in regular sessions, the appearance of another professional in their group is explained on the basis that their therapist is, by himself, insufficient for the task. The co-therapist's presence disrupts the distorted ties which form the matrix of the group.

The co-therapist is actually an unwanted intruder into the group. The cohesion which existed before is ruptured. The introduction of a co-thera-pist is similar to the introduction of a new patient in a regular group ses-sion. But the stranger (co-therapist) has a preferred status; she or he is a colleague and friend of the therapist and knows him in ways that the patients will never know him. The presence of the co-therapist reduces the transference bonds of patient to therapist. Some patients deny the co-therapist's presence by excluding her (him) from the discussion, by not looking at her (him), and by addressing only the original therapist. But the co-therapist's presence is keenly felt.

Remnants of the therapist's countertransference surface in the co-therapeutic extended session. The therapist admits to himself that he is not omniscient by inviting another professional to help him. In the extended session he may expose more of his unconscious to the group members when he describes his dreams and fantasies (See Chapter 7.)

The co-therapist should note and describe distortions in the relationship between the therapist and each member. If she (he) is intuitive and feels on a parity with the therapist, her (his) interpretation can help immeasurably in lessening the countertransference.

THE ALTERNATE SESSION

The alternate session is an opportunity to use in a productive way the members' ties to themselves and to their therapist. Group members meet before or after the group, so why not suggest that they formalize these meetings? (See Chapter 6.) In the absence of the therapist, silent patients sometimes become talkative, inhibitions are lessened, and aggressive and sexual feelings are often more freely expressed. Some patients who can exhibit only positive feelings for the therapist, with the help of the group, bring out some criticism during the regular group period. With the introduction of the alternate session without the therapist, this patient can begin to release pent-up hostility. Later, this anger can become part of the regular session until it is worked through. The transference shift, as the patient moves from the regular to the alternate session, makes the therapist seem first as a loving, and then as a hated, parental figure.

The alternate session is a proper step for the group members to take in their search for equality and freedom. It is like the child who moves from a complete dependence upon the parent (individual session), through the family life of sharing (group and extended session), into the world of adults (alternate session). All of these discrete sessions can take place in analytic group psychotherapy.

With the introduction of the alternate session, the therapist's countertransference continues to be reduced. For the beginning group therapist, this means that he has evolved sufficiently to let the group be free and mutual and to operate without his guidance. In successive groups and with successive patients, the use of the alternate hour lessens considerably the residual strivings of the therapist for omniscience and omnipotence. The therapist may excuse his not using the alternate method by claiming that he must know where his patients are and what they are up to. But this is impossible. When the patient leaves the therapist's office, he is on his own. Still, alternate meetings should not be used as a method unless the therapist permits his worries and misgivings to come to the surface.

Reconstruction in group psychoanalytic therapy occurs without the conscious efforts of either the therapist or the patients. Before reconstruction, gradual regression must occur, evidenced by the activation of many infantile transferences. Behavior will be quite irrational for a while. If the therapist's goal is the *change* of the patients' personalities, he will not worry. Gradually, the ties that bring the group members together will be replaced by less distorted relationships, and eventually the fundamental human needs found in treatment will be found outside of the therapy group. Termination, therefore, is never consciously arrived at; it is merely another point reached by each person in his own time and in his own way.

References

(1) WOLF, A., and SCHWARTZ, E. K. Psychoanalysis in Groups. In Kaplan, H. I., and Sadock, B. J. (eds.), Comprehensive Group Psychotherapy. Baltimore: William and Wilkins, 1971.

(2) BERMAN, L. Psychoanalysis and Group Psychotherapy. Psychoanalyt. Rev., 37 (1950), 156–63.

(3) FREUD, S. The Dynamics of the Transference. Collected Papers, II. London: Hogarth Press, 1948.

(4) FREUD, S. The Future Prospects of Psychoanalytic Therapy. Collected Papers, II. London: Hogarth Press, 1948.

(5) FREUD, S. Recommendations for Physicians on the Psycho-Analytic Method of Treatment. Collected Papers, II. London: Hogarth Press, 1948.

(6) BUCKLEW, J. The Subjective Tradition in Phenomenological Psychology. Phil. Sci., 22 (1955), 289–99.

(7) ALLPORT, F. H. The Theories of Perception and the Concept of Structure. New York: Wiley, 1955.

(8) WHITAKER, C. A., and MALONE, T. P. The Roots of Psychotherapy. New York: Blakiston, 1953.

(9) FROMM-REICHMANN, F., and MORENO, J. L. (eds.), Progress in Psychotherapy. New York: Grune and Stratton, 1956.

(10) DREIKURS, R. Techniques and Dynamics of Multiple Psychotherapy. Psychiat. Quart., 24 (1950), 788–99.

(11) MORENO, J. L. Transference, Countertransference and Tele: Their Relation to Group Research and Group Psychotherapy. Group Psychotherapy, 7, No. 2 (1954), 107–17.

(12) HORNEY, K. Neurosis and Human Growth. New York: Norton, 1950.

(13) GOLDSTEIN, K. Human Nature. Cambridge, Mass.: Harvard University Press, 1940.

(14) FROMM, E. Man for Himself. New York: Rinehart, 1947.

(15) FREUD, S. Further Recommendations in the Technique of Psychoanalysis. Collected Papers, II. London: Hogarth Press, 1948.

(16) ROSENBAUM, M. Co-Therapy. In Kaplan, H. I., and Sadock, B. J. (eds.), Comprehensive Group Psychotherapy. Baltimore: William and Wilkins, 1971.

(17) DEMAREST, E. W., and TEICHER, A. Transference in Group Psychotherapy. Psychiatry, 17 (1954), 187–202.

(18) LOESER, L. H., FURST, W., ROSS, I. S., and BRY, THEA. Group Psychotherapy in Private Practice: A Preliminary Report. Am. J. Psychotherapy, 3 (April 1949), 213–33.

(19) SLAVSON, S. R. Transference Phenomena in Group Psychotherapy. Psychoanalyt. Rev., 37 (1950), 39–55.

(20) SHARPE, E. F. Collected Papers on Psychoanalysis, No. 36. London: International Psycho-Analytical Library, Hogarth Press, 1950.

(21) STEIN, A. The Superego and Group Interaction in Group Psychotherapy. J. Hillside Hosp., 5 (1956), 495–504.

(22) BEUKENKAMP, C. The Multidimensional Orientations of Analytic Group Therapy. Am. J. Psychotherapy, 9 (1955), 477–83.

(23) BEUKENKAMP, C. Further Developments of the Transference Life Concept of Therapeutic Groups. J. Hillside Hosp., 5 (1956), 441–48.

(24) HULSE, W. C. Transference, Catharsis, Insight, and Reality Testing during Concomitant Individual and Group Psychotherapy. Internat. J. Group Psychotherapy, 5 (1955), 46.

(25) FOULKES, S. H., and ANTHONY, E. J. Group Psychotherapy: The Psychoanalytic Approach. London: Penquin Books, 1965, rev. ed. 1973.

(26) WEIL, S. The Need for Roots. Boston: Beacon Press, 1955.

(27) LOESER, L. H. Editorial. Internat. J. Group Psychotherapy, 1 (1951), 3.

(28) ROSENBAUM, M. The Challenge of Group Psychoanalysis. Psychoanalysis, 1, No. 2 (1952), 42–58.

(29) FOULKES, S. H. Concerning Leadership in Group Analytic Psychotherapy. Internat. J. Group Psychotherapy, 1 (1951), 319–29.

10 Emergency, Crisis, and Emergence

Hugh Mullan
Max Rosenbaum

IN GROUP PSYCHOANALYTIC THERAPY, emergencies and crises occur. They appear to be more frequent in groups that have been in existence for some time because of the nature of the group process. The emergency is felt at much greater depth. The patient must alter his frame of reference; he relates emergency to crisis and demands an immediate solution. The psychotherapist should relate emergency to change. The patient keeps referring to the potholes in the pavement, and the therapist notes that the entire street is sinking, suggesting a more total change that is taking place.

Emergency, crisis, and emergence is a continuum. A definition of *emergency* is "an unforeseen combination of circumstances which calls for immediate action" (1). Emergency and crisis in regressive-reconstructive group therapy should always be considered as part of the patient's process of change. The emergency leads to the crisis. *Crisis* means the decisive moment or turning point. It comes from the Greek word *krisis*, meaning *separate*. This separating leads to emergence and change. The patient wants the therapist to relieve the emergency without going farther to the crisis and the necessary change. The *emergence* is the movement forward (2, 3, 4, 5). Through all of this, the therapist must differentiate his *own* anxiety from the patient's expression of emergency and crisis.

The patient who seeks treatment is in a crisis or an impending crisis. Others (6, 7) have noted that the crisis represents both an opportunity for growth and a danger to the individual as its resolution can reflect a change in his precrisis coping to a more or less adaptive level. (Some therapists would stress that the crisis state is the individual's emotional response to an external hazard.)

In crisis intervention clinics, there is an active intervention by the therapist in the course of which alternative methods of coping are introduced. The patient remains rather passive in this type of setting, whether it be crisis intervention centers or suicide prevention centers (8, 9, 10). Once the immediate problem has been resolved, therapy terminates. In this type of definition of crisis, most crises are resolved in either a maladaptive or adaptive fashion from four to six weeks from the outset of the acute distress. The techniques are based upon a limited definition of crisis.

The First Emergency

Those who enter psychotherapy do so because they feel that the family, culture, and society in which they live have failed them. This is for them an emergency, or a set of circumstances calling for immediate change. For most of these individuals, the internal stress is quite unbearable. When they are introduced into the psychoanalytic group, a new emergency arises, which is far more related to emergence or change. This new emergency is related to the intensified transference relationships that are established and to the archaic patterns that come to the surface (11). Related to this powerful emotional experience is the awareness that they must begin to take responsibility for others as well as for themselves. This awareness is intensified when these individuals move into the alternate session and are in a peer relationship (12). The process of change is intense at these times; giving up the old and risking the new are both the crisis and the path to emergence, but all of this is seen by the patient as an emergency. It is important that the beginning group psychotherapist distinguish between the crisis as the patient sees it—fixed and intolerable—and the crisis as it moves the patient to constant growth—dynamic and ever changing. The psychotherapist must avoid adopting the patient's point of view.

We can restudy every crisis in terms of its deeper meaning and its relationship to the patient's unwillingness to make major moves forward. A person who comes for even one consultation is coming because he is in a state of emergency. This state can be moved forward constructively, changing the status quo, or backward neurotically, reinforcing the status quo. All our efforts toward this person become essential. His resistance to change will include all of the techniques that he can use to hold on to his neurosis, which in turn makes his early treatment so difficult. This is sharply defined when a patient asks for help and at the same time raises a series of objections to time of appointment, cost of therapy, and so on.

Emergency and the Group

For the new patient, since the group is the therapeutic environment, extremely deep relationships begin to appear. The intensity and meaning of these new relationships are greater than in any of the social groups of which the patient is part. The patient at first may fight the group in a variety of ways (sometimes even prior to his entry) (12). As he expresses his objections to group participation and moves away from the group, he seemingly makes sense and is supported in his endeavor by his friends and family, who generally support him in his neurosis.

If the psychotherapist were to accept these objections at face value, he would be deceiving himself as well as the patient. Because the therapist, for the most part, has no vested interest aside from therapy, he is in a position to be more objective about the desired move. He will often find that the patient is in *psychic emergency*, and the position that the psycho- therapist now takes will alter his relationship with the patient and will establish values for himself and the patient (6). The therapist must look behind the conscious, "rational" purpose. If he looks deeply, he will often find the motives within the group at that moment. The patient who wants to leave is very often disturbed by the intrapsychic shifts within his own personality. He finds these shifts quite intolerable, and he develops osten- sibly valid reasons (emergencies) for leaving. After a patient has been in group psychoanalytic therapy for some two to four years, however, his rea- sons for leaving are generally more valid. He may say that he feels ready to leave, or he may present other feelings, but he will probably not present seemingly rational reasons that actually clothe resistance.

Henry came to the group and stated that since some of his em- ployees didn't know "how to run the business," he would have to spend more time at work and absent himself from the group. It was, he stated, an emergency!

Neither the group nor the therapist permitted themselves to be side- tracked by the "valid" emergency but moved toward the deeper issue. The therapist probed toward the intrapsychic problems as the patient con- stantly attempted to conceal them. In fact, Henry was getting closer to examining his own controlling behavior.

Emergency and Change in Group Configuration: The Loss of Members

The group's solidarity, its experience, and its purpose are dependent upon its stable makeup, or group configuration. Marked and sudden changes lead to a good deal of anxiety (13). Loss of a member changes the group form. The resulting anxiety appears to relate historically to previous relationships. Sometimes the change is so radical that an emergency exists for many group members. The need for constancy in the group configuration seems to be a requirement for all but a few, and is related to the quasi-constant, but actually unsettled, relationships that existed in the family of the patients who come to us.

Regardless of the reason, the loss of a member is generally opposed by the group members. This opposition appears to be related to feelings of anxiety, guilt, rejection, helplessness, and hopelessness, and all of these feelings appear to have had their origins in the historic family milieu.

Jack was an extremely intelligent, but basically dependent, adult male. From the outset of his entry into the group, his behavior was extremely provocative. The group members showed increasing resentment of his lack of relatedness and his disruptive behavior, but they were unwilling to reject him outright, because all of their historic reactions to the disturbed familial figure who needed, but rejected, aid came to the surface.

The group's reluctance to remove Jack was related both to their historic reaction and to their need to hold onto the "constant" group configuration.

THE DEATH OF A GROUP MEMBER

The death or severe illness of a group member has tremendous impact upon the group.

John, a group member, committed suicide quite suddenly. The news was communicated to the therapist during an individual session with a patient, and the therapist expressed his feelings by crying readily and easily. This may be explained by two factors at work: First, after considerable experience in work with groups, the therapist was able to express his feelings with ease. Second, the patient being seen during that individual hour was in another group.

John's group met the next day; when the members had assembled they were told of John's death. They were all very shocked and upset. The therapist suggested an "emergency session," which was very important and meaningful to the group. The honest expression of feelings on the part of the therapist was also very important. The emergency became emergence, as all factors relating to death, hopelessness, and helplessness came to the surface.

Some group therapists become more active or directive when a group member commits suicide. This serves to relieve the therapist's anxiety, but often obscures the dynamics and impact upon other group members. It also avoids facing the despair that we all *must* face at different times and on different occasions (14, 15).

At times death is somewhat expected.

A therapist decided to continue group psychoanalytic therapy for a cardiac patient because therapy was needed and because there was no indication that the emotional impact of the group had an adverse effect on his heart. Eventually the patient died, and the therapist and group members attended the funeral. The feelings that came to the surface as a result of this emergency were part of each group member's emergence.

THE DEATH OF THE GROUP PSYCHOANALYTIC THERAPIST

If the group psychotherapist dies, unlike the patient in individual analysis, the group members are able to explore reactions with one another. Patients are not left stranded.

Some years ago, a colleague died suddenly. His death occurred about five o'clock in the afternoon while he was being rushed to a cardiologist's office after he complained of chest pains. The suddenness of this tragic episode was upsetting to all concerned. Patients who arrived several hours later, as well as those who came the next day, were told of the death by a note on the door of the office. Later, several of the groups met for a while and attempted unsuccessfully to "hire" another group therapist; finally, each patient had to make separate arrangements for further therapy.

As a result of the experience, a group of us evolved a plan. We have left instructions requesting that each patient be called immediately in the event of such an occurrence and that a therapist be suggested to him if he feels the need for one at that time. This involves a systematic filing of each patient's name, address, and phone number so that the plan can be carried through with some ease. It is advisable to include the names of several colleagues in such instructions. Another colleague became very ill, and several of his colleagues were able to use a modification of this plan with considerable success and rather minimal patient distress.

The practice of group psychoanalytic therapy permits the patients to carry on temporarily during this kind of crisis. Again, the process of emergence takes place as patients find themselves able to relate to one another and to carry on for some time without the therapist. This is in sharp contrast to individual analytic practice, where patients indicate marked anxiety when sudden death or illness of the psychoanalyst occurs. A psychoanalyst noted that when he told those patients he was treating individually that he was leaving for a vacation, much anxiety would arise. However, when he began working with groups, his vacation announcement was greeted with much *less* anxiety since the group members had one another. This analyst was disappointed at the group's matter-of-factness. Rosenthal (16) took over a group which met in an outpatient clinic, when the previous group leader died suddenly. She stated:

> It thus devolved upon (me) to help adjust these abandoned patients to the death of the father-figure, a task beyond the psychological means at (my) disposal . . . the reaction to the death of the leader . . . ranged all the way from apparent indifference to fear of annihilation (16).

THE ILLNESS OF THE GROUP PSYCHOANALYTIC THERAPIST

If the therapist becomes ill, he should personally call the patients whenever possible. This call is reassuring to the patient, since he generally reasons that the therapist is not too sick if he can still call.*

If someone else does the calling, a brief and accurate statement of what is wrong, how serious it is, and the possible duration of the illness is extremely helpful to the patient. It may be suggested that the patients meet together during this period in alternate meetings. This suggestion is rarely needed in an established group that makes arrangements for alternate meetings. The established group will also arrange alternate meetings if the therapist takes a lengthy vacation. Absence on the part of the therapist touches the core conflicts of relatedness with the parent figure, and the dynamics must be carefully explored.

The experience of the alternate meeting enables the patient to cope with any possible loss of the therapist. There are two factors present: on the side of the therapist, there is the reduction of his own omnipotent image and, from the patient's viewpoint, there is the surrender of the all-important figure, which is not unlike the death of the therapist. The alternate meeting moves the patient further because it enables him to face the emergency of the parent's death (11, 12, 17).

> I fractured my ankle. I met with one group while still unaware of the seriousness of the injury. I walked with difficulty and needed a cane. The group members expressed concern, but many of their hostile feelings came to the surface. In marked contrast were the reactions of patients seen individually, who all expressed stereotyped concern. A

* Some group psychotherapists may not physically feel well enough to deal with the patient's anxiety or anger at the idea of the group leader's illness. The group therapist's illness may bring back memories of a parent's illness. This in turn brings up the anger, frustration, and guilt that the child experienced when the parent became ill.

few days later I was wearing a cast. Love, hostility, and guilt quickly surfaced in the group. For the patients in individual analysis, it took some time for these feelings to come forth.

THE ILLNESS OF THE GROUP MEMBER

Physical illness of a group member is generally upsetting because of the identification that takes place. The therapist is carefully scrutinized by the patients in the group at this moment. All of the feelings about the parent's concern or lack of concern come to the surface. Very often test situations occur.

Hospitalization and illness of members always provokes intense, deep feelings. At these times the therapist should act as he feels most comfortable. Sometimes a visit to a patient is indicated; often it is not. It is always important for the therapist to explore what he is doing at these times. He should also look for the transference reactions as they occur and delineate them. The intent of the therapist's questions is toward the emotional, and should go beyond socially appropriate behavior (the stereotyped).

THE PERIPHERY OF A GROUP AND DEATH OR ILLNESS

The death or illness of a patient's relative or close friend is a frequent source of disturbed feeling, which is valuable if it furthers therapy. Death or severe illness brings up this possibility for any group member or for a similar member of their own immediate family. Many guilt feelings related to either expressed or concealed aggression become evident. For those in the group who have already lost someone close, there is a chance to renew these feelings and to put death in its proper perspective once and for all. At these times feelings of helplessness and despair predominate. If there is marked identification with the dead or ill person, the patient may ask for individual hours. Sometimes the patient becomes so upset that he wants to stay away from the group. In this case the therapist might say: "Your group would want to know about this. In your sadness, you need not stay away from us. You can feel with us about this death (or illness)."

The death of a significant person in our society causes disruption in the group. The question of how the group therapist should cope with the death of a person meaningful to his own life may be handled in one of two ways: the therapist may cancel his appointments for a day or for as long as he wishes, or he may come to the group and express his sense of disturbance. This second way is extremely helpful both to the therapist and to the group, for, in doing this, the therapist shows himself to be part of the

group, holding nothing back, and he is seen as a very human being, capable of feeling and suffering. Fromm-Reichmann noted:

> In this connection, I recall a very disturbed schizophrenic who had heard of the death of a very close friend of the psychiatrist. The patient was completely blocked in his communication when the psychiatrist first resumed work with him following the death of the friend until the psychiatrist made a remark to the effect that she realized he knew of her loss (18, p. 212).

The therapist should not use the group as a therapeutic medium for himself, but he should not deny painful feelings. Knowledge of the therapist's suffering and of his responsible relationships with the world often aids patients in structuring their own ego ideals.

Group members frequently bring up the deaths, accidents, and suicides of prominent persons. They are discouraged from a mere presentation of the event, but are asked about their own feelings and involvements with the occurrence. No cultural event is isolated, and it should never be treated as an event without meaning for all. When both Kennedy brothers were assassinated, there was much grief expressed. The grief, for some group members, masked rage at the tragedy which cut short the lives of two vital young people. The investigation and subsequent resignation of Richard Nixon stimulated enormous rage. He was perceived by some group members as a ruthless parent who was insensitive.

EXPLOSIVE AFFECT AND THE EMERGENCY IN THE GROUP

Patients sometimes leave a group angrily in the middle of a session, stating that they will not come back.

When patients under attack become upset and leave the room, the therapist may also leave to speak to them quietly in the waiting room. This often encourages their return. Later, it is important to inform the group that, although the therapist does not forbid such behavior, it would be helpful for all concerned if the desire to leave were discussed and worked through rather than acted upon. The angry exit, like all impulse-motivated behavior, is upsetting to the group. All of the urgent, emergency feelings come to the foreground as group members debate their mutual responsibility.

DIVORCE, REMARRIAGE, AND ENGAGEMENTS IN THE GROUP

A change in marital status of group members is significant. Patients who divorce become more totally dependent upon the group. The fantasies of group members about another member's divorce and the guilt when a fantasied divorce actually takes place are extremely important. Be-

cause divorce is a painful process, this emergency is generally sympathetically handled.

The group is usually supportive and concerned about the dissolution of a marriage. However, they are far from casual and, beyond their own identification, express strong convictions about the permanency of marriage. Even when it is apparent that a marriage is doomed, the group seems to struggle to save the relationship. This appears to be related to the larger societal norm of preserving the family.

Marriage and remarriage structure new constellations in the group. Those who get married are seen as withdrawing from the group and less available to the group. Sometimes the marriage, or even the engagement, of a member is seen as a rejection. The divorced person who remarries is also less accessible. The divorce has sometimes been far more acceptable than the subsequent remarriage.

VACATIONS AND EMERGENCY: THE THERAPIST AND THE PATIENT

Vacations are separations in a very deep sense, and they are emergencies. The therapist's assurance that "we will all be back together again after two weeks (or a month)" is a denial of the anxiety caused by the separation. The therapist here becomes the supportive parent. He can give no real assurance that "we will all be back together again." This may be his wish. Anxiety about the therapist's departure should be explored. The therapist will find that he has feelings about a patient's departure. After vacation, it appears that everyone has made progress.

The patient's feelings of rejection at the departure of the therapist represent a familiar pattern in individual analytic practice. Often, the patient will take vacations earlier as a punitive measure, as if to say, "if you can leave me, than I can leave you." This pattern is even stronger in the group, where the family history comes up. A patient may say, "You are taking your vacation when it pleases Martha [a group member]. It is very difficult for me to take a vacation at the same time as you. Why do you prefer Martha?" Or a group member will say, "Don't expect to find me here when you return." Occasionally this pattern is "acted out," and the group member stays away for some time after the therapist has returned.

This type of behavior is an effort to maintain a status quo relationship —denial that we are born, grow up, and die. The patient may plan activities to "fill up the time." This is an effort to cope with the emergency by denying its existence—denial of the loss of the therapist. The most real emergency the patient has to face is that the therapist may not return and that the patient will have to emerge from the safe and protected relationship into a new life situation.

Demarest and Teicher have noted:

When Demarest was preparing to leave on her vacation, the group in various ways expressed its feeling of being rejected and deserted . . . the therapist encouraged fantasies concerning her vacation. Joe, as spokesman for the group, had a fantasy in which the entire group went to a Florida beach with Demarest, "There we would live together as a family" (19).

Emergency and Change: The Addition of a New Member

The configuration of the group can be altered by the admission of new members; when the open-end, continuous-group principle is adhered to, there is constant change as new members enter and old ones depart. Many feelings emerge, especially rivalry and competition. These are important dynamics. Papanek noted: "Most interesting are the reactions to and in a new member; unconscious hostility is mutual at the beginning; it is as if at first the old members attempted to eliminate the new one" (13). The dynamic appears to be related to that of the birth of a new baby and is additionally complicated if the new member replaces a member toward whom there are still many unresolved feelings. Many fantasies and dreams come up about the new member—that the new baby will get all the love and all the food. Often anxiety is expressed that, since a new member has entered, it is time for an older member to leave before he is told to leave. One member commented, "It's too early to bring in a new person. I still have to be the baby here a while longer."

The family concept appears particularly applicable here, because the group members react in terms of childhood memories and fantasies concerning father, mother, and siblings; and it is particularly pertinent because one of the endeavors is to change the patient's externalized concept of mother, father, and family. Group psychoanalytic therapy is quite different from individual psychotherapy, for in the group there is greater opportunity for altering the fundamental symbols within each psyche.

The New Member Who Is Not a Patient

New members may be introduced, not to receive psychotherapy, but to enhance it. Such members might include co-therapist, participant observers, observers, student therapists, and others. These people are often perceived as allies of the therapist and not of the group members. If two therapists begin the group together, the patients appear to believe that both therapists are present for the patients, not to exploit them (19). If the co-therapist is introduced *after* the group has begun, the members usually think that they are being exploited. This reaction may be dormant for some time before it is exposed. It may be avoided altogether if both the therapist and the new co-therapist are experiential and genuine, for the patients then feel less isolated, less the objects of clinical scrutiny. When co-therapists are ultra-analytic, the patients appear to be hurt and to feel used. This is overlooked by therapists who, in recording group sessions, exploit the research possibilities of group therapy at the expense of the feelings and dynamics that are involved. The patient often views the therapist as the omnipotent parent, and his resentment of a research procedure may be dormant for a considerable period of time or may never come to the surface.   .

Signs of disagreement between the co-therapists deepen the feelings of insecurity and helplessness in the patient. These anxieties appear to be similar to those that the child experiences when his mother and father are arguing. The patients often forget their own needs and take on the burden of helping to quell the argument or disagreement. Often patients become upset when they realize that the therapist can be wrong, can make mistakes, and needs help. At this point, there is crisis and emergency. The more genuine the therapists are with one another, the more the group will relate to them. It is helpful at times for patients to experience co-therapists who disagree, but only if the two therapists are able to be honest with one another and resolve their difficulties.

THE INTRODUCTION OF THE STRANGER

On rare occasions, a group member will bring a relative or friend to a group session. This practice occurs more frequently in the alternate meeting, to which a patient will bring a person who is important to him. On occasion, when the group leaves the office to attend an alternate meeting, a relative or friend of a group member may be encountered in the waiting room or in the restaurant where the alternate meeting is being held. A group member may use this device to introduce a friend to the idea of psychotherapy, or a husband may bring his wife along to "prove" that those in therapy with him are not "seductive." These intrusions are quite upsetting and startling to the group, but no feelings are expressed while the stranger is present. Later, tremendous feeling comes to the surface. All of this is "grist for the mill" in group psychoanalytic therapy.

Emergency and Change in Group Configuration: Inner Stress

The group may be altered in yet another significant way—by violent and sudden changes in the lives of the members. Crises, inside and outside of the group, constantly move therapy and deny the status quo.

The failure or incompetence, real or imagined, of significant figures in the culture and society provokes helplessness and anger. Although overtly a circumstance outside of the group, it is related to the inner stress of the patients. The therapist's capacities and values are carefully scrutinized.

When Senator Joseph McCarthy was a strong political figure in the 1950's there was a good deal of agitation in the groups and a feeling that information revealed in the group might be used against the patients.

In 1950 the director of the Federal Bureau of Investigation wrote a guest editorial for the *Journal of the American Medical Association*, which contained the following passage: "The President, in a directive dated July 24, 1950, called on all . . . individuals to report any information coming to their attention concerning espionage, sabotage, and subversive activities to the FBI. . . . The physicians of America, like any other citizens, can best help in the protection of the nation's internal security by reporting immediately to the FBI any information of this nature which might come into their possession" (20).

A patient with a past history of affiliation with a left-wing political organization read this editorial and came to the group in a panic, fearful that he would be "turned in."

Careless public announcements about military action or war by important officials evoke despondency from many patients, who ask, "Why come to therapy? What's the use?" Political leaders who deceive the public evoke the patient's despair. Those feelings came to the surface during the Watergate era. Disclosures about such political affiliations as communism or fascism occur in the group; descriptions of theft, embezzlement, or homicide also came up. The *mutual trust* developed in the group seems sufficient to counter any disclosure possibility. Some therapists, prior to placing patients in a group, caution them not to discuss such material in the group. We do not agree with this practice.

Groups often ask the therapist to what lengths he would go in order to withhold professional confidences. None of the so-called critical areas, such as disclosure of political affiliations, seems as critical when finally brought to the surface. Homosexual experiences or fantasies, as well as incestuous experiences or fantasies, appear more difficult to bring to the surface. Descriptions of extramarital relationships are very painful to present. There is expression of guilt, but usually there is a good deal of reassurance from the other group members. Although there is fear of losing the love and admiration of group members, the patient's reluctance to disclose the basic problem masks a desire to hold on to the neurosis. At these moments, it is wise for the therapist to express feelings of warmth and to support the patient's courage in presenting this painful experience.

THE SUDDEN SHIFT AND THE EMERGENCY

At certain times, there is a shift in the patient's orientation from love to hate. In therapy groups of long standing, many patients go through this shift, with ensuing aggressive, hostile activities. Aggression may be directed toward many members of the group, including the therapist. The agitated group member may threaten to throw ashtrays or turn over furniture, or may make threatening remarks to other members.

When a sudden shift occurs, it is important that it be handled immediately, with the transference gone into directly. The therapist might say, "John, she is not your mother," or "You would like to kill your mother, but this is Joan." Although each therapist will do it differently, the therapist must express his deep sense of concern about the patient's behavior.

SEXUAL "ACTING OUT" AND THE EMERGENCY

Although many patients have been involved in sexual "acting out" prior to entering psychotherapy, sexual intercourse between two members of a group is an emergency. This is not to deny the possibility that members may find lasting and significant relationships in the group (17). All of the group members become involved in the dynamics. The therapist should not make any prohibitions in this regard, only insisting to those involved that they be aware of what is going on and attempt to interpret and analyze this behavior beforehand. If they fail to do so, the analysis of such behavior *must* continue.

EMERGENCY AND OVERT PSYCHOSIS IN THE GROUP

There have been very few experiences of overt psychosis in the group. Some group psychotherapists have reported a shift from compensation to decompensation.

In one group, a manic-depressive patient experienced an overt psychotic period, during which she was quite manic for several weeks. The patient was seen individually and offered considerable time, but it was the reassurance and warmth that she received from other group members at this time that was most successful in helping her. Their genuine expressions of concern and compassion were extremely stabilizing for her.

There are many varieties of this behavior, and each patient has to be considered individually. His fear at this time appears to be primarily related to identification. A policy of frankness is most helpful. Sometimes another patient who has gone through the experience of overt psychosis or near breakdown can be extremely helpful. The therapist may confuse deep anger with psychosis, because of his own fears.

EMERGENCY AND GENERAL DESPAIR IN THE GROUP

Close to the development of overt psychosis in the group is the expression of paralyzing anxiety, despair, and depression in the members. A group composed of too many dependent and depressed individuals may not interact sufficiently, but this is a different phenomenon. Every patient must go through a period of despair and depression as he changes markedly. During this period the risk of suicide is real, and all talk of suicide in the group is serious and must be explored. When a particular patient is going through a depressed period, other group members become aware of their own helplessness and their inability to help; they feel that their affection and attention are not enough. They help, however, by constantly showing their concern, by freely expressing their feelings, and by sharing experiences. At this point the therapist's ability to withstand the despair of those who are close to him is essential.

Termination of Group Psychoanalytic Therapy and Emergency

A patient's termination of group psychoanalytic therapy is an emergency. It creates crisis and fear; it should be experienced slowly and developed over at least several months' time. Sudden decisions to leave psychotherapy should be questioned, and the patient urged to remain. The therapist should stress that there cannot be departure with assurance of return. The therapist should not say, "You can always come back." There is no *guarantee* of a future patient-doctor relationship with the therapist. This is not punitive, but the existential reality.

Some therapists inform patients believed to be ready to leave the group that they will be accessible if in the future the patient desires to return to discuss any problems. This practice appears related to unresolved transference. If there is a potential incident that will require the transaction to be established again, the time to leave has not come; and if the patient feels that he can always return to the therapist for help, an important area has not been worked through.

To sum up, emergencies seem to occur with greater frequency as the group continues. Each emergency is related to emergence and change. A patient's avoidance of the therapy group during his emergency is resistance. He must be encouraged to come to the group and share his emergency. Intense feelings emerge and inner stress results when the configuration of the group changes. The therapist's activity is directed toward permitting the feelings to emerge, toward interpretation and analysis, and toward closure and maintenance of the configuration. Emergencies are never to be avoided but, whenever possible, are to be worked through in the group.

References

(1) Webster's Collegiate Dictionary, 5th ed. Springfield, Mass.: Merriam, 1941.

(2) DEWEY, J. Experience and Nature. Chicago and London: Open Court, 1926.

(3) WHITEHEAD, A. N. Process and Reality: An Essay in Cosmology. New York: Macmillan, 1929.

(4) JAMES, W. Essays in Radical Empiricism. New York: Longmans, Green, 1912.

(5) MURPHY, G. Personality. New York: Harper, 1947.

(6) BERMAN, L. Countertransference and Attitudes of the Analyst in the Therapeutic Process. Psychiatry, 12 (1949), 163–64.

(7) CAPLAN, G. An Approach to Community Mental Health. New York: Grune and Stratton, 1961.

(8) LANGSLEY, D. G., and KAPLAN, D. M. (eds.). The Treatment of Families in Crisis. New York: Grune and Stratton, 1968.

(9) LESTER, D., and BROCKOPP, G. M. (eds.). Crisis Intervention and Counseling by Telephone. Springfield, Ill.: Thomas, 1973.

(10) ALLGEYER, J. Using Groups in a Crisis-Oriented Outpatient Setting. Internat. J. Group Psychotherapy, 23 (1973), 217–22.

(11) WOLF, A. The Psychoanalysis of Groups. Am. J. Psychotherapy, 4 (1950), 525–58.

(12) ROSENBAUM, M. The Challenge of Group Psychoanalysis. Psychoanalysis, 1, No. 2 (1952), 42–58.

(13) PAPANEK, HELENE. Combined Group and Individual Therapy in Private Practice. Am. J. Psychotherapy, 8 (1954), 679–86.

(14) BOWERS, M. K., MULLAN, H., and BERKOWITZ, B. Observations on Suicide Occurring during Group Psychotherapy. Am. J. Psychotherapy, 13, No. 1 (January 1959), 93–106.

(15) KIBEL, H. A Group Member's Suicide: Treating Collective Trauma. Internat. J. Group Psychotherapy, 23 (1973), 42–53.

(16) ROSENTHAL, PAULINE. The Death of the Leader in Group Psychotherapy. Am. J. Orthopsychiat., 17 (1947), 266–77.

(17) WOLF, A. et al. Sexual Acting Out in Psychoanalysis of Groups. Internat. J. Group Psychotherapy, 4, No. 4 (1954), 369–80.

(18) FROMM-REICHMANN, F. Principles of Intensive Psychotherapy. Chicago: University of Chicago Press, 1950.

(19) DEMAREST, E. W., and TEICHER, A. Transference in Group Psychotherapy. Psychiatry, 17 (1954), 187–202.

(20) HOOVER, J. E. Let's Keep America Healthy (Guest Editorial). J.A.M.A., 144, No. 13 (November 25, 1950), 1094–95.

11　The Last Group Session: The Departure

Hugh Mullan
Max Rosenbaum

Of all the moments in the group treatment of patients, the moment of departure from the group is the most significant. The significance of this very last meeting is based upon (a) the patient's irrevocable choice and decision to leave, (b) the risk involved in this separation, and (c) the patient's willingness and ability to give up an environment that permits regressive activity in fantasy and to move to an environment that demands progressive activity in reality. The terminal period for a group member is difficult for all concerned, therapist and members alike, because this process causes an emergency in the group (see Chapter 10).

Separation Related to the Kind of Group Psychotherapy

Although a member has difficulty in leaving any kind of treatment group, he has the most difficulty in separating from the regressive-reconstructive kind. In this method he has been permitted such a degree of freedom to express himself in his own vernacular that it is difficult for him to contemplate leaving. The relationships that have been established are not unlike family ties, often being of equal strength and, indeed, less distorted. The patient's sense of individuality and of belonging have been nurtured and heightened, but as yet they have not been fully tested outside the treatment situation.

In group psychotherapies that are more *repressive* and *constructive*,

208

leave-taking is a simpler procedure. Here the ties have never been so deep, the duration of the treatment period has been shorter, and the goals have been less intense. These three factors allow the patient to leave more easily, for the therapeutic climate is less emotionally involving. However, even in the more regressive therapies there must be a stage of repression and construction as the patient contemplates leaving his group and then, finally, does so.

In the repressive types of group therapy, when a time limit is set upon the duration of therapy, leave-taking is a relatively simple affair. Setting a time limit may have certain procedural advantages, but it is not advocated. It denies the individual needs of the patient and also distracts him from more intense involvement with the therapist and other members, since he wonders, "Why get involved in this or with this person when the therapy will be over in six weeks?" Even more important, the ultimate decision to leave or to stay, which should be the patient's, resides with the therapist. Thus the member's achievement of a more certain responsibility is forever removed from him.

A patient leaves his therapy group in his own peculiar way. Any departure based upon the therapist's procedure—such as the time of vacation, or the moment of increasing fees—is to be considered untimely. Any leave-taking based upon the patient's new commitments outside of therapy is to be carefully questioned and analyzed. Noteworthy here are marriage, pregnancy, divorce, remarriage, shift in vocation, loss of position, and so forth. Although these significant happenings are perhaps related to emotional growth, the fact of their accomplishment is not a suitable indication that the moment for terminating therapy has arrived.

When he decides to leave, the patient must focus upon these emotional ties and experience the anxiety of severing these bonds once and for all. There can be no consideration by the leave-taking patient that should he desire or need to return that he *can* return to the group. The therapist must make this point abundantly clear. The patient must realize that his decision to leave, once made, is irrevocable.

Not all group psychoanalytic therapists consider termination final. They do not agree that the achievement of many therapeutic goals is assured only when and if the patient leaves the group on his own accord. Wolf states: "The departing patient may be advised that, should he at some time feel a recurrence of his neurotic disorder, he should feel free to consult with the therapist again, and if necessary, will be permitted to rejoin his group" (1).

During group sessions, for the patient who has decided to leave, it is indicated that there is no conceivable emergency that can warrant the return of the patient to the group. Of course, the group, after the patient's departure and with the addition of new members, becomes organically different, so that he would not return to the same group. The departing group member must be told that if returning to any therapy is contemplated, he should not leave at this time.

The Attainment of Goals: The Timing of Departure

A goal in group psychoanalytic therapy is the development of sufficient strength in the member's personality for him to be able to take responsibility for leave-taking after discussing the move with the other group members and the therapist. When does the patient leave? He usually leaves after two and one-half years of intensive group interaction. Technically, he leaves only after there is sufficient reduction in his transference relationships to his peers and to the therapist. This indicates that he no longer requires gratification from the maintaining of distorted group relationships. He has found that satisfaction can be achieved not only in the real (new and evolving) group relationships, but also in the real relationships in society's natural groupings, outside of treatment.

Many patients, upon introduction into the treatment group, express an intense loyalty to their parents. Later, they express hate and criticism for their parents' shortcomings. Still later, there is a recognition of what the parents did, and, finally, before departure, there is a new assessment. Parents are no longer seen as either good or bad but as adults who had, and still have, problems. There is a new meeting between the patient and his parents, one of mutual respect.

FALSE TERMINATION

False or nontherapeutic terminations occur in group psychoanalytic psychotherapy. They are *less* likely to be found in the regressive-reconstructive therapies where strong transference relationships have been established, which foster a truly workable cohesion. In addition, a careful individual preparation of the patient prior to group introduction prevents his too early departure because of his bond to the therapist.

False terminations are related to the emergence of repressed feelings, usually of a conflicting nature, within the personality of the one who leaves. Bross, in considering "deserters" from group psychotherapy, mentions five factors that prompt this action:

1. Feeling of inadequacy in a situation where others are better versed in psychotherapeutic dynamics: "I don't know what they are talking about."
2. Fear of loss of control over one's own irrational impulses: "What may I do to them?"

3. Fear of the unknown and the unpredictable as seen in the irrational behavior of the group: ""What will they do to me?"
4. Flight from one's own sexual drives and the fear of facing these in the presence of others: "I am ashamed, they will find out."
5. Flight from any situation repetitious of a transference phenomenon (2).

Terminations of this kind are characterized by (a) suddenness, (b) unexpectedness, (c) untimeliness, (d) irrationality, (e) superficiality of stated reason for leaving, and (f) unfavorable response by both the group and the therapist. "Out of the blue," toward the end of a session, a patient may state, "I am not coming back any more!" The other members, deeply involved with the one who makes this statement, are shocked by its abruptness and callousness. There seems to be no real reason for this leave-taking, and it is felt by the members to be "crazy." The stated reason for leaving, when it is expressed by the patient, contradicts everything that has been going on in the present session and in the ones immediately preceding. When the patient is more involved, and more emotional than ever before, the danger of too early termination sometimes occurs. The group members and the therapist should attempt to analyze this determination to leave and its accompanying behavior in the few remaining moments of the session. Sometimes the patient will fit his desire to leave the group into some social commitment that has never been discussed before. Often, he reaches for an excuse that in no way minimizes the hurt feelings of those he intends to leave behind. At this point, if the group psychotherapist can observe that the patient is not so much taking leave of the therapist and the group as he is taking leave of a part of himself that he is not yet strong enough to face, the situation is likely to come to a therapeutic conclusion. The patient may either stay or come back after a short absence, if the therapist does not respond as though the patient were actually terminating. The therapist should state that he will not cancel the patient, would like him to stay, feels that he can be helped and can be helpful to the others, and he should suggest that it is natural to get upset in group therapy. If the therapist feels hurt and responds in kind, the patient may leave permanently, only to seek help in another group or in individual therapy. A patient is not lost if he stays away, yet maintains contact with the group through any of its members. In this case, the therapist should let it be known that he is waiting for the patient to return to therapy. An opening in the group cannot be held indefinitely. A good practice is to suggest individual sessions if closeness to the therapist is considered essential at this moment of improper leaving.

THE GROUP'S AND THE THERAPIST'S ROLE IN MEMBER'S LEAVING

It is not sufficient for the patient alone to determine the time for his departure, and it is important for the group as a whole, and particularly the therapist, to be of the same mind. Readiness for and the moment of departure are the function of the entire interacting group.

It is good practice for the therapist to elucidate the group's opinion concerning the pending departure of a patient. This is distinctly different from individual therapy, where the therapist and patient decide between themselves when separation should occur. In the group the therapist attempts to discover the many feelings that each member has for the person who wants to leave. This procedure relates to the multiple transferences and the rational feelings of loss that each member and the therapist have for the departing patient.

The therapist is also called upon to state whether he thinks it is timely for a patient to leave. If the patient himself does not confront the therapist with this question, another group member surely will. The therapist should separate his own neurotic affect concerning the one who wishes to leave, because countertransference residuals may block a more valid perception of what the patient contemplates.

A patient may be induced to stay longer than necessary because of the needs of his group, of a member, or even of the therapist. There is no justification for prolonging therapy and for holding on to one who has grown sufficiently to warrant leaving. The therapist must face this possibility squarely, revealing to the group its existence or the chance of its presence. Or a patient may sometimes refuse to leave because of the weakness that he perceives in the group composition or in the personality of the therapist. Here the therapist must be alert and describe the situation by using dream and fantasy material to substantiate it, and he must indicate to the patient that termination is imminent. The introduction of new members is helpful in removing the hesitant patient who is staying for the sake of the group. As new patients enter, he sees that the group will continue and that there will be others to help after he has gone.

ENFORCED DEPARTURE

The therapist who conducts many groups may encounter a patient who must be told to leave his group. The most common problem of this kind is the very aggressive patient who endangers the therapeutic group process by indiscriminately acting out. Those who introduce psychopathic persons into their groups have to remove them if they exploit the other members.

Enforced departure of a member is determined by the therapist, with or without the sanction of the other members. Its purpose is to insure therapeutic interaction, followed by an analysis of this interaction. The continual usurpation of the therapeutic meeting for the egocentric needs of a single member, which serves only to gratify him, cannot be allowed. The therapist is solely responsible for preventing this by excluding this member.

The excluded member should be referred to another group whose composition is better able to tolerate him. If this is not feasible, he should be continued in individual therapy until the time comes when he will be more amenable to the group process. He may then reenter his old group or be introduced into a new one.

After a patient has been removed from his group, the therapist must allow for and encourage the group's expression of feelings concerning the incident, how it was handled, and so forth. The therapist should admit to his feelings of fear, if present, and to the fact that this action was for the departing patient and the other group members.

ADMINISTRATIVE DEPARTURE

In institutional settings, a patient's leave-taking may be determined by administrative need. In a psychiatric hospital a patient may be brought before staff to determine his fitness for discharge, or his hospital stay may be determined by an insurance or hospital policy that offers treatment for a limited time only.

Administrative separation, which does not help the patient or the group, can be handled in one of two ways. After discharge, the patient can be encouraged to return to his old (inpatient) group, or he can be referred to another (outpatient) group. If a decision is made to discharge a group patient, sufficient time should be allowed so that he and the other group members can express their feelings about the termination. Close cooperation and communication between the discharge board, the head of psychotherapeutic services, and the group psychotherapist will lessen the chance that the separation will be a harmful experience for the departing patient and for the remaining group members.

DEPARTURE OF THE THERAPIST

At times it becomes necessary for the therapist to leave his group. Therapists move from a community or leave a clinic for an appointment more to their liking. When the therapist has determined that he will leave, he ceases to introduce new patients into the group. Normal attrition will account for certain patient departures. Then, usually one month to six weeks before the departure date, the therapist tells the group members of his decision. If it has been arranged, he tells them that their needs have been considered and another group therapist has been appointed to conduct the group. Members should be allowed to make up their own minds about whether they wish to continue or to separate.

The therapist should point out to the group members that he is leaving for his own personal reasons and not because he wants to leave them. If he feels free enough, he explains his decision to move in more detail. He should elicit feelings from the members concerning the pending separation, and should analyze their reactions, referring them to earlier traumatic separations if there have been any. If practical, he may introduce the new therapist to the group.

In a highly mobile society, there are many lonely people. Among these lonely people, one is apt to find some group psychotherapists. Their loneliness is relieved by constant involvement in a psychotherapy group. These are the "experts about living" who are not "expert in living." On occasion, these group therapists make a departure from the group but maintain control. In one situation, a very controlling group therapist introduced a rather passive psychiatrist as her replacement. Of course, the group, which had become dependent upon her, rejected the ineffectual "parent." She (the controlling group therapist) went through a series of replacements, but did not appear to be able to find a new group leader. In fact, she did not want to leave the group and was sabotaging it rather than surrender her control.

A group therapist who replaces another group therapist should be clear as to what dynamics are at work. Sometimes his eagerness to work with the group obscures the fact that the previous group leader does not really want to leave. This fact must be shared with all concerned.

"HEALTHY" GROUP DEPENDENCY

Some patients remain in therapy groups for long periods of time. This suggests the development of group dependency. In the severely ill person, this clinging to his group is understandable and to be expected.

The therapist should suggest and promote group departure if he believes that the patient can successfully participate in his environment without the therapy group.

Group dependency does become a relatively healthy dynamic for those persons who, without their group, cannot function in society. To keep a person interested in his work and living outside a psychiatric hospital is a goal that some therapists believe to be a worthy one. Alcoholic patients require the therapeutic group environment for long periods in order to remain sober and become vocationally committed.

Goodbye

Should a patient continue with his group or should he leave? In the final analysis, only he can decide. The therapist and the others in the group should make clear what is being chosen and that the choice is *his*. Once made, the decision is irrevocable.

Fromm-Reichmann has noted:

No one living in this era and culture is expected either to be or to remain consistently free from any inklings of anxiety after the termination of treatment . . . but former patients should potentially be able, after treatment, to solve their conflicts and to spot and resolve their anxiety without the help of a psychiatrist (3, p. 190).

Help in the future cannot stem from an omnipotent father; it must come from the collective and cooperative effort of peers, the extended group—society and the culture.

References

(1) Wolf, A. The Advanced and Terminal Phases in Group Phychotherapy. The Development of Group Psychotherapy in Various Existing Settings. Proceedings, Second Annual Institute, American Group Psychotherapy Association, New York, January 22–23, 1958.

(2) Bross, Rachel. The "Deserter" in Group Therapy. Internat. J. Group Psychotherapy, 6, No. 4 (October 1956), 393–404.

(3) Fromm-Reichman, F. Principles of Intensive Psychotherapy. Chicago: University of Chicago Press, 1950.

III

ALTERNATIVE METHODS OF
GROUP PSYCHOTHERAPY

Introduction to Part III

Psychoanalysis emerged during the Victorian era. In many ways it was a therapy to deal with the conflicts that ensued because of the repressions that a Puritan culture demanded. Today we live in a hedonistic era. Many modern therapeutic approaches emphasize that the person is to express his impulses or feelings. Often the therapy is "physical." The psychoanalytic approach is more reflective, stressing insight.

The struggle between different therapeutic approaches is not as recent as the reader may believe. A bit of history is appropriate.

Otto Gross was one of the first German psychoanalysts. He was the only son of Hanns Gross, the Austrian criminologist, yet father and son were hostile toward one another. The father was a big man with a dominating personality. He was the epitome of Bismarck's Germany, which stood for nationalism. Otto Gross, the son, trained as a physician, neurologist, and psychiatrist, repudiated everything his father represented. The son rejected the authority of his father. He advocated sexual freedom and eroticism and was drawn to the Schwabing section of Munich, Germany—a great center for modern art where eroticism was valued. By 1900, Otto Gross became interested in psychoanalysis, and since he was charismatic, he soon attracted a group of followers.

Ernest Jones, the British psychoanalyst and biographer of Freud, met Otto Gross in Munich in 1908 and described him as "a romantic genius." In that same year, Freud believed Gross to be brilliant, but by the following year, 1909, he wrote that Gross' cocaine addiction and sexual excesses were inappropriate for a psychoanalyst. Since Otto Gross was extremely promiscuous and preached this approach to life, Freud believed that Gross was making a mockery of psychoanalysis and would lead people to identify Freud's teachings with Gross' anarchic approach to life.

Although Carl Jung was Otto Gross' analyst, it is claimed that he

218

received much from Gross—a kind of mutual analysis. Jung, in one of his books, expressed gratitude to Gross for what he had learned from him, but later he did not refer to him.

Gross believed in a sexual revolution, and stressed that "pleasure is what we should all strive for." The institution of marriage should be dissolved; he described monogamy as "submission to tyranny." He believed in an "orgiastic" approach to psychotherapy, and in psychoanalysts as proponents of revolution.

He evolved an approach based on Freud's psychoanalysis, but used Nietzsche's values. Many of his ideas were later incorporated in the writings of R. D. Laing and Timothy Leary. Gross' belief in eroticism can also be found in the writings of early philosophers of the Nazi movement in Germany—"joy is a way of life."

Otto Gross' influence upon his followers was enormous. He encouraged them to use drugs, to oppose family life overtly, and to be sexually promiscuous (although he described "promiscuity" as a term used by the bourgeoisie). He described this as "exploration of the self." Society was "sick and controlling." For a man to be truly free, he must explore his very depths, and this could only be done by experiencing erotic love of all kinds—heterosexual, homosexual, group sex, and so on.

In 1913 Hanns Gross, with the aid of Carl Jung, committed his son to a psychiatric hospital. Otto Gross escaped from the hospital and continued his activities, but he became so physically deteriorated that by 1920 he was hospitalized in Berlin, where he died soon after. Many of his ideas are to be found in the "new" psychotherapies which stress sexual fulfillment.

In the decade following Otto Gross' death, Wilhelm Reich began to write about his approach to psychoanalysis. There is nothing in Reich's writings to suggest that he knew Gross, but their ideas are remarkably similar, encompassing the importance of the political revolution and of sexual life, and the insistence that man return to basic roots found in the orgasmic experience.

Like those of Otto Gross, Reich's theories began to find favor in a period of societal upheaval and cultural change. With Gross, it was the period just after Bismarck's ideas lost favor in Germany when the nation began to question its values. With Reich, the entire American community after World War II and during the Vietnam catastrophe began to feel disoriented, estranged from familiar roots. Both men opposed the patriarchal and stressed a matriarchal culture.

An approach that has attracted a lot of attention is the Gestalt therapy approach of Frederick (Fritz) Perls, who was influenced by Wilhelm Reich, with whom he entered psychoanalysis in 1931 and 1932. In 1933 Perls participated in a seminar led by Reich. Perls was influenced by Reich's early work and by his stress on "muscular armor" and strong affective responses.

The therapies described in the following chapters are more instrumental, firmly rooted in a "here-and-now" approach. They are peripherally concerned with the "image of man." Of all the psychotherapies, the psychoanalytic approach is most directly concerned with this image — not just a "now" man, but one whose behavior represents a responsibility to the present, an awareness of the past and its traditions, and a hope for the future. He is both an emotional and a thinking person, faced with the problem of remaining true to himself and yet being part of the group.

It is possible that some of the methods presented in the next chapters reflect another aspect of the American culture that has been constantly pragmatic—the patient's insistence upon a quick result and restlessness with a more introspective approach. Also, some of the approaches presented appear to satisfy the needs of those individuals who may distrust professionals and who express a distrust of pure rationality.

While there are many professionals who look askance at what they perceive to be an attack upon scientific reason, there are many who would support an approach which questions over preoccupation with reason. Many therapists, in their desire for better outcomes, are willing to modify traditional methods. We are willing to support "new" methodologies which attempt to help large numbers of emotionally distressed people. Time and further research will assess the effectiveness of these alternative approaches.

Finally, there are those patients who are bored and distressed because the technology and pragmatism of our culture will not help them find answers to life. These people attempt to structure a society and find a therapy which they believe to be "older" and simpler. "Older," for them, refers back to the past, an idealization of a past where life appeared to be less complex. There is a longing for the simpler social structure which would ostensibly provide more happiness and less distress. This hope expresses itself in the desire for a simpler form of therapy.

12 Art Therapy and the Psychoanalytic Group

Hugh Mullan

Art Prepares Patients for Group Treatment

IT IS MY BELIEF that psychoanalytic groups can easily and dynamically be started by the use of art therapy in preliminary sessions. Further, it is our contention that under proper therapeutic circumstances, members by drawing, readily come together, quickly become involved in each other, and easily reveal themselves without the need for the others and the co-therapists to probe excessively and confront constantly.

A group begun in this fashion can continue as the definitive group, or it can be merely an intake or transitional group. In the latter case it functions as a reservoir of newly prepared and readied patients awaiting permanent assignment to specific analytic groups for prolonged therapy.

In any event it has been found that cohesion, the single most important ingredient in treatment group structure, is quickly established and maintained around the shared effort of members drawing. The group with this task, it seems reasonable to say, becomes homogeneous, in both its operation and in its goal as well. But, unlike other homogeneous treatment groups which have for their purpose the correction of a commonly held deficiency, usually by repression of it and by construction of a suitable defense, the one which focuses upon art production allows its members to create. Through this medium of drawing, patients open up emotionally, talk about very personal things, face solid blocks in their development, and acknowledge strengths as well as weaknesses in their personalities. In addi-

I am indebted to Joyce Tenneson Cohen, M.A., Assistant Head of the Northern Virginia Community College Photography Department, for her invaluable assistance in this experience and in its description.

tion, when art is the members' focus, nervousness and self-consciousness are considerably reduced.

This chapter is devoted to the art therapy method of beginning a psychoanalytic treatment group: the advantages and disadvantages of this method, the use of an art teacher as co-therapist, the diagnostic and therapeutic functions of the use of art, and in general the dynamics of this process.

Preparation for Entry into the Art Sessions

Our use of art is limited to the early sessions of group psychotherapy. The entire segment of art treatment, six two-hour sessions, therefore, becomes a preparatory period prior to a patient's placement in his final treatment group. The homogeneous aspect of drawing—that is, the task orientation of this portion of group treatment—allows patients to accept group introduction readily. Even though this is the case, careful preparation of the patient in individual sessions is still essential, but now the period of diadic interviews can be lessened considerably.

Preparatory individual sessions focus upon five necessary duties to be performed by the therapist: (1) the establishment of a diagnosis and prognosis; (2) the formation of a therapeutic bond (transference); (3) the confrontation of the patient with the idea of group therapy; (4) the reduction of resistance to group therapy; and (5) the orientation to group psychotherapy. However, when one uses art therapy as a preparatory period before definitive group placement all but the first task, that of diagnosis and prognosis, can be partly performed after group drawing sessions have started. *Thus, by using art therapy the whole period of individual preparation for an analytic group experience is shortened.*

The Function of Drawing in Preparing Patients

While it is true that the art productions of a circle of patients contribute to the therapist's diagnostic understanding of each one, this is not the primary purpose of this activity. The therapist, having previously had private sessions with each person, has already established a diagnosis. However, a patient's art productions, along with his fellow members' unrehearsed verbal responses, give the leader a chance, in this interactional situation, to check his original diagnostic impression. Many times it is confirmed, sometimes it must be modified, and infrequently it is to be completely altered.

To use art in the treatment group solely as a means of patient diagnosis would be non therapeutic, even if the patients were told that this was our purpose. This would be similar to using the patient's dreams, fantasies, and free associations only to diagnose his illness in a repetitive fashion. To use art as an occupational therapy alone would be equally nontherapeutic. In this instance we would be giving the group member a task, something to keep him busy, and we would expect a reasonable degree of competence to be exhibited in the finished product.

Art is used as a preparatory exercise in order to establish cohesion, cause the patients to relate to one another, define and identify for them their innate humanness, point out commonalities in their background, and bring conflicts into awareness. As a byproduct of this, transferences are activated, members are confronted with the idea of their permanent group, resistances are reduced, and a sense of well-being develops. Thus, the long period of individual preparation is shortened.

Generally, then, art work in group psychotherapy does describe each member's fantasy life, his rigidities, his ability to risk, his conscious and unconscious conflicts, his sexual identification, his view of life and of the cosmos, his perception of the human condition, his ability to participate, his degree of aloneness, and so forth. For example, take May's drawing "The Long Road" (Figure 1). Done in black and white, almost endless in its intent; regular, always the same; well paved, no persons, no scenery. The goal to be reached way up the road is a large red square with a red dot in it. Picked up by the group members immediately are the following characteristics exhibited by the drawing, all pertinent to May: "Your life contains many elements related to struggle." "You can work only by yourself." "You seem compulsive." "You're doing the same thing always." "Your life is always a struggle." "Your goal is at the end of the road." May is quite alone and can participate intellectually, but not in an affective fashion.

THE ART THERAPIST IS CHALLENGED TO BE SPONTANEOUS

Before the therapist applies art therapy to his treatment effort he must first of all develop, and then accept, his spontaneity. He must be aware that it plays a most decisive role in the process of growth and maturation of the art group members. (Naturally, we hold that the therapist's spontaneity is significant in all treatment endeavors.) Once the therapist acknowledges this, his group treatment, from structure to interpretation, is modified by a shift in his agenda, in his behavior, and in his concept of his professional role. This development in the therapist allows him to support the members' creative efforts and to blend this into past and present behaviors through affective interpretations.

One of us has pointed out that when the therapist sees himself less as a therapist and more as a person, a fundamental treatment relationship develops in the therapy group. "Therapist and patient become *being and*

Figure 1.   "The Long Road."

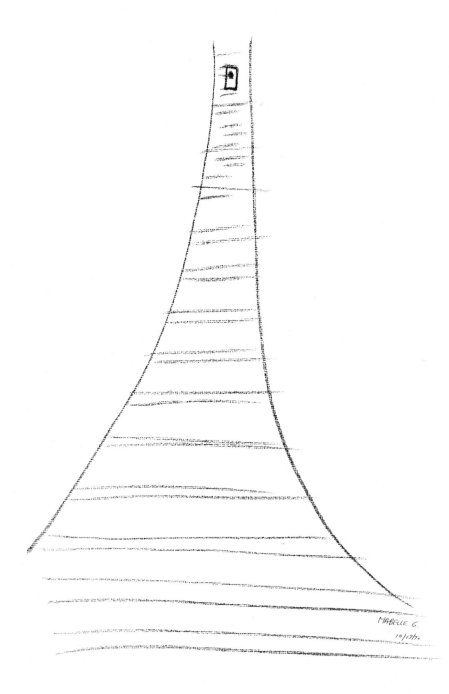

being; leader and led become *being and being;* male and female become *being and being;* the younger and the older become *being and being;* the infirm and the sturdy become *being and being;* the neurotic and the healthy become *being and being"* (1). In order, then, to use art therapy successfully in group treatment, the therapist must relinquish his overdetermined status of psychotherapist, do less role playing and become more of a person.

THE REQUIREMENT: NONTELEOLOGICAL DRAWING

Free and self-acting therapists, in contrast to rigid and formal ones, promote the necessary creative atmosphere where patients can draw without inhibition. In a paper written in 1956 I emphasized the significance in mental health of nonteleological behavior—that is, thinking, feeling, and acting which do not have a carefully-thought-out purpose. In this article it was suggested that "in order for an act to be nonteleological, its causality, meaning and purpose can only be reflected upon and sought retrospectively. If these are subjectively known before the act has passed, it is necessarily teleological" (2). We hold that if art is to be used in preparatory sessions it must be introduced and used without coercion. Patients, therefore, are to be given the materials but at the same time told to use them or not, or to use them in any way that they see fit. The ideal situation would be to have the materials present and make no comment about them whatsoever, and still have them employed in any way the group member chooses.

Spontaneous, free behavior—that is, behavior which is nonteleological —is, we believe, all-important in the healthy personality development of the child. Similarly, for patients in psychoanalytic groups we see that uncompelled, free activity is of singular importance in both the regressive and reconstructive phases of treatment. Group members, in their permanent groups, are therefore encouraged to find their own level of regressed behavior, to transfer on to the therapist and their peers whatever they will and in amounts individually determined, and then to reconstruct their personalities by their own trials and errors, at their own pace.

Our requirement that the use of art be nonteleological in the preparatory group, rather than that its use be an experience in learning, is consistent with our system of treatment in general. Drawing for the beginning patient is a further means for him to express himself. In a fashion similar to his words, emotions, and physical behavior, drawing gives him a chance to communicate in a still more holistic manner. In addition, drawing in a group calls upon the person to respond not only to his own work, but to the other members' as well. Thus, an interaction occurs which is longitudinal as well as cross-sectional: the patients respond to each other's unconscious productions, to each other's childhood traumas and conflicts, to each other's parents, and, in addition, to each other in the ongoing group process *in the present.* Naumberg, from the standpoint of an individual therapist, states the nature and purpose of art in treatment in even more inclusive terms:

> The process of dynamically oriented art therapy is based on the recognition that man's fundamental thoughts and feelings are derived from the unconscious and often reach expression in images rather than in words. By means of pictorial projection, art therapy encourages a method of symbolic communication between patient and therapist. Its images may, as in psychoanalytic procedures, also deal with the data of dreams, phantasies, daydreams, fears, conflicts and childhood memories. The techniques of art therapy are based on the knowledge that every individual, whether trained or untrained in art, has a latent capacity to project his inner conflicts into visual form. As patients picture such inner experiences, they frequently become more verbally articulate. Through the use of graphic or plastic expression, those who originally blocked in speech often begin to verbalize in order to explain their art productions (3).

Practicalities of the Art Method

When art preparatory sessions are used, the therapist, after making his diagnosis and determining suitability for group treatment, suggests to the patient that he enter the art group. Specific techniques to ready the patient for this experience center around reassurance concerning his drawing ability. The fact that the group is task oriented, a work group, with an understood purpose in mind, allows the patient to make this step although at this point he is not ready for his permanent group. A prospective member is not told how to behave once in the art group. He can be told that drawing will "free him up," and will be helpful to him and to the group. The resistance encountered when transferring the patient from individual sessions to his intensive psychoanalytic group is not met when the therapist proposes the less intensive, art preparatory group of short duration.

The therapist who brings the preparatory group together by focusing upon the art production of its members, soon finds that he has a pool of prepared patients who can easily be transferred to other groups for the long haul of group psychoanalytic treatment. However, as this is one's purpose, at the outset it is necessary to let the art group patients know the temporary nature of their group. When the therapist does not make the temporary nature of the art group known, it causes painful feelings when members must separate after six sessions. Mutual drawing stimulates such strong ties that it becomes exceedingly difficult for members, who are not warned beforehand, to leave one another at a later date. The closeness that members develop in the art sessions is not transient. A patient, long after assigned to his permanent group, will continue to remember another's name, his prominent characteristics, and distinctive features in his drawings.

THE USE OF A CO-THERAPIST FROM ANOTHER DISCIPLINE

The art group therapy described in this chapter can be enhanced by a co-therapist from the discipline of education. Co- or multiple * treatment forms employing two mental health specialists are felt by most to be advantageous, suggesting that two heads (and two hearts, for that matter) are better than one (4, 5). There is a further gain in the use of an artist-teacher as co-leader, for by doing this we support the patients' fragile self-esteem. A teacher who is a co-therapist is a person whose background and training is somewhat similar to the patients', *and vastly different from the therapist's*. Because of this, the patients tend to see the co-therapist as their advocate. This feeling is reinforced when the co-therapist is untrained in dynamic psychology, when she experiences the members as potentially creative, and when she sympathetically displays knowledge and understanding about their task (drawing).

If we observe the group for a moment with two leaders from different disciplines, we see a group divided in form and purpose. It becomes a *basic assumption group*, on the one hand, with no clear end in sight and led by a mental health specialist while, on the other hand, it is a short-term *work group*, with drawing its principal task and co-led by an artist-teacher. We believe that the benefits to be derived from this fusion stem from the characteristics of these two enterprises. Turquet states, in referring to task oriented groups, the following: "The sophisticated work group is a group called into being for a predetermined, clearly defined primary task which has been openly accepted, at least at the conscious level, by its members and at which, again consciously, they have agreed to work" (6). Contrast this to Hartman and Gibbard's description of Bion's basic assumption group, quoted in part as follows:

> Bion (1959) has proposed that at various times in a group's life all of its members share a common assumption about the group—an assumption that has little basis in fact, obstructs the purpose for which the group meets, and springs from deep emotional sources. These unverbalized and largely unconscious "basic assumptions"—of "dependency," "fight/flight," or "pairing"—stand in the way of the more rational problem-solving agenda of the "work group" (7).

Paradoxically, it is the confusion in the leaders' methods and purposes, and again in the patients' double response to work and to therapy, that is

---

* The term "multiple therapy," first used by Whitaker and Malone, suggests that the two therapists are of equal therapeutic stature and that their mutuality is a prime dynamic in the treatment process (5).

the vantage ground in the preparatory stage. Patients find it easier to enter a work (art) group than a basic assumption (therapy) group. Once in the art group, however, it is a simple task for the therapists to continue to ready the patients for the more intensive experience in the near future.

The use of a co-therapist from a different field causes an occasional patient anxiety. This group member initially questions the co-therapist's purpose while at the same time resisting her presence.* This early opposition seems to be directed toward the status of the co-therapist as artist-teacher. But, later, the response focuses upon the fact that the co-therapist is a woman. For example, Joan's concern at the very first meeting of the art segment was the female art therapist. Joan, who had a very close relationship to the male therapist, asked him, "What can I draw?" He answered, "Anything that you want." Joan then started to draw and for thirty-five minutes worked away quietly. The result (see Figure 2) was her conception of the art therapist.

Figure 2.   "The Woman Therapist."

---

* Maximum therapeutic value occurs when the multiple therapists are of the opposite sex.

Questions about the art "therapist"—for example, why an artist or teacher and not a mental health specialist—must be answered frankly. The inquiring patients are told that an art teacher describes the materials, assists when called upon by patients, and suggests methods which allow for free drawing. The art therapist's role, however, is vastly different from that of the usual teacher, even though viewed as a teacher by the group. Both therapists are mainly interested in the creative style which characterizes each person; through the art therapist the patient unearths and expresses his creation, and through the therapist the patient acknowledges and uses this creation.

Method: An Outline of Six Art Sessions

The outline below indicates the time allotment and the kinds of activities in preparatory art sessions. The sessions are not to be rigid and should have a flowing quality; some members may be engaged in one activity while others are caught up in an earlier one and others are reaching ahead to a later one. Thus, the duration of actual drawing as compared to the segment devoted to reflection and response is different in each session, in each group, and with each member. Patient reflection and members' and therapists' response is a time of growing awareness about the patient, involving establishment of a close and affective tie.

Session No.	Time	Activity	Time	Activity
1	45 mins.	Free Drawing	75 mins.	Patient reflection, members' and therapists' response
2	45 mins.	Free Drawing	75 mins.	Same
3	45 mins.	Focused Drawing: "Birth"	75 mins.	Same
4	45 mins.	Focused Drawing: "Intercourse"	75 mins.	Same
5	45 mins.	Focused Drawing: "Death"	75 mins.	Same, and discussion of selection for definitive group
6	60 mins.	Focused Drawing: "Collective Mural"	60 mins.	Same, and assignment to definitive group

While the beginning drawings, both in manner and content are left up to the individual group member after the second period and for the next three, the content is suggested. At the start of sessions three, four, and five the therapists propose that the members focus their drawing on "birth," "intercourse," and "death." The final session, the sixth, is devoted to drawing a collective mural.

It is not unusual for the patients, sometimes seriously and sometimes in jest, to ask the therapists to draw too. The request must be taken seriously but, even though strongly inclined to draw, the therapists must refrain. Should the therapists draw, mistakenly, the focus would be upon them rather than upon the patients who require attention, support, and interpretive activity. When therapists draw, they remove themselves from the circle of patients and patients take second place, ignore themselves and each other, and, in general, resist the treatment process. In addition, it is never recommended that the art therapist draw because her technique and talent sets an example "hard to follow," and one difficult to compete with. This intrusion is noxious to the treatment process.

The First Two Sessions: Free Drawing

The first two sessions are set apart for seven to nine patients to draw freely. The therapists keep their suggestions to a minimum. The instructions are simple: "Draw anything and any way that you want." "Take about an hour's time and then we will talk about what you and the others feel about what has been drawn." The atmosphere is relaxed in these sessions devoted to art. Shifting seats and positions is common at first, to get better light or to arrange one's pad. Almost immediately, the therapist feels a difference in the art group as compared to one not so constituted. For example, in a *deeply* involved treatment group of long standing, the therapist feels central with attention focused upon him. But in this situation, as the patients turn to their tasks, their focus, at least for a time, is removed from the therapist. The members' thoughts seem to be directed toward their innermost beings and toward the tasks at hand. (The therapist's feeling of isolation in this setting is similar to that of many leaders conducting homogeneous groups, that is, alcohol treatment groups.)

As we have pointed out, the main objective of the therapists is to have the assembled patients draw easily and without inhibition, to assume this task with almost no direction from the leaders, to risk putting something on the paper which may be different from what is intended, and to allow others to look at it both during its drawing and after its completion.

A group formed in this manner, that is, around the element of drawing, comes together with little resistance. Patients meeting on the very first day are already aware that they will have the opportunity to draw. On entering the group room their attention is divided between observing the art therapist and the other members and inspecting the pastels and pad. They seem to want to get down to work. Brief introductions can be made. Especially is it important to introduce the unknown therapist, telling briefly the nature of her purpose. The two therapists, although from different disciplines, attempt to be of equal status and of identical value to the members: they make independent observations, suggestions, interpretations; they answer patients' questions openly and frankly about the immediate experience; and they admit to feeling awkward, upset, nervous, tense, and so forth, *if in fact they feel this way.* However, in the area of their personal lives and histories, they remain an enigma to the patients. Thus, in psychoanalytic fashion, the patients are required to fantasize about the two therapists and it is just this fantasy, if it can be encouraged, that many of the drawings reflect. (See Figure 2, "The Woman Therapist.")

During the first two sessions, particularly in the very first, the members become wrapped up in their drawing books, with little observation of the others' work and almost no group conversation unless it is promoted by the therapists. The original therapist very cautiously begins to introduce his earlier understanding of each patient. For example, he might say, "You see, Tom, your fears are not being realized. It is quite easy to just draw as Joyce (the art therapist) suggests. Last week you were so worried. Did you have any dreams since that last session with me that might tell us why you were so worried about these drawing sessions?" In this manner the therapist brings in much more of each patient, something of his previous therapeutic experience, of his unconscious functioning, and so forth. However, the therapist is careful not to bring into the art session *content* that would undo the confidential nature of their early relation. Usually this kind of questioning-observation is so low key that the other members, although hearing the conversation, do not look up from their tasks.

A good rule is to pay attention to comments made by patients immediately. To the statement often heard, "I told you I couldn't draw," the therapist might say, "You don't have to. What you are doing is *you*, and this is all that counts." The co-therapist, if she is a teacher, can intervene here and restate the therapist's position: "It's not necessary to have any ability at all. Just do what is natural. We are not judging your ability. There are no marks and absolutely no comparisons. You can't really make a mistake. I like being here with you, the end product does not alter my liking you at all." It is in this vein that the two therapists can reduce the patients' apprehensions, encouraging them at the same time to continue without inhibitions.

It is not necessary to explain or describe the process of art therapy. Questions or members' observations about drawing, however, can be answered or responded to. If, for example, Ruth complains that drawing is work, the therapist might say, "Too bad it can't be play." Or, to the query, "Why do we have to do this?" the therapist might state, "Yes, why?" If the therapist observes a change in Tom he might state, "Tom, you certainly seem more 'with it' today. Your colors stand out and can be seen. They seem to be a part of your mood. I like this." If an anxious patient directs a question at the leader, "Is it true that you can tell all about me from this drawing?" a response might be, "No, but with your help perhaps we can untangle some things that are troubling you." The perfectionistic group member asks, "Can you see any change in me from last week to this week by looking at my drawings?" The therapist must answer accurately. "Yes, I think your second drawing is very different from your first. It has a dream-like quality. Did you have a dream that you can remember? Why not share it with us?"

When the art therapist is a teacher her method, if authoritarian, must be dropped. Even the original therapist, trained in dynamic psychology, tends to become dogmatic when the group members have a task to perform. The art therapist has a position both advantageous and disadvantageous. Advantageous because she does not consider the members as patients, and so is not biased by their diagnoses and prognoses. However, her position is disadvantageous because she has had no previous history-gathering period with members and, therefore, has no past ("in depth") knowledge of them. In this setting, then, the purposes of preparation are best served when the art therapist enters the group "cold," with no briefing whatsoever, on a "here-and-now" basis. Having no psychological understandings as to why the patients are in the group and behave the way that they do, the art therapist, in contrast to the original therapist, expects something quite different from them. The art therapist observes, interacts, and handles the group members while asking them to draw and to draw spontaneously. Reality oriented, her expectations in the treatment group are somewhat similar to those in the classroom.

Properly matched group co-therapists, one from psychology or psychiatry and one from art or art teaching, offer to the circle of patients a beneficial composite of understanding and interpretative activity. The former operates in the area of hidden motivations, unconscious conflicts and strivings based upon reported historical events both real and imagined. The latter operates in the area of present feelings and activities, in the task (drawing) and in its accomplishment, in the struggle with technique and with the need for acceptance and approval. However, the art therapist must quickly learn the names of each patient and respond to them individually. Quickly, bits of their history, including their position in their families, their relational and sexual activities, and, most important, the depth and manner in which each member responds to the original therapist, must be observed by her. Later, the quality and intensity of this tie to the therapist is brought to bear on the interpretations of the drawings.

In the two drawings which follow, done in the first two sessions, the two patients involved describe their defensive structures. In Figure 3, Faith worked with great care and persistency for the allotted period and more to present the series "Houses, Bridges, and Piers" in black and white. She hardly glanced at anyone and did not speak until her work was complete. Faith, a professional photographer, stated that she had just returned from

Figure 3.   "Houses, Bridges, and Piers."

Figure 4. "Secure Man Looking Out Window"

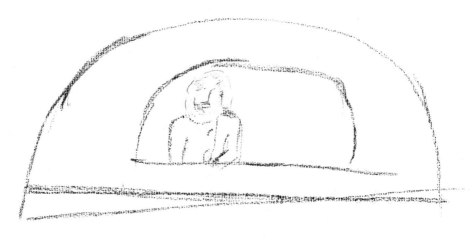

an assignment where she attempted to concentrate on the geometrical design of structures which border on the sea.

It takes little imagination and no great intuition to identify Faith's struggle in life. The compartmental design, its concreteness, its repetitive quality, along with her preferences for black and white, suggest a rigid character structure, hemmed in and divided. The group members noticed and responded with concern and question to this use of black on white only, to the stylized and rigid quality of her work. Some pointed out to her that her drawing lacked people, color, activity, and so forth. Others contrasted her drawing to the way she appeared in our group, pointing out striking inconsistencies. For example, it was noted that she dressed as if she were a Saks Fifth Avenue model, modeling a sports outfit, different each time. Subtly at first, and then directly, Faith was confronted with pertinent observations and, especially, contradictions. Members wanted to know if her dress represented an attempt to compensate, to neutralize, or to cover up something. An inner questioning began to stir Faith; she became anxious and defensive.

Joe's early drawings, Figure 4 and Figure 5 of this series, indicate where he is in life and how he considers himself to be. Joe, in Figure 4, seems to seek a simpler life, in which he would be secure and cared for. Members plied him with questions as to why he was in group treatment and his answers, paraphrased, were of two kinds: "My doctor thought it would help" and "I have many problems related to my stomach."

At a later time, another of Joe's drawings, Figure 5, seems to describe more accurately why he is in treatment:

Here group members indicated the destructive quality of this drawing and how in content and tone it was the opposite of the "Contented Dog," the earlier drawing. Someone suggested that Joe was afraid that he would

Figure 5. "Autos Colliding and Parts."

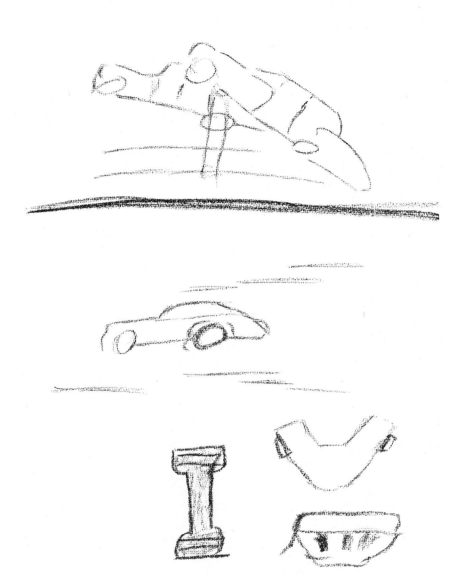

have an accident, did he believe that he was uncontrollable? Another wanted to know which car was his? And why weren't there drivers in the car? The contrast between Joe's two drawings (as well as others not illustrated here) became the foci of questions and discussions. Naturally, group cohesion is established and maintained when the person ruminates out loud about his work and the other members and the therapists respond with question, interest, and emotion.

THIRD, FOURTH, AND FIFTH SESSIONS: FOCUSED DRAWING

The following is an instruction sheet:

ART GROUP THERAPY

Third Session   Date

Describe through your drawing the three central biological events of our existence:

Death

Birth

Intercourse

DISCUSSION: Group Interpretation

In describing the common emergencies which confront both patients and therapists, I have suggested, "The therapist's function is to make the lines of communication open [between therapist and patient] so that authenticity is audible and meaningful to both. He is assisted in this as he [the therapist] becomes concerned with those biological events of (a) birth, (b) intercourse, and (c) death, which are irrefutable common experiences in the life of everyone (1). These central human experiences have in their wake anxiety" (7).

When art sessions are preparatory to psychoanalytical group therapy, it is necessary to ready patients for their definitive groups in six weeks. Certain steps must be taken by the therapists to increase the tempo and depth of interaction. Therefore, during the third, fourth, and fifth periods the therapists suggest that members focus upon birth, intercourse, and death in any order they choose. During these three periods, to be sure, there is a reversal from our previously held position: "Draw anything you like." Now we suggest, "Be immersed in this event (death, birth, intercourse), what it means to you and your experience with it, and draw." However, even with this directive, which does indeed limit, the therapists make no further suggestion as to procedure. Responses and questions such as "Which do you want first?", "I don't want to think about death," "You mean my birth or birth in general?", or "I have never seen a birth so I can't draw, can I?" are handled sympathetically, with interest and support.

As the patient draws "birth," he is confronted with his own presence and the debt that he owes his parents. Ignoring this or overstating it is easily picked up by the fellow members and therapists. The often-heard remark "I didn't choose to be born," as the disturbed patient struggles with his pastels, opens up a dark and gloomy aspect of the patient's existence, his anger toward his parents, his fundamental belief that he is not responsible for his *own* behavior, and so forth. Naturally, the therapists note this significant disclosure. However, at this time, before placement in his definitive group, the therapists refrain from a detailed probing. Later, when patient and therapist are securely ensconced in the permanent group, the statement "I didn't choose to be born" is used as the opening wedge to face the patient with his despair.

Jennifer, a mother and grandmother, is older than the usual group members. In her drawing, Figure 6, she describes birth as a usual and painless event. There is confusion, however, between the mother who is giving birth and the same mother who is very childlike and who could almost be the infant. This discrepancy was pointed out to her by a member who said, "Who is being born, you or your child?" Fruitful discussion followed, with the patient's naïveté becoming the focus of our attention.

Figure 6. "Child Mother."

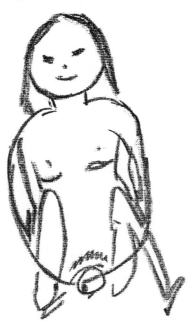

As for the requirement to draw intercourse, group members handle this task in a variety of ways. Two extremes are noted in Figure 7 and Figure 8. As sexual intercourse is the closest of all interpersonal events, a description of this act and in this case a drawing, will contain many clues as to the self-image of the group member, his concerns and fears about sex, and his method of relating to the opposite sex.

Louise, in the following picture, Figure 7, obviously suggests that the woman is higher placed than the man and that the sexual contact is at a distance and perhaps mostly for the man's benefit:

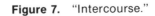

Figure 7. "Intercourse."

Both participants seem to be aware of a force outside of themselves to which they are overattentive. In their postures and facial expressions, they demonstrate some defiance of this outside authority. The man seems more interested in his sexual pleasure than does the woman, and he seems more intent on gaining satisfaction for himself than in sharing it with the woman. All of these perceptions, paraphrased here, were originally offered by Louise's peers in the art group. Thus, a drawing of intercourse opens up the much larger area of human relatedness, male and female differences, idealized self-images, creativity, authority, and so forth. Again, the value of drawing is not only for the one who draws but, as it becomes the production of the entire group, the members and therapists giving their impressions and feelings, its value extends to the entire Gestalt.

Peggy's drawing of intercourse (Figure 8) contrasts sharply with

Figure 8. "Intercourse."

Louise's. While drawing this Peggy became very quiet and intense, being carried away with her task and with her innermost thoughts and feelings. Someone told her later during the discussion period, "You seemed so intent, so serious, you weren't with us."

In this drawing, the sexual act is portrayed abstractly. It is seen as flowing, equal, rhythmic, and so forth. The participants, who seem inseparable, are lost in their sexual gratifications. There is the loss of identity with a merging of the two.

In a psychotherapy which treasures life and freedom, not only do we focus upon birth and intercourse, but upon death as well. Death, then, because of its crucial significance, is a proper area to dwell upon in therapy. Taking our cue from the existentialists, we note that patients are prone to give up ordinary insignificant pursuits, break with convention and habit, and become self-propelling and creative when confronted with their finite state. In the art section of group treatment, we merely get an indication of each patient's conflict about death and how he handles it. Later, these disclosures form the content of further analytic work in the definitive group.

Peggy (see Figure 8, "Intercourse") sat for a long time pondering death. The result, realized in less than a minute after she began her scribble, is reproduced in Figure 9.

Peggy's effort indicates that rumination about death is foreign to her, that this activity causes her some distress, and that perhaps she does not want to be reminded of her finiteness. The members questioned Peggy, wanting to know why she was so quick to complete her "death" drawing. Peggy's reply came quickly and with tears. She told the group that her mother had recently been found to have cancer and that, although the treatment had been started early, neither her mother nor anyone else was taking the illness lightly. It made it difficult, if not impossible, to go home, and yet Peggy felt a strong need to reach her mother in some way before she died. Thus, in Peggy's situation the potential loss of her mother was expressed through her drawing. This in turn allowed Peggy, with the help and *presence* of her group, to face the loss of a parent, to consider meeting her mother in a brand new manner, and to try to do something about her own life before time would run out for her too.

From the therapists' observations concerning the interactions caused by the "death," "birth," and "intercourse" drawings, plus indications of positive transference, commitment to treatment, regular attendance, and so forth, they begin to determine a patient's readiness to enter a particular psychoanalytic treatment group. Naturally, certain practical considerations such as time of group meeting and frequency and duration of each session play a part in selecting not only the patient for a proper group, but a proper group for the patient. From the third to the seventh session, then, the therapists consider definitive group placement for the members of the art group. When, as frequently occurs, members express the desire to continue as a unit, the therapists respond that "this was not the agreement" and that group treatment can best be realized in a specific group where members have been selected for a variety of reasons. The therapists have noted conflict areas in each patient, and they are also aware of the potential support or confrontation capability of each continuous long-standing group. Take, for example, Edward. In his drawing "Mother and Father," Figure 10, he reveals to the therapists and group members an entire sphere of deep-seated conflict: the sexual and reproductive areas. The

Figure 9. "Death."

therapists noted, too, the gingerly and carefully sensitive way in which Edward's peers responded to the drawing and to its obvious message.

Taking all of this into consideration and, in addition, Edward's general behavior in the group, the therapists selected as Edward's definitive group one whose membership would support him for a long time before getting him to face up to his many and deep-seated difficulties. In all drawings produced by each patient during the art treatment segment, the therapists

Figure 10.   "Mother and Father."

are being told of the patient's readiness (or lack of readiness) to enter the highly charged, interactional group, and perhaps which group to enter. Drawings depicting intercourse and death are most relevant to the therapists' decision.

THE COLLECTIVE MURAL: SEARCH FOR "THE DESIGNER"

The last period of the art treatment segment, lasting two hours, is again task directed; members are told what to do. However, rather than suggesting content, the therapists now suggest method. The group members are instructed to draw a mural, to spend an hour on it, and then to discuss the project.

As this is the sixth session, members know one another and are to a degree spontaneous, whereas earlier, say in the first or second session, this was not the case. However, even so, on being given a seemingly simple task, they do not readily translate this into action. Minutes of the last period slip by as members search among themselves for a leader, while at the same time they halfheartedly plan a joint drawing.

In one such session thirty minutes elapsed as the frustrated members sought a design and "grand designer." As this was not forthcoming, and perhaps for other reasons also, some members hesitated to participate, while one refused to draw at all. Naturally, these preparatory deliberations tell much about each person's ability to lead, risk, cooperate, and so forth. Once again the therapist is given many clues as to how each person will behave after placement in his definitive group. If a decision has been pending about proper permanent group placement, the manner in which the patient faces this task, his participant drawing, its content, and the discussion which follows all aid the therapist in proper group placement.

Conclusion

In both the private and clinic practice of group psychotherapy, patients can be pooled in art groups for an indefinite period while awaiting assignment to open-ended, permanent analytic treatment groups. The system outlined in this chapter is easily modified to meet the needs of most office and clinic regimens, and yet the patients may benefit while awaiting their definitive placement.

The use of art therapy allows the clinic or practitioner the opportunity to place patients in groups quickly, thereby offering group therapy almost immediately while cutting waiting lists to zero. Thus, art can become the focus of an intake group.

Art therapy sessions are adjunctive to the preparatory phase reducing the time of preparation, thus saving both patient treatment time and therapist hours. In addition, the competent group leader, while observing and responding to the patients, can more accurately place each patient at the proper moment in his permanent treatment group.

The selection of an art therapist from the ranks of educators is beneficial to the patients. The group, through this device, becomes partly task oriented, thus allowing the members to move more gradually into a total therapeutic ambience, the definitive treatment group. A spinoff from this procedure can easily be the training of beginners in the group method.

References

(1) MULLAN, H. Status Denial in Group Psychoanalysis. J. Nerv. & Ment. Dis., 122 (1955), 345–52.
(2) MULLAN, H. The Nonteleological in Dreams in Group Psychotherapy. J. Hillside Hosp., 5 (1956), 480–87.
(3) NAUMBURG, M. Dynamically Oriented Art Therapy: Its Principles and Practice. New York: Grune and Stratton, 1966.
(4) MULLAN, H., and SANGIULIANO, I. The Therapist's Contribution to the Treatment Process: His Person, Transactions, and Treatment Methods. Springfield, Ill.: Thomas, 1964.

(5) WHITAKER, C., and MALONE, T. The Roots of Psychotherapy. New York: Blakiston, 1953.

(6) GIBBARD, G., HARTMAN, J., and MANN, R. (eds.). Analysis of Groups: Contributions to Theory, Research, and Practice. San Francisco: Jossey-Bass, 1974.

(7) MULLAN, H., and SANGIULIANO, I. The Discovery of Existential Components Inherent in Contemporary Psychotherapy. J. Exist. Psychiat., 1 (1960), 331–45.

13 Core-Energetic Processes in Group Therapy

John C. Pierrakos

The Principle of Mutuality

"No MAN IS AN ISLAND," John Donne wrote, "complete unto himself."
Human beings harvest their highest individual fulfillment in relationships
with other human beings. The person evolves from within outward, ra-
diating outward, according to the principle of mutuality: interaction between his parts and between them and the parts of another person.

Mutuality means that there is a fusion of different aspects of people in
a comprehensive whole. They open toward each other, creating a new
entity in the incorporation and contact. An idea, according to the principle of mutuality, must be followed and focused on with the intention of
executing it—and execution requires conscious and persistent effort. Creation, on the one hand, and execution, on the other, must synthesize for
inspiration to bear fruit. Both must be present for creative living. The balance between these two factors is the mutual pool existing in the human
relationship—the balance, for instance, in an exchange of love. Mutuality
is a movement toward unification.

For mutuality to take place, there must be an expansive movement
from each person toward the other, two "yes" currents approaching one
another, and there must be receptivity on both sides for the currents to
fuse. The ability to sustain increasing pleasure and a richer life has to be
obtained gradually through mutuality. The capacity to develop and to
tolerate more pleasure, to become integrated as a whole person depends
upon saying yes when yes is offered. In actuality, many times we say "no"
to the yes of another, forcing the other person to close up, so that when we

open up, he says no to our yes. This puts us in a hellish cycle of negation.

There are cultural and historical reasons behind every no to pleasure, expansion, and growth. Society, beginning with parents, impose restraints on the person. Authorities such as organized religion forbid what they perceive as sin or wrongdoing. At bottom, the human habitat requires people to act or not act in certain ways they want or need. Often these restrictions are legitimate, if not necessary, and the person must fluctuate between opening to pleasure and withdrawing from it.

But many aspects of external reality bind the human being unnaturally. The child who experiences capricious constraints, cruelty, or any other abuse of his innate dignity knows this at the core of his being. The lesson is digested that certainly the negative emotions—and perhaps even the positive ones—cannot be expressed freely without punishment. To use Sigmund Freud's description, the mind internalizes the lesson, and the threat of self-punishment may reach such proportions as to force the person to deny that he even has negative *feelings*.

Wilhelm Reich, the creator of the basic bioenergetic concepts, saw the internalization process in terms of the whole organism rather than the mind alone. It was Reich's seminal perception that the human being is a unified energy system rather than a composite of psyche and soma, and that when the person denies his primal emotions—whether positive or negative—his energy flow is blocked. Blocks distort the whole of the person's functioning, and they reveal themselves not just in the way the suffering one feels and looks at life, but in how he holds his body and moves. The therapeutic techniques developed by Reich and later by bioenergists, particularly Dr. Alexander Lowen and myself, focus on removing these blocks to allow "the living substance [to] express itself in the way that is natural to life," as Reich said.

Many years ago, I discovered that I could see—see with my physical eyes—the energy of living things in what are called auras. The *aura* is pure energy that emanates from an organism into its surroundings in something of the same way that heat radiates from a stove or perfume rises from a flower. Each kind of living thing has its own characteristic aura formations that vary according to the state of the organism: rest or excitement, sickness or health. The human aura furnishes essential diagnostic information through its rate of pulsation, colors, and extension from the body. It is my conviction that many people could be trained to perceive these energy envelopes, and in fact a Russian process called Kirlian photography seems to record parallel effects.

The auras of patients have confirmed and added to the invaluable concepts of bioenergetic analysis. As Reich discovered, when a person is not aware of his negative primal emotions and rejects his potential for destructiveness, hatred, and rage, he traps a great amount of energy in that denial. His energy slows down, in a sense thickens, stagnates, and then freezes. But that isn't all. Emotions are made up in one yarn, for they are moving energy currents. So blocking negativity also blocks the positive primal emotions: faith, compassion, joy in others' existence—love.

Love is the impulse behind the principle of mutuality—within a person as between people—and it rises from the innermost being of the organism, which I call the *core*. This word represents an essential concept behind my vision of the human person, and shapes my approaches to individual and group therapy. It is a convenient but evocative acronym: *center of right energy*. "Right" does not imply a moral judgment; it means direct energy, energy flowing as an unobstructed river of life.

One other concept makes a major impress on the methodology of core therapy. It is that the essential energy in the human being perceives itself, and that this power of knowing is consciousness. The core process, the flow of life from and to the center, creates as well as comprehends. *Consciousness* in this sense means not only the intellectual functions of assimilating, synthesizing, and analyzing internal and external events. It means the capacity to intuit, innovate, and know the truth about one's state.

Most people rarely touch the nucleus, the core of their inner being. Why? Because a great number of emotions are blocked. As a result, the feelings—the person's perceptions of his emotions—are deadened. When feelings are not felt through many successive years, a paralysis develops in the person, a dullness, a "laziness." This is caused by fear, no longer the direct fear of pain as suffered by the child, but *fear of that fear*. The fear of fear becomes a habit and then a pattern, miring the person in slowed, viscous energy.

The principle of mutuality can't operate where there is fear of fear. And as many schools of psychiatric treatment have discovered, explaining the divisive emotions is often not enough to integrate the person, either in himself or with others. Core therapy works to tap energy as the ultimate healing agent. It sees the division between the person and the group as a necessary outcome of the division within the sufferer, because the person who is alienated from himself will deny the possibility of expansion and therefore of mutuality; he will remain separated and "safe" in his isolated state. When he does experience an impulse toward unification, he withdraws sooner or later in anxiety or even panic, throwing up internal walls against perception of the emotion and external walls against the person who has activated it.

We see this continually in individual therapy. The suffering one has no more than opened his core emotions than he goes into a frenzy and rids himself of the positive feelings as fast as he can. A typical comment of patients is, "I'm in a hurry. I want to get out of here, I want to get going."

And, oddly enough, that feeling—though taken in a different way—was a principal reason for my decision to try to utilize the core process in group therapy.

Some Aspects of Group Dynamics

About a decade ago, I began to observe the auras of groups of people, particularly lecture audiences, which relate as a collective to one person. At the beginning of a meeting, I have found, audience members seem a little detached or tired; the energy field over the head and shoulders of each person pulsates slowly and independently, though there is some inter-penetration of the fields because the people are seated close together. Then, as the speaker addresses them, remarkable things happen to the auras.

If the lecturer's voice is vibrant and energetic, and the concepts he discusses make an impact on the audience, a resonance phenomenon sets in: each person's aura vibrates increasingly faster, rising from about 15 pulsations per minute to perhaps 35, and at this rate all the fields coalesce and set to moving up and down *in unison*. Conversely, if the speaker isn't getting his ideas across to the audience, the individual auras dull and slow down, showing that the energy level of each member has dropped. The same thing happens when an audience or a section of it is hostile to the speaker.

The feedback in either case is palpable as well as visible in the energy fields. I have invariably found that when I'm speaking to a receptive group, my words practically fly out of my mouth, because the tremendous unified energy of the audience reaches out to include me. But when I'm expressing myself badly, or when the audience is feeling resistant, my words seem to be hitting a barrier, and it takes a lot of energy to get through to them.

Anyone experienced with audiences senses these things. What struck me was the potential of the resonance phenomenon as a therapeutic instrument. If one person's self-expression could heighten a whole group's energy fields in simply a lecture setting, what might happen if suffering human beings came together for the direct purpose of affecting each other energetically? Could group work, using the resonating energy generated by several people at once, break through to the core of each member more intensively and more persistently than individual therapy? The possibility was tremendously exciting.

By 1972 core therapy had evolved into an approach distinct from its matrix of bioenergetics, and work with individual patients suggested many orientations that group treatment might take. I realized, of course, that a group of people would function on a different dimension, with different dynamics, from a single person. New applications and techniques had to be invented, and some of these will emerge in the following pages. What I couldn't foresee was how far core therapy can penetrate the whole fabric of each group member's outside world.

Group work, like individual therapy, has two main thrusts. One is to elevate the energy level, which is the quantitative aspect of the organism. The other is to increase each person's consciousness, which is the qualitative differentiation of the emotions—of the energy currents moving in the organism.

Both processes unfold in two directions simultaneously—from without inward and from within outward. Raising the energy level entails not only removing the blocks in the character structure but drawing core energy outward. In the beginning, group participants work a great deal with their bodies to expand and free their energies. Enlarging the consciousness relies heavily at first on analysis of the body structures, the feelings, the underlying emotions and blocks, and their interconnections as expressed in the character of each member.

As the group matures, these processes gradually merge, because consciousness is a fundamental attribute of energy. Thus consciousness increases as energy increases. Again, everybody has had some experience of this effect. If a person feels vibrant and rested, he is able to perceive many more things during the day and to have greater variations and depths in his perceptions. When his energy level is low, he carries a minimal level of activity. So in the group, increasing the energy quantitatively also increases its qualitative aspect, the specificity and clarity of the emotions.

Generating New Energy

At this point let me give a few very brief examples of movements used in group therapy to energize the participants. These parallel the successive steps used with individual patients, and the progression in both contexts mirrors the growth of the human being from birth to adulthood.

We begin with *breathing*, the most fundamental of the life-sustaining actions that a person must perform from the moment he is born. Breathing gives the immediate energy for movement of the body. The patient lies on his back, in the position of the infant regarding the outside world, which allows the therapist to observe everything that happens in the body with the energy flow: whether the breathing is a unified cycle, moving up and down rhythmically; or whether it is blocked and caught, and where—in the diaphragm, in the neck, in the throat.

Then the person is encouraged to make the movements of infancy, and the focus is first on the negative movements, the actions that say no. These include vibrating the legs, sticking the heels out, turning the head from side to side, and using the voice with expressions such as "No!" and "I won't!" and "Go away!" The patient may also lie face downward to pound with his fists. Many times, the energy that is freed by these movements carries the person into expressions of protest, like "Why is this happening to me?" and "I want. . . ." And with the desire to receive, the core has been touched and opened—if only for a moment.

From the position of infancy, the patient comes to standing, assuming the posture of the child and the adult. Beginning with the negative feelings, again, the person makes further contact with his destructive emotions. In the standing position the arms move freely, and the person will use them to whack a couch or a chair seat. The feet learn to kick and stamp, the lower torso to thrust aggressively, the jaw to jut forward, the voice to bellow, the eyes to glare. It is a magnificent thing when a person can integrate the negative emotions with negative gestures, even if the therapist sometimes has to duck fast.

Like the direct expressions of negative feelings in the reclining position, these movements target the energy blocks on the periphery of the patient's being. They are only the beginning of the intensive, multifaceted therapy required to free the functioning of the core.

Early in my core work with groups, I thought of asking the participants to lie down in a circle with their feet in the center. The idea may have been prompted by the basic longitudinal movement of energy in the human body. It flows in the shape of a figure 8, or in Reich's description a kidney bean, streaming counterclockwise—from left to right—around the head and shoulders, and clockwise in the lower torso and legs. Reich spoke of two distinguishable currents meeting at an angle and sustaining the spinning circle that is visible in each sector.

The circular arrangement of people in a group, which I call the *mandala* position, has proved to be a veritable cyclotron, vastly more energizing to a group as a whole than any other placement I have observed. As I said, the participants lie initially with their feet in the center and their heads at the periphery of the circle, their bodies like the spokes of a wheel, and they touch or hold each other's hands. Three basic energy formations appear.

One is the *longitudinal stream* in each person, moving up and down each spoke in a systole-diastole pulsation; the rhythms differ from person to person. As the group members begin to work with their bodies, usually through breathing and vibrating and at first without the voice, their independent energy systems accelerate. Above the rate of about 25 pulsations a minute, a second and third energy formation appear, one at the center of the mandala—where the feet are—and one on the periphery. The single energy currents have begun to fuse, and because of the differing rhythms the new formations move in a continuous flow. The diastoles of each individual pulsation are filled in by the systoles of the others. The central energy stream moves clockwise and the peripheral stream counterclockwise.

The cyclotron is a far more powerful exemplar of the resonance phenomenon than the unified energy of an audience, and it charges the group vitally. Group members report that when it has cumulated, they feel themselves brought together almost as a new entity—a mutuality not of separate beings, but of the parts of a single being.

The cyclotron seems almost to take on a life of its own, independent of its immediate sources. For instance, when one or two group members are critically blocked, the new body of energy bridges over them, connecting the people on either side who are contributing to it. This resolution is like the sweep of a river; if there is a deep groove in the riverbed, the water fills it and runs forward on its course. The person who is in the groove feels pressured and miserable, to be sure, but there is value in this: the new energy streams outline starkly the contours of the blockage, and if they don't break through the person's resistances, they show the group who needs most to be focused on during that session.

These are only a few of the energy movements in the mandala; the moods, points of contact, and body placement of the members create variations so numerous that we are still discovering them. The effect of position warrants some further comment here. The feet-in mandala drives energy toward the legs, increasing awareness of the negative emotions. The body work used in this position, such as kicking and screaming, grounds the participants. When we want to bring out positive primal emotions, the group members lie with heads at the hub of the mandala, and they may use verbal expressions of longing, such as "Mama, Mama," or "Help me." It creates a tremendously strong circuit if each person turns on his side and places one hand behind the neck and the other under the pelvis of his neighbor.

When a group has coalesced and matured to some degree, we introduce the standing position, the stance of the adult. Now the participants face each other, taking responsibility for themselves as persons vis-à-vis each other—their looks, their reactions to each other's expressions of feeling, their interrelationships. Arranged again in a circle, members work particularly with movements that vibrate the body and then may progress into big gestures with the arms, legs, and torsos. The voice is used frequently in this position, which makes the body's inner tube vibrate as well. Combining vocalization with leg vibrations resonates the whole organism and enormously amplifies the individual energy pulsations, which again mount in intensity until they join in a new energy formation. The rise in energy occurs faster if participants touch the outer edges of their feet and hold hands.

The new energy formation created by the standing circle spins counterclockwise and, like the cyclotron in the mandala position, it curves into a haystack shape. If the therapist is standing in the middle of the circle, the manifestation can quite literally be felt between the hands, as an elastic medium. Also like the cyclotron, but more so, the unified aura shimmers with light, surrounding each person in a glow that brightens as the excitatory process between the individual fields and the new formation accelerates.

The infusions of energy reach to the core of the group members, awakening each person's awareness of how it feels truly to live. But the work of core therapy has only just begun. If the core is to remain open, accessible to the person within and the world without, the suffering one must press through the blocks in his character structure again and again, examining how they sunder inner harmony and distort relationships with others. The heightened consciousness that is the heightened energy gives the mind something with which to work.

Exploring the Inner Person

A human being is made up biologically of billions of cells that Nature intends to function in harmony as an integral whole. Each atom in each cell is like a drop of water, and the drops join in rivulets and brooks that form bigger waterways and eventually a river in which billons of organisms live. The river flows, and this is the river of human life.

The whole who is the person appears to us superficially in a conglomerate of "personality traits," but he is immensely more than this shell, which acts as a mask or filter between internal and external events. The mask is only the surface of the river. There is a deeper self, which is identified in classical psychoanalytic terms with the negative primal unconscious, the locus of the negative emotions in man. But the essential substance of the person streams from his core, which comprises the positive primal emotions. Thus, the purposeful movement of energy from the core gives the person his fundamental identity.

Core therapy works constantly to remove the obstacles that block the river of life and distort the identity of the person. Its goal, however, is restorative rather than only corrective. Therapies that lose sight of the river itself forget that it has a special course and myriad purposes and destinations. Yet the river is what makes the person unique and beautiful, not the obstructions in it or its deviations.

The analytic focus in core therapy, therefore, is directed toward the person's self-perception and perception of others as unique and immeasurably wonderful beings. His horizon is not "What is my sickness? How do I stop my pain?" but, rather, "What is my task in life? Where do I want to go? How do I unify myself to go there?"

This vista calls on the group members to envision themselves at the core level rather than according to appearances. It helps overcome the common tendency—therapists have it, too—to pigeonhole people as types, whether attractive to oneself or not. There are patterns of human behavior, of course. Psychiatry uses terms like "masochist" and "schizoid" and "paranoid," and not without reason; people do manifest definable nexuses of illness as well as "personalities." But it does a person a great injustice to equate him with his problems or his mask. Groups come to perceive this rapidly through the energy exchange, and their understanding carries them across even barriers of dislike that some members might ordinarily have for each other.

Participants approach themselves and each other analytically from the surface as well as from the center. Much of the early work concentrates on displacing the virtually universal belief that the negative emotions are "evil." They are not; on the contrary, they are expressions of the life force—in terms of the core process, they are alterations of energy caused by constrictions of the core. For example, when a person is made to feel worthless, as by a rejection from without or self-contempt from within, anger flares in the negative unconscious, like a spark on a shorted circuit.

Evil, in fact, derives not from the negative emotions but from denials or negations of emotions—both positive and negative. Every block is a denial; so is every sickness, every ungenuine feeling. Group members begin their perceptual exploration by examining the denials embedded in their masks: the bland smile on the face that gainsays an interior rage, the smug superiority that veils a sense of inadequacy, the apologetic droop of the shoulders that hides a fear of doing murder. These indications show in the body, not only in the words of each person.

There is an appearance of laziness in some people that covers a deep-reaching inertia; this is the case, as I have said, when the feelings have remained untouched for years. The deadness causes great suffering, which the person may misrepresent with an attitude of "I don't care." Others may deny the completion of a movement of energy. An employee may sense rising anger against a boss and skew it, sending out instead a complaint or a whine. A date may flirt seductively, but run when the prospect of intercourse arises. A wife may make love and then turn on her husband in coldness, finding fault and picking a quarrel so as to cut off the flow of warmth between them.

All these and countless other ways demonstrate withdrawal behind the mask, the periphery of the human being. Group members scrutinize such mechanisms in their own makeup and exchange observations with each other. The purpose is "to see ourselves as others see us," never to criticize as such; criticism is merely projection.

The subject of each person's exploration in the group is always himself, his own mask, his own negative emotions behind it, and ultimately his own positive affirmations of life. The assumption that "I am right and you are wrong" is not allowed to stand. For if he attacks someone's character in this way, the person is doing two destructive things: he is rejecting his responsibility to discover the negations lurking behind his mask, because everyone has the capacity for "wrongness" that he's attributing to the other person; and he is provoking the other into a counterdenial or a counterattack. At worst, he is actively reaching out to inflict cruelty.

In the group, no one needs to keep up pretenses, and no one is allowed to for long. The participant who paints himself as a Don Juan has to confront the fact that underneath he really hates women and wants to punish them. It is far better for him to admit this fact openly than to hide from it.

Projection and transference are among the commonest defensive tactics that we use to avoid dealing openly with our true emotions, and the sicker a person is, the more he will blame others for his suffering. A healthy person accepts others as they are. If they cause him pain, he tries to see this as an accident or as an honest collision of interests. He tries to say, "That hurt me," rather than "You did that to me deliberately!" Transference and acting out may take positive forms that give others pleasure, but at the same time they misconstrue each person's inner reality. These devices usually cast other people in images stemming from early childhood, so that the adult encounters and interacts not with the human being who is really there but with a phantom. Group work utilizes transference and acting out to penetrate to the neurosis, but the substitution should always be pointed out for what it is—a misguided target for the genuine feelings.

The keynote of group core therapy is responsibility for one's emotions. Each participant concentrates on how he feels, where his blocks shackle him, what his reactions to other members mean. Each learns to drop his mask and grapple directly with his primal movements. Each regresses to infancy, so to speak, supported by the profound mutuality that the group has created. Negativities, each participant learns, do not destroy others or goad them into throwing him into an abyss. The terror he suffers, the fear of the fear, has given him the illusion that if he lets himself go, he will drown in the river of life. Fellow group members give him the experience again and again that this is not so—that they will accept negative as well as positive expression from him. They work with each other energetically and analytically, steadily gaining and granting untrammeled access to their cores.

Because a group constitutes a society for each participant, the therapeutic process does not stop at releasing the primal emotions. The participants are adults, no longer babies dependent on parents for their meaningful relationships; they have grown-up bodies, they can move as they wish, they can support themselves, marry, and have children of their own. All these strengths entail encounters with other human beings that call for the responses of a whole person. By the responsibility demanded of each participant, by the exchange of trust and faith, by the intensive experience of mutuality, the group moves in its mature stage to reintegrate the person not only within himself but with the outside world.

Initiation and Development of the Group

The energizing processes and perceptual penetration just discussed invest every group I have worked with; it doesn't take special "types" of people to compose an effective therapeutic setting. I feel that it is actually good if participants represent a broad sample in terms of character structures, ages, and backgrounds, and I make up the group of about half men and half women. A mixture encourages a lot of things to happen fast. Consider the confrontation, for example, of an oral person with a masochist, the first saying, "Give it to me, do it for me," and the second retorting, "I won't." An older participant will gravitate toward a parent role, and if the group contains a young member, they may pair up. There are people who can be disruptive and who have to be removed from the group. These are usually psychopathic personalities who monopolize the group, sucking its energy, so that the work cannot be focused on anybody else.

The maximum number of people is fourteen and the minimum eight; a greater number would be crowded in the mandala, and a smaller number would find it hard to reach each other's hands. I have worked with as many as eighteen in workshops, but not in a continuing group. Sessions run two and a half to three hours, and members meet once a week, usually alternating a session with me and a session with a body therapist. This specialist works with the participants to heighten the relationship between physical movement and emotions, though the characterological analysis of the interconnections is undertaken only in the meetings with the core therapist.

The nature of core work makes it necessary for group members to be in individual therapy at the same time; the emotions evoked can be overwhelming and must be guided independently as well. Moreover, a person should enter individual treatment up to a year before joining a group, for his own sake as well as for the other participants. My colleagues and I have found that an unprepared person cannot stand the impact and pace of the group movements and that his resistances expand geometrically in the contact, so that the whole group is stymied.

The content of the individual sessions is intentionally linked to the material unearthed in the group. The patient may focus on repressed feelings that fellow members have pointed out. He may work through a negative reaction to another participant that he is not yet able to express directly in the group, or I may bring up feelings that I think he should carry into the next meeting.

There are few rules for group members, but these few are firm. Participants are asked to commit themselves to one year of work and to attend every session. If a person doesn't come twice in a row without a compelling reason, fellow members decide in their next meeting with him whether they feel that he should drop out. We have found that people rapidly develop the attitude that the group work is centrally important to them, and members rarely leave it after the first weeks.

Confidentiality is as binding on group participants as it is on the therapist; people cannot discuss with any outsider, not even their spouses, any revelations that have been communicated in the sessions. From the outset, group members are encouraged to try to trust each other and to discard the supposition that any expression of feeling, from themselves or the others, derives from ill intent. The work requires much patience and permissiveness, far beyond the thresholds of toleration encountered in the outside world. Social conventions, in large part, need to be laid aside.

I caution people coming into a group to be careful about acting out, because most of us can use this ad infinitum as a pressure valve without exploring the impulse. Once the group has made some headway, participants who feel an urge to hit or wrestle with each other may do so under supervision, as the following pages will describe; but they are not allowed, of course, really to hurt each other.

I also ask members to guard against being drawn into a close friendship with one or two other participants outside the sessions. This is not a hard and fast rule but, rather, a guideline to keep the group from subdividing into cliques. I discourage outside sexual relations between group participants on the same grounds. Sexual partners will find it particularly hard to bring up their relationship in the meetings, and their efforts to hide their attraction to each other militate against the openness and honesty that must infuse all the participants together. It is my feeling, too, that a group member who takes up a sexual relationship with a fellow participant early in the work is most often acting out a negation, such as vengeance against the spouse or resentment because sexual feeling for the therapist has not met with a response.

The group leader in core therapy does not stand apart from it but becomes one with the participants in a very real sense, sharing their goals and their work. He must bring the members a profound sense of warmth for their uniqueness as persons, and he must also impose on himself the same rigorous openness and honesty they are called upon to sustain. His attitude has to be that the group members have come together to cure themselves, not to be cured by him.

Participating does not mean that the therapist abdicates his responsibilities as the group leader, for that way lies chaos. His raison d'être is to give group members his insights and guide them in their work, but he must not force explanations on them or herd them in directions he wants them to take. Insofar as is possible, the group should tell him how and where it wants to move in each session. If he is puzzled or unsure of what the members need to do at any point, he has to admit it; they will get him back on their track.

Above all, the group leader may never use the notion of truthfulness as an excuse to feed his own ego or to let out his own unconscious drives. There have been groups in which this has happened—the therapist has attacked a member who has annoyed him or taken a patient to bed who attracted him. This is manipulation, not openness. Openness in the therapist means accessibility to his core. From the birth of a group and throughout its life, I interrelate with the members as a physician, yes, but I am first and foremost simply John, another human being.

The evolution of a group, as I mentioned earlier, is like the evolution of a human person. The group develops from infancy into adulthood as the core work advances, and it follows a rhythm of growth in terms of the material it comes to grips with during its successive stages.

In the early phases of the group's life, people concentrate on themselves, as do children. Their attention is riveted on the "me" that each one is, and for a few sessions the members will speak fairly freely of their sufferings and of their major problems. Then there comes a point where they sit back and wait, looking for the therapist to take them in hand and produce solutions for their difficulties. The leader's task now is to help them begin moving toward unification as a group, for it is their coalescing energy and consciousness that will integrate them individually.

Gradually, the participants open their focus of concentration to include each other. Their attention broadens from the "me" to the "us," and transferences inevitably ripen as the people reveal their true character structures. Masks begin to drop, and negative emotions emerge to the surface. Much work is done at this stage to intensify the positive feelings, and as the members grow in mutual trust, they bring in dream material and fantasies for the group to explore with them. Their sense of responsibility for each other strengthens markedly in the process, and the group moves into its last stage of growth.

The mature group combines the "me" focus with the "us." Participants examine their human condition, assess their functioning relationships, and work toward integration with their outside worlds. They need increasingly less guidance from the therapist in this phase. Emergencies that arise are likely to be taken up with fellow members directly rather than with him. The group has fused within itself, and in the process it has raised each person's gaze from the pain of life to the promise of life. It has opened his river to the sea.

Let me now trace some specific applications of core therapy during the various stages of a group's growth. No single technique is uniquely reserved for one phase; methods introduced early may be utilized throughout the life of a group. The work in each session does not follow a preestablished program, but evolves as needed to deepen the members' font of energy and consciousness. Nor are the stages mutually exclusive; again, like the human person, the group swings back and forth between negative and positive, between clearing the river and strengthening its flow. But, broadly speaking, there are aspects of therapy that pertain to each phase, from infancy to adulthood.

Stages of Development: Infancy and Childhood

When a group assembles for its first meeting, its members are apt to feel a little shy and nervous. They are already calling me by my first name, and I use theirs to introduce them. This eases the tension; it also strips them of roles to which society assigns a hierarchical value—lawyer, clerk, janitor.

Ordinarily, we do not take up physical work in the first several sessions, for I feel it has a mechanical quality until there is some real sense of acquaintance among the members. We start, rather, with each person telling the group why he wants to join it and what he wants to accomplish through it. This is the short period of airing problems, and during it or in the following few sessions, the work of observation and analysis begins.

For this purpose, I ask each participant in turn to stand and move before a mirror while fellow members watch him. All of us, himself included, speak of what we see in his physical body. The body, revealed in a leotard, can't lie, and group members are attuned to its messages from their individual treatment. "You look like a tall, thin cypress," one person may learn. "You seem to be cut in half at the waist, like a wasp," another hears.

The group draws inferences from each person's physique about where his blocks are, what they indicate of his character structure, and how his defenses relate to the problems he has described. I may point out to a woman, "There is a narrow structure to your hips and pelvis, like a boy's, as though you aren't recognizing this part of your body." Or a participant may comment to another, "Your neck looks stiff. Are you mad at the world?"

Commentaries like these provide the group with a good deal to work on, for they not only give the people knowledge of each other but stimulate reactions. The therapist asks each member how he feels about the others, given their observations. Some people are embarrassed. Other are frightened. Still others are outraged. Each is encouraged immediately to try to perceive why he is experiencing his particular reaction.

The body work introduced in these early meetings depends on my perception of what the group as a whole is prepared for. If the people are already active and moving, I may ask them to take the mandala position and launch into some rather evocative gestures, such as kicking. If I feel them withdrawing into themselves, as is more often the case, I will proceed with only gentler warming-up exercises, done usually in a standing circle. I work particularly with their breathing, focusing their attention on what parts of their bodies they feel moving with their respiration, what parts they don't feel, where they have pressure or pain. These movements, too, the group members observe in each other and comment on. Observation of the body, incidentally, is an instrument that the group uses periodically throughout all its stages of development.

Following these introductory sessions, the people will usually draw back into themselves. They have information about each other, but as yet little sense of cohesion. A stillness sets in, a resistance that the therapist must break through to begin shifting the group's attitude from dependency on him to self-reliance. This is a complicated stage, and we use many techniques to advance it.

I may start with perceptual work on the group as a whole. I ask the people to sit in a circle and speak in rotation about their sense of several other participants—not rational judgments, but gut feelings. The group goes the round, attempting to expose true if surface reactions, and this can stir up a lot of emotions. Then, working with the people who have spoken most vehemently, we take up each emotional response and move it from the fact—the "I don't like you" or "You annoy the hell out of me"—to the why. We connect the projection with the person's inner self: his resentments, his patterns of response to authority figures, his predispositions toward men and women in general.

It may seem better, on the other hand, to involve the group first in physical movement, and I will ask the members to lie down in the mandala formation with their feet toward the center. They begin with breathing and add leg vibrations, continuing with a long series of movements that may last half an hour or more, to open the energy transmission of the group. Resistance can't be allowed to persist because it creates an atmosphere of futility.

Work like this through a number of sessions generates some awareness of unification in the group, and participants arrive at subsequent meetings more ready to move. Collective withholding does recur, of course, and there are times when I let the stillness and waiting develop until discomfort provokes one or more people to break through. This is a useful tool for bringing out resentments between members. But generally, from this time forward, the group increasingly shows the leader where it wants to go, and the participants need less and less stimulus from him to get to working.

The leader continues to guide each meeting, particularly in deciding how to start it. I take my cue from what I find on evaluating the members as the session opens. Several things enter into this evaluation. The auras of the members are the surest index of their energy level, but there are many other kinds of evidence. Most therapists learn to sense the "mood" of patients the way you can feel what the temperature of a hot stove is at some distance from it. Facial and body expressions tell a lot. A participant may be making conversation but his face may be blank and colorless; this person is holding in. Another may enter the room and lie on his back; he doesn't want to participate. Neither does the member who sits down and hunches forward, arms around the knees. Many positions denote anxiety: a rigid back, tightly clasped hands plunged into the lap, hunched shoulders, shallow or held breath. People who show such tension states need to be focused on specially during the session.

I will ask the person who seems to be suffering the most to come lie down on a mattress with the rest of the group sitting around him in a circle. By this stage, the other participants can usually see right away that this person is in a tremendous bind, caught in the blocked emotion, the denial of the need to let go. It takes a little physical work to open him up. He is asked first to kick his legs and let his breathing expand; he may use his voice as well, perhaps beginning with a vibratory "Ahh" and then using a negative term.

When his movements are flowing, he is urged to shout out his destructive and irrational feelings at each member of the group. He isn't permitted to express judgments or opinions but is turned toward his own feelings, the movements that he perceives in his own organism. For instance, he can say to the others, "I hate you, I want to kill you," but not "I hate you because you're hostile." The "because" isn't necessary; it's a copout of his responsibility for these emotions. The group members for their part are guided to accept his negativities, to let him scream at them without cutting him off.

When he has worked through his hatred and rage, it often happens that he experiences a welling up of positive emotion, and he begins to ask the group for help. He extends his hands to the others, and they gather closely and tightly around him, touching him. A heartbreaking surge of despair and suffering courses through his organism, an agony that we all carry within us but that we deny and sidetrack; it bursts out of him like a torrent, convulsing him with sobbing. And this emotion is so deeply enriching and moving that it can draw his comforters to weep with him, each perceiving his own deadness and despair, each confronting his own conflicts. So it is that one member, cleansing himself of his negations, can open the hearts of the whole group. This is the resonance phenomenon at work creating an enormous amount of energy. The experience gives the participants a profound sense of unity among themselves and a feeling of belonging to the human race. It humanizes them.

If no one participant at the beginning of a session needs urgently to be focused on, I may place the whole group in the mandala position to work into the primal feelings together. The people lie on their backs, their feet toward the center, and start kicking their legs as would a small child in a temper tantrum. I may ask them to bring up negatives without a target, or I may suggest that they visualize an early authority figure and pinpoint rage against that person.

Sometimes a participant will become so energized that he will spontaneously get to his feet in order to have more freedom of movement. He may then take a bataka—this is a foam-rubber bat we use for some of the hitting gestures—and beat a mattress, yelling at a parent image: "You goddam monster, you fucked me up, you hurt me, you hurt me!" He may rev up so much hatred and anger in other participants that everybody will grab batakas to beat their parents.

When these explosions have worn off, the people will often sit close to each other in a circle and explore their problems in a way that is cleaned out of rationalizations and the need to protest. Without any prompting from the leader, they will discard the accusations against their parents and take up the negative emotions and their implications in their present-day lives. When this happens, it is clear that the group is maturing.

Stages of Development: Youth and Adulthood

Though the emphasis in the youth stage of a group's development is still laid on the negativities, we are aiming always for the positive emotions. Sometimes, in a session, the people work for a while in the feet-in mandala position, but do not build up the momentum to open their positive movements. So I reverse them to the head-in mandala to channel the new energy formations upward in their bodies and evoke the heart feelings. They vocalize their distress, their pain, and especially their fear of fear: "I am suffering," "I'm going to fall apart," "I don't want to die!", and "Help me, help me!" Many people will weep, and the deep empathy around the entire circle makes the participants realize that they are not alone in their misery. Most important, it makes each one experience total expression and total acceptance—a total mutuality—of the positive emotions.

The group is by this time deeply cohesive; it has become a family, and the members are ready to assume not only more of the direction of the work but a greater share in carrying it out with each other. I am still guiding them, but only intermittently, and after an initial suggestion from me, they may move through an entire session on their own.

For example, a meeting may begin with a member lying down, his fellow participants sitting in a circle around him. As the person in the center expresses his negative feelings, the others react to these in kind. Suppose he

is saying, "I hate you." They answer, "*I hate you!*", accentuating his movement while at the same time feeding it back into themselves. If he regresses to denial and tries to blame any of the others for his hatred, they
are quick at this stage to refocus him (as well as themselves) on the inner
sources of the negativity.

In this stage, too, the group is increasingly using the adult standing
position, bringing big movements into play to stimulate the self-contained
energy flow in each organism. These are particularly helpful if I feel that
the group is becoming undercharged. I may line the men up on one side
of the room and the women on the other, each subgroup facing the wall.
I have each line hold hands and I set them to vibrating, and little by little
their jaws go out. Then someone begins to say, for instance, "Damn you."
The message spreads along each wall, so that all the women are soon
shouting things like "You're a bunch of sadists!" and the men are giving as
good as they're getting with "You bitches, you tricky mothers!" After a
while, one or more people will turn around and make threatening gestures
at the subgroup opposite, and two people may lock eyes in a glare of rage.
If I feel they can handle themselves well, I'll let them zero in on each
other with batakas.

Participants are not allowed to act out hostility on each other physically
until the group as a whole has developed considerable maturity. This is
not because they will do each other bodily damage; by this time, the core
emotions are moving freely enough to prompt bystanding members themselves to intervene before an interaction turns into a fistfight. It is because
physical attack is so provocative that it can emotionally disintegrate a person who has not learned to accept negativity. Consider, for example, what
might happen to the man and the woman in the following case if either
were in an unstable condition:

A man who is very fearful of women comes to a session one day in a
crisis. He has had a fight with his wife, or, rather, she has given him a
tongue-lashing that he hasn't been able to stand up to, and it is driving him
to despair. "The bitch, she's smashing me, and I can't say boo to her. I'm
stuck with the feeling and I can't move." He has worked a great deal on
this problem already and he has faced the denial of negativities that sus-
tains it, but he hasn't been able to break through the block in his life
situation.

The group listens to his story, and then a woman member says, "Let's
try to bring this thing out. I'll be your mother, okay?" Then she starts
imitating an overbearing mother, babying him, treating him like a helpless
creature and putting him down. The man begins to get mad, and she continues to needle him until he catches fire. At this point, I ask her to get
under the mattress, and I give the man a bataka. She sticks her head out
and keeps on provoking the daylights out of him: "My bitsy boy, didn't I
tell you not to hit other little boys?" She taunts and he whacks until he is
pouring out rage.

The response can be cataclysmic throughout the group. As the man flails away, people who identify with his problem scream at the woman under the mattress, venting their own rage at their mother or at all womankind. The man's breakthrough is a tremendous victory for them. Others— men and women—empathize with the person under the mattress and grieve with her as she cries out, "Don't hurt me, don't hurt me! I love you, don't desert me!" The sense of loss and separation can sweep through both camps like a wind through a wheat field.

Much of the technique in the youth period is devised to sharpen the assertiveness of the group as a whole and the capacity of the individual members to express it. If I feel that they don't want to work against each other, I may put myself in the middle of the standing circle and call myself their father, goading them to attack me. The movements in this situation begin with vibrations and progress quickly into aggressive fist-shaking and yelling. The therapist, of course, serves as a fine authority figure for transference purposes, and more than once I've just missed getting a bloody nose. Group members have always stepped in to restrain any free-swinging co-participants who looked seriously bent on murder. It's worth mentioning at this juncture that in all the years I have used physical provocation and retort, in individual as well as group therapy, there have never been any injuries outside of a minor scrape or bruise.

Most sessions during these phases need no stimulus at all from the leader. For weeks at a time, my contribution will be supervision and analysis only, not piloting. The group moves itself, and there will be more than ample material.

It can still happen that the group as a whole doesn't get off the ground. The weather may be heavy, or several people may have just come back from vacations and may not want to move. Perhaps the group will be caught in a verbal streak so that everything is flying all over the place with no focus, no integration, no real work. At times like these, I will give the participants five or ten minutes to take flight themselves, and if they don't, I will put them in one of the circular positions—usually the mandala first—to work until they are moving on their own. A mature group can take the full force of the mandala, so that the participants may choose to stay in it for an entire session.

The mature group will often sense for itself at the beginning of a session who needs its concentrated attention most. Then the members, not the therapist, lead the person into working through his suffering. They may form a circle around him and guide his physical movements, all of them pushing him ahead, goading him, helping him open up. This may seem bullying, but it isn't, for they are simultaneously working their own feelings out parallel and conjoined to his.

Participants now have little patience with evasions or deviousness; they will cut through whining or rationalizing with a speed that verges on brutality. They are a good deal more abrupt with each other than the therapist would be with any of them. Yet rarely does this give offense, for they know themselves well; they know each other's character structures and blocks, conflicts and resources, values and hearts. Together they have built a reservoir of common trust.

Banking on this trust, they spend a great deal of time at this stage discussing their most troubling problems, their deepest emotions, their grestest shames. They compare and explore the meaning of their fantasies, existing relationships, and expectations in life. They assess their success in applying the strengths developed in the group work to the outside world. They give each other courage, motivation, and love—energy from the core.

The organismic movement of the mature group reintegrates the participants beyond the measure that I feel the individual treatment can accomplish. This is not to devalue the central importance of independent therapy; it is to recognize that group work translates core therapy onto new dimensions.

There is, first of all, the significant differential of energy. The new formations generated by the group vastly surpass the energy mass available to the single patient. An immediate implication of this is that the core contact, which is the foundation of the entire therapeutic process, can be established virtually at once among group members but may require a tremendous infusion from the therapist in the one-to-one relationship. Until that contact arises, there will be no vitality in the treatment, which not only leaves the patient in his suffering but denies the therapist full perceptual enlightenment.

The effects of transference are tremendously magnified in a group setting. The therapist will accept and utilize the identities that the individual patient clothes him in—as the patient's mother, father, sibling. But these cloaks can't all be worn at once. By dint of its numbers and composition, a group enables a person to reincarnate his entire family in one sweep. Because each of at least ten people is transferring to the others simultaneously and reciprocally, the permutations are myriad. Then too, one group member may really resemble a person's boss, another his spouse, and a third his testy next-door neighbor.

Individual core therapy also uses the mirroring effect to help the patient intensify emotions and feelings: the therapist may shout along with the patient, exchange glares with him, hit the couch alongside him. But he is constrained by professional ethics not to give rein to his negative unconscious. A patient's fellow group members have the opposite obligation—to vent their negativities as fully and as irrationally as they can, short of physical mayhem. The cumulative acceleration and intensification of the energy flow feeding back into each person can shatter blocks that it might take months for individual therapy to chip.

The quality of personal responsibility that evolves in group therapy surpasses anything to be found not only in individual treatment but in life relationships. The single patient is obliged to account for his feelings to his therapist, but not vice-versa. Lovers may urgently need open communication of emotions, but cultural inhibitions as well as passion foreclose the negativities. As for the human mask, the filter we all maintain between our inner selves and others, I have often seen group members reveal vile actions to their co-participants that they have not so much as hinted at in their individual sessions.

Granted the need for a society to place restraints on its members. Granted the right of any person to say "no" to another's "yes." Granted the internal struggle latent in humankind because we have primal negative and primal positive emotions. Granted all this, I nevertheless ask myself: What might we not accomplish, we people of the earth, if we could replicate the mutuality of the core therapeutic group throughout our societies?

14 Transactional Analysis, Gestalt Therapy, and Psychoanalysis in Group Psychotherapy: A Synthesis

Richard G. Abell

GROUP PSYCHOTHERAPY TODAY is an exciting field, a growing, expanding, experimental field in which new methods are continuously being tested. This chapter will describe the philosophy and techniques of transactional analysis (TA) and will then show how it can be combined with Gestalt therapy and psychoanalysis in one ongoing, flowing method of group psychotherapy.

Eric Berne's method of diagnosis and treatment, which he called "transactional analysis," became a permanent part of the psychiatric literature with his publication of a paper entitled "Transactional Analysis: A New and Effective Method of Group Therapy" in the *American Journal of Psychotherapy* in October 1958.

According to Franklin H. Ernst (1), "Historians will describe Eric Berne as the most outstanding contributor to the theory and practice of Psychotherapy and Psychiatry since Freud." Berne was himself trained psychoanalytically and was deeply affected by the work of Freud.

Eric Berne worked out a set of principles for doing psychotherapy which were scientific in the sense that the results secured by their application were predictable, verifiable, and consistent. He defined the unit of social communication as a *transaction*, which consisted of a stimulus from one person and a response from the other, and went beyond previous investigators in isolating the exact origin of the stimulus and response in aspects of the personality which he described as *ego states*. The isolation and description of such ego states is, according to Ernst, Eric Berne's most significant contribution. Other important aspects of TA are strokes, time

266

structuring, injunctions, counterinjunctions, counterscript drivers, early decision, script, counterscript, games, rackets, stamps, permission, redecision, and contracts. I will later explain briefly those aspects of TA which are essential to an understanding of my group treatment in group therapy of the patient I am describing in this selection. The methods of Gestalt therapy and psychoanalysis are described elsewhere in this book.

Strokes

One of the most currently emphasized aspects of TA is strokes. *Strokes* are units of recognition. They may be physical, verbal, or nonverbal. The reason why strokes are so important is that the kind of personality a person has, and the way he thinks about himself and experiences himself, depends upon the kind of strokes he received in infancy and childhood. If they were positive he feels good. If they were negative he feels bad.

Eric Berne (2) described four kinds of strokes: (1) positive unconditional (I love you just for being), (2) positive conditional (I'll like you if you do well in school), (3) negative conditional (I won't like you if you don't do well in school), and (4) negative unconditional (I won't like you no matter what you do). The most intolerable situation of all is to receive no strokes, for without strokes the child cannot survive.

In the beginning, strokes are given by the parents to the child, who can't really determine what kind they will be. A grown-up person, when he knows how, can determine to a large extent the kinds of strokes he gets.

How to do this—how to get the strokes you want from others and how to give the strokes you want to others—is one of the basic subjects with which TA deals.

Ego States

It is generally accepted that Eric Berne's most significant contribution is his concept that every person's personality is composed of three ego states, which he called Parent, Adult, and Child, as illustrated in Figure 1.

Berne states that the Parent ego state (P) consists of a set of feelings, attitudes, and behavior patterns which result from messages received by him from his own parents. These messages consist largely of slogans, directives, moral precepts, prejudices, and such other material as the parents believe (rightly or wrongly) are essential to the welfare of their child. These messages are colloquially called "Parental Tapes." The individual continually replays them throughout his lifetime, and because of this they exert an ongoing effect upon his behavior. Once implanted in his cortex,

Figure 1.   Structural Diagram of the Personality.

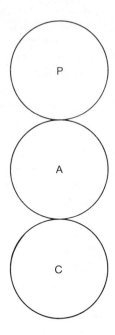

the individual may express these directives at himself or at others in his environment.

A typical parental message is, "Work hard and be a credit to your family." A typical parental gesture is pointing the finger at a person when telling him what to do. Typical parental words are: "should," "shouldn't," "do," "don't," "must," "mustn't," "ought to," "have to," and sometimes "never" and "always."

The Parent ego state may be subdivided into the "Nurturing Parent," which contains an OK part and a Not OK part, and the Critical Parent (which also contains an OK part and a Not OK part). The OK part of the Nurturing Parent says such things as, "I love you just for being," "I am really pleased with your good report card," and "It is all right for you to have fun." It is nurturing, permissive, growth promoting.

The Not OK Nurturing Parent says such things as, "I'll bake that cake for you, Susie, and you won't have to do any of the work," the Not OK part of the Nurturing Parent is smothering and growth inhibiting.

The Adult ego state (A) is concerned with dealing with reality. It is involved with data processing, rational thinking, working out options.

The Child ego state (C), according to Berne, "is a set of feelings, attitudes and behavior patterns which are relics of the individual's own childhood." There are two aspects to the Child ego state. These are: the Free or Natural Child (Prince or Princess) and the Adapted Child (Frog). The

Figure 2. Descriptive Aspects of the Personality.

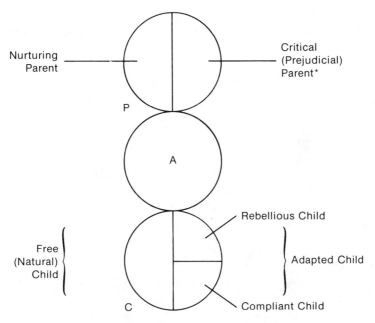

Prejudicial was the term first selected by Eric Berne. In his last book he changed *Prejudicial* to *Critical*. Some writers prefer one and some the other.

Adapted Child itself can be divided into two parts, the Compliant part and the Rebellious part.

Figure 2 illustrates the ego states and their subdivisions as described above.

A typical Free Child statement is, "Let's have some fun, let's go swimming." A typical Free Child word is, "Wow." A typical Adapted Child feeling (Compliant part) is, "I wish I were popular." A typical Adapted Child (Compliant) word is "can't." A typical Rebellious Child word is, "No." A typical Rebellious Child phrase is, "You can't make me."

I have described ego states in more detail than I will other aspects of TA theory because of the importance I place upon knowing what ego state a patient is in when I am working with him. It is important that each group member learn to identify what ego state he is in and what ego states the other group members are in, since the identification of these ego states leads to valuable information concerning the nature of the person's problems and how to resolve them.

With the development of ego states, Eric Berne created a terminology which can be used for understanding precisely what is going on in a patient at any moment of time, both by himself and by others in a way that is more accurate, or refined, than previously possible.

Figure 3.   Egogram showing a person with a highly developed Prejudicial Parent (PP) ego state and a correspondingly high Adapted Child (AC). Nurturing Parent (NP) and Free Child (FC) are low. Adult (A) is moderately developed.

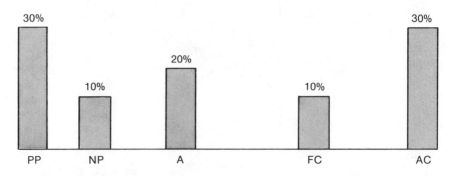

The concept that ego state boundaries are permeable, so that a person may be in one, and then another due to a movement of energy from one to another was developed by John Dusay (3). In this paper he states that if the total amount of energy in all the ego states is 100 percent, and it cannot be increased or decreased in total amount, then if there is an increase in the energy of one ego state, such as the Parent, then there must be a decrease in the energy in one or more of the other ego states.

He devised a bar-gram graph to indicate the amount of energy in each ego state in a given individual at a given moment of time. Such a graph is shown in Figure 3.

In this graph you will observe that there is much more energy in the Prejudicial (Critical) Parent than in the Nurturing Parent, and much more energy in the Adapted Child than in the Free Child. This is the distribution I find in most patients when they first come into my office.

Figure 4 shows the distribution of energy in most patients following therapy. You will see a marked increase in the amount of energy in the Nurturing Parent and a corresponding decrease in the amount in the Critical Parent. There is also an increase in the amount of energy in the Adult, in consequence of increased autonomy (more Free Child and OK Nurturing Parent, the latter indicating internal increased permission to grow and develop). In consequence, the Adult becomes "decontaminated" from the undesirable effects of the Adapted Child and the Critical Parent.

Such changes I specifically and intentionally facilitate in patients in group therapy, first by inviting the patient to move out of his counterscript drivers, and second by helping him to neutralize or reverse the effect upon him of his parental "injunctions."

This brings me to a description of the different types of messages that parents give their children that are crucial in determining the type of personality their children have, and the character of their ego states.

Figure 4. Egogram of the same person, showing change that has occurred during therapy in the percentage of energy in each ego state. PP and AC are now low and NP and FC are both high. A has been released from the directives of the PP and the contamination from the AC and is now more active and effective.

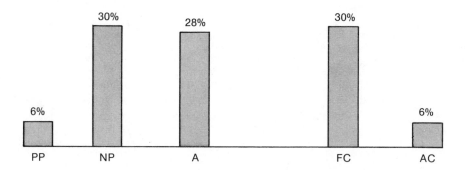

Counterscript drivers (6) are messages (admonitions) which are passed from the Parent ego state of the parent to the Parent ego state of the child. The parent is aware that he is giving these messages to his child. *Injunctions* (also called stoppers) are more powerful and devastating messages that are passed from the irrational part of the Child ego state of the parent to that part of the Child ego state of the child that is termed the "electrode" (P_1). Usually these injunctions are outside of the awareness of the parent. This is illustrated in Figure 5.

Counterscript Drivers

Kahler and Capers (4) describe five counterscript drivers. These are (1) "Please me," (2) "Try hard," (3) "Be perfect," (4) "Hurry up," and (5) "Be strong." Usually a child who receives these messages will feel good only if he obeys them. If he received all of them he will make every effort to please his parents (and others), will try hard (yet never feel that he accomplishes what he wants), will try to be perfect (which is impossible and hence frustrating), will hurry up (and yet never feel that he is hurrying up enough), and will keep a stiff upper lip, "keep his chin up," and not show his real feelings (which is what "be strong" means). Kahler and Capers deal with such drivers by inviting the patient into what they term "allowers," which are the opposite from the drivers. For example, the allower for "Please me" is, "It's all right for you to please yourself, to do what you want."

When patients are unable to give up their drivers even when invited to substitute allowers for them, Kahler and Capers say this is because these

Figure 5. Script Matrix (P^2, A^2, and C^2 refer to the three ego states in the complete person, P^1, A^1, and C^1 refer to the Parent, Adult, and Child in the Child ego state of the whole person).

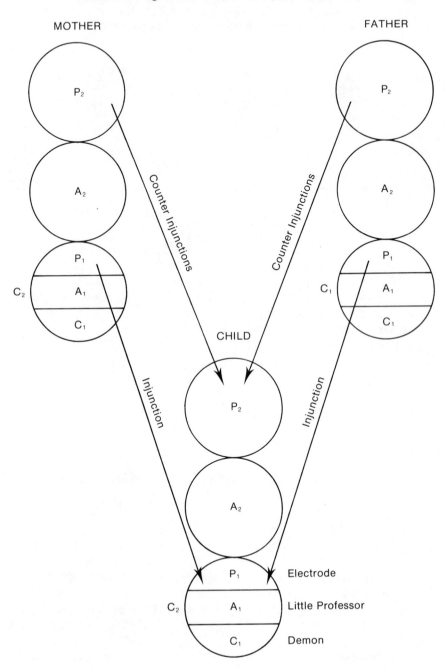

patients have received injunctions which make it impossible for them either to fulfill the demands of their drivers or to give them up. Thus they are locked into an anxiety-provoking situation for which there is no resolution until the effects of the injunctions have been neutralized.

Injunctions, Early Decision, and Life Script

According to Robert Goulding (5), "By definition the Injunction is a message given to the child by the parent's internal Child, usually, but not always without the awareness of the parent's Adult. In essence it tells the child how he can receive recognition, i.e., under what circumstances he can expect to receive strokes from Mother or Father."

Goulding lists the following injunctions: "Don't Be," "Don't Be You," "Don't Be a Child," "Don't Be Grown Up," "Don't Be Close," "Don't Make It," "Don't Be Important," "Don't Belong," "Don't Be Sane" (or well), "Don't Show Your Feelings," "Don't Have Your Feelings," and just plain "Don't". Other injunctions are "Don't Trust," "Don't Think," and "Don't Have Fun."

These injunctions are not usually given in the words used above, though occasionally they are. The child intuits them empathically from the actions and behavior of his parents.

What can a child do who receives such an injunction? Since he is dependent upon his parents for strokes (recognition, food, shelter, and so on) and since without strokes he cannot survive he is literally forced to make a decision early in his life about what to do and how to behave. This decision is made in the Adult of the Child (the Little Professor), as shown in Figure 6.

One common response to the "Don't Be" injunction listed by Goulding is: "I'll show you even if it kills me."

When the child (Little Professor) responds to the injunction by deciding to accept it and behave accordingly (the early decision), he gives up his autonomy and becomes Adapted. This is the way the Adapted Child ego state originates. Having made this decision, the child begins to formulate plans by means of which he can fulfill during his lifetime the expectations placed upon him by the injunctions. Each injunction leads to a special kind of life script. The force which impels a child to respond to an injunction as he does is his need for strokes.

Games

One way that individuals maintain their Not OK existential position is by playing games. The player (agent) of a game pretends to be doing one

Figure 6.   Second Order Structural Analysis.

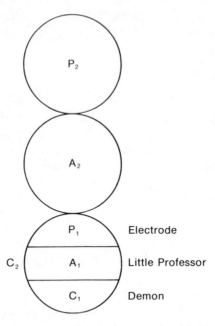

NOTE: Electrode: point of response to the injunctions in the Child ego state of the child. Little Professor: Adult ego state of the Child of the child. Demon: The Child of the child. What is intrinsically ours at birth—the essence of creativity.

thing when he is in fact doing another, so that, as Eric Berne says (10), all games contain a "con." A con works only if there is a receptivity to it in the respondent. This receptivity Eric Berne calls the "gimmick." Such a gimmick may be interest, involvement, fear, greed, sentimentality, or something else. Once the game player hooks the "mark" (respondent), he does the opposite of what he is pretending to do (pulls a switch), as a result of which he collects his "payoff." Following the switch is a moment of confusion in the mark, who tries to figure out what happened to him. Following this, both players collect their payoffs, and the game ends.

The payoff consists of feelings. In some instances the player collects bad feelings, in others, false good feelings, when the respondent is put down. Those who wish to know more about games should refer to Eric Berne's *Games People Play* (6, 7).

Rackets

The bad-feeling payoff of games reinforces the bad feelings that we hold onto from childhood that, in TA language, are called *rackets*. Such feelings are often copied from parents, and the child collects strokes for developing them. Some of the most common rackets are sadness, inadequacy, depression, regret, anxiety, confusion, anger, helplessness, fear, and guilt.

Redecision

If the Not OK life script is based upon an early decision in response to the counterscript drivers and the injunctions, then it can, as stressed by Goulding subsequently be reversed by a redecision. Most TA techniques and methods are directed toward facilitating such a reversal.

This *redecision* is a new decision to reverse the effects of the counterscript drivers and injunctions, to reverse the Not OK script to an OK script and to achieve autonomy. In the process the Adult ego state becomes decontaminated from the prejudicial effects of the Critical Parent and the phobic and delusional ones of the Adapted Child.

How are these changes brought about, and how is group therapy used to facilitate them? To begin with, I teach group members the principles of TA outlined above. I say "outlined" because the group members learn much more than I have space in this chapter to describe. I find that this knowledge is invaluable to them in helping them to understand the nature of their problems and in diminishing their resistance to change.

T.A., Gestalt Therapy, and Psychoanalysis in Groups

I will now describe how I do therapy in a group, using the principles described above.

What I am going to say applies to psychoneurotics. I do not make a similar claim for schizophrenics, though I don't rule it out.

Step 1. *First I ask the patient to identify his problem.* If he has trouble knowing what his problem is, or verbalizing it, I find it useful to ask him, "How do you want to be different?" I will illustrate with several examples. The first concerns a twenty-eight-year-old former client of mine named Tom, who said that he wanted to get married, but was afraid to be close to girls.

Step 2. *Formulation of a contract.* A transactional analysis contract is a statement by the client that he will work on a specific problem, a specific way that he wants to change, and a statement by the therapist that he will cooperate with the patient in bringing this about. Tom said that he would like to work in group psychotherapy on learning to overcome his fear of girls so that he could be close to them.

Step 3. *Exploration of the problem in the patient's current life.* I asked Tom how he was affected by this problem in his everyday life and he explained that when he came home he felt lonely, found this intolerable, and wanted to find a compatible woman with whom to share his life. He then went on to say that when he does meet a possible candidate for this position he immediately begins to look for some flaw, or blemish, in her. When I asked him why he did this he said, "I want to have some way of breaking off the relationship if I want to later."

An example of the way Tom creates distance when involved with a girl occurred in the case of Grace, of whom he approved, and to whom he planned to give a birthday card. He showed me the card before giving it to her. Grace was slightly plump, more so than Tom liked, and he had been urging her to lose weight. The card had a picture on the front of a fat girl trying to get out of a tight-fitting bathing suit. Upon turning the page, the reader was confronted with the greeting "Happy Birthday," and under this were the words, "You can't get out of this one." The barb is obvious. I pointed this out to Tom and encouraged him to send a card with a simple and affectionate message on it. Similar examples were given by Tom from his experiences with various girls. Even after Tom realized that playing the game of Blemish kept him from getting close to women, he was unable to change.

This in spite of his recognition that when he behaved with hostility toward girls he was in the Not OK part of his Critical Parent (looking for some flaw) and in his Adapted Child (afraid to be close).

Step 4. *Going back to an earlier scene.* It became clear that trying to solve Tom's problem by dealing with contemporary experiences alone, even in conjunction with permission, does not work. I am now in a position to go on to step 4, which is to uncover the earlier conditioning which led to his present behavior. What I want to determine are what injunctions, what counterinjunctions, and what counterscript drivers he was given as a child, and by whom.

I did this by asking Tom, "What occurred in your earlier life that is related to the way you feel about women and the way you treat them now?" He recalled that his father felt very bitter toward women, said that they were bloodsuckers and that they would take advantage of you. In addition, his mother was extremely seductive, even during adolescence, which increased Tom's fears of women. For the sake of brevity, however, I will discuss only the effect his father's attitudes had upon him since this is adequate to illustrate my methods. When Tom told me the kinds of things his father said about women, I drew a script matrix for him and put on it the injunctions, counterinjunctions, and counterscript drivers he received from his father (see Figure 7).

Figure 7. Script Matrix.

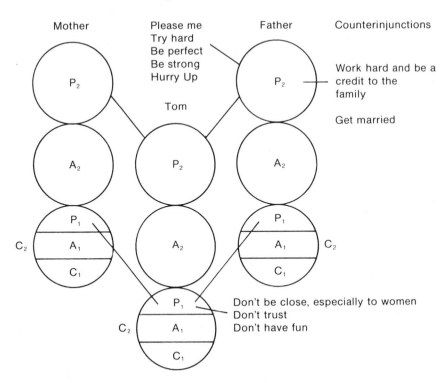

The injunctions that Tom received from his father were:

1. Don't be close, especially to women.
2. Don't trust, especially women.
3. Don't have fun.

His counterinjunctions were:

1. Get married.
2. Work hard and be a credit to the family.

His counterscript drivers were:

1. Please me.
2. Try hard.
3. Be perfect.
4. Be strong.

It is obvious that the conflict of wanting to get married and being afraid of women was based upon the contradictory directions given to him by his father: "Don't be close to or trust women" (injunction) and, at the same time, "Get married and work hard to support your family" (counterinjunction). Tom's early decision was to avoid women and not get close to them, and this aspect of his script was based on that early decision. His desire to be close to women (a natural instinct) was reinforced by the counterinjunction: Get married.

In his life Tom was alternately isolated from women (script) or in an unsuccessful relationship with one (in an attempt to fulfill his counterscript).

His drivers pushed him into the impossible task of trying hard to be perfect and strong and please his father—and, by generalization, everyone else.

Step 5. *Reverse the effect of the counterscript drivers.* The next step is to attempt to reverse the effect of the counterscript drivers.

I invited Tom into the appropriate allowers. For example, I said, "You don't have to please your father by not getting close to women. You can please yourself by getting close to one," and so on. Tom said he understood this, but he was still unable to get close to a member of the opposite sex. This knowledge was real, but intellectual, and he was unable to change his behavior simply by knowing it. The reason for this was that the effect of his father's injunctions, "Don't be close to women," and "Don't trust," made him anxious when he tried to be intimate with a woman, so that he continued to create distance.

In order for Tom to move beyond this point, it was necessary to reverse the effect of the injunctions.

Step 6. *Neutralize the effect of the injunctions.* In my experience this cannot be done *by intellectual means alone.* Such a change requires deep feeling accompanied by regression of the patient to the period in which the injunctions were implanted, followed by or accompanied by a redecision. This requires that the patient relive relevant parts of the early scene in as must intensity as possible—he must, as Freud described it "abreact."

How can the patient be helped to do this? Often he cannot recall enough significant details to reinvoke the early emotions. This is where Gestalt therapy comes in. Gestalt therapy is a method which facilities the development of deep emotions, whereas transactional analysis leads to intellectual comprehension. Both are excellent methods, though neither in my opinion are adequate alone to produce the most significant change. When combined, the effect is like dynamite; the feelings, when properly invoked in the therapeutic setting, blast away resistance, and facilitate moving into new areas of "being" previously considered inaccessible; the intellectual comprehension broadens and consolidates this new position.

The Gestalt "double chair" technique is particularly useful when the patient has reached the point at which it is important for him to become deeply immersed in the emotions that were originally caused by implantation of the injunctions. In Tom's case this was in childhood (probably even in infancy), at the time when his father was by example showing in many different and devious ways how he did not trust women, and how he, in fact, despised them. Tom had many feelings about this then, but he had suppressed them since he needed strokes from his father for survival. What he experienced was an uncomfortable and unexpressed sense of pervasive resentment, the resentment being partly based on his father's continuously discounting his mother in his presence.

It was now time for Tom to reexperience and express these emotions.

I put an empty chair in front of the one that Tom was sitting in and said, "Imagine your father is sitting in this chair. Be whatever age you want to, talk in the present tense, and say to your father in fantasy whatever things you have always wanted to say to him."

The first thing Tom did was to push the chair farther away. Then he said, "I am going to be eight years old." He continued as follows:

TOM: Dad, I don't like you to say those bad things about women in front of Mother. Don't you see it hurts her feelings?

THERAPIST: Now sit in the other chair. Be Dad in fantasy, and answer your question.

TOM: *(Playing Dad's role.)* I don't mean Mother, she's different.

THERAPIST: Now play Tom's role and sit in the other chair.

TOM: *(Playing his own role.)* How do I know that? I'm just a little boy. I keep hearing what you say, and it scares me. *(Tom's voice sounds weak and frightened.)*

THERAPIST: Sit in Dad's chair again and be Dad. "Dad, did you hear that you frightened Tom when he was a little boy. Talk to him about that."

TOM: *(Playing Dad's part.)* I didn't think about that. When I was in World War I, I went out with this French girl, and then she was always bothering me, always trying to get things out of me.

THERAPIST: Be Tom.

TOM:*(Playing his own role.)* When we went out to restaurants, when a little girl went by, you would say, "Look at that pretty little girl. Isn't it a shame she is going to grow up to be such a viper." You would say it in a voice that was loud enough for others to hear, and they would turn and look at us.

THERAPIST: Now be your own age and tell Dad what his being this way about women and saying these things has done to you.

TOM: *(Playing his own role as an adult.)* Your being this way spoils my life. I'm afraid to be close to a woman. I'm afraid she'll hurt me. *(Tom's voice is rising.)* I'm angry at you.

THERAPIST: Say that again, say, "I'm angry" ten times *(I put a pillow on the chair in front of Tom)* and hit the pillow every time you say, "I'm angry."

TOM: I'm angry at you. *(Hits pillow.)* I'm angry at you, Dad. I'm angry. I'm angry.

THERAPIST: Say it louder each time.

TOM: I'm angry, I'm angry, I'm angry. (*He is now yelling loudly. His face is flushed. Then he suddenly exclaims, "And I'm sick and tired of having my life spoiled just because you are scared of women. I'm fed up with it. Fed up, do you hear me?" Tom is literally screaming at this point.*) Fed up with it and fed up with you. All my life I've been scared and frightened and I'm sick of it. I don't believe women are out to get me and I'm giving that up. (*Redecision.*)

THERAPIST: When?

TOM: Right now.

THERAPIST: Go to each girl in the group, look directly at her, and say, "I'm giving up my scare of women, and I'm not scared of *you.*"

Tom did this with each of the six girls in the room, and each of the girls responded with remarks such as, "I'm glad," "That's great," "I'm glad you worked that out," "I like you," and so on.

After Tom finished he sat down, and I said, "How are you feeling now?"

Tom said, "I feel great, I feel lighter, I feel like the weight of the world has been lifted off my shoulders."

Step 7. *The redecision.* The redecision is never easy to achieve. I would not usually attempt it with a patient without going through the steps previously described. It is not something that a therapist can "do" for a patient. The patient makes the redecision himself when he is ready for it. The most the therapist can do is to facilitate its emergence by setting up the circumstances most favorable for this. Even then, the patient makes the redecision with difficulty and usually under great emotional stress (as in Tom's case), at a time when he experiences his frustration intensely and finally finds it intolerable.

Tom reached a redecision during the Gestalt fantasied conversation with his father. His father was still alive at the time Tom was in therapy with me, so that I did not suggest that he say goodbye to his father, and then bury him, as I often do in similar cases when the parent in question is actually dead. However, Tom had a somewhat equivalent experience one week after the session I have just described. He decided that he would have an encounter with his father in the flesh and tell him to his face how his attitude toward women and his criticisms of them and his vituperations about them had affected his (Tom's) life.

When Tom did this (from his Adult ego state), his father initially took it as a rejection of himself rather than as his paranoid behavior. He felt hurt and angry, and broke off communications with Tom for about a month. He then approached Tom, saying that he was sorry for what had happened and that he hadn't realized what effect it would have upon him. Following this, they had a serious and friendly talk, and are now on better terms than ever before. Tom neutralized the effects of the injunctions from his father and made a redecision to be close. His fear of women diminished; he learned to be close to the women in the group, and concurrently with women outside of the group as well. Sometime later he fell in love with an attractive girl and after a period of adjustment asked her to marry him. She accepted. They have now been happily married for three years.

Tom required two years of therapy to achieve autonomy and marriage. What I have described included excerpts taken from this entire period of time. I am now going to present verbatim excerpts taped in just one group therapy session of another client whom I will call Philip. In this session we worked on (1) identification of the problem, (2) formulation of a contract, (3) exploration of the problem in the patient's current life, (4) going back to an earlier scene, (5) reversing the counterscript drivers, (6) uncovering the injunctions and neutralizing their effect, and (7) redecision.

Philip is a talented thirty-four-year-old writer. In the group session he began as follows:

PHILIP: Grace, I have been thinking about what I said to you before the group started tonight, when we were talking about Spain. You said you didn't like Barcelona when you were there last summer, and I felt you didn't stay there long enough to know what it was really like, and I had. I was feeling contemptuous of you.

GRACE: Yes. I know. I was angry.

PHILIP: That's a problem of mine, being contemptuous. It gets in my way. I have a feeling of contempt for other professionals, and I cut off the possibility of exchange . . . and as a result I often act on half or a quarter of whatever information there is. I stop the interchange.

THERAPIST: Is this a problem you would like to get over?

PHILIP: (Seriously.) Yes, I would like to work on that.

GRACE: Who first did that to you?

HENRY: And made you feel full of shit.

GRACE: Made you feel that you didn't really know what you were talking about?

PHILIP: My father . . . my father . . . my father . . . my father!

THERAPIST: (Putting a chair in front of Philip.) Put him on the chair in fantasy and talk to him.

PHILIP: I don't think he ever told me that, but it was an injunction. (Don't be close.)

THERAPIST: How about putting him on the chair and telling him how you feel. (Indicates chair.)

PHILIP: I had intended not to put him on the chair.

THERAPIST: OK. . . . Now suppose he is sitting right here.

PHILIP: He's coming through very strongly. . . . I first want to know you are there. (Pause.)

THERAPIST: What are you feeling right now?

PHILIP: (*Snorts, with a sudden exhaling of air through his mouth.*) I want to talk to you very reasonably, Dad. (*His voice is reasonable and even.*) I want to very much. You make me cry a lot—and—I think I understand (*pause*) . . . I think I understand what you did. You had a very hard time when the world was very cool to you . . . and your need for my love and recognition of you was so great and uncontrollable that . . . I believe that you didn't want to hurt me, that you didn't intend to.

THERAPIST: How did your . . . are you hurting?

PHILIP: You are hurting me . . . you are hurting me.

THERAPIST: Tell your father how he is hurting you.

PHILIP: (*Exhales loudly, makes little sounds of grief and anguish.*) I feel I can never please you and that . . . I still need your approval . . . ah . . . (*Sighing.*)

THERAPIST: Tell your father what you want from him right now.

PHILIP: (*Long pause.*) I want you to look at me. . . . I want you to love *me* (*voice charged with emotion*) and not *yourself*. I want you to see *me* for *me*. Not for your needs—you make me feel so helpless—to help you feel better. I wanted to help you feel better.

THERAPIST: Tell him why you wanted to help him.

PHILIP: Because you were in such pain, always. Physical pain, spiritual pain. You never felt that you could complete anything. (*Voice filled with emotion, a pleading kind of nonverbal sound.*) That hurt me so . . . all of your frustrations hurt me . . . made me feel helpless. (*Loud exhaling.*)

THERAPIST: Will you be your father and respond to what Philip just said? (*Philip has come to the point where he doesn't know where to go next. It is very important at this point that the therapist be with him and direct him. Philip moves to his father's chair, sniffing and blowing his nose and breathing hard. Then he begins to make a low wail.*)

PHILIP: Oh . . . oh . . . oh . . . oh. (*Long pause.*) I don't want you to feel bad. I really don't. It hurts me that you should feel so bad. I want only the best for you. . . . My life is so hard.

THERAPIST: What's hard about your life?

PHILIP: (*Playing father's role.*) Nobody here understands me. . . . They don't know what I can do (*breathing hard*) . . . I get no recognition for my work. They're stupid. Everybody succeeds around me. (*Long pause.*) And they're stupid.

THERAPIST: What do you do that keeps you from succeeding when everyone else does?

PHILIP: (*Still playing his father's role.*) I feel some anger in me that stops me. I can think better than most people that I work with. When I was important I was the apple of everybody's eye . . . but it didn't last. (*Pause.*)

THERAPIST: What happened to it?

PHILIP: *(As father.)* The mill in Mississippi was sold and I lost my job as foreman. I wasn't good from then on. You know that.

THERAPIST: Be Philip and respond to your father.

PHILIP: *(Shifting chairs.)* I know all that. I know you had it rough. But you took it out on me and Ruth (his sister). *(Voice rising in anger.)*

THERAPIST: Tell him how he did that. What did he do?

PHILIP: *(Grief in his voice.)* You only saw yourself. You screamed at Mother . . . you threatened my sister continuously . . . then you pretended to love me *(struggling to breathe)* . . . and you were good at making me believe that. I don't believe you now. I don't believe you love me. *(Anguish in voice.)* I don't believe it. *(Voice drops and is very intense.)* I don't believe you love Mother. I don't believe you love Ruth. You used us opportunistically when you needed us. And when we needed you *(voice rising in intensity and pitch)* you weren't *there.*

THERAPIST: Say that again.

PHILIP: You weren't there *(Yelling loudly and with anger. Long pause as he breathes heavily.)*

THERAPIST: How did you feel about his not being there? Tell him.

PHILIP: I didn't mind it when you weren't there physically, when you were working away from home . . . but I hated it when you were there. How could you walk out of the house and leave Mother crying on the floor? *(Philip begins to cry.)* And me standing at the door and not knowing what to do . . . and thinking that it was Mother who was driving you out of there . . . and hating her *(breathing hard).* Whew . . . that's what I didn't like most. When you were there. When you weren't there I could imagine that you loved me. *(Groaning.)* It was a lot easier when you weren't there. *(Heavy grieving.)* But I missed you. I was always so proud of you . . . the way you talked, the way people were attracted to you. I even liked it when you were *contemptuous* of other people, because you seemed so smart, and that gave me some security. You are smart. Very strong intuitive sense about people. You meant things well . . . but you didn't love me. *(Sobbing.)* It hurts me every day of my life that you didn't. *(Long pause.)* You didn't know what was going on in me. You didn't know how much I wanted to please you. You didn't know how much I loved you. *(Voice small, like a child.)* And you scared the living shit out of me. You were very violent.

THERAPIST: What kind of things did he do that were violent? Tell him.

PHILIP: He screams. He throws textbooks at me that I won't memorize. He tells me that he won't love me unless I do better in school. He demands that I agree with everything he says.

THERAPIST: How did you feel about that?

PHILIP: I felt that all my power was you. And when you died, I thought that I died with you . . . I gave you all my power. (*Voice full of grief.*)

THERAPIST: Do you want to take that power back now?

PHILIP: (*With conviction.*) I want the power I gave you *back*. I don't want you to have my power. (*Whispering, but with certainty and conviction.*)

THERAPIST: Say that again.

PHILIP: I don't want you, Dad, to have my power. I don't want you to have my power, Dad, to *have my power*. (*Louder and more definite.*)

THERAPIST: Will you change that a little bit and say, "I won't let you have my power" . . . if that feels OK.

PHILIP: That feels fine. I won't let you have my power, Dad. (*Voice rising in intensity.*) I won't let you have my power, Dad. I won't let you have my power, Dad.

THERAPIST: Is that true or false?

PHILIP: I don't know.

THERAPIST: Tell Dad why you don't know.

PHILIP: You're strong. You're holding on tight. I don't know if I'm as strong as you. I want to be stronger than you. I want to be . . . I want my power back from you, bastard.

THERAPIST: Say that again.

PHILIP: I want my power back. *I'm going to take my power back from you, whether you want to give it to me or not.*

THERAPIST: How are you going to do that?

PHILIP: I'm not going to let you make me feel bad. I am not going to let you have power over me. (*Speaking in a small voice with a new tone.*) I'm not going to go to you for love.

THERAPIST: Will you be your father now?

PHILIP: (*Changes chairs and speaks as father.*) Ah . . . it's interesting that I need to have power over you. I need to know that when I am sad you are sad, and when I am happy you are happy. I need to know that, because it's the only way *I* can be happy and the only way I can feel potent. So you've got *some fight* on your hands.

THERAPIST: Be Philip and talk back to your father.

PHILIP: I guessed that. I had you figured. I knew that you would fight. But I *have to live*, and you're dead. *I'm going to live, and you're dead.*

These redecisions, to take back his own power and to live his own life, were made at a time when Philip was regressed to childhood in an early scene which occurred during the fantasied confrontation with his father during the double chair Gestalt work. While doing this, he was able momentarily to come out of the regression into his present-day Adult ego state. He then viewed the early scene in the light of his current knowledge, which is that he was not at fault in not being able to make his Dad happy and successful, and that he can now take back his own power and lead his own life.

At first sight much of this work seemed to be unrelated to the original contract Philip made to resolve his attitude of contempt for others, but on closer inspection it is right on target, since by taking back his own power Philip undercut his need to be contemptuous of other people's opinions, as his father had been contemptuous of his.

Nevertheless, I wanted to go back to the original contract and find out where Philip was with it. "How do you feel now about being contemptuous toward your friends and colleagues?" I asked.

"I don't need to be contemptuous," Philip said. "I've taken back my own power, and that's much better. I'm going to live for me now." When Philip said this, the other group members broke out into spontaneous cheers and applause.

Often, redecisions like these need further working through, and in Philip's case he later reconfirmed them through further work on reversing the injunctions and by enacting a wrestling match with his father (in fantasy), which he won decisively after a hard struggle. With this increased awareness of his own power he was able to stop trying to please the incorporated Not OK Critical Parent in his own head, and to see his father as a man who had many problems and who was struggling with them. With this knowledge he was finally able to contact feelings of affection toward him, and to let him go.

For some patients, the impasse between dependence upon parents and autonomy is so difficult that they despair of ever resolving it. They are unable to get beyond the stage of grief and anger. Even the recognition that their parents could not have been any other way does not seem to help. I was working with such a case just recently, a woman named Anne, twenty-eight years old. For the nth time she was trying to work through grief and anger in a double chair fantasied conversation with her mother, but again nothing came out but irritation at her mother's criticisms of her, and anger at her.

"There must be some other way of getting through this impasse," I thought, and then I had a flash, an image of what her mother might have been like if she had had psychotherapy. So I said to Anne, "How would you like to try out something new, that I have never used before, and have no experience with?"

Anne looked at me, nodded her head, and said, "I would like to try it."

"Imagine that your mother has had therapy and that it worked. That she knows everything you know, and that she is just the kind of mother you want. Now put her on this chair in front of you in fantasy and have a conversation with her."

Anne looked at me for a full minute and said nothing. Then she looked at the empty chair. Then she said, "I want to sit in that chair and be my mother first." She got up and moved to the chair. After a few moments of silence she said, "Anne, I always wanted to have you. I always wanted a girl just like you." Her voice was soft and warm, amazingly different from the whining, irritated, and angry tone she had used in her conversation with her mother before.

"Now sit in this chair and be Anne," I directed.

ANNE: *(As herself.)* I love it when you talk to me like that, Mother. Can we play and do things together?

THERAPIST: Be Mother.

ANNE: *(Playing her mother's role.)* Yes, yes, that's what I want. We'll take walks together, and go down to the brook, and go wading.

THERAPIST: Be Anne.

ANNE: *(Playing her own role).* Oh, mother, that will be such fun. *(Clapping her hands.)* And will you hold me and cuddle me?

THERAPIST: Be your mother.

ANNE: *(As her mother.)* Yes, yes, I will. *(Voice excited.)*

THERAPIST: Be Anne.

ANNE: *(As herself.)* Oh, Mother! *(Anne's voice was soft and warm, her face relaxed and glowing.)*

This conversation continued for a longer time than I have recorded, but I will not reproduce it in its entirety in order to save space. Its essence is that in this fantasied experience Anne feels loved by her mother and Anne loves her mother. Anne's Adapted Child asked Mother's OK Nurturing Parent for what she wanted, and Mother's OK Nurturing Parent gave it to her. Anne's Adapted Child received permission to do and be, and was happy. At this time energy passed from Anne's Adapted Child to her Free Child. Literally, this was for Anne a new kind of experience.

Before the session ended, I suggested that Anne have such a conversation with her mother for ten minutes every day. She has now done this for two weeks and feels and looks radiant. With the help of this technique, she finally broke through the impasse that had previously blocked her in many months of therapy.

I have used this method with seven other patients, all of whom are enthusiastic about it. I know two other therapists who have used it with favorable results.

It is too early to estimate the long-term effects of this maneuver, but several theoretical advantages are obvious. Resistance to change is undercut because the patient gives herself permission from her parent's OK Nurturing Parent to be herself with approval and protection. She is also giving herself permission from her own OK Nurturing Parent to be herself. Her Adapted Child gets the message, relaxes, and feels freer. Her Little Professor (the Adult in the Child of the child) takes in this new information and is able to use it more easily (than if it has been fed from the outside) to make a redecision to give up the old fears, to relax, and to be autonomous. All of the patient's ego states concur (a necessity for a successful redecision) since the entire series of transactions is carried out by the patient herself, and hence with her own approval.

Goulding helps the patient move toward a redecision by asking him "to fantasize where he will be in five years, or ten years, or fifteen years, if he continues to smoke" (or something else), letting him realize the full implications of his life pattern. We let him feel enough organismic disgust so that at this moment he will make a redecision, feel the change in his guts, feel the flood of relief at having made a real decision to "grow, or play, or live" (5).

Another help toward redecision, as indicated by Goulding, is to point out to patients that such words as "try, can't, won't, should, why, because" are all copouts. The person who uses them does not really intend to do what he says he wants to do. The correct words when the intent is to avoid a redecision are, "I won't." The correct words to use if the determination is to make a redecision are, "I will." Here we see an intertwining of TA and Gestalt. "Copout words" are TA and "organismic change" is Gestalt.

Step 8. *Saying goodbye to parents.* After patients have gotten far enough along in their therapy and have completed most of the Gestalt work, I ask them if they would like to say goodbye, once and for all to the undesirable things that their parents did to them, and then to the parents themselves. This requires that the patient has already worked through the grief and anger that he felt toward his parents, and uncovered at least some feelings of love. If the patient is still angry at his parents, saying goodbye to them as a step toward regaining personal autonomy will not work, since as long as he is angry, he remains in his Adapted Child ego state and still needs them. This is why such anger toward parents is called the "holding-on bite," in Gestalt. The person with the holding-on bite cannot chew up the food, cannot swallow it, and cannot spit it out. He is stuck with it.

Usually, after the anger at parents is fully expressed, the patient does experience feelings of love toward them that were previously repressed. As this occurs, most patients recall some positive experiences with their parents. Then they remember the pleasant things and finally they recognize their parents as real people who had problems and who loved them to the extent that was possible for them.

Step 9. *Making a new "life" contact.* Having given up his injunctions, counterinjunctions, and counterscript drivers, and, in consequence, much irrational behavior, the patient needs now to substitute new ways of being for old. It is not enough to stop behaving irrationally. The patient needs to "learn" new ways of being, new patterns of behavior, which are health promoting. Heretofore this was difficult to do, because much of the patient's energy was bound up in his Not OK Critical Parent and Adapted Child. New ways of behaving were looked upon with fear and suspicion and were rejected. Now that the patient is released from the effects of the irrational messages from his parents, this is no longer the case. A kind of psychological vacuum exists at this time. It is filled by "retraining," which follows the redecision. Strictly speaking, this began even before the redecision, with the new type of relationship which the patient gradually learned to have with the therapist and the other members of the group, one that is frank, direct, open, nondefensive, stroking, and nurturing. The group participant learns this way of behaving in the group and transfers it to others outside the group—members of his family, friends, business acquaintances.

This new type of learning now needs to be intensified. The group member who was too much in his Adult ego state now can devote time to giving his Free Child permission to play. The person who was too much in his Critical Parent needs to learn to be nurturing and stroking, both to himself and others. The person whose Adapted Child was too much in the Executive discovers that he is better liked if he is autonomous rather than rebellious or placating.

Such new behavior can best be learned in a group setting. My groups meet once a week for two to three hours, and then the members of all the groups come together for a twelve-to-fourteen-hour minithon once a month. This is supplemented with weekend and five-day marathons and workshops. Such group sessions, minithons, and marathons constitute a special environment for personal growth.

Therapeutic Value of the Group

I do a great deal of individual therapy in the group setting. I literally go through the steps in therapy descriped in this chapter, and sometimes more, according to the needs of the particular patient and depending on my creativity in improvising new ways and new methods of dealing with specific problems and impasses. Usually I do not spend more than a half or three quarters of an hour on any one patient, though sometimes exceptions to this may occur, when an individual may require almost the entire session during a crisis, or when on the verge of breaking through some longstanding impasse, such as the second- or third-degree impasses described by Goulding.

In such a case the group member who is requiring all this time usually feels that he is taking up *too* much time, and that the other members of the group will object. When this occurs I ask the patient who is working to check with the group members and ask if they do object. Usually the response is, "No," with a shake of the head, or, "I'm getting a great deal out of this, I want you to keep on," and so forth.

When I am working intensively with one patient, the other group members are usually so deeply engrossed in the way what we are doing affects their own lives that they do not become restless. Sometimes the individual work involves the patient going to each of the other members of the group and asking some question of him or making some statement to him. After the intensive work is done, the patient who is working usually goes to certain or all of the group members and asks for whatever he wants to know or have from him. He may want to know what playback that person has about the work he did. He may want a hug. He may want additional nurturing.

The intimate and direct exchanges that occur in such encounters are extremely important and facilitate change.

In the discussion that follows each piece of work, each person says what he feels, how he reacts to the person who was working, and what he did. Group members are discouraged from telling the other person what he "should" have said, or that he didn't know the meaning of what he said. They are taught to react with personal feelings, and to share these feelings with each other.

I am going to illustrate the importance of group interaction and positive support by describing briefly how, on one occasion, the group gave strong, united support to one of its members who was struggling with a severe emotional crisis.

Linda is a bright, personable woman who was severely discounted by both parents. She does not remember ever having received a positive stroke from either of them. She was discounted both for "being" and "doing" and she received all of the injunctions, with special emphasis on "Don't exist," "Don't have sexual feelings," "Don't be close," "Don't trust men," and "Don't be sane." In consequence, she married a man who was distant, dominating, and critical, reinforcing her distrust of men and her inability to be close or to have an orgasm. Subsequently, she divorced her husband. Both her mother and father increased her feelings of guilt and inadequacy by insisting that she was a failure as a wife and a mother, and that she should have stayed with her husband even though he became increasingly violent—since, as her mother said, "Everything is your fault."

Linda arrived one Saturday morning at a minithon upset to the point of hysteria, having received an unusually heavy barrage of discounting from her parents the night before. She had made considerable progress in the group in getting close to the men but, in consequence of the latest battle with her parents, she regressed.

This was really a crisis. Linda was crying uncontrollably. In a videotape session, including the group, which lasted over two hours, she described the unexpected confrontation with her parents the night before in which her father criticized her for not talking with him about divorcing her husband (who had threatened to kill her), when the fact was that she had tried to discuss it with him previously, but he had remained aloof and withdrawn, as usual, and had now forgotten the episode. The interchange escalated. Linda accused her parents of driving her sister into schizophrenia and ultimately suicide by their continuous discounting of her. (There seems to be some reality in this accusation, because every time her sister began to get well, her parents took her away from the doctor who was treating her.) Linda's great fear was that her parents would do the same thing to her, and she said to them the night before this minithon, "I would like you to give me just one compliment before I die." Her mother replied, "You will never get a compliment from me." When Linda accused her parents of driving her sister crazy, both parents began screaming, "You're crazy, you're crazy!" The evening ended with Linda literally running out of the house in despair.

As she talked about what had happened with rage and anguish, the members of the group listened with very deep concern. I am now going to describe here the steps in which Linda, after a series of Gestalt double chair exercises with her parents, got into her own power. My purpose in describing this particular case is to show how the group interaction encouraged, supported, and facilitated the work.

In reversing the effects of the injunctions, after going into them in detail in the Gestalts and realizing their irrationality, Linda finally took a piece of Kleenex for each injunction and tore each up. At this time the group, like a Greek chorus, which I led, fed her positive messages (the reverse of the injunctions).

"Linda, it's all right to exist."

"Linda, it's all right to have your feelings."

"Linda, it's all right to be close to men."

"Linda, it's all right to have an orgasm."

These positive messages, which are in reality new tapes and permissions to which she can go back in the future, affected her deeply. As she listened, her face and body relaxed, and she became radiant and beautiful.

After this work was done, each man in the group went up to her and in his own way expressed his feelings toward her, in an intimate and close exchange.

Then, at my instruction, the whole group picked Linda up and rocked her gently for about five minutes, humming at the same time, "Om."

I then directed them to put her down gently. She lay on the floor looking trustingly from face to face as everyone stroked her gently, in silence.

After this, I asked her how she felt. She sighed contentedly and said, "I would like to feel this way forever."

Then she made close individual contact with each member of the group.

Finally, she stood up before the whole group and said, with a radiant smile, "I'm a pearl of a girl."

Conclusion

As noted previously, I usually work intensively with one person for only half to three quarters of an hour. During that time I frequently go through all of the steps I have outlined, from identifying the problem, formulating a contract, and determining the injunctions, counterinjunctions, counterscript drivers, and rackets, to the Gestalt double chair work, redecision, and the formulation of new ways of behaving to replace the old.

In such a case I am dealing with only one specific problem, such as being afraid to speak up in a group, or to talk in front of an audience. In the latter instance the therapy usually ends with the patient giving an impromptu talk to the group, followed by applause.

The way I proceed, then, is to solve one problem after another. Frequently, *individual problems* can be resolved in a short period of time, but a whole lifetime reorientation usually requires one or two years or more. The final result, leading to a termination of therapy, occurs as the consequence of previously solving each individual problem as it arises.

However, as in the case of the "whole being greater than the sum of its parts," so the final resolution, which leads to autonomy, also transcends the "sum of *its* parts," and is a unified attitude and way of looking at oneself and at the world. It involves accepting oneself as OK. If a person does this, he will accept others as OK unless there is evidence to the contrary. His existential position will be "I'm OK—You're OK." He will have learned to ask for the kinds of strokes he wants and to give the kind of strokes he wants to give. He will not feel that he needs to accept any strokes from others that he does not want. He will feel comfortable about stroking, or nurturing himself. There will be a shift of energy from his Critical Parent to his Nurturing Parent and from his Adapted Child to his Free Child. His Adult will be free from parental prejudices and childish illusions, and will thus be able to function freely without contamination. In short, he will be a whole, autonomous person.

References

(1) ERNST, F. H., JR. The Diagrammed Parent. Transactional Analysis Journal, Eric Berne Issue, 1, No. 1 (January 1971).

(2) BERNE, E. Transactional Analysis in Psychotherapy. New York: Grove Press, 1961.

(3) DUSAY, J. M. Egograms and the Constancy Hypothesis. Transactional Analysis Journal, 2, No. 3 (July 1972).

(4) KAHLER, T., and CAPERS, H. The Miniscript. Transactional Analysis Journal, 4, No. 1 (January 1974).

(5) GOULDING, R. New Directions in Transactional Analysis: Creating an Environment for Redecision and Change. In Sager, C. J., and Kaplan, H. S. (eds.), Progress in Group and Family Therapy. New York: Brunner/Mazel, 1972.

(6) BERNE, E. Games People Play. New York: Grove Press, 1964.

(7) BERNE, E. What Do You Say after You Say Hello? New York: Grove Press, 1972.

Supplemental Bibliography

TRANSACTIONAL ANALYSIS

ABELL, R. G. Own Your Own Life. New York: McKay, 1976.

BERNE, E. Transactional Analysis in Psychotherapy. New York: Grove Press, 1961.

BERNE, E. The Structure and Dynamics of Organizations and Groups. Philadelphia: Lippincott, 1963.

BERNE, E. Games People Play. New York: Grove Press, 1964.

BERNE, E. Principles of Group Treatment. New York: Oxford University Press, 1966.

BERNE, E. Sex in Human Loving. New York: Simon and Schuster, 1970.

BERNE, E. What Do You Say after You Say Hello? New York: Grove Press, 1972.

HARRIS, T. A. I'm OK—You're OK. New York: Harper and Row, 1969.

JAMES, M., and JONGEWARD, D. Born to Win. Reading, Mass.: Addison-Wesley, 1971.

McCORMICK, P., and CAMPOS, L. Introduce Yourself to Transactional Analysis. Transactional Publications, 1772 Vallejo St., San Francisco, Calif. (1972).

MEININGER, J. Success through Transactional Analysis. New York: Grossett and Dunlap, 1973.

SCHIFF, J. All My Children. Philadelphia: Evans, 1970.

STEINER, C. Games Alcoholics Play: The Analysis of Life Scripts. New York: Grove Press, 1971.

STEINER, C. Scripts People Live By. New York: Grove Press, 1974.

Transactional Analysis Bulletin. Formerly official publication, International Transactional Analysis Association. Vol. 1 (1962) to vol. 9 (1969).

Transactional Analysis Journal. Official Journal, ITAA. Vol. 1 (1971) to current issue.

WOOLLAMS, S., BROWN, M., and HUIGH, K. Transactional Analysis in Brief. Huron Valley Institute, 3318 Williamsburg, Ann Arbor, Mich. (1974).

GESTALT THERAPY

FAGAN, J., and SHEPHERD, I. L. Gestalt Therapy Now: Theory, Techniques, Application. Palo Alto, Calif.: Science and Behavior Books, 1970.

PERLS, F. S. Ego, Hunger and Aggression. New York: Random House, 1947.

PERLS, F. S., HEFFERLINE, R. F., and GOODMAN, P. Gestalt Therapy. New York: Delta, 1951.

PERLS, F. S. Gestalt Therapy Verbatim. Lafayette, Calif.: Real People Press, 1969.

emporary Western man, especially in the United States, is ren-
potent by two primary effects of the technocracy. On the one
is caught by the systematized, impersonal, invisible, referentless
of the culture whose scope and complexity he must fail to com-
and whose ethic of scientific objectivity is no longer acceptable to
the other hand, he is hemmed in by his technocratically condi-
ability to pit his self against the world on the basis of faith alone.
the solution of compromise. It promises power without merit, in-
thout risk, victory without battle. But, if you think of it, magic is
ate technique. If you do it right, it will produce everything. As
ears no relation to the human values which it professes to serve.
econd source of the need to see these techniques as magic resides
henomenon of "I only work here," to borrow Philip Slater's
y observant phrase. Again, because of the vastness and complex-
psychosocial and psychophysical environments of contemporary
dividual participation in the design and outcomes of the world
grossly limited. Creative private action is blocked in the realm of
primary concerns. The effect is a paralysis of the will, an atrophy
ertion, and finally an irreparable loss of the sense of responsibility
mmunity and for the self. "I only work here" is a sickening ex-
f the powerlessness and captivity of defeated beings. Magic be-
imaginary antidote. Without risk or struggle, without the threat-
dow of further defeats, magic makes the world malleable and
subject it to sudden total control. Therefore, it promises what
century man lacks and craves: personal influence.
ird interrelated source of the need and the error of regarding
magic has to do with the early practitioners. As I said, Gestalt
s initially practiced by a handful of charismatic people, whose
ower, exceptional stage presence, and idiosyncratic creativity
pressive, with good reason, to numbers of people. But the gap
lent and magic is wide. What contracts it is our contemporary
e Celebrity and the delusion of visibility through identification
rities. What I mean is this. The anonymity of the individual in
has increased in proportion with the size and complexity of our
ters. Neighbor has become stranger to neighbor, supermarket
lo not call their customers by name, Bloomingdale's department
s nothing of the lady or gentleman who drops in for a look-see
Personal visibility, especially for those not expert in some spe-
a, has declined and can amount to the number of immediate
bers. In very large cities like New York, for many people, it is
lmost zero. Those, then, who succeed in making themselves
me unreasonably overvalued and worshiped. They are endowed
ies which in reality they do not possess in the hope that they
on the projector. In other words, the Cult of the Celebrity is

POLSTER, E., and POLSTER, M. Gestalt Therapy Integrated. New York: Brun-
    ner/Mazel, 1973.

PSYCHOANALYSIS IN GROUPS

ABELL, R. G. Personality Development during Group Psychotherapy. Am. J.
    Psychoanal., 19 (1959), 53.
KADIS, A., KRASNER, J., WINICK, C., and FOULKES, S. H. A Practicum of Group
    Psychotherapy. New York: Harper and Row, 1963.
MULLAN, H., and ROSENBAUM, M. Group Therapy, 2nd ed. New York: Free
    Press, 1978.
ROSENBAUM, M., and BERGER, M. Group Psychotherapy and Group Function.
    New York: Basic Books, rev. ed. 1975.
WOLF, A., and SCHWARTZ, E. K. Psychoanalysis in Groups. New York: Grune
    and Stratton, 1962.
WOLF, A., and SCHWARTZ, E. K. Psychoanalysis in Groups. In Kaplan, H. I.,
    and Sadock, B. J. (eds.), Comprehensive Group Psychotherapy. Baltimore:
    William and Wilkins, 1971.
WOLF, A., SCHWARTZ, E. K., McCARTY, G., and GOLDBERG, I. A. Psycho-
    analysis in Groups: Contrasts with Other Group Therapies. In Sager, C. J.,
    and Kaplan, H. S. (eds.), Progress in Group and Family Therapy. New
    York: Brunner/Mazel, 1972.

15 Gestalt Group Psychotherapy

Magda Denes-Radomisli

The Promise of Gestalt Therapy

GESTALT THERAPY THESE DAYS reminds me very strongly of the status of the United States in the early 1900s from a European perspective. America was then widely perceived to be, through hearsay, a place of great promise, a land of unequaled opportunities, a refuge for the routed, a breeding ground for the daring, a haven of rich and certain rewards for the diligent. True, rumor also had it that the country was rather wild and unruly, a bit lawless, and that it lacked any definite direction in its progress; nevertheless, these purported disadvantages paled in comparison with the vision of streets paved with gold.

Also, firsthand accounts seem to have been scarce. Information filtered back to the citizenry of the Old World as if by osmosis, always titillating, always speaking to dreams and desires, to dormant yearnings for vast spaces, to latent longings for freedom and for uncluttered wealth in all realms of life. And yet, for all its power to grip the soul, America remained vague, perpetually shrouded in the mysteries of a long, unpredictable, and generally one-way sea voyage.

Currently, Gestalt therapy seems to suffer a similar fate. Propagated for almost two decades by a handful of charismatic people, primarily through verbal means, Gestalt principles both spread and diminished. In the absence of any significant published text from 1951 (1) to 1969 (2), Gestalt passed into the public domain as legendary hope for the afflicted as well as uncharted territory to be developed or exploited by practitioners, including many whose actual knowledge of Gestalt therapy all too often lacked intellectual substance.

It is only from 1969 on that some written works began to appear, like welcome maps to a fabled country. These texts notwithstanding, the "romance" of secret, facile miracles continues to haunt Gestalt practice.

Concommitant with, and because of, this also developed a second prevalent attitude to somewhat more conservative, Thomist circle tice, Gestalt came to be regarded as one n sprung, "humanistic" movement. In this vie entirely on the particular therapist's persu scope of treatment depending on the practi peutic outcomes reflecting the random di coveries.

Both assessments are false. I also think t deeply rooted contemporary cultural mala highlights twentieth-century man's desire—e that comes from mattering to himself.

The Industrial Revolution of the ninet quent automation in the twentieth, brough ture that have resulted in pervasive psychi isolation, mechanization of work, intrapsyc creasing reliance on experts to interpret th not specifically trained in the newly evolve ford, Paul Goodman, and more recently I the sphere of influence and personal signific steadily since the nineteenth century, with population being composed of nonpersons.

Today we are witnessing a massive r There is a resurgence of the need to mak and a revitalization of the belief that subje source for interpreting the reality of the w

It is to these positive strivings in the c therapy speaks. And incidentally, as I h Gestalt therapy is in a position to accor strivings.

Magic and Gestalt Therapy

I regard, then, the quality of magic t ment (attached as well to some of the o erating therapeutic techniques) as the though interrelated processes of social di nocracy are apt to succumb.

Magic, sorcery, witchcraft, secular mi come significant in times of crisis in th themselves as helpless.

Con
dered ir
hand, he
realities
prehend
him. On
tioned in
Magic is
tegrity w
the ulti
such, it l

The
in the
felicitous
ity of the
culture,
becomes
day-to-da
in self-ass
for the c
pression
comes th
ening sh
appears t
twentieth

The t
Gestalt a
therapy w
personal
proved in
between
Cult of t
with cele
our societ
urban cer
managers
store kno
every day.
cialized a
family me
down to
visible bec
with quali
will reflec

fed through projective identification, whereby anonymous people expect to regain a measure of their selfhood. Thus charisma becomes handmaiden to magic in weaving the insidious dream of secondhand self-affirmations.

Gestalt therapy, then, is no magic, and if it were it would be worthless and counterproductive to the very notion of psychotherapy or emotional wholeness.

Next, I should like to tell you what I think Gestalt group therapy—or, as I prefer to call my particular brand of it, existential Gestalt group therapy—is. Before I do this, however, I want to say a few words about the opposing, prevalent view in the field: namely, that Gestalt is faddish hocum.

I want to stipulate that to the extent that it is seen as, or pretends to be, magic, it is mere faddism, and distrust in it is fully justified. To the extent that Gestalt, as well as some of the other new movements, is nothing but a conglomerate of techniques, often devised on the basis of flamboyance alone, or devised in the service of narcissistic gratifications for the practitioner in the spirit of "why not?", it is indeed no psychotherapy. Further, the very emphasis on technique goes contrary to existential humanistic aims, because it reasserts the technocratic ethic of objective manipulation.

Primary Assumptions

Gestalt therapy, individual as well as group, rests on two primary assumptions advanced originally by Fritz Perls.

1. According to Perls, the phenomenal world of a person is always organized by his most pressing need, which becomes figure, until the need is satisfied and recedes into the background to give way to another organizing need. He regards the elasticity of this figure-ground formation as the base in which selfhood is rooted.

Since need satisfaction takes place in the context of the environment, *awareness* is the boundary experience of contact between the organism and the environment.

The theory is deceptively simple and ingenious since it provides a criterion for organismic health purely in terms of the elasticity of figure-ground formation. Or, differently put, illness is regarded as a function of disturbance at the contact boundary.

2. Awareness gives the self cohesiveness and enables the individual in a state of health to choose his being in an active mode. Awareness is to be distinguished from insight in that the latter is the product of primarily cognitive operations, whereas the former—that is, awareness—is a total organismic response of attention transmuted into knowledge. As such, awareness is also the basis for the individual's reality orientation and perception.

Perls has devised a series of what he refers to as "exercises" or "games" designed to enhance and broaden awareness. He assumes that increased awareness produces a shift from the need for environmental support to self-support; that is, maximum awareness results in maximum field independence, a condition which he regards as crucial to healthy organismic functioning.

The exercises, which are used in both individual and group treatment, although preset by Perls, in practice must remain as flexible models to be modified and altered by the particular therapist using them. Also, they must be transformed to fit the specific patient and the specific context within which they are employed.

The Contracts of Gestalt Therapy

Generally speaking, the Gestalt group is organized around a set of "rules." These are to be distinguished from exercises in that they represent contracts between the therapist and the group members. They are explained at the first session, and transgression of them is always immediately brought to the group's attention. As is the case with most recurring interpretive interventions on the part of the therapist, eventually the group takes over this regulatory function in relation to individual members.

The rules are as follows:*

THE PRINCIPLE OF THE NOW

The group is instructed that communications are to be made at all times in the present tense. Thus if a past event is being related, the patient is asked to put himself, in fantasy, back in the situation and to describe the event as if it were taking place now.

The aim of the rule is to remobilize affect in relation to the past and to give both the patient and therapist an opportunity to become aware of the authenticity with which the patient is related to the past event. Rote "stories," rehearsed "injuries," rationalized "explanations" for current ills rather quickly reveal themselves through this technique.

The same applies to future concerns. Projected anxieties, fears, forebodings of defeat, or anticipations of pleasure, success, and so on, are all dealt with in the now. The expected, often obtained result is an increase in the genuineness and reality of the experience.

---

* These rules were first set forth in *Gestalt Therapy* by Perls, Goodman, and Hefferline (1).

I and Thou

Communications are to be made at all times *to* someone. Usually the "someone" is either the therapist or a group member. Occasionally, it can be a fantasy figure, provided that it is named, described, defined, and located in a particular place in the room. Thus one can speak directly to one's dead grandmother, dressed in black, sitting on the chair in front of the window, so long as the old lady is addressed as "Grandma" and her imagined reactions to the address are reported.

The rule aims toward the awareness of the distinction between talking *to* and talking *at* someone. It also aims at a heightened sensitivity that human interactions involve a respondent, an other, who must be regarded and therefore not treated as object but as person. Talking *at* someone is assumed to be a manipulative rather than a communicative activity. As such, it reduces both the speaker and the listener to objecthood.

"It" Language and "I" Language

Group members are asked, when talking about themselves (often regarding their physical beings), to convert "It" expressions into "I" expressions. For example, referring to one's jaw: "It is clenched" becomes "I am clenching." In the case of one's hand: "It trembles" becomes "I am trembling." "It is sad to think" changes to "I am sad to think," and so on.

What at first glance appears to be a rather simplistic semantic shift, has in fact some far-reaching consequences. Its references, on examination, tend to reveal both dissociated and passive attitudes. The person using them implies that he is "acted upon," not responsible, not in charge. Further, that he disowns not only his autonomy, but often his anatomy as well: "The head hurts." Contrasted with "my head hurts" or, even beyond, "I am hurting my head," this clearly highlights major differences in self-perception. The device of a deliberate semantic shift nearly always brings this self-perception into awareness.

No Gossiping

This rule has to do with the stricture against referring to anyone present in the room in the third person.

Thus, "You see, Mary, what John means is ———" is not acceptable. John has to be addressed directly, even though the clarification may be intended for John's respondent, Mary. The requisite sentence then becomes "John, what I think you mean is ———." The same applies, of course, to commentary, such as "John is doing that in order to ———." It must become, under our rule, "John, you are doing that in order to ———."

The rule aims to facilitate direct confrontation of affect. The assumption is that the "gossip" is motivated, and his indirection is in the service of not revealing his feelings and not taking responsibility for them.

ASKING QUESTIONS

Perls distinguishes two types of questions: those which genuinely seek information, and those which are manipulative in intent. Naturally, the latter type are discouraged in the group. Again, as with several of the other symptomatic behaviors, which these rules attempt to interrupt and bring to awareness, the manipulative question is seen as being in the service of passivity, helplessness, and denial of responsibility—in short, in the service of perpetuating reliance on environmental support, as opposed to achieving a self-supportive stance. Technically, the manipulative questioner is asked to convert his question into a statement. Most frequently the conversion automatically—that is, without further interpretation—reveals the questioner's underlying motive as well as his accompanying affect.

The Awareness Continuum: The Cornerstone of Gestalt Therapy

A sixth item, which Perls classifies under rules, but which I regard as the cornerstone of Gestalt therapy as well as its most creatively innovative feature, is the use of "The Awareness Continuum" and its two corollary techniques "Can You Stay with This Feeling?" and "Take a Reading." (In some ways the "homey" language of Gestalt therapy pains me, for it fails to reflect adequately the importance and seriousness of these notions.)

The Awareness Continuum represents an immediate, direct translation into practice of the existential aim of phenomenological observation. It reveals the "how"-ness of experience, and changes the individual's relatedness to reality in that his grasp of it becomes sensorially immediate.

Specifically, it consists of asking the patient to list all the extroceptive and proprioceptive events of which he is aware at any given limited period of time. The specific instruction is something as simple as saying, "Please make up some sentences all beginning with 'Here and now I am aware that . . .'"

It is the therapist's task to call attention to the discrepancies that occur between verbal report and organismic expression, such as the patient saying "Here and now I am aware that I am happy" while his tone is sad and the corners of his mouth point downward. Also, to call attention to the discrepancies between the verbal report and consensually demonstrable reality, such as the patient in a group setting reporting "I am aware that everyone here is laughing at me" while in reality the group looks deeply touched. Confrontation in the first instance gives rise to issues of psychic integration, denial, repression, authenticity, responsibility, the battle of introjects, and so on. Confrontation in the second instance gives rise to issues of projection, stereotypy in function, reality testing, and so on. In either case, and whatever the specific problem that arises, the patient is in firsthand organismic contact with his discrepant functioning.

A closely allied technique or perhaps even an integral part of the Awareness Continuum is what is referred to as "Can You Stay with This Feeling?" The purpose here is to confront resistance in the face of the discovery of a discrepant state. The patient is asked to familiarize himself with his discomfort in staying with the feeling in order that he may contact its ramifications and overcome his phobic avoidance of the feared state.

A third technique, really an abbreviated form of the Awareness Continuum, is what I call, "Take a Reading." "Take a Reading" as an invitation to pinpoint, at a given instant, one's internal experiential state in order to orient oneself in relation to one's momentary being-in-the world. The instructions run something like this: "Please take a reading, by which I mean pay careful attention to where you are at this moment in your fantasy, here or perhaps someplace else. What is your most outstanding feeling at the moment? How is the comfort level of your body? Name what is the most important thing of which you are intellectually aware."

The aim is to sharpen awareness of the figure of the Gestalt of one's momentary being-in-the-world so that some relevant stance may be adopted in relation to it. I say "stance" and not "action" because often action is suppressed by other considerations even though one's stance is clarified. Thus, on becoming aware that one is angry at one's boss, one may or may not choose to act on this awarenesss. But it is through the awareness— that is, through the clarification of one's stance—that the action (or inaction) inescapably becomes a matter of *choice*.

Since awareness in Gestalt therapy is regarded as the single most crucial factor in effective human functioning, the Awareness Continuum and its two allied techniques become focal in both individual and group treatment.

Individual Treatment in the Group

In traditional Gestalt therapy as practiced by Perls and some of his followers, no real distinction is made between individual and group treatment. Group therapy consists of the therapist working serially with each person while the other members look on. The primary interaction is one to one, between the therapist and one patient at a time. The rest of the group members serve as what has been referred to in the literature as a Greek chorus; that is, they underscore and from time to time facilitate the action between the two main protagonists, but they do not directly participate in this action.

The rationale for this method is the assumption (in some ways correct) that the onlookers, although ostensibly passive, do become internally mobilized and are able to derive therapeutic benefits through identification with the momentary patient. The disadvantage of the procedure, among others, is that there is no way to tell with which member of the performing dyad a given onlooker will identify. If the subject of identification is the therapist, it seems to me that the onlooking patient, far from deriving therapeutic benefits, may be receiving fuel for his "symptoms fire" in the form of grandiose, sadistic, manipulative fantasies. I am not implying that these qualities characterize the therapist but, rather, that from the point of view of the audience the interaction between patient and therapist lends itself to such distortions, given the confrontive nature of most Gestalt techniques.

In my own group work I use the Gestalt Rules. I also use the Awareness Continuum and its allied techniques, as well as various exercises. I regard the exercises as useful primarily at points of impasse, whether they occur in the group process or in the working of an individual patient. At the same time, I encourage member interaction, albeit within the Gestalt framework, in order to actualize what I conceive to be an existential aim of treatment, namely, facilitation of the development in each member of a sense of intersubjective responsibility. Far from Perls' philosophy of "I do my thing, you do yours," I see as the most advantageous aspect of group psychotherapy precisely the opportunity of learning to establish an "I and Thou" relatedness with many persons simultaneously.

Concerns and Reservations

Before I describe, however, what I think to be the unique advantages of group treatment, let me say a few words about my concerns and reservations.

It seems to me that the proliferation of the practice of group therapy in the past two decades must be regarded as more than simply a breakthrough in mental health techniques. It represents, at least in part, a cultural phenomenon in that it fills a felt need within the population at large. As such it is extratherapeutic, and its strictly therapeutic claims should be subjected to very careful scrutiny.

What I mean is this. My delineation earlier in this chapter of the cultural conditions which induce people to see Gestalt therapy as magic also applies to the need for joining groups. Thus, the experience of helplessness, isolation, insignificance, invisibility, lack of autonomy, and loss of influence which the vast technocratic culture engenders in its individuals, creates as well the need for belonging to small human conglomerates where, as we know, these ills are in some measure alleviated. Consciousness-raising groups are a case in point.

The question is: Are therapy groups therapeutic for the individual in the same sense as individual treatment is, or are they meeting primarily extratherapeutic culturally induced needs?

The distinction is important. If the latter is true, then therapy groups, far from being therapeutic, represent an impediment to appropriate social change by acting as palliatives to social ills under the guise of providing health services for needy individuals.

Further, if all the above is true, a process of mystification takes place in which each individual comes to believe that his private emotional condition places him in the group; therefore, what he needs is treatment. He does not ask himself if a generalized cultural condition brings him to the group so that what is needed is a change in the culture.

The question then, in summary, is: Has group therapy proliferated to such an extent because people need therapy or because they need groups? Whatever the answer, the question itself brings to mind a second, somewhat related concern. Except when a group is run in the most classically analytic manner, with the appropriate prohibitions, it has a tendency to act as a social arena where "making it" within the group in terms of group values and mores becomes a prized aim. In my experience, the phenomenon is extremely resistant to confrontation or interpretation. Now, to the extent that one conceives of treatment as only aimed toward intrapsychic reorganization and not also toward real-life interventions, to this extent the group ceases to be a therapeutic agent.

One could agree that making it in the group leads to transfer of learning and thereby facilitates finding other, more appropriate social settings. This argument seems questionable. For one thing, the group tends to satisfy social needs, and this reduces the motivation to search elsewhere. For another, there is the problem of reentry. Very few social settings permit their members emotional expression and behavior comparable to that which therapy groups encourage.

And here I come to my third and final concern. It has to do with habits of interaction that group therapy patients are inevitably taught. The notion that discharge of unmodulated affect toward the person who elicits it is desirable and health-promoting is dubious. And yet, that is the ground rule of most therapy groups. No wonder the therapy group becomes more satisfying than any other social situation, or that it produces problems of reentry into other less permissive social settings.

On the positive side of the ledger, there is no question that the therapy group increases greatly, and in a way that it is difficult for individual treatment to do, the members' sense of empathy and intersubjective responsibility. And it does one more thing, and perhaps therein lies its greatest benefit and power. It demonstrates convincingly and teaches concretely that all of us, to use Sullivan's words, "are more human than otherwise."

References

(1) PERLS, F. S., HEFFERLINE, R. F., and GOODMAN, P. Gestalt Therapy. New York: Julian Press, 1951. Reprint. New York: Dell, 1965.
(2) PERLS, F. S. Gestalt Theory Verbatim. Lafayette, Pa.: Real People Press, 1969.

16 Basic Encounter Groups: Their Nature, Method, and Brief History

Jim Bebout

Introduction

THE OVAL OFFICE, September 15, 1972 (as John Dean comes in the door):

> PRESIDENT: Hi, how are you? You had quite a day today, didn't you? You got Watergate on the way, didn't you?
>
> DEAN: We tried.
>
> HALDEMAN: How did it all end up?
>
> DEAN: Ah, I think we can say "well" at this point. The press is playing it just as we expect.
>
> HALDEMAN: Whitewash?
>
> DEAN: No, not yet—the story right now. [later]
>
> PRESIDENT: It is a big story. . . . Just remember, all the trouble we're taking, we'll have a chance to get back one day. . . .
>
> DEAN: Well as I see it, the only problems we may have are the *human* problems and I will keep a close watch on that.
>
> PRESIDENT: Union?
>
> DEAN: Human.
>
> HALDEMAN: Human frailties (italics added) (Gold, *The White House Transcripts* [New York: Bantam Books (General Edition, *New York Times*), 1974], pp. 57–62).

An encounter this is not. The men in this group are deadly serious; they are, or were, important to our nation, and their responsibilities were grave. But something is lacking in their interaction. If you can set aside, for the moment, your politics and value judgments, and bracket your personal opinion of the powers in office at the time of this group meeting—then let's examine what is missing from this group interchange.

The President asks Dean how he is and seemingly offers some sympathy for his trying "day." But he preempts any personal answer by asking another question—to the point of his major concern: Watergate. Dean responds ambiguously, "We tried." We who? Does he mean "I tried"? Does he mean "my staff and I gave some failing effort to it"? Is he feeling humble, or trying to cope with both sides of Nixon's comment, the personal interest and the problem solving? Or does he mean to communicate "Yes, I worked by ass off for you, like it or not, and had considerable success," covering his proud but injured but righteous feelings with the "we" and the "tried"? Haldeman leaves out token personal concerns for Dean and wants "facts": "How did it all end up?" One message could be, "So what if you tried"—I couldn't care less. What did you accomplish?" Again vague, Dean thinks it went "well"; he forgoes, as if by tacit understanding, any further mention of himself or his "day." "Well" means a "whitewash" to Haldeman but that is a projection and not what Dean meant, as he begins to give a more complete story. Nixon seems to offer a slight stroke by building Dean's importance ("a big story"), followed by an invitation to join him in a paranoid revenge ("we'll . . . get back one day"). No one responds to this invitation. Later, the group takes note of "human frailties" (except that the President misunderstands the idea). Dean is talking of interoffice bitterness.

The basic reason this is not an encounter group is that these people are *out of touch with each other as persons,* and out of touch with their own "human frailties."* The members of this group do not reveal their personal discomforts; they are not open with each other. They do not discuss their fears, struggles to maintain respect, to avoid failure, to further noble causes, or to save their own necks or pass the buck. They do not personalize; they do not seem to care about each other as individuals as much as they care about "business" or political problems. Is it possible, then, that had they dealt with their humanness, had they "encountered" one another, then this period of history—the subsequent national disgrace, prison sentences, resignations, disbarments, impeachment actions—would not have been so inglorious? I think this is quite possible.

Encounter groups do not avoid feelings; they do not ignore personalities; they insist on personalizing. They do not long suffer third-person statements or abstract generalities (like "we tried" or "we'll get back") to take the place of individual responsibility. They tend to insist on personal

---

* "The [Nixon] administration admired people who could be cold and dispassionate in making personnel decisions. To make concessions to people's feelings, to recognize that a particular objective was not worth destroying people in the process was not something that elicited any admiration. Such a concern was viewed as a fatal flaw" (J. Jaffe, White House staff psychiatrist, 1971–73; *San Francisco Chronicle,* January 18, 1976).

honesty and openness, sometimes in the extreme; and encounter groups would not sit still for totally uncaring relationships. These characteristics are common in encounter groups, but still they are surface descriptions. Traditional group therapy seeks honesty and openness, emotional depth, and group affectional ties, if only to further the treatment of each individual. Encounter groups are distinct from these in some major respects.

In the following pages I will try to show that there is one overriding principle that characterizes basic interpersonal encounter groups, and that is "direct experiential contact." I suggest that such human contact is a powerful change agent in itself; and that it also gives rise to a secondary but equally impactful interpersonal phenomenon that I call "experiential communality" or co-experience. The nature of these processes will be described with a capsule review of techniques and their background, and a position taken on the putative dangers of encounter groups.

Basic Encounter—Toward a Definition

It is possible to reeducate paramecia, to facilitate insight in a chimpanzee; it may even be possible to self-actualize a parakeet—but it is not possible to encounter anything other than another human being in the sense given here. Just what is this process called "encounter"?

In the literature of the last decade or so, there are two general approaches to a general definition of encounter and encounter groups, both of which are inadequate. The first general definition amounts to a listing of desirable human traits, ordinarily scarce, particularly in groups, such as "authenticity," "freedom," "wholeness," "transparency," "love," and "joy" (1). Among other criteria, Lieberman, Yalom, and Miles point out that encounter groups:

> encourage openness, honesty, interpersonal confrontation, self-disclosure, and strong emotional expression (2, p. 4).

Within an existential-phenomenological point of view, Blank, Gottsegen, and Gottsegen indicate:

> The existential stress on meaningfulness, involvement, and immediacy is a crucial feature of encounter phenomena. So too is the humanist emphasis on maximizing human potential, development, and communication and respect for other humans (3, p. viii).

And similarly, from Burton:

> In this book on encounter . . . there is only the ancient understanding that *community*, set in a framework of honesty, openness, and responsibility, is enlivening and healing. And this "community healing" is vastly different from group therapy or group recreation (4, pp. 1–2).

Jack and Lorraine Gibb describe their rendition of community growth groups as TORI experiences, which is an acronym for "trust-openness-realization-interdependence" (5).

The second typical definition of encounter in groups amounts to a "method" definition, relying on a common set of techniques used and usually adding the component existential values above. Two examples will be given. Schutz, a pioneer of the movement, describes his version of "open" encounter in this way:

> The open encounter group . . . is a specific technique. . . . The philosophy and theory underlying open encounter lead to very specific ways of conducting a group and their consequences can be expressed as a set of rules for group interaction (6, pp. xii, 148).

And elsewhere:

> Encounter is a method of human relating based on openness and honesty, self-awareness, self-responsibility, awareness of the body, attention to feelings, and an emphasis on the here-and-now. It *usually* occurs in a group setting. . . . Encounter differs from most other group methods in that it stresses body methods, nonverbal techniques, and guided daydream fantasies. . . . Encounter is also unusual in its attempts to integrate methods from a particularly wide variety of approaches (6, pp. 3, 20, 21).

Egan recognizes "laboratory learning" groups as the genetic source of most other new groups. The essential framework of laboratory groups consists of "learning through experience," "experimentation," "feedback," "communication and emotion," "support," "ambiguity," "exercises," and so on (7, pp. 4–9). From this "genus" sensitivity and encounter groups form parallel species. Egan states:

> Sensitivity training . . . is a particular kind of laboratory learning *in which personal and interpersonal issues are the direct focus of the group.* Other goals such as learning about group processes . . . are incidental (7, p. 10).

This author's particular version of encounter is called a "contract" group, which

> has a much higher degree of structure and of "visibility" (the opposite of ambiguity) . . . (and) the major features of the contract experience are outlined either by lecture or in writing. . . . Secondly the contract . . . provides a certain degree of structure for the laboratory; it establishes definite goals . . . and definite interactional means to achieve these goals. . . . The kinds of interaction seen as facilitating growth are self-disclosure, total human expression, including honest expression of emotion and the use of . . . language to translate oneself to the other members of the group . . . , support, and responsible confrontation (7, pp. 18–19).

Gibb* points out that

> during the past decade there has been a growing emphasis . . . upon authen-
> ticity, openness, transparency, encounter, and confrontation. In response,
> there has been a rise of quasi-therapeutic sensitivity training groups . . .
> sometimes called "growth groups" or "encounter groups," these experiences
> are an extension of methods found to be effective in dyadic therapy . . .
> leaders . . . rely upon time tested methods of feeling expression, personal
> feedback, mirroring, role playing, confrontation, and fantasy analysis (5,
> p. 371).

Marathon groups are almost always thought of as encounter groups because of their compacted timing and intensity, and they are usually called
"marathons"; if people also take off their clothes, they are said to be in a
"nude marathon." If some members are black and others white, the same
kind of interaction may be termed "black-white encounter." As the reader
can see, the labeling of new groups can proliferate without end—every
time someone thinks of a new application, a new technique, or a new structure. But we are no further along toward an understanding of the essential
nature of "encounter," or what it means to say "encounter group."

Clearly, traditional psychotherapy, whether individual or group, depends for its success on some measure of openness or self-disclosure, on
emotional interactions, and on a degree of intimacy between participants.
It is not the case that encounter simply means having *more* of these and
similar events. Moreover, group therapists have borrowed techniques from
a wide variety of sources over the past decade, and it is more common than
not to find body reference, fantasy techniques, expressive media, psychodrama methods, and the like used in standard practice. Techniques are
adopted or dismissed according to their utility in producing a desired
psychological process, but they do not thereby *define* that ultimate process. Technique and "trait" definitions have not helped our basic understanding. Investigators who use trait or technique approaches to a definition of encounter miss the central point—the question of what encounter is. And how, if at all, is this process special and basic in a group
experience?

Direct Experiential Contact

Encounter represents one of the most fundamental and complete
modes of "being-together-in-the-world" that is possible between people. Its
earliest referent is to Buber's philosophy of "I and Thou" (8). The experi-

---

* Gibb distinguishes eleven "varieties" of "sensitivity training groups." For the purposes of this selection, and for most practical purposes, groups are differentiable by
their emphasis: T-groups emphasize learning and group process; encounter/personal
growth groups emphasize holistic growth; Gestalt groups stress Gestalt therapy principles, and so on.

ence of encounter enters a directness and intensity which is extraordinary in social exchange. In another paper, I described this aspect of encounter as follows:

> An encounter between humans is first of all psychological touching. It is a meeting of emotions and minds. The first prerequisite for encounter between persons is *contact*. To follow this physical image, to be touched is to be felt. . . . But, in being physically touched by the other, one "feeling" another is also felt by the other. In touching (feeling) me, I also feel you and your touch if I allow it. *Our feelings occur together.* So it is psychologically—or it can be so. I can feel me feeling you. Contact is made (9, p. 372).

To be more precise, the use of the term interpersonal "feeling" borrows from the essential definition given by Plessner:

> Direct intimacy with the other or self-awareness of a contact that excludes all distance (distanzlose sächverhaftung) (10, p. 17).

Also, from Strasser's adaptation of this concept in which he states:

> Our original feeling and emotional mode of awareness . . . rises to the surface whenever the situation appears to the ego in such a manner that he cannot maintain a distance (emotion) or whenever, in the nature of things no distance exists (feeling). When I am present to the other, no distance exists. The most elementary of all human experience—we together in a surrounding world—is not at first perceived, thought or sought after; it is primarily lived, through feeling (11, p. 306).

It is strange that after a century of scientific theorizing in psychology and psychiatry we still do not have an adequate language to describe this most basic and natural form of human transaction—direct and conscious psychological contact. Technical language does not lack for terms describing internal and interpersonal distance, the absence of contact: "projection," "alienation," "defense," "denial," "transference," "character armor," and so on. But what are the qualities of an interaction in which none of these deflections of experiential contact occur?

Perhaps the best analogy is the state of being "in touch" with oneself, in its most ideal form.

One may notice that ideation simply flows, uninhibited and without being identified as such; that attention is entirely focused; that one is undistracted (such descriptions are possible "looking back" on the process). There seems one voice inside which is your voice rather than several or a babble. But what is "inside" and what is "outside" is the same; the inner voice *is* the outer voice; and this is not a separate "voice" but a total action. Spontaneity exists in that there seems to be no cognitive or evaluative mediation between perception and action, or between impulse and behavior, or between intention and impulse (12), though these might arise on reflection. One's body, along with one's mind, seems in "tune." Sometimes athletes say "my hands felt thin" when they are giving an outstanding performance, as if to indicate that nothing "on" them is in excess; that there is an easy deep synchrony.

There are not many selves but one self; an experience of self-unity. There is an organismic awareness rather than *self*-consciousness. There are not, everywhere, doubts for what is "real" because what is real is what is being experienced—or, more exactly, *the flow of immediate experiencing constitutes reality*. Frequent questions like "What am I experiencing?" and "How do I really feel?" do not occur in this state of "intouchness" with oneself. The "meaning" of the experiencing is contained within the experiencing—for the moment it "means" itself. Knowledge and experience are both givens; in this sense, one feels whole.

Csikszentmihalyi (13) calls such a state a "flow experience," found in some forms of play, ritual, creativity, religious and meditative practices, and in what has been called "peak experience." He points to three essential characteristics (among others):

1. the merging of feeling and action
2. the centering of attention
3. loss of ego

He relates this subjective state to de Charms' (14) concept of an "origin" state. This state is like the "bare attention" of Buddhist meditation in that all of awareness is "present" (15, p. 41). It is as if there is no "fat" on the mind, the will, or the body.

Certainly, much of our daily life is spent in a condition of fractured experience, piecemeal awareness, and sufferance of the omnipresent self-concept." There are many gradations of self-contact; rarely is the organic self unitary and focused. But those ideal times exist; and they exist between people in what is called "encounter." The terms for self-contact can be used as well to describe being in touch with another. Magda Denes-Radomisli says it well:

> Encounter refers to the full relationship that exists between two people as they are together in the world. It is always characterized by *presence*. . . . The central characteristic of encounter, as I see it, is that it consists of a dialogical relatedness between two people. . . . Encounter always occurs in the Mitwelt ("with" world), so that *by definition it implies the presence of another* . . . if the other . . . is physically absent or *is psychologically abstracted, diffused, uncommitted, unpresent, no encounter can occur* (italics added) (16, p. 26).

Now in this case, in interpersonal encounter, "we" are not many selves, but a somehow expanded single self; there is again an experience of *unity*. There is a *spontaneity* and an original *emergence of relationship*, without cognitive or judgmental screening. Knowledge and experience of each "other" occur together, directly, simultaneously, and as given. There is a direct feeling contingency (but not necessarily equality). However momentary, during this interaction there is no question (for each) that all or both persons are in contact or in touch; there is no question that *the experience of contact* is real. The sense is that another or others live in your "self" space and you live in theirs. A focused, mutual attention (borrowing from T. Burrow's theory discussed later, a "cotention") exists, a merging of consciousness(es). The "presence" of each is itself present to each, without reflection. There is not, for the moment, a self that examines the self that is in relationship. And again there is a unity of feeling and action, intention and impulse, and motive and perception—this time between people.

It is this holistic, direct experiential contact that is the core meaning of encounter, the basic nature of complete encounter. Carl Rogers was one of the first writers to emphasize this kind of transaction as central to psychotherapy. In 1955 he wrote:

> The essence of some of the deepest parts of therapy seems to be a *unity of experiencing.* The client is freely able to experience his feeling in its complete intensity . . . without intellectual inhibitions or cautions [or] . . . having it bounded . . . and I am able with equal freedom to experience *my understanding of this feeling,* without any conscious thought about it, without any apprehension or concern as to where this will lead, without any type of diagnostic or analytic thinking, without any cognitive or emotional barriers to a complete "letting go." . . . *When there is this complete unity, singleness, fulness of experiencing in the relationship, then it acquires the "out-of-this-world" quality* which many therapists have remarked upon. . . . In these moments there is, to borrow Buber's phrase, a real "I-Thou" relationship, a time-less living in the experience which is between the client [and therapist] (italics added) (17, pp. 267–68).

Notice that in this early theory, a theory of therapy, the nature of the experiencing in the therapist is of a different order—Rogers is careful to speak of "my understanding of this feeling." While the client was to be fully present and fully living his or her experience, the therapist's participation in the relationship was limited to empathic understanding and was fully present in those terms only.

Modern client-centered theory (a better term is neo-Rogerian) renders the therapist co-present. In a more recent statement, Rogers says:

> I find that I have changed in the willingness to express myself and my feelings openly, as data for the other person to use. . . . If I am angry, I will express that anger as something within myself. . . . I am much more freewheeling in stating personal feeling reactions (18, p. 519).

Other theorists in the neo-Rogerian school underscore the quality of this relationship:

Genuine relating is simultaneously a coming to be of each person. . . . Without making real touch with what is there in another, one cannot relate to that other (19, p. 217).

The client simultaneously perceives the living vitality of himself and his therapist. . . . This duality [in] encounter may be of decisive importance in psychotherapy, for in [it] . . . the participants become both the knower and the known (20, pp. 176–77).

This view is not exclusive to Rogerians, or to psychotherapy. Within a psychoanalytic framework, Maurice Friedman (21) draws on the work of the Swiss psychiatrist H. Trüb (himself strongly influenced by Martin Buber's teachings) to explicate the concept of "healing through meeting":

For Trüb the dialogical meeting is both the starting point and the goal of therapy. . . . The therapist must experience the patient as a partner in his own meeting with him. It is through this eye-to-eye confrontation that the patient's capacity for meeting begins to be restored. . . . Thus the equality of respect for which the humanistic psychologist seeks is attained . . . by the recognition of the betweenness itself as the place where real meeting, real healing, and real finding take place. . . . Healing through meeting is not restricted to psychotherapy . . . the whole encounter movement has within it the seed of the happening between and among people (22, pp. 256, 261–62).

From the point of view of this definition, dialogical meeting is not a small part of the promise of encounter groups, but, in the sense of direct experiential contact, it is the core meaning of encounter.

From the above it would seem that there is little distinction between encounter and therapy; indeed, in some therapies they are the same thing. In the following there is again a prime emphasis on contact, but encounter is distinct in *how* it comes about. The late Fred Stoller puts it this way:

The encounter group . . . is a setting in which people come together to rub up against one another so that they may experience others and, ultimately, themselves, more fully . . . the casual or unexpected nature of the meeting is what is essential to the goals of the [encounter] group. . . . [In] interaction terms, *this means unprogrammed and spontaneous contact*—a coming together without the necessity for maneuver, filtering, or distortion; it means allowing various levels of the person to be known as freely as possible . . . the opposite of encounter . . . can be seen as handling or dealing with, *rather than making contact* (italics added) (23, pp. 85–86).

A personal, phenomenological point of view comes from Malone:

Encounter literally means to be *in against* . . . it is a very warm image . . . it is physical, deeply personal, tactile, meeting, not nice nor careful, exploratory, sensual, but not necessarily sexual. . . . It most clearly is *not* culturally programmed . . . the encountering experience [is] essentially passionate, phasic and flowing, gratifying and enjoyable, essentially involuntary, novel, neither highly culturally programmed nor anti-cultural, but essentially personal, and more natural than neurotic (24, pp. 130–32).

In what Rogers calls a "unity of experiencing" from a client-centered therapy viewpoint; what Denes-Radomisli identifies as "presence" and "dialogical relatedness" in terms of Gestalt practice; what Friedman argues is "healing through meeting" consonant with the thought of Buber and Trüb; and what is otherwise termed a "spontaneous coming together" or a "passionate, phasic flowing" by Stoller and Malone—the core meaning in these concepts is what I refer to as "direct experiential contact." What essentially distinguishes basic encounter groups from other group models is their total reliance on this single factor. Encounter groups are groups of people that encounter. The goal of a basic encounter group is to bring each person into full contact with at least one other member, but hopefully with *all* other members, including the leader, and thereby, into full contact with himself. It is difficult to make an exception. As Rogers states:

> As time goes on the group finds it *unbearable* that any member should live behind a mask or front. The polite words, the intellectual understanding of each other and of relationships, the smooth coin of tact and cover-up . . . are just not good enough (25, p. 7).

It is not sufficient that the therapist or leader *either* be the sole purveyor of relationship *or* the least personally known member of the group. This fact generally distinguishes encounter group leaders from traditional group therapists (and many "new" group therapists). Just as encounter—direct experiential contact—is lessened when we deal with pieces rather than with the whole of a person, it is not enough to deal with pieces of a group. Subgrouping is antithetical to holistic contact. Similarly, if a group leader stands at a distance, apart from full and mutual contact with each person and thus the whole group, encounter is diminished, distorted. Some group leaders like to practice therapy on other people's encounters. This puts into effect different levels of the reality associated with human contact—a status hierarchy—and renders an encounter group minus one: the leader. In this context it is probably *not* true that degreed professionals automatically make good encounter group leaders (nor does it necessarily follow that good encounter group leaders are ipso facto good clinical therapists).*

The existential "traits" identified earlier in some definitions of encounter (openness, authenticity, and so on) lead to and follow from the fact of direct experiential contact. It can readily be seen that *direct* experiential contact is not obtainable if participants are mainly defending themselves,

---

* A disappointing finding from my five-year study of community-based encounter groups (TIE Project, NIMH grant 17330) was that roughly four out of five professionally trained therapists were not found acceptable as group leaders. The main selection criterion was nomination by fellow group members (nonprofessionals) as having encounter group leadership talent (9).

disclosing only under the protection of social roles, or filtering emotionality through intellectual constraints, and the like. These behaviors enforce a distance and reduce contact; in fact, that is their purpose. What happens in individual therapy and in many types of group therapy when nondefensiveness is achieved is a greater contact with oneself and a "working through" of intrapsychic problems, often accompanied by strong emotion which surrounds the conflicts themselves. What happens in encounter is a contact that is similarly intense but with another, engaging in the moment all of oneself, problems included, and all of one other (or all others), their problems included, too. When this happens, a strong intimacy develops between people. With such holistic direct experiential contact, people *come to* value the trust, openness, and feeling interaction involved; and they further value its occurrence in everyday life. Such contacts lead to growth. When such direct contact takes place members often experience a further event—an event that is equally or even more prized. I call this process "experiential communality."

EXPERIENTIAL COMMUNALITY

The first basis of encounter is bringing people together into intimate and direct psychological contact with each other and with themselves. This insures that they do receive and respond to each other's feelings and existential condition. However, the fact of this contact brings about another possibility: that people realize, through direct experience, the essential communality of their human condition. This component of encounter has been given slight recognition in the literature. Carl Rogers gives this definition:

> A man tells, through his tears, of the tragic loss of his child, a grief which he is experiencing fully for the first time, not holding back his feelings in any way. . . . Another man says to him, also with tears in his eyes, "I've never before felt a real physical hurt in me from the pain of another. I feel completely with you." *This is a basic encounter* (italics added) (25, p. 33).

A much earlier example comes from Nick Hobbs' transcription of a therapy group in which the discussion turns to an absent member:

> MR. H: I thought that there was so much difference in our two ages that there might be a gap there. Somehow he closed the gap the other day. I feel that underneath we all have the same feeling. . . .
>
> THERAPIST: I am not sure . . . that I understand just how you see that relationship.
>
> MR. H: Well, I had the feeling that somehow I couldn't quite understand the scope of his problem and how much this problem really meant to him. Yet, as he spoke on Monday, I had the feeling of great empathy with him. Not so much that I have the same problem, but because I could see how another person feels carrying a burden like

that around with you all the time. Because even though we may have different problems, the feelings these problems create are pretty much the same . . . well, thinking about it made me feel much closer to him.

Miss W: That is better said . . . that is what I was trying to say.

THERAPIST: You feel closer to him not because of a similarity of problems but because of a similarity of feeling.

Mr. H: By and large, I think that has been typical of the whole group (26, p. 288).

It is important to note that the contingency of feeling and the realization of communality these members experience is not merely the practice of empathy, as that is usually understood. The availability of empathy is important, but the degree of richness and intensity, the directness of psychological contact, and the mutuality involved in the above examples cannot be understood in the standard terms definitive of empathy—terms such as "imaginative project," "role taking," "perceptive awareness," and so on. Rogers points out:

> To carry on psychotherapy . . . is to take a very real risk. . . . If I enter, as fully as I am able, into the private world of a neurotic or psychotic individual, isn't there a risk that I might become lost in that world? (27, p. 333).

Surely, there is no great risk of losing one's identity (or self) in an "imagined role taking," but there is such a risk in encounter where two or more people are deeply embedded in an essentially equal and holistic experiential state. David Bakan proposes that one fundamental aspect of human nature lies in

> communion [standing] for the participation of the individual in some larger organism of which the individual is a part. . . . Communion manifests itself in the sense of being at one with other organisms . . . in contact, openness, and union . . . in noncontractual cooperation. . . . The healer-role is one which entails . . . coming into intimate contact with [the other]. . . . In the healing relationship . . . *the separation between the two people is overcome as the paradigm of the overcoming of all other separations* (italics added) (28, pp. 99–101).

In the above examples by Rogers and Hobbs there is intense experiential contact, but there is also a "unity" of experience, a co-experience, and the existential condition of another is directly shared. In the encounter described by direct experiential contact two people's feeling states are "met" or joined, but they are not necessarily equivalent or even compatible. We may, for example, be in direct experiential contact when I become angry at your fear of me; or when you (and I) feel my impatience with your calmness. Our feelings are co-present; we are in touch, but our experiential states are very different. Martin Buber creates an allegory in his original conception of the I-Thou relationship or encounter:

A man belabours another, who remains quite still. Then let us assume that the striker suddenly receives in his soul, the blow which he strikes; . . . that he receives it as the other who remains still. For the space of a moment he experiences the situation from the other side. . . . A man caresses a woman, who lets herself be caressed. Then let us assume that he feels the contact from two sides—with the palm of his hand still, and also with the woman's skin. The twofold nature of the gesture, as one that takes place between two persons, thrills through the depth of enjoyment in his heart and stirs it. . . . A transfusion has taken place after which a mere elaboration of subjectivity is never again possible or tolerable to him (29, p. 90).

Most traditions in Western philosophy seem to have rejected the notion that it is possible to "directly know" another, and science followed this example. The argument seems to be that since I cannot know what is in your mind, we can never truly share our existence. But the man in Rogers' example who feels the "physical hurt" from another is doing just that, and such events are frequent in the best encounter groups. After a successful encounter experience, many members testify to the values inherent in experiential communality:

It has had great value. I've never been close (intimate) to people . . . always held [them] at arm's length. The group was and in part still is a family—the family of man is what I needed to feel and see. . . . [Now] I think I *will* much more.

Interacting with the other members . . . made me aware that my feelings are not that different from everyone else's. That I was not alone in my feelings.

Listening to other people's problems and how I felt toward them made me realize the uniformity of human experience.

I'm able now to be more direct with other people, more honest. I'm more in touch with my feelings; I'm better able to "see" myself in relation to others. I understand how very similar all human beings really are in terms of basic needs.*

Elsewhere, I offered a formal definition of experiential communality in this way:

The spontaneous, simultaneous, and more or less conscious coexperiencing of functionally equivalent . . . affective-meaning processes . . . in two or more people in face-to-face interaction and contact, which contact implies the perceived lack of psychological distance (9, p. 377).

As early as 1918, Trigant Burrow contributed a theoretical base for such a concept as experiential communality, from a psychoanalytic (or "phyloanalytic") framework:

* Data from the Talent in Interpersonal Exploration Groups Project; NIMH Grant No. 17330, sponsoring institutions: Wright Institute, and Stiles Hall, University YMCA, Berkeley, Calif.

Burrow's formulation regarding a "principle of primary identification" was presented before he initiated group analysis. . . . He spoke of a "primal mode of awareness" associated with the original identification of infant and maternal organism. . . . Burrow [found] evidence of a *cohesive and unifying trend* preceding Oedipal conflict and *persisting as a powerful integrative force in adult life* (italics added) (30, p. 116). (See also [31, p. 145 ff.].)

Thus the twin principles of direct experiential contact and experiential communality define the nature of basic encounter groups and their purpose. Any group in which such maximum interpersonal "meeting" is both the primary goal and medium of exchange can be said to be a basic encounter group. Characteristics of openness, trust, authenticity, intimacy, emotionality, and the like are valued accompaniments, preconditions, or outcomes of encounter groups, but they may also describe other group processes. Although a definition of encounter in terms of technique is insubstantial, it may be instructive to look at certain approaches that facilitate contact and communality.

Encounter Methods: A Capsule History

Encounter needs no method. Carl Rogers has repeatedly shown this to be true. If it is desired and worked at, direct experiential contact and communality can be achieved by "merely" facing another, and being honest while open to and continuously in touch with the other's present being. (Of course, the other must do the same.) What has been written on the history of encounter takes a "mass movement" view of these groups, identifying them in terms of philosophy, or a set of values, or a group of techniques. Oden (32) traces the roots of the encounter movement to Hasidism and eighteenth-century Protestant pietism, Back (33) compares the encounter grouper to a modern-day pilgrim, Schutz (34) finds the hot bath spa in the ancient Greek city of Epidaurus an ultimate historic model, and Max Lerner (35) points to Thomas Jefferson. What's wrong with the twelve apostles? I don't believe we are much informed by such retrojections. There are a few general methods that are widely used in basic encounter groups and these have a fairly short, clear, and recent derivation.

In 1923 Trigant Burrow, on a challenge from his student analysand (Shields), "switched roles." He, Burrow, took the couch position and his student assumed "the authoritarian vantage ground Burrow had relinquished. [Surprisingly] the therapist-patient situation . . . remained in all essentials the same" (30, p. 116). This might have remained a private, novel experimentation (now familiar as "role reversal") by an established and heretofore traditional psychoanalyst. But Burrow's resistance to analysis became as strong as that of his previous patient and this bit of pathology he would not let slip through his intellectual grasp. No theory explained the difference: while he was healthy and mature of mind behind the couch, he was full of conflict on it.

To understand this mystery, he and his pupil assembled "friends, associates, patients, and family" at a summer camp, establishing a "consensual laboratory" for the "study of normal interaction" (30, p. 117). Galt compares this early group with encounter in terms of a deliberate orientation to the "here and now" and the priority given feeling material;* and Anthony views Burrows' group as possibly the first "sensitivity training" group on record. Aside from the preoccupation of this group with intellectual and theoretical analysis of their interaction, the essentials of encounter—direct experiential contact and communality—were present.

It is striking that his experimental community, still partly active today, was an outgrowth of an almost casual reversal of roles by an analyst and his patient. In effect, their role change brought about, in Burrow's later work and theory, a profound realization of the distancing of people through the acceptance of "culturally neurotic" role postures (the "mask" or "front" referred to by Rogers (27, p. 13).

But Jacob Moreno had previously introduced the use of role playing and role reversal, the intensive small group context, and emphasis on the here and now and on feeling material, in his practice of psychodrama. Moreno (36) was discontented with the traditionally passive and introspective behavior expected of psychoanalytic patients. He was impressed with the dynamic nature of the "theatre of spontaneity" which he explored in Vienna in 1911, and by the 1920s he had developed a set of techniques and theory which emphasized (1) action, (2) trying out new behaviors, (3) reenacting the interpersonal dynamics in one's present and past life, (4) the use of spontaneity, (5) role analysis, and (6) fantasy (37). Each of these features lead toward more direct experiential contact with oneself, with internalized others, and with objective others. Their opposites—immobility, control, role-boundedness, unemotionality, and so on—establish or reinforce distance between people. Martin Buber's translation of the Tierra del Fuegian word for "far away" is appropriate here:

> They stare at one another each waiting for the other to volunteer to do what both wish, but are not able to do (29, p. 18).

Like Burrow's concept of "primary identification," Moreno advanced the notion of "tele relations" or deep insight in encountering another, and this interpersonal mode is clearly allied with experiential communality.†

---

* Galt points up differences in terms of the "phyloanalytic" group being composed of significant others and the fact of their concern with home, money, children, and so on. Defining encounter in terms of experiential contact and communality works against this distinction (30).

† It is a dilemma of psychodrama methods that the emergent spontaneity so much sought after is approached through a highly structured (staged) method involving manufactured or directed role taking. This sometimes adds a degree of "indirectness" in groups.

Moreno's dramatic flair was matched by the flamboyant personality of Fritz Perls, the principal originator of Gestalt therapy. Perls arrived in New York in 1946 and at first aligned himself with the interpersonal orientation of the (Sullivanian) W. A. White Foundation, and then later became involved with an artistic-intellectual circle of people with Paul Goodman at the center. According to Shepard, "Goodman articulated the desire of this group to end the discrepancies between their professional lives and their private lives (38, p. 57) (as did Burrow). Like Moreno, Perls was taken with the possibilities of the New York "living theatre," promoted by one of the circle, Julian Beck, with its stress on "honesty and on exploring the limits of behavior and feeling. In Beck's words,

> [Fritz] was always . . . trying to bring the meeting, the encounter, to its frontier. And the device was always honesty, frankness, and a certain shock technique. These forms of address were very important to our own work . . . for instance, in . . . scenes . . . concerned with bringing that kind of candor and . . . honesty into a direct I-and-Thou relationship between the actor and the audience (38, p. 60).

And, again, this circle (including Goodman, Elliot Shapiro, Paul Weisz, Isadore From, Ralph Hefferline, and Jim Simkin) became an intensive training group, led by Laura and Fritz Perls in 1950, reminiscent of the Burrows' community and the Morenos' group focus.

Perls was influenced by the sensory awareness techniques of Charlotte Selver (a student of Else Gindler), the here-and-now focus and self-responsibility of Dianetics, the action and fantasy techniques of Moreno, the Zen teachings translated by Paul Weisz—in fact, almost any other lesson he could learn from practitioners in America. He confronted; he avoided interpretation and intellectualization. His original psychoanalytic article, "Ego, Hunger, and Aggression," is an apt description of his interpersonal style. From a 1966 lecture, he states:

> I have one aim only: to impart a fraction of the meaning of the word *now*. To me, nothing exists except the now. Now = experience = awareness = reality (39, p. 14).

The "now" is the principal technique in the "rules" of Gestalt therapy groups. It requires a constant effort to maintain present awareness, the subjective, first-person tense in speaking, constant reference to one's immediate experiencing, undisguised language, and so forth. Each of these recommendations is specifically designed to promote greater and more direct experiential contact; their alternatives are usually tactics establishing distance between oneself and another or within oneself. Levitsky and Perls summarize:

> True communication involves both sender and receiver. The patient often behaves as if his words are aimed at the blank wall. . . . Thus the patient is

often directed to invoke the other's name. . . . He is asked to be aware of the distinction between "talking to" and "talking at" the listener. He is led to discover whether his voice and words are truly reaching the other. Is he really touching the other with his words? . . . How far is he willing to touch? . . . Can he begin to see that this phobic avoidance of relating . . . , of making genuine contact with others is also in his . . . verbal behavior? If he has slight or insufficient contact, can he begin to realize his serious doubts as to whether . . . he is truly *with* people or feeling alone and abandoned? (40, p. 141).

And, again:

Gestalt techniques train people precisely in the ability to acquire and sustain presence, and in the requisite contact for meaningful encounter. . . . To be in contact is the natural state of the awake, healthy human being (40, p. 29).

The core Gestalt concepts of here and now and awareness can be clearly seen to be aimed at *contact*, or "presence," as they prefer. I have not, myself, found practitioners of Gestalt encounter very interested in a recognition of co-experience.

Lots of things happened right after World War II, in the late forties and early fifties. As Perls was spreading word about Gestalt therapy, and Moreno was promoting a string of psychodrama institutes across the country, the systems of Wilhelm Reich and Charlotte Selver relating to body integration were gaining acceptance, Carl Rogers and Abe Maslow began articulating their humanistic theories of therapy and self-actualization, W. R. Bion continued experimenting with a psychoanalytic model for adult "rehabilitation" which amounted to self-led groups, and a small group of social and educational psychologists under the guidance of Kurt Lewin stumbled onto the basic principles of "open group feedback," later iconified as "T-groups" or sensitivity training.

In 1946 Ken Benne, Leland Bradford, and Ron Lippitt were the leaders of a professional staff conducting a workshop for educators focused on individual learning and group dynamics. They spent evenings analyzing the progress of the workshop. On impulse, some teachers in the workshop appeared at one nighttime staff analysis session and began objecting to the interpretations given of their own and their group's behavior. Lippitt states:

And the next night the whole fifty workshop members were there and were every night, and so it became the most significant training event of the day (33, p. 8).

Back calls this event the "starting point of the T-group movement" since it promoted "group-confrontation, encounter, and process-analysis (33, p. 9). The T-group movement, sponsored by the National Training Laboratories (NTL), proliferated into thousands of workshops, each incorporating the principle of "feedback" (a God-awfully cryptotechnical term for honest and open communication of personal views and feelings). Members and leaders were brought into more direct experiential and interpersonal contact by this expedient. Experiments with lack of structure, role expectations, different leader styles, shared perceptions, and exercises were carried out between 1950 and 1965. At about that time, some NTL leaders began to concern themselves more with personal growth than with skill training or organizational or community development. Among these were Jack Gibb, Charlie Seashore, William Schutz, Fred Massarik, and Michael Kahn. Nonverbal techniques were included in the T-group armamentarium, along with techniques of fantasy, role enactment, and consciousness raising, plus emphasis on intimacy, cohesion, self-actualization, expression, and psychological community. Many of these group leaders had one thing in common—California.

It was in California in the early 1960s that the encounter "movement" can be said to have started. The Esalen Institute at Big Sur, founded by Michael Murphy, brought together an extremely varied assortment of practitioners plying the frontiers of psychology, generally humanistic and eastern psychology. Esalen was the utmost in eclecticism. Fritz Perls and Bernie Gunther (later known for sensory awareness work) were invited to a weekend at Big Sur by Gene Sagan in 1963; ultimately both became residents. A number of Perls' students held workshops during this period, as did a number of psychodrama and most of the NTL "groupers" mentioned above. The teachings of Alan Watts lent a here-and-now, "center" yourself, "do your thing" philosophy to the place.

Simultaneously, Carl Rogers became a resident at the Western Behavioral Sciences Institute in La Jolla, invited by Richard Farson, a former student. WBSI attracted another score of humanistic therapists and theorists. Many chose to concentrate, as Rogers did, on the small-group field; among these were Jack Gibb, Larry Solomon, and Betty Berzon. Rogers began his extensive work with basic encounter groups here, as a logical extension of his theory of helping relationships and of psychotherapy. The techniques of marathon encounter were being developed by three other Californians: George Bach (1966), Fred Stroller (1968), and Paul Bindrim. Approaches to community encounter were advocated by Jack and Lorraine Gibb (1970); and about the same time Berzon, Solomon, and Reisel (1972) assembled programs for self-led encounter groups. The components of these tape-recorded programs present a résumé of the most common and usually effective methods in the then current practice of encounter:

> The first session, "a series of short, timed meetings and a variety of activities" includes each person telling every other in the group his initial impression of them while looking directly at them and touching them to make contact; physically "breaking in" to the middle of a tight circle formed by

all other group members, or "breaking out" of it; being physically passed along inside a group circle putting oneself "in the hands of the group." The second session "emphasizes the importance of expressing feelings and of learning from the immediate, shared, here-and-now experience of the group." The program proceeds to areas of self-disclosure, feedback, fantasy descriptions of members, giving and receiving, and support and criticism (41, p. 211).

Why the emphasis on physical touching, "handling," motor expression ("breaking in/out")? Physical or nonverbal methods have become widely adopted in encounter groups. Will Schutz is the most vocal spokesman for their use. In his discussion of the "physiological basis of encounter," he quotes Izard (42) on the allegiance of body and mind:

1. The organism is unified as expressed by the interdependence of various levels of functioning.
2. The body is central in understanding emotions. Motor activity is crucial to the expression of feelings.
3. Natural feelings expressed through motor action are suppressed by cultural factors (34, p. 28).

These cultural factors are the same as those invoked by Burrow (cultural neurosis) and Wilhelm Reich (character armor). Many leaders draw on the concepts and practices of Reich, Lowen, Rolfe, Assogioli, Feldenkrais, and the eastern disciplines combined in Aikido, Tai Chi Chuan, Yoga, and so on (in particular for methods of centering, breathing, concentration, grounding, "bare" attention, body "flow," and flexibility and freedom of expression). The theory is that mind and body are inseparable; they are one and the same. The most complete and direct experiential contact with oneself includes body awareness, motility, and sensitivity; contact with another also includes physiological involvement and reactivity. At times body techniques are a desirable "short-cut" approach to establishing contact in encounter; but, more important, the synthesis of body and mind states is presently viewed as a criterion of "normal" self-actualization and growth.

The Basic Encounter: Fad or Panacea?

In its heyday, the decade between 1962 and 1972, a reasonable estimate would be that several million people participated in some form of encounter group. In a recent survey I conducted of fifty-five growth centers throughout the country, it was found that approximately one hundred thousand people joined such groups in 1973.* Since this sample is a much smaller part of the total national and international picture (not including

* Sponsored by the Association for Humanistic Psychology, San Francisco, Calif.

educational, religious, mental health, or business institutions or private practice) it is safe to guess that another 2 million people will have experienced some form of encounter process between 1972 and the time of this writing. This would indicate that roughly 10 million individuals have come in contact with encounter groups to date.

During its peak popularity, the encounter group movement received mass media coverage that was rarely favorable, sometimes violently opposed, but in either case, always sensational.* Right-wing literature appeared to meet the challenge in such articles as "Hate Therapy: Sensitivity Training for Planned Change," (43) and "Aren't Our Teachers Being Subjected to 'Sensitivity Training' to Prepare Them for the Dictatorial Control Which Is the Essence of Nazism and All Socialism?" (44). Encounter was traced to the brainwashing techniques practiced by Nazi youth in the 1930s.

On the heels of such alarm came reports that encounter and similar groups were responsible for inducing widespread psychological damage. Articles appeared suggesting that up to 50 percent of those attending groups suffered "acute pathological reactions," "borderline psychosis," and "anxiety and depressive reactions" (45); "insomnia," and "distractedness" (46); and "deviation in self-concept" (47). At least two cases were reported of encounter group members who later committed suicide, and a strong implication of causality was left without direct evidence being given (48).

A later sophisticated study of Lieberman, Yalom, and Miles found that 16 out of 175 continuing members in encounter groups showed evidence of "significant psychological injury" eight months after their experience (2, p. 174). Their criterion included seeking emergency psychiatric aid (2 cases), dropping out of the group (5 cases), peer ratings of "hurt" (12 cases), negative self-report (7 cases), beginning therapy following the group (8 cases), and other indicators (most of the 16 cases had multiple signs). These negative effects were directly related to "attacking" or "rejecting" leaders or groups and to members' overly high expectations. The need for caution with encounter groups appeared proven—no method that entailed a 10 percent "casualty" rate could be tolerated.†

However, some rather serious criticisms of the method and results in the Lieberman, Yalom, and Miles study have recently appeared, which in their totality reopen the whole question. Schutz (49) argued that a number of

---

* For example, "Inhibitions Thrown to the Gentle Winds," Jan Howard, Life, July 12, 1968; "A Marathon Assault on Your Hang-Ups," Family Circle, November 1969; "See Me, Feel Me, Touch Me, Heal Me: The Encounter Group Explosion," Linda Francke, New York, May 25, 1970; "The Group: Joy on Thursday," Newsweek, May 12, 1969; "Encounter Groupers: Up against the Wall," Bruce Maliver, New York Times Magazine, January 3, 1971; "Encounter Groups versus Psychiatrists," David Perlman, San Francisco Chronicle, May 18, 1970.

† The actual reported figure is 9.1 percent; however, the authors repeatedly suggest that this is quite a conservative estimate.

the groups in the sample were mislabeled encounter groups, as does Russell (50). They point out that several of the groups and leaders would better be identified as therapy oriented, and some leaders had little experience with encounter. Realigning the groups shows that negative effects occur about equally often (by the original data) in the therapy-oriented groups as in the encounter groups. Schutz maintains that the control group used was not comparable and the method of establishing "casualties" was faulted (no interviewer reliability was carried out). Rowan (51) criticizes the sample selection, the random group assignment, and the reportage; and Smith reanalyzes data to show that the rate (percent) of adverse change in the control subjects is roughly equal to, or *possibly much higher than,* that for the encounter members. Smith concludes that "there is at present no dependable evidence as to . . . adverse effects" (52, p. 618); and Cooper states that "there is some evidence that indicates that [encounter] may be less stressful than university examinations or perceptual isolation experiments, or indeed, that it may enable participants to cope better with . . . stressful periods in their life" (53, p. 258).

Perhaps most precipitous and negative were the sometimes scornful attitudes voiced by social science academicians, who themselves had little or no experience "inside" an encounter group. Most notable of these was Sigmund Koch. While he concedes that "the group movement has become the most visible manifestation of psychology on the American scene" (p. 111), he also claims that

> the encounter process becomes an *extraordinarily ritualized kind of game* [which] carries every earmark of a shallow fad [that] . . . will soon . . . fizzle out . . . [the encounter movement] . . . provides, in effect, a convenient psychic whorehouse for the purchase of a gamut of well-advertised existential "goodies." . . . One enters for such liberating consummations but inevitably settles for psychic strip-tease (1, pp. 112, 124, 127).

Koch sees encounter as a strip mine in a Japanese garden of human refinement and sensibilities, for, in the "simplistic lexicon" of encounter,

> love may be seen as a barter of reinforcements; honesty as transparency; or trust as a state engendered by . . . falling backwards. . . . We often [prize] "depth" rather than "transparency" . . . the charm of certain forms of reticence; the grace of certain kinds of containedness . . . the communicative richness of certain forms of understatement, allusiveness . . . that kind of modesty which is the outward form of the capacity to prize personhood and to love directionally rather than diffusely (1, pp. 118–19, 127).

Bernard Rosenthal (1971) joins in Koch's indignation:

> The encounter Movement reveals its affective promiscuity and evaluative Limbo . . . for it is ready for all experience, all states of being, and all explorations of sensation. . . . Indeed, it is often the character of the Encounter Movement to stimulate sexual interest, intimacy, personal revela-

tion and the like without . . . significant understanding. . . . Do not these types of contacts often result in excitement without purpose and fulfillment? (54).

From atop a sociological mountain, Kurt Back's detachment is great. Combining T-groups and encounter as one animal, he arrives at two conclusions: (1) the movement is a powerful force to be reckoned with, and (2) it is a form of "adult play":

> [When effects are weak] . . . the groups serve a kind of recreational function, which has given the "psych resorts" such great popularity and mass recognition . . . sensitivity training might turn out to be a rather interesting but not very consequential movement. . . . Perhaps ultimately it will be remembered as an example of the middle class at play (33, pp. xxi, 384).

Most of this author's historical treatment begs the last premise. So we are led to believe that 10 million Americans took up encounter groups when they got tired of their finger painting and frisbees.

In summary, with the gratuitous help of social science sophistry, we should beware that the intensive group movement is either a fad, a hoax, a plot, a puffed-up game, an excuse for cheap religion, or a ritualized entertainment, or that encounter has the inherent general properties necessary to reduce 1 million Americans (10 percent) to psychiatric casualty status. Something is amiss in this overview.

What seems most lacking is some perspective. Surely the newness of encounter groups is gone and the height of their popularity is over. However, one hundred thousand to five hundred thousand people are engaged each year, *for fifteen years*, in some form of encounter group, this could hardly be called a "fad." In fact, the philosophy and technique of encounter has gone into the fabric of all manner of institutional programs, psychotherapy groups, and training procedures. For example, a number of larger universities regularly offer "group process" or "human relations" courses which are actually mild forms of encounter; a great many service organizations, such as hospital staffs, day care centers, army psychiatric units, and experimental college programs are being conducted along encounter lines; dozens of conferences are conducted annually in which there is a steady diet of "encountering." Carl Rogers and his colleagues have engendered the use of encounter methods in an entire religious diocese, in a large city school system, and with "warring" factions in North and South Ireland (55). If only by virtue of enterprise, the "hoax" theory of encounter is no longer viable. The "plot" theory never was.

It is necessary, after Lieberman et al.'s research, to suppose that some encounter-type leaders are bad leaders and that "browbeating" methods can hurt some, probably quite small, percentage of people. Some psychotherapists, group or otherwise, are bad therapists. "Some counselors and therapists are significantly helpful, while others are significantly harmful"

(56, p. 301). Recent surveys of sexual relations between professional therapists and their patients indicate a predominantly negative effect. What is
the psychological "fallout" base rate from institutionalization in a mental
hospital, from new movements like Erhardt Seminar Training (EST) or
the "Moonies," or from the Vietnam war? What should be our basis for
comparison in terms of when to get alarmed?

Alienation is still our current cultural heritage. It is because so many
Americans sense their lives to be "plastic," lonely, unfulfilling, and bru-
talized (and this, partly due to cynics in robes) that they have turned to
the human potential movement and to encounter groups. This is a "human
problem," not a union problem; it is not a clinical problem. I have tried to
show that basic encounter is a process involving two apparently simple, but
passionately human, events—establishing *contact* with another by direct
experiencing, and realizing, at the same time, the uniformity of human
existence. There is good evidence that this approach is of some help (57,
58).

References

(1) KOCH, S. The Image of Man Implicit in Encounter Group Theory. J.
Human. Psychol., 11, No. 2 (1971).
(2) LIEBERMAN, M., YALOM, I., and MILES, M. Encounter Groups: First
Facts. New York: Basic Books, 1973.
(3) BLANK, L., GOTTSEGEN, G., and GOTTSEGEN, M. (eds.). Confrontation:
Encounters in Self and Interpersonal Awareness. New York: Macmillan,
1971.
(4) BURTON, A. Encounter: The Theory and Practice of Encounter Groups.
San Francisco: Jossey-Bass, 1970.
(5) GIBB, J. TORI Community. In Egan, G. (ed.), Encounter Groups:
Basic Readings. Belmont, Calif.: Brooks/Cole, 1971.
(6) SCHUTZ, W. Here Comes Everybody. New York: Harper and Row, 1971.
(7) EGAN, G. Encounter: Group Processes for Interpersonal Growth. Belmont, Calif.: Brooks/Cole, 1970.
(8) BUBER, M. I and Thou. New York: Scribner's, 1958.
(9) BEBOUT, J. It Takes One to Know One: Existential-Rogerian Concepts
in Encounter Groups. In Wexler, D., and Rice, L. (eds.), Innovations
in Client-Centered Therapy. New York: Wiley, 1974.
(10) PLESSNER, H. Lachen und Weinen. Bern: Francke, 1950.
(11) STRASSER, S. Feeling as Basis of Knowing and Recognizing the Other as
an Ego. In Arnold, M. (ed.), Feelings and Emotions: The Loyola Symposium. New York: Academic Press, 1970.
(12) LANGER, S. Problems of Art. New York: Scribner's, 1957.
(13) CSIKSZENTMIHALY, M. Play and Intrinsic Rewards. J. Human. Psychol.,
15, No. 3 (Summer 1975).

(14) DE CHARMS, R. Personal Causation. New York: Academic Press, 1968.

(15) THERA, N. The Heart of Buddhist Meditation. London: Rider, 1962.

(16) DENES-RADOMISLI, M. Existential-Gestalt Therapy. In Olsen, P. (ed.), Emotional Flooding. New York: Human Sciences Press, 1976.

(17) ROGERS, C. Persons or Science? A Philosophical Question. Am. Psychologist, 10 (1955), 267–78.

(18) ROGERS, C., and HART, J. Looking Back and Looking Ahead: A Conversation with Carl Rogers. In Hart, J., and Tomlinson, T., (eds.), New Directions in Client-Centered Therapy. Boston: Houghton Mifflin, 1970.

(19) GENDLIN, E. Client-Centered and Experimental Psychotherapy. In Wexler, D., and Rice, L. (eds.), Innovations in Client-Centered Therapy. New York: Wiley, 1974.

(20) BUTLER, J. The Iconic Mode in Psychotherapy. In Wexler, D., and Rice, L. (eds.), Innovations in Client-Centered Therapy. New York: Wiley, 1974.

(21) FRIEDMAN, M. Healing through Meeting: A Dialogical Approach to Psychotherapy—I. Am. J. Psychoanal., 35 (1975), 255–67.

(22) TRÜB, H. Individuation, Guilt, and Decision. In Friedman, M. (ed.), The Knowledge of Man. New York: Random House, 1964.

(23) STOLLER, F. A Stage for Trust. In Burton, A. (ed.), Encounter: The Theory and Practice of Encounter Groups. San Francisco: Jossey-Bass, 1970.

(24) MALONE, T. Encountering and Groups. In Burton, A. (ed.), Encounter. San Francisco: Jossey-Bass, 1970.

(25) ROGERS, C. Carl Rogers on Encounter Groups. New York: Harper and Row, 1970.

(26) HOBBS, N. Group-Centered Psychotherapy. In Rogers, C. R. (ed.), Client-Centered Therapy. Boston: Houghton Mifflin, 1951.

(27) ROGERS, C. On Becoming a Person: A Therapist's View of Psychotherapy. Boston: Houghton Mifflin, 1961.

(28) BAKAN, D. The Duality of Human Existence. Chicago: Rand McNally, 1966.

(29) BUBER, M. Between Man and Man. London: Kegan Paul, 1947.

(30) GALT, A. Therapy in the Context of Trigant Burrow's Group Analysis. Group Process, 5 (1973), 115–28.

(31) ROSENBAUM, M., and BERGER, M. (eds.). Group Psychotherapy and Group Function. New York: Basic Books, 1963.

(32) ODEN, T. The New Pietism. J. Human Psychol. (Spring 1972).

(33) BACK, K. Beyond Words: The Story of Sensitivity Training and the Encounter Movement. Baltimore: Penguin Books, 1973.

(34) SCHUTZ, W. Elements of Encounter. Big Sur, Calif.: Joy Press, 1973.

(35) LERNER, M. American Precursors of the Human Potential Movement. Address, University of California, Los Angeles, December 1972.

(36) MORENO, J. Who Shall Survive? New York: Beacon House, 1953.

(37) YABLONSKY, L. Psychodrama and Role Training. In Solomon, L., and Berzon, B. (eds.), New Perspectives on Encounter Groups. San Francisco: Jossey-Bass, 1972.

(38) SHEPARD, M. Fritz. New York: Bantam Books, 1975.

(39) FAGEN, J., and SHEPHERD, I. L. Gestalt Therapy Now: Theory, Techniques, Applications. Palo Alto, Calif.: Science and Behavior Books, 1970.

(40) LEVITSKY, A., and PERLS, F. The Rules and Games of Gestalt Therapy. In Fagen, J., and Shepherd, I. (eds.), Gestalt Therapy Now. Palo Alto, Calif.: Science and Behavior Books, 1970.

(41) BERZON, B., SOLOMON, L. N., and REISEL, J. Audio Tape Programs for Self-Directed Groups. In Solomon, L., and Berzon, B. (eds.), New Perspectives on Encounter Groups. San Francisco: Jossey-Bass, 1972.

(42) IZARD, C. The Face of Emotion. New York: Appleton-Century, 1971.

(43) ALLEN, G. American Opinion. John Birch Society, January 1968.

(44) STANG, A. The Review of the News, April 9, 1969.

(45) GOTTSCHALK, L. A., and PATTISON, M. Psychiatric Perspectives on T-groups and the Laboratory Movement: An Overview. Am. J. Psychiat., 6, No. 126 (Devember 1969).

(46) JAFFE, S., and SCHERL, D. J. Acute Psychosis Precipitated by T-group Experiences. Arch Gen. Psychiatry, 21 (October 1969).

(47) REDDY, W. Sensitivity Training or Group Psychotherapy: The Need for Adequate Screening. Internat. J. Group Psychotherapy, 20 (1970), 366–71.

(48) MALIVER, B. Encounter Groupers: Up against the Wall. New York Times Magazine, January 3, 1971.

(49) SCHULTZ, W. Not Encounter and Certainly Not Facts. J. Human. Psychol., 15, No. 2 (Spring 1975).

(50) RUSSELL, E. W. Encounter Groups: First Facts?: A Reexamination. Unpublished manuscript, 1976.

(51) ROWAN, J. Encounter Group Research: No Joy? J. Human. Psychol., 15, No. 2 (Spring 1975).

(52) SMITH, P. B. Controlled Studies of the Outcome of Sensitivity Training. Psychol. Bull., 82, No. 4 (1975b), 597–622.

(53) COOPER, C. L. How Psychologically Dangerous Are T-groups and Encounter Groups? Human Relations, 28, No. 3 (1972), 249–60.

(54) ROSENTHAL, B. Address, Annual Conference, American Association for the Advancement of Science, Philadelphia, December 1971.

(55) RENHOLD, R. Encounter Movement, a Fad Last Decade, Finds New Shape. New York Times, January 13, 1974.

(56) TRUAX, C., and MITCHELL, K. Research on Certain Therapist Interpersonal Skills in Relation to Process and Outcome. In Bergin, A., and Garfield, S. (eds.), Handbook of Psychotherapy and Behavior Change: An Empirical Analysis. New York: Wiley, 1971.

(57) BEBOUT, J. The Use of Encounter Groups for Interpersonal Growth: Initial Results of the TIE Project. Interpers. Develop., 2 (1971/72), 91–104.

(58) SMITH, P. B. Are There Adverse Effects of Training? J. Human. Psychol., 15, No. 2 (Spring 1975a).

17 Group Psychotherapy Toward Increased Sexual Response

Ruth T. Caplan
Stanley W. Caplan
Joan B. Scott

Introduction

TRADITIONAL PSYCHOANALYSTS and psychoanalytically oriented psychotherapists have assumed that if individual constructive changes occur in two partners while undergoing treatment, their sexual intimacy will automatically improve. Over the past decade, however, we have become increasingly aware that this is not necessarily the case. Many couples have reported that, despite a tremendous improvement in their interpersonal relationships in areas like communication, playing, and fighting, they were experiencing the same or greater problems in the bedroom. Consequently, we embarked on a program of intensive study and training. The sexual modification treatment program presented here is the result.

The following criteria governed the development of this therapy: (1) Since we are experienced group psychotherapists who value the group process, our treatment efforts would take place in the group. (2) The costs (about eight hundred dollars per couple in 1975) would be within reach of our middle-class patient population. (3) The program would be conducted locally to further minimize expense and to allow for continuity of treatment and followup. (4) The program would be geared to the relatively conservative fabric of the community in which we practice.

What evolved is a unique treatment form that employs some aspects of the basically positive reinforcement strategies of Masters and Johnson (1) and Hartman and Fithian (2) and of the teaching model of the National Sex Forum, in addition to intensive ongoing individual and group psychotherapy, transactional analysis, and Gestalt therapy, reinforced by multimedia materials. The basic aim of this method is *an increase in the intimacy flow in the partners' relationship, primarily through their learning to leave any sexually toned encounter feeling better about the self and the partner.*

For the first three years our only participants were couples in our regular psychotherapy groups whose problems were primarily in the sexual area. Since then sex therapy has become increasingly popular as a result of a number of changes in the society as a whole: the impact of the women's movement, the impetus of the research publications of Masters and Johnson, the more open attitudes of both schools and religious organizations, the wider acceptance by the general public of discussions of sexuality (primarily in television and the movies), and the increased acceptance of sexual therapy by the helping professions. Eventually, too, participants in the group intimacy workshop, the primary treatment event in our evolving program, came to feel more open in discussing with close friends their improvement in sexual function. Thus we gradually started including couples who had not been in therapy with us and who were directly referred for sexual difficulties.

Referrals now come to us from other sources such as physicians, ministers, and social workers. One couple, when asked for their referral source, gave the names of three couples who had been in previous workshops, in addition to that of their minister! Many couples come to us after a considerable length of time in other kinds of psychotherapy and are able to change their overall feelings about intimacy in their relationship within a matter of a few weeks. Such positive, rapid results attest the importance of sex modification group therapy.

The components essential to the speed and effectiveness of this program are: (1) the "transparent," open therapist who is willing to disclose many facets of himself; (2) a schedule of behavioral modification, which employs the established principles of learning for the purpose of changing neurotic behavior, backed by a strategy of positive reinforcement consisting of small, step-by-step exercises in which there is a minimal chance of failure; (3) the attitude change achieved rapidly by the use of films and group therapy sessions during the workshop weekend; and (4) a continuous and consistent interlocking of all these elements throughout the program, combined with the therapists' optimistic expectations of positive change.

Since in our group psychotherapy practice we do not differentiate between or segregate married and unmarried couples, we have not done so in the group intimacy workshop. With the changing mores of society today, the rapid increase in divorce rates, and the expanding variety of life styles, we view as unrealistic an insistence on the convention of a marriage certificate as an admission ticket to a group where partners diligently, honestly, and earnestly work on improving either their personal interaction or their sexual relationship. Our only requirement is that the couple be committed to the relationship for the entire treatment period—the preparatory sessions, the intensive group workshop, the six weeks of followup sessions, and the six-month period of integration after the workshop that appears crucial if the life styles of the partners are to be truly modified. The presence of both married and unmarried couples in the same intensive workshop has never been a critical issue.

The treatment described in this chapter is suitable for couples over a wide range of age groups. One of the greatest rewards of the workshops for us is the number of "older" couples who say they wish this program had been available to them prior to or early in their marriage. One such couple gave their son and new daughter-in-law a gift certificate to a workshop as a wedding present; the younger couple felt it was the most thoughtful *and* practical gift they could have received. We also find that an increasing number of partners contemplating a second marriage seek our assistance, either before making a final decision or to confirm a decision already made.

While we are aware of the use of surrogate partners by some sex therapists for specific purposes, such as phobic reactions to the opposite sex (3), we are unwilling to use them in our treatment plan for several reasons. The major one, of course, is that since our therapy centers upon increasing the intimacy between partners, commitment to the partner (which would not exist with a surrogate) is essential to the basic principles and eventual success of our efforts. Further, we feel that we can accomplish much the same results by the use of other procedures (like fantasy exercises, gradual relaxation, and desensitization) without infringing on the mores of the community in which we practice or on the sensitivities of other patients who are already highly anxious about the propriety of this kind of therapy. When surrogate partners are used many moral, ethical, and legal problems arise that could jeopardize the entire treatment program.

Principles and Goals

Therapeutic goals at the start of psychotherapy vary considerably, depending on the patient's strength and his ability to risk and on the therapist's theories, methods, and abilities. During initial sessions with a couple for either the ongoing couples group therapy or the sexual intimacy program, we attempt to assess what each partner views as the basic difficulties in their relationship in order to determine whether we may be able to help.

Sue and John, for example, wanted to resolve all their conflicts immediately, and Sue said that she wanted "to be happy and to make John happy." The therapist rejected these goals as unrealistic: "I simply don't know how to eliminate conflicts between partners, but I can help you learn how to argue fairly without as much damage to each other and how to make up quickly after a fight. Sue, I can help you feel more comfortable about yourself and to change in ways you consider important. But I can't assure you that you'll always be happy. And you can't *make* John happy; no one can *make* another person happy. Let's work toward a practical goal. In what specific ways would you like to change, individually and in your relationship?" Gradually, Sue and John narrowed their expectations to attainable goals acceptable to them and to the therapist. For example, one of their high-priority objectives was "to learn how to resolve our fights quickly so we can be close again."

When the joint patient-therapist decision is to begin preparation for the intensive intimacy program, in addition to discussing the aims of the treatment we also give the couple basic information regarding time, place, cost, preparation, and followup, and an outline of what occurs during the weekend workshop. We emphasize the ways in which our method differs from others, that is, in the use of the group process and in the goals to be realized by those participating, both as individuals and as partners. The long-term therapy goals of our program are that (1) each member of the couple will learn to leave each sexually toned encounter feeling better about himself or herself and about the partner, and (2) each partner's attitudes and feelings of freedom regarding sex will change as a result of participation. As we frequently and emphatically tell patients—initially and throughout *all* sessions—our treatment focuses not only on relief of symptoms, but on establishing and maintaining intimacy flow between partners. Increased emotional sharing, exchange of warmth, and recommitment to the relationship are integral goals of our program.

It is crucial to lasting success that the couple gives top priority, in terms of both time and energy, to their joint endeavor to improve their intimacy. Even then, we occasionally meet with resistance by one or both partners regarding the use of group therapy, and it is not uncommon for a patient to state flatly, "I would be too embarrassed to discuss my problem in front of others." This type of overt resistance, however, can usually be reduced during the preparatory phase.

Three interrelated principles of our program underlie the fundamental attitude change that is expected in patients (paradoxically, they are the reverse of attitudes originally held by most patients who seek our help in the area of sex). They are: (1) that sexual intercourse is not a "right" to be demanded ("no-demand sex"); (2) that "performance criteria" in sexual activity are to be eliminated gradually; and (3) that the couple will proceed through the program at a pace at which the slower partner feels comfortable.

By "no-demand sex" we mean that each partner has the right and responsibility to take "time out" from any sexual activity that he or she feels unable to cope with at the moment. Further, it is the responsibility of the partner who requests time out to reinitiate contact, emotionally or physically and verbally or nonverbally. The deliberate deemphasis on standards of "performance" in sex (in terms of orgasms, erections, duration of intercourse, and the like) permits couples to relax and become aware that truly intimate lovemaking demonstrates caring rather than adding points to an imaginary scoreboard. Pacing the program to the more fearful, resistant, or anxious partner further decreases the pressure for performance.

Kay and Jack, a couple in their twenties who had been married for six years, exemplified the way these attitudes operate and how the true acceptance of these goals can gradually reverse past resentments that cause many intimacy problems. Kay initially felt that Jack "demanded" intercourse much more frequently than she wanted it and that it was her "duty" to agree. She believed her arousal to be too slow for Jack and that she was inadequate because she could not always satisfy him by having an orgasm. As it turned out, Kay was sometimes correct in feeling that Jack wanted intercourse more often than she did, but she also frequently *assumed* a demand without checking this out with Jack, "gave in" passively and resentfully, and felt guilty because she should but could not satisfy him. Later her resentment increased and she got even by denying her own body feelings, but she continued to feel guilty because she set up an arbitrary deadline by which she "should" be orgasmic.

Jack admitted during the intensive workshop that he was angry and impatient with Kay. Both he and Kay were relieved and reassured when one of the therapists told him that he had every right to express his feelings of impatience and Kay agreed to listen to him without construing his feelings as a demand on her. After hearing repeatedly from various members of the therapy team that attitudes and behaviors acquired over a span of twenty years were unlikely to be reversed in six weeks, this couple became more relaxed and less demanding and concentrated more on the intimacy aspects of the program. They were amazed at the changes in both their feelings and their sexual experiences together.

The group experience during the intensive workshop proves to be significant in still another way. For example, another couple in the group had a sexual history similar to that of Kay and Jack and had also felt defeated by the old cycle of performance, perfection, and guilt. "We thought we were the only ones who got bogged down this way," Kay said, after the other couple had opened up about this common experience. No amount of reassurance from the therapists has quite the same impact as this kind of exchange among group members.

An impasse such as the one experienced by Kay and Jack invariably elicits a reiteration by a member of the therapy team of the major intimacy goal of the program: that each person must learn to leave every sexually toned encounter feeling better about himself or herself and about the partner. This concept is the vital one in our therapy and embodies several other basic tenets: (1) that sexuality and sensuality are on a broad continuum and that genital intercourse occupies a very narrow space on that continuum; (2) that the quality of sex and intimacy rather than the quantity are crucial to a positive, flowing relationship; (3) that any form of sexual activity is a form of adult fun and play; and thus (4) that genital intercourse is simply one way of expressing caring in a relationship, not necessarily the ultimate goal of a display of affection. We stress repeatedly that a "sexually toned" encounter can include anything on this broad continuum of sexuality and sensuality: holding hands, a smile across a room, sitting together watching a sunset (or a favorite television show), playing with children or pets, sharing joint fun activities, cuddling together, and any form of intercourse that both partners enjoy.

We cannot overemphasize the fact—proved by our experience with more than three hundred couples—that the ultimate success of our treatment depends on the degree to which patients accept as *fundamental* the goal of leaving any sexually toned encounter feeling better about oneself and about one's partner. The importance of this position, which represents a profound change from the initial stereotyped, performance-oriented attitude of most couples, has been confirmed by extensive followup and research.

Sex therapy, therefore, is designed to assist individuals and couples in a specific aspect of behavior: intimate sexual response. However, we often find that positive change in sexual attitudes and behavior tends to spill over into other areas of the partners' lives, affecting their sense of self-worth and their feelings toward each other in nonsexual parts of their relationship. When this happens we encourage it; it is an exciting phenomenon, seldom verbalized, which frequently stimulates the partners to explore new ways of relating.

Theory

The purpose of this group therapy is to intervene directly in the area of sexuality and thereby to effect both intrapsychic and interpersonal change. Throughout the course of treatment the therapists, with the help of the group members, work to modify cultural influences that have caused psychosexual abnormality and sexual dysfunction.

The sex drive is different from other drives (such as hunger, thirst, and sleep) in two important ways: (1) it is essential for the survival of the species, but not of the individual, and (2) it is a learned behavior. A considerable body of evidence in anthropology and sociology as well as in psychology and psychiatry suggests that cultural and, more directly, familial pressures shape many aspects of sexual behavior (2, 4, 5, 6, 7, 8, 9).

Since sexual behavior is learned, it can be unlearned and then relearned.

Further, since sexual behavior is both a sociological and an individual phenomenon, it is easily influenced in a deeply involved therapy group, which is in some ways a microcosm of society.

Numerous cultural factors play an important role not only in the original acquisition of attitudes regarding sex, but also in the continued shaping and reinforcement of these attitudes. The most important factor in the early acquisition of sexual concepts is the position that one's parents take concerning sex and the display of feelings. This is reinforced by the extended family and is influenced by peer groups and in many cases by religion. The attitudes of these groups and the manner in which they are transmitted regarding birth, nudity, early sex play and experimentation, natural physical processes of maturation, sex roles and expectations, and self-concept and body image are often critical to the psychosexual development of the child and adolescent.

Frequently, facts or family myths about a child's birth—whether he or she was wanted or planned or of the hoped-for sex, and the birth order of the children—affect the evolving sexual concept of the individual and determine his or her adult sexuality. For example, one sexually well adjusted patient said she knew she was a wanted child, assumed from the ages of her brothers and sisters that she was planned, and had often heard the family story that her mother was in labor for so long that her father and grandfather missed the opening of dove season waiting for her to arrive! Another patient knew from an early age that he was unwanted and unplanned, that his parents had married because his mother was pregnant, and that his birth had interrupted her plans to complete college. He received a strong "Don't be" message from his parents that he is still striving to overcome.

Children also receive extremely powerful nonverbal messages from their parents. For example, the child whose hands are removed from the genitals during exploration or masturbation often interprets this action to mean that masturbation or touching oneself is bad. If there is no discussion of sex in the home and no nudity, the child (and later the adult) often comes to feel that sex in general is bad. A child who is not touched or held by either parent and who sees little or no physical demonstrativeness between parents has no model for learning how to touch or how to show a partner that he cares. An adult with such a childhood background may have an extremely large amount of what we call "skin hunger"—a need to be touched, which we believe is universal, although many patients are unaware of it and try to satisfy it by genital intercourse alone. Montagu's book *Touching* is strongly recommended reading for those who are withdrawn from their own and others' needs to be touched (10).

Another factor that strongly influences and reinforces what we view as unrealistic views toward sex are messages communicated by the mass media. Sometimes these messages are delivered subliminally; often they are blatant: "Use the right mouthwash if you want to be sexy and popular."

Over and over, in movies, on television, and in pulp magazines, the pretty woman or the handsome man wins. There is tremendous superficiality in the media view of sex and little that involves true intimacy: feeling good about oneself and about one's partner.

Our culture also overemphasizes the physical aspect of sex at the expense of interpersonal and intimacy-based aspects. Our group therapy team now sees more and more women who feel inadequate in that they are not *always* orgasmic and men who feel they should *always* satisfy their partners. In other words, the formerly unspoken criteria for "successful" sexual behavior have surfaced, with a resulting set of "shoulds" and "oughts." These demands affect not only those people whose sexuality or sexual relationships are already somewhat tenuous, but also those who thought they had—and probably do have—a good and mutually satisfying sexual adjustment.

Our program of sexual therapy, based on the belief that sexual behavior is learned, consists of having our patients take extremely small steps toward increased intimacy, with frequent review and provision for (and insistence upon) returning to a previous level whenever one partner experiences discomfort or fear of the next step. This safeguard provides for the maximum number of successes and minimizes failures. Any small setback during the intensive workshop is discussed within the group if the person concerned feels able to express his or her feelings of failure—usually to the relief of others in the group who are experiencing the same feelings.

We are firmly convinced of the importance of involving, mutually supportive group therapy in treating sexual dysfunction. We believe that a strong supportive group operating as a dynamic kind of family can speed up and intensify a behavioral, albeit humanistic, approach to treatment in the couple area. The use of such a group approach during the intensive workshop and during the followup sessions accounts for our high success ratio (86 percent) in terms of both symptom relief and increase in feelings of self-worth on the part of the participants. This method strongly differentiates our approach from that of Masters and Johnson (11), Hartman and Fithian (2), and Kaplan (12), all of whom treat one couple at a time at what we feel are unnecessary expenses and a loss of efficiency. We find ourselves closer to the theoretical stance of the University of California Medical School Unit on Human Sexuality and the National Sex Forum in San Francisco, which also use a group *teaching* if not a group therapy approach.

The Sex Therapist

Intrinsic to this mode of therapy is the therapists' frankness about their own experiences and difficulties in the sexual as well as other personal areas of their lives (the "transparent therapist" concept), whenever this is relevant and supportive to the patients (13, 14). It has been especially helpful that two members of our team went through the sex therapy program several years ago and have been willing to discuss the feelings they had about the program when they were patients. We strongly urge, therefore, that anyone preparing to become a "sex" therapist experience, *as a patient*, sex treatment similar to that described in this chapter.

Besides being open and self-revealing, the therapists attempt to model the positive behaviors that are constantly being emphasized in the program: smiles, closeness, touching, holding, and other warm and affectionate responses to each other become an important part of the group workshop. At times, too, minor irritations and frustrations develop between team members and are worked through as openly as possible. Group members often express appreciation of the leaders' openness.

Extensive experience with and understanding of individual and group processes is crucial for the sex therapist. He or she should have a solid background in individual, group, and marital counseling, as well as knowledge of the ways in which partners function with each other, how these interactions influence their sexual activity, and how the sexual relationship may in turn influence the other aspects of their life. A practical understanding of the physiology of normal and abnormal sexual behavior is important for the therapist interested in the sexually dysfunctional person. Further, it is necessary that this therapist understand the effects of drugs (particularly alcohol), aging, life trauma such as birth and divorce, physical or emotional illness, and physical handicaps on a person's or a couple's sexual life.

A sex therapist must be especially sensitive to the unique needs of each individual, couple, and group. If partners tend to sabotage each other with "game playing" (15), for example, we spend time in bringing this to their attention and helping them to stop it. The three most common games between partners in the intimacy groups seem to be: (1) "If you really loved me, you would . . ."; (2) "Be more like me"; and (3) "If only you . . ." Couples with long-established patterns of communication usually play these games in their financial dealings, in child rearing, and in the bedroom. In the brief sex therapy workshop we can concentrate only on those games played in the sexual arena. Most attempts to control one's partner are a way of alleviating one's own anxiety. A therapist who is sensitive to the underlying dynamic of anxiety can frequently help the person who is experiencing this to verbalize his feelings; and his partner, thus becoming aware of those feelings for the first time, can often learn to act in ways that provoke less anxiety.

In this program our group therapists must cope with the same problems of transference, countertransference, resistance, and acting out that are present in all psychotherapies. We direct and encourage patients to use all effective techniques—psychodrama, Gestalt therapy, and transactional analysis—when the need arises. Should it be necessary during the intimacy weekend workshop, we refer the patient back to the original therapist. It is always our responsibility to maintain objectivity in monitoring the group process. As stated earlier, the major curative dynamic begins to operate when the partners begin by word and by sign to reinforce each other whenever a step toward greater intimacy occurs. And (although we allow ourselves to be models) we are never members of the group itself, but try to create an atmosphere conducive to change and growth. We guard against members of the group competing in a "power" or status struggle, to "go faster," or to be the "best" patient. We try to stay alert for possible misuse of the group by persons with marked exhibitionist or voyeuristic needs or by couples who try to use the workshop to "prove" that their relationship is not tenable, thereby providing themselves with an excuse for divorce.

Selection

The success of this treatment program depends in part on the motivation of the patients to change. The problem of sufficient motivation is greater when the attempt is to effect change in one of the most sensitive parts of their relationship, such as sex. The interactional dynamics between the partners, and the way these are used by the couple in maintaining the balance of control between them, are at the same time subtle and powerful. The selection process for our program begins with an initial interview in which the couple seeking sex therapy is seen conjointly by a member of the therapy team. During this initial interview the therapist assesses (1) the stability of the patients in their relationship, and (2) the stability of the relationship.

In evaluating the stability of the relationship, several questions are pertinent. Can the couple play and vacation together without the intermediary of children or friends? Do religious, ethical, or aesthetic conflicts spill over into the sexual area? Does each partner consider the other a friend? Do they share common interests, talk, play, and closeness as well as sexual intimacy? Do they look forward to aging in each other's company? (A "yes" answer to this question indicates a strong commitment to the relationship.) Finally, can they fight and make up with minimal damage to each other? Partners who do not fight cannot resolve conflicts; on the other hand, some couples fight with so much ensuing damage that it is impossible for them to be close again for days afterward.

If it is determined that both partners are highly motivated and that their relationship is stable enough to survive intervention, the couple are admitted to treatment. For those patients who have not been examined by a doctor in the last six months, a physical examination is required prior to the onset of therapy.

Preparatory Sessions: Individual and Conjoint

The six-week preparatory period of weekly fifty-minute sessions is an integral part of the program. These individual or conjoint sessions allow the therapists to establish strong therapeutic ties, as a result of which the patients' fears are reduced and new intimate sexual behavior is learned and practiced. During this phase the couples renew their commitment to remain together, are "desensitized" to unhealthy attitudes about sex, and learn to explore their bodies and to give themselves tactile pleasure. Beginning with the second preparatory session, the therapists also work with the patients to broaden and enrich their sexual fantasy life because individual and mutual fantasies help a couple reestablish their sexual feelings and direct them toward more intimate coupling. Patients learn that a sexual fantasy need not be a long, involved story with a beginning, a middle, and an end—it can be a brief flash, a thought, or a feeling—but that it should make them feel alive and happy.

We wish that time of entry into treatment and financial constraints had not, up until now, limited our ability to bring the group together at the beginning of the treatment process—before the intensive workshop. We are convinced that the use of a group therapy approach throughout the entire program would yield even better results than we have achieved, if we could overcome the practical difficulties.

First Preparatory Session: The Sex History

A sex history taken during the first preparatory session begins the success-oriented, step-by-step program. For male patients a male therapist, and for female patients a female therapist, obtains information concerning the patient's sexual background, traumas, fears and forbidden practices, and other long-established problems. The frank and open discussion of sex lessens the patient's anxiety and begins the slow process of desensitization. The sex history outline should cover the following, and close attention should be given chance remarks of the patient.

1. Birth history, myths surrounding the birth: wanted or planned child, birth position in the family, early health, sex, and so forth.
2. Messages concerning what each parent valued or expected of the patient in childhood and adolescence: "Be a good boy"; "Study hard"; "Don't touch!"; "You'll be the death of me!"
3. Affection displayed between the parents and toward the child: "They were always hugging each other"; "All I remember is horrible fights."

4. How nudity was handled in the home: "I always bathed with my brothers and sisters"; "I never saw my parents naked."

5. Statements and inferences about sex acquired from family, peers, books, and so forth: "Don't play with yourself"; "Don't get pregnant"; "Sex is exciting."

6. The history of sexual trauma, if any: "My uncle played with me when I was four and I was really scared."

7. Information and misinformation about masturbation, intercourse, conception, and so forth, where and how it was acquired, and feelings of guilt, curiosity, and excitement transmitted at the time: "My dad kept pictures of nude women locked up in his desk"; "They told me I'd go insane if I masturbated."

8. Early sexual exploration or play with the other sex, attitudes concerning this, and punishment for it: "We played doctor a lot"; "I got caught playing in the nude with another girl and got a switching for it."

9. Attitudes about sex acquired from church and school: "Sex is only for married people to have babies"; "The priest said I would go to hell if I masturbated."

10. Heterosexual and homosexual activity up to the age of eighteen or twenty: "We used to have contests to see who could urinate the farthest"; "I had a steady girl and we petted but we never went all the way."

Adult sexual activity is described by the patient as he or she learns to trust the therapist. Toward the end of the first period it is not uncommon for emotionally laden material regarding masturbation, fetishes, deviations, affairs, fantasies, and so forth to be revealed.

To counteract the misinformation and confusion of most patients regarding sex, during the entire preparatory phase the therapist supplies simple, accurate sexual information in a casual, nonthreatening manner: "No man can *give* a woman an orgasm"; "No man can *will* an erection"; "There is no difference between 'clitoral' and 'vaginal' orgasm." The therapist often establishes rapport and further reassures the patient by revealing similar childhood experiences: "Masturbation was considered sinful in my family, too. I decided my family was wrong and I was right."

SECOND PREPARATORY SESSION: THE PLEASURING EXERCISE

During the second preparatory session, each woman is given an explicit set of homework assignments to follow. The first is to take a half hour each day that is completely her own. She is told to buy a "special" bottle of lotion or oil and to give herself a very slow hand, foot, or face massage during the first half-hour "pleasuring session," and to experiment with some of the following exercises: to spend five or ten minutes running her hands over a piece of fur, silk, or satin, and draw this material slowly over her body; to stroke her cheek or the palm of her hand with a feather or a flower; and to put on her favorite gown or bathrobe and move around the house noticing the feel of the texture on her skin. She is also encouraged to use her own imagination in finding out precisely what pleasures and pampers *her* the most. Many women find this assignment very difficult to do because they feel that they must finish the housework and attend to husbands and children first. Learning to be their own highest priority is one of the most important steps in their sex therapy.

The male partner is also instructed to take a half hour a day to pleasure himself and become more aware of his body and its sensory experience. We do not yet have as fine a list of suggestions to offer men as we do for women, so we ask them to translate the suggestions given to their wives into their own experience. An underlying goal of these pleasuring exercises is to get the patients used to putting themselves in top priority, so that eventually as a couple they will put their intimacy in higher priority.

The partners are also told, as a couple exercise, to snuggle together nude for five minutes each day, taking turns at who holds whom. No other sexual activity is to take place before, during, or immediately afterward. Partners learn that physical stroking and displays of affection neither have to start with a genital sexual impulse nor must always end in intercourse.

Third Preparatory Session: The Leisurely Sensuous Bath

The second homework assignment is a bathing exercise. Both men and women are asked to take a long, leisurely bath—separately—using a bath oil, bubbles, or whatever else they can to make it special and pleasing. During the bath they are to do three specific tasks: wash slowly without using a washcloth, learning what their bodies feel like to their own hands; go over their bodies from the tips of their toes to the tips of their fingers, deciding what they like and what they don't like in order to make peace with their body images; and find areas of the body other than breasts and genitals that are particularly sensitive to the touch, a first step in eroticizing the entire body so that the genitals are not the only erogenous zones in lovemaking.

Again, as a couple exercise, the partners are told to extend their cuddling sessions to include a head, hand, or foot massage, in which the partner giving the massage pays attention to the other's needs and follows his or her directions about what gives him or her special pleasure.

Fourth Preparatory Session: Genital Examination

The next homework assignment is to continue the pleasuring half hour and for both men and women to spend five minutes during the pleasuring session looking at their own genitals. Although many men have already done this in some measure, most women are entirely unacquainted with their genitalia and feel that they are somewhat "strange" and "unattractive." Women are asked to separate the labia and really look closely at their genitals, using a mirror, for five minutes each day until they become bored—at which point they are asked to find something pretty about their own genitalia. This is the most difficult step in the preparatory sessions and, perhaps the most powerful. Once men or women can find something pretty or positive about their genitalia, they seem to be able to integrate these parts of their anatomy into their total body image instead of feeling that they are something to be ashamed of.

FIFTH PREPARATORY SESSION: THE VIBRATOR

At this point we sometimes ask women to begin using a vibrator during part of the half-hour pleasuring session, to get used to a hard, cold, noisy instrument and to find some way in which it can give them pleasure. They are also to continue any other kind of pleasuring they enjoy. Some men need a great deal of time to work through their fear that the use of a vibrator is abnormal and that their partners may come to prefer it to intercourse with them. Once these fears have been allayed, we ask the men to consider at this time ways to "court" their wives, because many men (and women) today have so little knowledge of what their partners really like.

The use of the vibrator and the practice of masturbation were formerly somewhat controversial. However, Masters and Johnson (1), Hartman and Fithian (2); Kaplan (12), and McCrary (6) all agree that masturbation is pleasurable, harmless, and natural, that it relieves sexual and other tensions, and that it is a healthy way of learning one's own sexual responses. In a different way the use of a vibrator assists the person with a low-key sex response to discover more about his or her individual modes of sensual and sexual pleasure. For those people who have less difficulty in getting in touch with their changing and unique patterns of response, it is an added, fun way of exploring and sharing with one's partner.

SIXTH PREPARATORY SESSION: MASTURBATION

During the last week before the workshop both men and women are encouraged to masturbate, although if any patient feels religious, moral, or aesthetic constraints against masturbation we do not insist on this step. Most women who are preorgasmic when they come into the program become orgasmic during this exercise. They are instructed to masturbate daily with a vibrator and experience all the pleasure they can, but not to *try* to reach an orgasm. Men are asked to become aware of their point of "ejaculatory inevitability" so that they will be prepared to learn the "Semans squeeze technique" * during the workshop (16).

---

* This technique is described on p. 348.

At this time women are also taught the Kegel exercises for tightening the pubococcygeus muscle (17). This exercise involves contracting and relaxing the muscles in the vagina, starting at thirty and working up to four hundred contract-relax sequences each day. The exercise, which tones the muscles in the vagina and makes the nerve endings there more sensitive to stimulation, also gives the woman more control over her own stimulation and satisfaction during intercourse. Voluntary use of this muscle can be fun for both partners.

Prohibition against Sexual Intercourse

Genital intercourse is prohibited only during the last two weeks of preparation for the intensive group workshop and for the two and one half days of this workshop. The couple is told honestly that we want their maximum interest to be on broadening their sexual life to more than genital intercourse and that we want the more anxious partner to learn that genital intercourse is not the be-all and end-all of an intimate life. As a result most patients feel more free to explore each other in new, exciting, and at the same time less frightening ways. We believe this "prohibition" is essential in diverting the couple's attention from their symptoms to the worth and value of their relationship. Almost all couples have obeyed this injunction, and the few who have rebelled have usually told us about it laughingly afterward. We have had no problems with patients being attracted to members of other couples or of any sexual acting out between couples. We believe this is because of our emphasis on the "couple" and its interdynamics as the basic treatment unit.

The prohibition against intercourse is mandatory, as this program is based on a sequence of small successes. When patients fail in intercourse during the last two weeks before the intensive workshop, they find it quite traumatic. The prohibition helps couples to realize that there are other satisfactory ways to "make love," and this removes any pressure to "perform" just before and during the workshop.

The Intensive Group Workshop

After the preparatory sessions, a group of five to ten couples meets at a pleasant local motel. The workshop continues the guidance, support, and intervention of the five therapists, one of whom is a physician-psychiatrist. The couples do not ordinarily know each other, unless by chance they have been in a therapy group together. People are asked to give their first names and say a little about their feelings. Most report they are a little apprehensive, anxious, and sometimes excited.

Some instructions concerning the workshop are given: eat lightly; use a minimum of alcohol (one drink before dinner maximum); report any medication being taken to the psychiatric consultant; call on any therapist any time during the weekend. Partners are told that before they can proceed to a next step in the program they must always complete the previous step. They are reminded that material discussed at the group sessions is confidential. The therapists discourage patients from discussing specific sexual dysfunctions in the group. Each person is given a notebook and must take his own notes during every session because everyone hears things a little differently. The first assignment after each group session is for each couple to discuss and come to a mutual agreement on the meaning of the notes they have taken.

The intensive group workshop is a series of ten sessions, starting on a Friday morning and continuing until Sunday noon. The time, duration, and content of these sessions may vary, but the goals, the step-by-step procedures, and the group dynamics are always much the same.

Friday, 9:00 a.m. to 10:15 a.m. (Whole Group)

Desensitization is begun during the first group session by showing several hundred erotic art slides until the group is actually bored with them. Then a humorous slide set called *Genesis* is shown to ease the tension. All participants are told to take careful individual notes and ask questions freely as the therapists outline the basic principles of the program. Instructions to each couple for the first exercise are: "Go to your room and remove as much clothing as you feel comfortable without, sit without touching your partner, and discuss the principles of the program until you agree on them. If you have time, talk about how you acquired ideas and attitudes about sex that are different from these principles." The simplicity of these steps is a relief to some couples; others feel that they are too easy, but we emphasize that the program will not be successful unless each couple understands and *accepts* its basic principles. At the end of this group session, a humorous, nonthreatening two-minute film called *Love Toad* is shown that demonstrates most of the principles just presented. Couples are given forty-five minutes to an hour for this step. Many do not complete it within the hour break, and they are told to take their time, go slowly, and use part of the next practice session to finish the first step.

Friday, 11:00 a.m. to 12:00 Noon (Whole Group)

The second group session begins with questions and problems not resolved during the first practice session; couples typically disagree about the principles. A great deal of support from other group members begins to take place during this session: "She heard you say that you should never initiate sex"; "No, what I heard Stan say was that initiation is better shared from time to time." Couples are cautioned again not to proceed to a new step until *both* agree that they have *successfully* completed the preceding one. The most effective curative dynamic that we know in sex therapy is mutual reinforcement and awareness of change and increasing intimacy. The simple success of being able to talk about sex in a calm and mutually supportive fashion is often a peak experience.

Following the group discussion, the therapists explain the importance of body image and fantasy in sexuality. Research has shown that people who allow themselves to fantasize easily and broadly about sex are much more likely to be responsive. Common male and female sexual fantasies (like bondage, multiple partners, and group sex) are discussed to help give participants "permission" to broaden this area of their lives. Two movies about sexual fantasies are shown. The first, *Unfolding*, a black-and-white film depicting a woman's sexual fantasies, makes the point that a sexual fantasy can include many things—the sight of the ocean, running through forests, laughter, and so on. The male fantasy film, *Watercress*, includes interracial and group sex material.

The second exercise in the program is then presented. Couples are to go to their rooms and undress. Each person is to stand in front of a mirror as the partner watches and examine his or her own body from head to toe, telling the partner which parts of it he or she likes and doesn't like. We also suggest that the person describe what he or she would change about himself or herself if it were possible. The onlooking partner is to remain absolutely silent. No touching is allowed. The next part of the exercise is for couples to begin revealing nonthreatening sexual fantasies to each other. Couples report that, although they find this exercise difficult, they feel much more comfortable with their bodies in each other's presence afterward. The thought of revealing fantasies usually causes apprehension, also, but most couples return feeling that they are quite normal and with the beginnings of some new ideas on how to experiment with each other sexually. We discourage the sharing of sadomasochistic or other violent fantasies.

FRIDAY, 1:30 P.M. TO 2:30 P.M. (WHOLE GROUP)

The third group session again begins with the discussion of questions and problems that have arisen during the break, but people usually also report that they are beginning to feel good about themselves and about each other. It is interesting to note the contrast between the tight, drawn, and sometimes angry faces at 9:00 Friday morning and the glowing, warm ones Friday afternoon.

This session is usually the most difficult because here the "taboo" subject of masturbation is introduced. The therapists discuss its positive and negative aspects without pushing it, but emphasize its rewards. A lengthy movie called *Susan*, demonstrating female masturbation techniques, is shown; even if a couple rejects masturbation, the movie does demonstrate many ways in which women like to be pleasured. We regret that we do not have a male counterpart to this film, but we have not yet found a male masturbation film suitable to our program.

The third exercise of the program is presented. Couple are to go to their rooms and, using the positions that have just been demonstrated, have a session on pleasuring (without genital or breast contact) to begin to learn what Masters and Johnson call "sensate focus." Lotions, oils, powders, and bubble baths are provided for use during pleasuring sessions at the workshop. We emphasize at this time the importance of applying the principles of the program, such as saying "yes" rather than "no" to your partner and giving alternatives during the pleasuring sessions. Couples are also encouraged to tell each other their feelings about masturbation. As in the previous step, the partner is asked simply to listen. Couples who successfully complete this step have a high chance of succeeding in the program.

Friday, 3:45 p.m. to 4:30 p.m. (Same-sex Group)

For this session men and women are split into two groups. For half the period they work with a therapist of the same sex and for half with a therapist of the opposite sex. In these groups people can safely bring up questions that they could not comfortably ask in front of their partners or perhaps anyone of the opposite sex; or, conversely, they can ask the therapist of the opposite sex to confirm facts about that sex: "Don't men suffer if they don't ejaculate enough or get enough sex?" "Do women really enjoy sex without an orgasm?"

Friday, 4:30 p.m. to 7:00 p.m. (Whole Group)

Couples are told to relax and are encouraged to have another nongenital pleasuring session before dinner. We reiterate that they must learn and practice pleasurable, caring alternatives to genital intercourse in their intimate behavior.

Friday, 7:00 p.m. to 9:00 p.m. (Whole Group)

The evening sessions are kept casual and fun with the group's fatigue level in mind. Usually the Semans squeeze technique is taught the first night, regardless of the nature of the couple's present sexual dysfunction. It is a procedure that will stand them in good stead in case future illness, fatigue, or aging cause problems of premature or retarded ejaculation or impotence.

In this technique, the male lies on his back, completely relaxed and passive, while the female slowly stimulates him first to erection and then almost to the point of "ejaculatory inevitability." He then signals to her that he has reached this point, and she immediately squeezes the penis as hard as she can, preferably with both hands, with her fingers above and below the coronal ridge and her thumbs on the back side of the penis, for about thirty seconds. The result is that the ejaculation is stopped and the erection partly lost. During the practice session in the rooms each couple is to repeat the exercise at least three times before the man is allowed to ejaculate. This technique, in which the male is absolutely passive and the female takes the initiative, helps immeasurably in teaching partners to relate differently to each other. A woman reported, "It's really fun to be able to tease and be seductive." Men like this shift in role, too: "It's nice to lie back and let you take charge. I'm tired of always being the aggressor."

All participants are to make "turnon" lists of deeply personal likings, three from each of the five senses (touch, sight, smell, hearing, and taste), and three favorite nonsexual activities. They are to share these lists with their partners and use them to please each other. New "courting" behavior can be drawn from these, and patients are impressed again with the fact that love can be expressed in many ways besides intercourse.

The last element in this session is a brief massage demonstration, which is emphasized here because through its use partners quite literally reach a state of physical and emotional closeness and mutual gratification.

Before leaving the evening session, couples are told to relax the next morning until noon. Also, it is carefully explained to them that it is quite natural for a partner to need some privacy and "distance" during the workshop (as well as in everyday life), but that the one who wishes to separate for a while must explain the desire to the partner, saying when he or she will be "back."

SATURDAY, 12:00 NOON TO 1:30 P.M. (WHOLE GROUP)

By the time of this meeting, couples need little encouragement to bring up frankly the problems they have been having in following the program. It is a demonstration of the cohesiveness and therapeutic strength of the group that its members now trust each other enough to open up about many intimate subjects. For example, one man said, "I didn't know other people were scared of getting together after a fight," and a woman asked, "Why do we always screw when we make up?"

The therapists use this session to restate the principles of the program and the lasting rewards that the participants can reap from it if they make a concentrated effort to apply it to their lives. Two films, *The Erogenists* and *Give to Get*, demonstrate caring massage techniques and suggest that the goal of lovemaking need not always be genital intercourse.

Before returning to their rooms, couples are instructed to develop jointly a list of alternatives to genital intercourse that they enjoy doing together. While other sexual acts such as mutual masturbation are readily agreed upon, many couples find it difficult to settle on a list of nonsexual activities—the theater, sports, concerts, music, vacations, and so on. After making the list, the couple is to have another genital pleasuring session.

Saturday, 3:30 p.m. to 4:45 p.m. (Same-sex Group)

This session allows men and women to discuss their successes, failures, and feelings of anxiety freely in the supportive group. Women now frequently report becoming orgasmic for the first time; men report having regular erections and those who have had difficulty with premature ejaculation or impotence often say they think the Semans squeeze technique is overcoming these problems.

Saturday, 6:30 p.m. to 8:00 p.m. (Whole Group)

The group dinner finds all the participants in high spirits. As partners have gotten close to each other, learning very private likes, dislikes, and preferences, acknowledging hard-to-tell fantasies, sexual impulses, and practices, and finally appreciating differently their own and their partners' bodies, a new bond develops between them. The dinner usually becomes a special celebration.

Saturday, 8:30 p.m. to 10:00 p.m. (Whole Group)

Two films—*Heterosexual Intercourse* and *Touching*—demonstrate that it is the responsibility of each couple to develop their own patterns of lovemaking. It is stressed that there is no one "normal" way to express love. While the films are being discussed, the group begins a massage session in which additional techniques for relaxing are first demonstrated and then practiced by partners.

Before the group members leave to return to their rooms for the evening the therapists confront them with the question, "How are you going to fit this program into your lives during the next six months?" Discussion now centers around this goal. It is pointed out that unless each couple is able to fit a pleasuring session three to five times a week into their busy schedules, their present feelings of success and closeness will dissipate. Back in their bedrooms, partners usually discuss seriously the ways in which they can insure the continuity of this part of the program. A pleasuring session is suggested before going to sleep.

Sunday, 9:30 a.m. to 10:15 a.m. (Whole Group)

The group discussion now centers around each couple's priorities: children, work, studies, entertainment, house, pets, hobbies, sports, and so forth. Keeping in mind the importance of fitting this program into their lives, they begin to juggle duties and time to fit pleasuring sessions regularly into their lives. The movie *Rich and Trudy* is shown, which illustrates that "lovemaking" can go on twenty-four hours a day.

Couples are instructed to return to their rooms and discuss the critical question, "How are we going to ease back into our home life today and retain the emotional flow developed in the last two and a half days?" The success of the program, both immediate and later, depends on their answers. In the future when their intimacy flow is endangered through arguments, illness, and other disruptions, they must be able to return to this program's principles and go through the steps they have learned in the workshop.

SUNDAY, 11:30 A.M. TO 12:30 P.M. (WHOLE GROUP)

In the final group session the therapists summarize the workshop and gives the couples time to work through their goodbyes. The prospect of leaving is often frightening after the protective, intensive environment of the workshop. Three group therapy followup sessions are scheduled—at one three, and six weeks following this weekend. During these later sessions, aided by the therapists, couples are to support one another in continuing with the program and offer each other suggestions as to how this can be done.

We caution couples at the end of the workshop and during the followup sessions against unrealistic expectations and against the common exaggerated emotional highs and lows that accompany many intensive marathon experiences. We emphasize that real problems must be handled, but that the priority of romance and intimacy must be kept foremost in their daily lives.

References

(1) MASTERS, W. H., and JOHNSON, V. E. Human Sexual Inadequacy. Boston: Little, Brown, 1970.

(2) HARTMAN, W. E., and FITHIAN, M. A. Treatment of Sexual Dysfunction: A Bio-psycho-social Approach. Long Beach, Calif.: Center for Marital and Sexual Studies, 1972.

(3) JACOBS, M., THOMPSON, L. A., and TRUAX, P. The Use of Sexual Surrogates in Counseling. Counseling Psychol. 5, No. 1 (1975), 73–77.

(4) BERKEY, B. R. Too Tired for Sex: Fighting the Fatigue Factor in Sexual Disharmony. Med. Aspects Human Sexuality, 6 (1972), 132–49.

(5) LAZARUS, A. A. Behavior Therapy and Beyond. New York: McGraw-Hill, 1971.

(6) McCary, J. L. Sexual Myths and Fallacies. New York: Van Nostrand Reinhold, 1971.

(7) Money, J., and Ehrhardt, A. A. Boy, Girl: Man, Woman. Baltimore: Johns Hopkins University Press, 1972.

(8) Packard, V. The Sexual Wilderness. New York: McKay, 1968.

(9) Reiss, I. The Social Context of Premarital Permissiveness. New York: Holt, Rinehart and Winston, 1967.

(10) Montagu, A. Touching: The Human Significance of Skin. New York: Columbia University Press, 1971.

(11) Masters, W. H., and Johnson, V. E. Human Sexual Response. Boston: Little, Brown, 1966.

(12) Kaplan, H. S. The New Sex Therapy. New York: Brunner-Mazel, 1974.

(13) Jourard, S. Transparent Self. New York: Van Nostrand, 1971.

(14) Kopp, S. B. If You Meet the Buddah, on the Road, Kill Him! Ben Lomand, Calif.: Science and Behavior Books, 1972.

(15) Berne, Eric. Games People Play. New York: Grove Press, 1964.

(16) Semans, J. Premature Ejaculation, a New Approach. Southern Med. J., 49 (1956), 353–58.

(17) Kegel, A. H. Sexual Functions of the Pubococcygeus Muscle. Western J. Surgical Obstetrics & Gynecol., 60 (1952), 521.

Supplemental Bibliography

Bach, G., and Goldberg, H. Creative Aggression. Garden City, N.Y.: Doubleday, 1974.

Bach, G., and Weyden, P. The Intimate Enemy. New York: Morrow, 1970.

Belliveau, F., and Richter, L. Understanding Sexual Inadequacy. New York: Little, Brown, 1970.

Caplan, R. T. Attitude Change of Couples Involved in a Sexual Therapy Program. Doctoral dissertation, University of New Mexico, 1973. Dissertation Abstracts International, 34A (1973) 3053A. (University Microfilms No. 73–27, 787.)

Goulding, R. L. New Directions in Transactional Analysis. In Sager, C., and Kaplan, H. (eds.), Progress in Group and Family Therapy. New York: Brunner-Mazel, 1972.

Mullan, H. The Psychotherapist Is Challenged by Existentialism. Pilgrimage, 3, No. 1 (1974), 1–10.

Scott, J. B. Attitude Change of Spinal Cord Injured Males and Their Marital Partner Involved in a Sexual Therapy Program. Unpublished doctoral dissertation, University of New Mexico, 1974.

Stephenson, W. The Study of Behavior: Q-technique and Its Methodology. Chicago: University of Chicago Press, 1953.

18   Psychodrama

Zerka T. Moreno

Historic Background

THE ROOTS OF PSYCHODRAMA go back to the Greek theater. It is generally conceded that Aristotle was the first to observe and describe the notion of "catharsis" in De Poetica. While dissecting the structure of tragedy, he stated it to be "imitation of an action, in a dramatic, not in a narrative form; with incidents arousing pity and fear, wherewith to accomplish its 'catharsis' of such emotions."

At the time Moreno arrived upon the scene, drama constituted a problem for him. His concern was with what would happen to the actor if the script were taken away—if, so to speak, the actor became poet-playwright, actor, and observer in one. He began to work with children in the gardens of Vienna, at first telling them the fairytales so beloved of the young. Gradually it occurred to him that the children, for whom play is a natural habitat, should be allowed to enact the tales rather than be passive receptacles of this cultural heritage, however valuable. Moreno began to let them choose their own roles, or to assign them as he sensed the needs of the child. When they enacted these fairytales for the first time they were wonderfully creative, inventive, and spontaneous. The more often they repeated the same roles, however, the less free became their expression; they became more rigid and frozen; rehearsals also reduced their spontaneity and creativity. The next step was, therefore, to discard the script, to permit them to develop their own roles, their own fairytales. In the course of organizing large numbers of impromptu play groups it became evident that the children not only enjoyed the drama, but that they learned and grew. Some unpleasant personality characteristics appeared to be modified, while various desirable ways of interacting with others were given a chance to emerge.

From these naïve beginnings, Moreno developed the theoretical foundations involving such concepts as the encounter, spontaneity-creativity versus cultural conserves, the spontaneity factor, the pathology of spontaneity, spontaneity training, the act in the here and now, performance neurosis, the warming-up process, the role and its pathology, the pathology of interaction, tele, and sociosis, and many others.

In 1921 he made his first attempt to establish a Theater of Spontaneity for adults (1). This took more the form of what he later came to designate as "sociodrama," that is, the enactment of a problem relating to and involving an entire group, rather than that of a specific individual. The problem was that of Europe in disorder. It was a time of ferment, a few years after World War I; the great Hapsburg Empire had collapsed, Russia was still in the throes of the aftermath of revolution, restlessness was everywhere. There was no powerful leader to guide the people of Europe. It came to Moreno that this was a time to test the potential for new ideological leadership. He secured a theater for one night and invited representatives from foreign countries in Vienna to this open house. The night of the performance, April 1, only an empty stage was visible, with an empty throne and a crown resting upon it. But there was neither cast nor play. There was only the stage director—himself. He addressed the audience and invited one after another of the illustrious participants to step upon the stage and address the audience, conveying their own ideas of how the problems of the world could be solved. Many tried but none were elected. The world remained as leaderless as ever.

The incident was less vital in itself than some of the questions that led to it and also from it, namely: First, how well will an individual perform in a role which, though proscribed by society, needs original inventiveness? Second, man is a role player in a drama which he is forming in an ongoing fashion with other human actors. He may have been spontaneous once but the more often he repeats the role, the less is his spontaneity. Is there, then, a method by means of which this spontaneity can be uncovered and reinfused? Third, can spontaneity be an art form in itself, apart from its therapeutic potential? Fourth, will making the actor more spontaneous also produce a deeper kind of catharsis in the spectator? Fifth, what is the nature of creativity? Are there several forms of creativity? In what ways does the creativity of a highly developed type, such as that found in a Da Vinci or a Beethoven differ from the type required to live life creatively, day by day? Sixth, what are the forces impinging upon spontaneity and creativity which render it pathological?

In opposition to the psychoanalytic view of man, the underlying assumption was that the human psyche is not a closed system, that it is the human being *plus* his interrelations with others that ought to be the concern of the psychiatrist. Individual treatment does not necessarily create change of behavior or improve human interaction. Insight alone may not produce cure. The main emphasis is on the primordial nature of the act. Moreno considered verbal communication both ontogenetically and phylogenetically, a rather late development in man. Below language is the action matrix. It is man as an actor and interactor who is the focus of concern. His insights developed from man in interaction with one or more significant others and not from the treatment of the individual in isolation.

Before attempting adult sociodrama in 1921, Moreno had tried out a number of other innovative approaches to groups. Among these was verbal group psychotherapy of prostitutes; another was the application of psychodrama to entire families, between 1910 and 1914. He was concerned about the differences between a natural group and an intentional one; the impact of emotional infection between group members; the pushes and pulls of emotional entanglement in a group; the effect upon man's creativity of the products of that same creativity such as machines, books, tools, and finished products of all types, and whether these children of man's mind might not constitute a danger to the children of his loins. He observed that because the male of the species cannot bring forth children from his body, he loves better and becomes more attached to the children of his invention, and that the latter might become enemies of the former, turning against their creators like a Frankenstein.

During World War I his assignment was as medical superintendent of a resettlement camp of Tyrolean wine-growing peasants who had been moved from their mountain homes. As they were largely "irrendenta" with sympathetic leanings toward Italy, they constituted a threat to the Hapsburg Empire. In the uprooting consequent to this resettling, their multiple interactional problems emerged starkly. Out of this setting, as well as out of his earlier family practice, Moreno developed the systematic study of group organization, a science of human relations which he called "sociometry," that is measurement of human society.

In the course of undertaking the treatment of entire families, he gradually forged the interactional, not solely verbal, form of therapy. The partners in a conflict were made to enact it, rather than to talk about it. This led to the idea of "redoing" the conflict scenes in many different ways, with an opportunity to experiment with more suitable alternatives. The idea of role reversal between the original partners emerged, each taking the role of the other, and, still later, the idea of the *auxiliary ego*. The latter became eventually the crucial instrument in the treatment of mental patients. The auxiliary ego was a therapeutic actor, enabling the relevant absentees to be portrayed so that the patient could present his inner and interactional drama completely. With the psychotic, especially, the auxiliary ego was fundamental in the patient's coming to grips with delusions, hallucinations, fears, dreams, body parts, and threatening objects, all of which could now be dealt with in concrete fashion.

Between 1922 and 1925 Moreno organized the Theater of Spontaneity in Vienna, the laboratory in which many of his ideas could be tested and further developed. Although it was originally conceived as an art form, it gradually became a therapeutic theater, and subsequently the psychodrama was established as a full-fledged approach to major mental disease. Its clinical application was begun in 1936 at Moreno's mental hospital in Beacon, although he spent several years in New York City with groups of actors in impromptu theater production at Carnegie Hall and at the Civic Repertory Theater between 1927 and 1932, as well as working with children at Mount Sinai Hospital and the Plymouth Church play school.

Moreno ascribed his faith in the psychodrama to the fact that he had been his own first patient, using the method on himself. He wanted to prove that a person could be what might be designated as insane, pushing himself to the brim of sanity, yet remaining creative and productive. One of his basic postulates was that unless man can make peace with his God-likeness, with what he termed "the I-God" within him, he could not endure and remain balanced in what appears to be an unfriendly universe. Therefore, he believed and put into practice the principle of God-playing as a systematic approach to emotional imbalance. This God-playing is evident in children and is the source of creativity and spontaneity. In our society, rather than supporting this God-likeness, it is suppressed, distorted, denied, negated, scorned, and pushed underground, and it is responsible for numerous forms of emotional illness. Obviously, this is almost the exact antithesis of the psychoanalytic view of man. One of Moreno's main theses is that if spontaneity and its twin principle, creativity, are denied healthy expression, they will find unhealthy forms in which to emerge. According to this view man is a multiple role player, an improvising actor on the stage of life. Denying him the ability to complete his numerous dramas will lead to unhealthy manifestations of his emotional needs. Rather than attempting to reach objectivity through analysis and rational interaction, Moreno advocated the completely subjective route to gain genuine objectivity. It is this delicate balance between objectivity and subjectivity which is one of the main axes of intervention for the psychodramatic therapist, and one of the main reasons why this approach is both so threatening and so difficult to learn. Moreno taught that incomplete living through of fantasy may cause eruptions into reality, which then become difficult to deal with and to control in life itself. He referred to psychodrama as a "kindergarten for adults" and as "a cosmetic for the psyche." We have come to look upon it also as "a small dose of insanity under conditions of control." Control can be taught only after expression in action has been completed. Psychodrama is often described falsely as "a method for acting out." It is obvious from the previous statement that it is just as much "a method for acting in." But whereas control is expected to be applied externally in other methods, in psychodrama it is taught to emerge from within the person. The psychodramatic position is that it is the autonomy of the actor which needs to be mobilized and guided into integrative rather than disintegrative channels.

Psychodrama is both an intrapersonal and an interpersonal method, a form of behavior training as well as body therapy, a form of psychotherapy as well as of sociotherapy. It has numerous areas of application: diagnosis, therapeusis, research, and education and training for a profession or vocation.

There are two main types of psychodrama: the confessional or direct form, and the nonconfessional or indirect form. In the first, the patient or the group makes a more or less open declaration of the difficulties which bring about the need for treatment. In the second, the mirroring of typical situations similar to those of the group members stimulates the spectators' own attempts at autonomous objectification and healing. This can be applied in minor maladjustments, incipient neuroses, and simple interpersonal conflicts. In more serious cases, however, this approach is but a prelude to the direct, confessional form of treatment, culminating in the personal presentation of problems on the stage.

Basic Concepts

MENTAL CATHARSIS

Two avenues led to the psychodramatic view of mental catharsis, the one as described above from the Greek drama; the other led from the religions of the East and the Near East. These religions held that a saint, in order to become a savior, had to make an effort; he had, first, to actualize and save himself. In other words, in the Greek situation the process of mental catharsis was conceived as being localized in the spectator—a *passive catharsis*. In the religious situation the process of catharsis was localized in the actor, his life becoming the stage. This was an *active catharsis*. In the Greek concept the process of realization of a role took place in an object, in a symbolic person on the stage. In the religious concept the process of realization took place in the subject—the living person who was seeking the catharsis. One might say that passive catharsis is here face to face with active catharsis, and aesthetic catharsis with ethical catharsis. These two developments, which heretofore have moved along independent paths, have been synthesized by the psychodramatic concept of catharsis. From the ancient Greeks we have retained the drama and the stage, and from the Hebrews we have accepted the catharsis of the actor. The spectator himself has become an actor.

DEFINITION AND OPERATIONAL DIFFERENCES OF SPONTANEITY

Spontaneity is defined as a new response to an old situation or as an adequate response to a new situation. The protagonist is challenged to respond with some degree of adequacy to a new situation or with some degree of novelty to an old situation. When the stage actor finds himself without a role conserve or the religious actor without a ritual conserve, they have to "ad lib," to turn to experiences which are not performed and ready-made, but which are still buried within them in an unformed stage. In order to mobilize and shape them, they need a transformer and catalyst, a kind of intelligence which operates here and now, *hic et nunc*—"spontaneity." Mental healing processes require spontaneity in order to be effective. The technique of free association, for instance, involves spontaneous acting of the individual, although it is restricted to expressing in words whatever goes through his mind. What is working here is not only the association of words but the spontaneity which propels him to associate. The larger the volume of word associations, the more significant and spontaneous is its production. Other conditions being equal, this is true of all methods of psychotherapy. In psychodrama, particularly, spontaneity operates not only in the dimension of words but in all other dimensions of expression, such as in acting, interacting, speaking, dancing, singing, and drawing. The significant event was the linking of spontaneity to creativity, in our view the highest form of intelligence, and to recognize them as the primary forces in human behavior. The dynamic role which spontaneity plays in psychodrama, as well as in every form of psychotherapy, should not imply, however, that the development and presence of spontaneity in itself is the "cure." There are forms of pathological spontaneity which distort perceptions, dissociate the enactment of roles, and interfere with their integration on the various levels of living.

ROLE THEORY

The *role* is defined as a unit of functional behavior. Role playing is prior to the emergence of the self; roles do not emerge from the self, but the self may emerge from roles.

"Role," originally an old French word which penetrated into medieval French and English, is derived from the Latin *rotula*. In Greece and also in ancient Rome, the parts in the theater were written on "rolls" and read by the prompters to the actors who tried to memorize their part by heart; this fixation of the word role appears to have been lost in the more illiterate periods of the early and middle centuries of the Dark Ages. It was not until the sixteenth or seventeenth centuries, with the emergence of the modern stage, that the parts of the theatrical characters were read from "roles" or paper fasciles. In this manner, each scenic "part" becomes a role.

Thus, role is not by origin a sociological or psychiatric concept; it came into the scientific vocabulary via the drama. It is often overlooked that modern role theory had its logical origin and its perspectives in the drama.

The function of the role is to enter the unconscious from the social world, bringing shape and order into it. Every individual has a range of roles in which he sees himself and faces a range of counterroles in which he sees others around him. They are in various stages of development. The tangible aspects of what is known as ego are the roles in which the individual operates, with the pattern of role relations around an individual as their focus. We consider roles and relationships between roles as the most significant developments within any specific culture.

Role Playing, Role Perception, and Role Enactment

Role perception is cognitive and anticipates forthcoming responses. Role enactment is a skill of performance. A high degree of role perception can be accompanied by a low skill for role enactment and vice versa. Role playing is a function of both role perception and role enactment. Role training, in contrast to role playing, is an effort through the rehearsal of roles to perform adequately in future situations.

Methods of Role Analysis

We consider: (a) how the expectancy of acting in a role in the future affects a subject and each member of the audience; (b) role deficiency of a subject; (c) adequacy and superiority in a role on the stage and in actuality; and (d) whether a role is dominant or secondary to the subject and each member of the audience, on the stage and in actuality. Expectancy of acting in a certain role may produce a fear of entering situations in which that role comes to expression. In another case, the expectancy of a role may produce the opposite effect; getting a chance at expressing this role may increase courage, self-confidence, and satisfaction in the role.

TELE AND TRANSFERENCE

Tele is defined as a unit of feeling transmitted from one individual toward another and is always considered in terms of mutuality. Tele differs from transference in that it pertains to the actual feelings between persons based on the reality factor within the personalities involved and the real feelings generated between them. A relationship is a stick with two ends; tele is responsible for facilitating two-way communication within a relationship. Tele includes both transference and empathy. Transference and empathy are, furthermore, one-way relationships and not two-way relationships. Tele is the tree trunk of which one branch is transference; the other is empathy. It is clear that these three categories of perceiving the other are not always mutually exclusive. But no relationship can be built on transference or empathy. Tele is the factor responsible for cohesion between two or more individuals in a group, whereas transference is the dissociative factor. Transference is built on fantasy; even the concept of countertransference is actually a misnomer. In *transference* the movement of feeling is from one person toward another; it is the projection from one person upon another and contains within it the fantasy construction of the projector. Since countertransference is also a one-way process, there are actually two parallel processes operating. Two lines in a parallelogram do not meet. There are, therefore, at best two parallel processes going on in transference-countertransference. In this context transference is considered the pathological aspect of the relationship. Empathy, on the other hand, first emerged in a situation of aesthetic behavior, that is, from a person upon an object as, a tall sculpture in a museum. A person standing in front of the sculpture might be seen to stretch himself to his fullest height to feel himself, so to speak, into the sculpture in all its dimensions. Obviously the sculpture was not reciprocating in kind. *Empathy* is a one-way projection of feeling from a person upon an object and does not require mutuality. Tele is the all-inclusive concept encompassing all three forms of perception and feeling.

THE SOCIAL ATOM

Man as an interactor creates a network of interrelations between himself and his relevant others. The individuals so related form together what is known as a "social atom," which consists, therefore, not merely of the single individual, but of the individual *plus* his significant others *plus* the relationships between them. In this context the relationship is as much the focus of attention as the persons concerned. When treating a dyad, husband-wife, mother-child, employer-employee, we are aware that we deal with three entities, not two, the two partners *and* their specific relationship. Thus, we are as much relationship therapists as we are psychotherapists.

The social atom can be employed in the exploration of the world of the psychotic as well as that of the neurotic or normal. It charts the delusional system in terms of the relationships and the personae which the patient has constructed for himself and which have replaced the objective or real social atom, that is, the real persons and their relationships to him and to one another. Once conceived and charted, the auxiliary egos can, under the direction of the chief therapist or director, represent these delusional roles, assisting the patient in clarifying and completing his needs for and with them. These same auxiliary egos, having been accepted by the patient on these terms, are now potential agents for therapeutic redirection and guidance into the real other world. In every sense of the word, they are auxiliary to the psychodrama director or chief therapist who does not become involved in the action. More important, they are auxiliary to the patient so as to help complete his inner psychotic drama which he is helpless to do on his own, and auxiliary to the world of the real persons to whom the patient must eventually return on some level of interaction. Thus, all the psychotic constructions of the patient can be embodied, concretized, and reintegrated. We consider the psychotic as a creative person who has been unable to complete his creation; the psychodrama provides helpers, midwives, in the creative process. We humans are unable to let go of those precious ideas, situations, relationships which have been left incomplete and unfulfilled. Once they have been brought to completion, it is easier to relinquish them. Psychodrama also offers what life itself usually does not, namely, the exploration of other possibilities and a thorough experiencing of the consequences of one's actions so as to evaluate the best route to take before trying it out in life itself. We have found the catharsis of action to be a more complete one than either interpretation, insight, or disillusionment can provide. Indeed, the psychotic profoundly resists these latter approaches, but psychodrama is his natural milieu; he is more comfortable with it and even enjoys it.

Once the patient has given up the delusional social atom and is coming out of the psychotic world, the objective social atom can be examined and the relevant others within it can be brought into the treatment situation. Indeed, the patient is not considered completely ready to resume going into the outside world until the outside world has been brought to him and made part of the treatment process itself. A comparison between the psychotic social atom and the objective one may point to the emotional needs not being met by the real one; there may have to be substitutions made or such corrections as will remedy the deficiencies experienced by the patient which supports his withdrawal from the real world and will precipitate him back into the psychotic world.

TREATMENT OF THE FAMILY

What is now known as "sculpting" in family therapy comes from the construction of the family into an action sociogram. Instead of depicting the relationships on paper, the family members are asked to place themselves spatially and mimically in relationship to all other family members, in such postures as they see themselves and each other. The family tableau is constructed subjectively by each family member, and each in turn can co-experience every other member's perception and experience of what the family interaction means to him. The elucidation of family conflict is then worked through in psychodrama and various other modes of interaction are tried out within the therapeutic setting. Thus, all participants in the conflict are simultaneously involved in diagnosis and treatment. This is a great step forward diagnostically; however, frequently it leaves something to be desired from the point of view of therapeusis. With all the family members being co-protagonists, the ability to be spontaneous in behalf of total self-expression or availability for the others' needs is notably inhibited. The usual pressures and interpersonal conflicts operate in the therapeutic sessions as they do in life. Under these conditions total family interaction may be or may become inadequate or even negative. Repeating the "normal" course of events within the therapeutic setting often reinforces interpersonal pathology rather than resolving it. It may also happen that one or another member is unavailable at a crucial moment, for instance, in the case of resistance to treatment, or illness, or other circumstances which prevent attendance. A frequent finding has been the special importance of deceased family members who continue to dominate family interaction; their presence needs to be brought actively into the treatment process. Here the introduction of the auxiliary ego is so felicitous. It may be a trained professional or a family member whose objectivity, sensitivity, and talent for interpersonal contact make him or her a useful assistant in the therapeutic intervention.

This was, in fact, how the idea of the auxiliary ego originally emerged. There are numerous advantages in the employment of the auxiliary ego: it is freer, more spontaneous, both subjective *and* objective at the same moment. He or she can assume any number of roles as available in his or her role repertoire; he or she can enact the special role of a pet, delusions and hallucinations, ideas, values, needs, body parts of the protagonist or relevant others, and so on. This makes possible intrapersonal as well as interpersonal guidance and retraining until such time that the relevant other(s) are ready and can be brought actively into the treatment process.

As each participant can work first with a suitable auxiliary, the onus of one family member is spotlighted as *the* patient is removed and the focus of attention is placed on the entire family, where it rightly belongs.

Group Oath

Group psychotherapists and psychodramatists frequently feel the need to convey to group members, at the beginning or in the course of a session, the nature of their responsibility during the process of treatment. The suggested group oath is not to be taken as a ritual, word for word, or as a dogma, but it tries to convey the spirit of such an oath which may be expressed or silent, or tacitly accepted by all.

This is the group oath to therapeutic science and its disciples.

Just as we trust the physician in individual treatment, we should trust each other. Whatever happens in the course of a session of group therapy and psychodrama, we should not keep anything secret. We should divulge freely whatever we think, perceive or feel for each other; we should act out the fears and hopes we have in common and purge ourselves of them.

But like the physician who is bound by the Hippocratic oath, we are bound as participants in this group, not to reveal to outsiders the confidences of other patients.

Like the physician, each of us is entrusted to protect the welfare of every other patient in the group.

Code of Ethics for Group Psychotherapists

The advent of group and action methods in psychotherapy—the procedures most popularly known are group psychotherapy and psychodrama —has brought about a radical change in the relationship of the therapist to his patients and to the general public. Urgently needed is an "open discussion" of new principles to guide practitioners in this field. Here is a list of applicable rules. The fact that they are put in numerical order from one to ten should not imply that there is any finality about the formulation of these principles or that ten is a holy number or that this is a rank order as to importance or that they cover all aspects of the potential problems.

These principles are addressed to all group psychotherapists. They are not laws, but standards for maintaining a high level of ethical conduct.

1. The principal objective of group psychotherapy is to render service to every member of therapeutic groups and to the groups as a whole.

2. A group psychotherapist should practice methods of healing founded on a scientific basis, approved by official professional boards.

3. The designation "group psychotherapist" or "psychodramatist" should be used only by psychotherapists who have obtained training in recognized institutes of learning. As the field is new and expanding, the therapists should continuously improve their knowledge and skill; they should make available to other therapists and their patients the benefits of their attainments.

4. A principal objective of the group psychotherapist is to protect the patient against abuse and to render service to groups of patients with full respect for the dignity of every patient.

5. Therapeutic groups should be so organized that they represent a model of democratic behavior. Regardless of the economic, racial, and religious differences of the patients, they should be given "equality of status" inside the therapeutic group.

6. Should patients of the same therapeutic group pay the *same* fee or not? Could charging different fees to members of the *same* therapeutic group produce feelings of inequality and thwart the therapeutic aim?

7. The patients should be free to choose the therapeutic groups in which they participate as members. The therapist, in turn, is free to accept or refuse to serve in behalf of a therapeutic group. Indications or contraindications for "coercive" placement in the groups should be carefully

weighed in exceptional cases, as in the treatment of deteriorated mental patients.

8. The Hippocratic oath binds the physician to keep all matters of his professional practice secret. *In group psychotherapy the Hippocratic oath is extended to all patients and binds each with equal strength not to reveal to outsiders the confidences of other patients entrusted to them.* Like the therapist, every patient is entrusted to protect the welfare of the co-patients.

Should group psychotherapy and psychodrama be televised, it would produce "leaks" of the confidence pledge difficult to control. Closed circuit television broadcasting for subscribers only is a tolerable but unsafe way out of the dilemma. But the "open" circuits may become the major route for mass psychotherapy. How can we utilize them without taking risks?

9. Every patient is expected to divulge freely whatever he thinks, perceives, or feels, to every other in the course of the treatment sessions. He should know that he is protected by the "pledge" and that no disadvantage will occur to him because of his honest revelations of crimes committed, of psychological deviations from sexual or social norms, of secret plans and activities. The confidence so entrusted may never be violated unless it is imperative to do so by law in order to protect the welfare of the individual or of the community. In extreme cases of improper conduct, therapists and patients may be disqualified from practice or treatment. How can this be brought into harmony with our therapeutic philosophy of taking care of every individual patient?

10. The timing of the "pledge" has to be carefully considered by the therapist responsible for the group. In order that it may not frighten the participants or produce the effect of an unnecessary restraint upon their freedom, it should not be discussed prematurely; the therapist should wait until the group is ripe and well formed and until the meaning of the pledge is clear to all members. The critical moment, for instance, may arise when a patient in the course of the treatment sessions is put on the spot and hesitates to reveal a highly personal event in his life. His hesitancy may be internal, as in feelings of guilt, or external, such as fear of gossip, public discomfort, or persecution. In such an intense situation the therapist can step forward and reassure the patient that all members of the group are bound by a pledge, just as the physician is bound. Thus, an atmosphere of confidence in the proceedings and a feeling of collective security can be established.

The Instruments

The psychodramatic method uses mainly five instruments—the stage, the subject or patient, the director, the staff of therapeutic aides or auxiliary egos, and the audience. The first instrument is the *stage*. Why a stage? It provides the patient with a living space which is multidimensional and flexible to the maximum. The living space of reality is often narrow and restraining; he may easily lose his equilibrium. On the stage he may find it again due to its methodology of freedom—freedom from unbearable stress and freedom for experience and expression. The stage space is an extension of life beyond the reality tests of life itself. Reality and fantasy are not in conflict, but both are functions within a wider sphere—the psychodramatic world of objects, persons, and events. In its logic, the ghost of Hamlet's father is just as real and permitted to exist as Hamlet himself. Delusions and hallucinations are given flesh—embodiment on the stage—and an equality of status with normal sensory perceptions. The architectural design of the stage is made in accord with therapeutic requirements. Its circular forms and levels, levels of aspiration, pointing out the vertical dimension, stimulate relief from tensions and permit mobility and flexibility of action. The locus of a psychodrama, if necessary, may be designated everywhere: wherever the patients are, the field of battle, the classroom, or the private home. But the ultimate resolution of deep mental conflicts requires an objective setting, the therapeutic theater. As in religion, although the devout may pray to his God in his own chamber, it is in the church that the community of believers attain the most complete confirmation of their faith.

The second instrument is the *subject or patient*. He is asked to be himself on the stage, to portray his own private world. He is told to be himself, not an actor, as the actor is compelled to sacrifice his own private self to the role imposed upon him by a playwright. Once he is warmed up to the task, it is comparatively easy for the patient to give an account of his daily life in action, as no one is as much of an authority on himself as he is. He has to act freely, as things rise up in his mind; that is why he has to be given freedom of expression, spontaneity. Next in importance to spontaneity comes the process of enactment. The verbal level is transcended and included in the level of action. There are numerous forms of enactment: pretending to be in a role, reenactment or acting out a past scene, living out a problem presently pressing, creating life on the stage, and testing oneself for the future. Moreover, there is the principle of involvement. We have been brought up with the idea that, in test as well as in treatment situations, a minimum of involvement with other persons and objects is a most desirable thing for the patient. An illustration of this is the "Rorschach." The Rorschach situation is reduced to ink blots. In the Rorschach the subjects change, but the situation is always the same. It is thought to be its greatest virtue that it is pure and therefore offers an "objective" test. The psychoanalytic interview in its orthodox form also tried to be pure and objective, by reducing the involvement with the analyst to a minimum. In the psychodramatic situation, a maximum of involvement with other subjects and things is not only possible but expected. Reality is not only not feared but provoked. Indeed, in the psychodramatic situation all degrees of involvement take place, from a minimum to a maximum. In addition, there is the principle of realization. The patient is enabled to meet not only parts of himself, but the other persons who are involved in his mental conflicts. These persons may be real or illusions. The reality test, which is mere verbiage in other therapies, is thus made true on the stage. The warming-up process of the subject to psychodramatic portrayal is stimulated by numerous techniques, only a few of which are mentioned here: self-presentation, soliloquy, projection, interpolation of resistance, reversal of roles, double ego, mirror techniques, auxiliary world, realization, and psychochemical techniques. The aim of these sundry techniques is not to turn the patients into actors but, rather, to stir them up to be on the stage what they are, more deeply and explicitly than they appear to be in the reality of life.

The third instrument is the *director*. He has three functions: producer, therapist, and analyst. As producer, he has to be on the alert to turn every clue which the subject offers into dramatic action, to make the line of production one with the lifeline of the subject, and never to let the production lose rapport with the audience. As therapist, attacking and shocking the subject is at times just as permissible as laughing and joking with him; at times he may become indirect and passive, and for all practical purposes the session seems to be run by the patient. As analyst, he may complement his own interpretation with responses coming from informants in the audience: husband, parents, children, friends, or neighbors.

The fourth instrument is a staff of *auxiliary egos*. These auxiliary egos or therapeutic actors have a double significance. They are extensions of the director, exploratory and therapeutic, but they are also extensions of the patient, portraying the actual or imagined personae of their life drama. The functions of the auxiliary ego are threefold: the function of the actor, portraying roles required by the patient's world; the function of the therapeutic agent, guiding the subject; and the function of the social investigator.

The fifth instrument is the *audience*. The audience itself has a double purpose. It may serve to help the patient or, being itself helped by the subject on the stage, the audience becomes the patient. In helping the patient, it is a sounding board of public opinion. Its responses and comments are as extemporaneous as those of the patient, and may vary from laughter to violent protest. The more isolated the patient is—for instance, because his drama on the stage is shaped by delusions and hallucinations—the more important becomes the presence of an audience which is willing to accept and understand him. When the audience is helped by the subject, thus becoming the patient itself, the situation is reversed. The audience sees itself—that is, one of its collective syndromes—portrayed on the stage.

The stage portion of a psychodramatic session has opened the way to action research and action therapy, role test and role training, situation tests and situational interviews whereas the audience portion has become the common ground of the better known forms of group psychotherapy, as lecture methods, dramatic methods, and film methods. Scientific foundations of group psychotherapy require as a prerequisite a basic science of human relations, widely known as sociometry. It is from "sociatry," a pathological counterpart of such a science that knowledge can be derived as to abnormal organization of groups, the diagnosis and prognosis, prophylaxis and control of deviate group behavior.

Now that we have described the five basic instruments required to run a psychodramatic session we may ask ourselves: To what effect? We will limit ourselves here to the description of a single phenomenon, mental catharsis (stemming from the Greek, it means purging, purification).

Breuer and Freud were ignorant of the psychotherapeutic implications of the drama milieu to which Aristotle referred. It remained for psychodrama to rediscover and treat the idea of catharsis in its relation to psychotherapy. We picked up the trend of thought where Aristotle had left off. We, too, began with the drama but reversed the procedure. It was not the end phase but the initial phase of the drama toward which we directed attention. Mental catharisis was to be found only in dramatic literature when we entered the scene with our investigations, in faded memories of Aristotle's old definition, and the term itself was practically out of circulation. The psychoanalysts, after a flareup in the early 1890s, had pushed it aside. As practically every human activity can be the source of some degree of catharsis the problem is to determine in what catharsis consists—in which way it differs, for instance, from happiness, contentment, ecstasy, need satisfaction, and so forth—and whether one source is superior in the production of catharsis to another source; indeed, whether there is an element common to all sources which operates in the production of catharsis. Therefore, our aim has been to define catharsis in such a way that all forms of influence which have a demonstrable cathartic effect can be shown as positive steps within a single total process of operation. We discovered the common principle producing catharsis to be spontaneity.

From studies of both phylogenetic and ontogenetic development of man, we observed that language is a rather late arrival. Yet the human infant is demonstrably an actor long before the onset of speech. I designated this need for action as "the act-hunger syndrome" and concluded that beneath the level of speech lies an older one, that of the act; that speech is not the royal route to the psyche; and that we need to concern ourselves with the deeper level of action to comprehend what the source of spontaneity might be.

Because of the universality of the act and its primordial nature, it engulfs all other forms of expression. They flow naturally out of it or can be encouraged to emerge verbal associations, musical associations, visual associations, color associations, rhythmic and dance associations, and every other stimulus which might arouse or inhibit the emergence of one or another factor: for instance, the use of psychochemical starters like sedatives, such as barbiturates, sodium amytal, sodium pentotal; or shock methods such as insulin, metrazol, or electricity. Endocrinological medications such as thyroid are fully within the scheme of total catharsis; they may condition and prepare the organism for psychodramatic integration. The need for action can be temporarily choked, for instance, by sleep or shock therapies. But the fundamental need for the realization of certain fantastic imageries cannot be "shocked away." Unless the subject is reduced to a brain invalid by surgery or prolonged shock treatments, the temporarily scared patient is bound to relapse and reproduce the same type of mental syndrome he had before treatment began. It is into the stream of action catharsis that all the rivulets of partial catharsis flow.

The treatment of audiences has become an important alternative to individual treatment. The relationship of the audience to itself in a psychodramatic session, being treated by its own spokesman on the stage, gives us a clue as to the reasons for the cathartic effect of psychodrama. According to historians of the Greek drama the audience was there first, the chorus, musing about a common syndrome. There were "keynoters" among them, but they remained within the chorus. Aeschylus is credited with having put the first actor upon a social space outside of the chorus, the stage, not speaking to them, but portraying the woes of their own hero. Euripides is credited with having put the second actor on the stage, thus making possible the dialogue and interaction of roles. We may be credited with having put the psyche itself on the stage. The psyche which originally came from the group, after a process of reconversion on the stage, personified by an actor, returns to the group—in the form of the psychodrama. What was most startling, new, and spectacular to see and to feel on the stage appears to the participants after thorough exposure as a process which is familiar to them and intimately known—as their own selves. The psychodrama confirms their own identity as does a mirror.

Psychodramatic Techniques

Psychodrama has been applied to a large variety of settings, clinical as well as educational. It is not our intention to cover all possible uses. The following is but a bare listing and description of techniques.

1. *Soliloquy.* A monologue of the protagonist in situ: for example, the patient is preparing to go to bed and, combing her hair, speaks to herself: "Why don't I cut my hair short again? It is such a nuisance, this long hair.

On the other hand, it really suits me better this way and I don't look like everybody else."

2. *Therapeutic soliloquy*. The portrayal by side dialogues and side actions, of hidden thoughts and feelings, parallel with overt thoughts and actions.

The patient is confronting her superior, who has called her on the carpet for participating in civil rights demonstrations. The auxiliary ego, as the superior, asks her to account for her whereabouts the previous evening. The patient tells her she went to visit a sick friend. The auxiliary ego states she has evidence that this is not the truth. The director stops the overt action, asks the patient to express how she feels, explains that "her superior" won't hear her and will not react, since she could not have known what was going on inside of her in the real situation. Patient states: "I really *did* go to that demonstration; she can't really do anything to me because I have tenure, but she can make it unpleasant for me." Director: "What do you want to do?" Patient: "Give her a raspberry, but of course I can't." Director: "Here you can." Patient belches lustily. Director asks her now to continue the scene as it was and end it on the reality level.

3. *Self-presentation*. The protagonist presents himself, his own mother, his own father, his brother, his favorite professor, and so on. He acts all these roles himself, in complete subjectiveness, as he experiences and perceives them.

4. *Self-realization*. The protagonist enacts, with the aid of a few auxiliary egos, the plan of his life, no matter how remote this may be from his present situation. For instance, he is actually an accountant, but for a long time he has been taking singing lessons, hoping to try out for a part in summer stock (musical comedy), planning eventually to make this his life's work. Alternatives may be explored: success of this venture, possible failure, the return to his old livelihood, preparing for still another one, and so on.

5. *Hallucinatory psychodrama*. The patient enacts the hallucinations and delusions that he is at present experiencing (though they may not be so designated by the director). The patient portrays the voices he hears, the sounds emanating from the chair he sits on, the visions he has when the trees outside his window turn into monsters which pursue him. Auxiliary egos are called to enact the various phenomena expressed by the patient, to involve him in interaction with them, so as to put them to a reality test.

6. *Double*. The patient portrays himself, and an auxiliary ego is asked also to represent the patient, to "establish identity with the patient," to move, act, behave like the patient. The patient is preparing to get up in the morning; he is in bed. The auxiliary ego lies down on the stage alongside of him, taking the same bodily posture. The double may start speaking: "What is the use of waking up? I have nothing to live for." Patient: "Yes,

that is true, I have no reason for living." Auxiliary ego: "But I am a very talented artist, there have been times when life has been very satisfying." Patient: "Yes, but it seems a long time ago." Auxiliary ego: "Maybe I can get up and start to paint again." Patient: "Well, let's try and get up first, anyway, and see what will happen." Both patient and auxiliary ego get up, go through the motions of washing, shaving, brushing teeth, all along moving together as if they were one. The auxiliary ego becomes the link through which the patient may try to reach out into the real world.

7. *Multiple double.* The protagonist is on the stage with several doubles of himself, each portraying another part of himself, one as he is now, another as he was five years ago, a third as he was when at three years of age he first heard that his mother had died, another how he may be twenty years hence. The multiple representations of the patient are simultaneously present and act in sequence, one continuing where the other leaves off.

8. *Mirror.* When the patient is unable to represent himself in word or in action, an auxiliary ego is placed on the action portion of the psychodramatic space. The patient or patients remain seated in the group portion. The auxiliary ego reenacts the patient, copying his behavior and trying to express his feelings in word and movement, showing the patient or patients "as if in a mirror" in terms of how other people experience him.

The mirror may be exaggerated, employing techniques of deliberate distortion in order to arouse the patient to come forth and change from a passive spectator into an active participant, an actor, to correct what he feels is not the right enactment and interpretation of himself.

9. *Role-reversal.* The patient, in an interpersonal situation with his mother, "steps into his mother's shoes" while the mother steps into those of her son. The mother may be the real mother, as in psychodrama in situ, or she may be represented by an auxiliary ego. In role reversal, the son is now enacting his mother, the mother enacting her son. Distortions of interpersonal perception can be brought to the surface, explored, and corrected in action. The son, who is still himself, must now warm up to how his mother may be feeling and perceiving "himself"; the mother, now the son, goes through the same process.

A mother of an eight-year-old girl, after showing how they argue for ten minutes every morning during the winter as to what clothing the child should wear to school, is asked, after their own roles have become clear, to take the role of Kay; Kay is asked to take the role of her mother. They are instructed to change place in space, assuming the role, the posture, and the position of the other.

Kay stretches a foot in height in the role of her mother, shows authority and certainty, whereas in her own role her anxiety was very evident. The mother now has to subdue her ebullience and restrain herself to be her somewhat withdrawn daughter. Both open their eyes wide at the image that each holds before the other. The mother remarks when this scene is ended: "Am I really as aggressive as Kay portrayed me? My poor Kay!"

10. *Future projection*. The patient portrays in action how he thinks his future will shape itself. He picks the point in time—or is assisted by the director to do so—the place and the people, if any, whom he expects to be involved with at that time.

The patient is an English major and has his bachelor's degree; he has been working toward his master's for almost eight years, but still has not attained it. The future projection shows him three years hence, teaching his first course in English at the university. The entire audience is his class; he is asked to face them and inspire them with the beauty of the English language. "My name is Mr. Johnson; it is a very ordinary and yet beautiful name. I should like to welcome you here today by asking you all to introduce yourselves to one another. But remember, that name stands for you. Try to present it in such a way that it sings, that it reaches out to the other as if to say, 'Here I am, who are you?' "

11. *Dream presentation*. The patient enacts a dream instead of telling it. He takes the position he usually does in bed, when sleeping; before lying down and taking the position of the sleeper, he warms up to the setting separately. The director asks him when and where he had this dream, to describe the room, the location and size of the bed, the color of his pajamas, whether he wears top and bottom or sleeps in the nude, whether he sleeps alone, with the light on or off, window open or closed, and how long it normally takes him to fall asleep.

The patient is asked, in the lying-down position, to breathe deeply and evenly, as he does in sleep, to move in bed as he does ordinarily while asleep, and, lastly, to relax and let himself drift off. The final instructions of the director are: "Try, without telling me about it, to visualize in your mind the beginning, the middle, and the end. Do you see it? Just answer yes or no."

When the patient has fixed the various images somewhat in his mind's eye, the director asks: "Where are you in the dream? Do you see yourself? Yes? Then step out of the dream. What are you doing, walking, swimming, sitting, running, what?" Patient: "I do not see myself, I am in the dream." Director: "You are acting, doing something?" Patient: "Yes, I am flying, over the rooftops of houses." Director: "Do you see the rooftops? Get up and start to take a position resembling flying, here, stand on top of this table." Patient climbs on table, leans forward somewhat. "Yes, I see the rooftops, in fact, I'm hardly able to fly over them, sometimes it seems I'm going to crash into them." Director: "Where are these buildings and what are they?" Patient: "This is a residential section, in fact, as I realize now, this is the suburb where I live!" Director: "Do you see your house?" Patient: "No, but I seem to sense this is my section." Director:

"Are you the only one who is flying? Are you alone?" Patient: "No, I am carrying a bundle in my arms." Director: "In both arms, or in only one? Look at your arms." Patient looks down at his arms which appear to be carrying something, then drops his left arm, and says: "My right arm." Director: "What is in the bundle, do you know its contents?" Patient (*looking intently at his right arm, crooked around an object, amazed*): "It's a baby." Director: "Whose?" Patient: "My parents'; it's my baby sister, we are eighteen years apart in age." The director motions to an auxiliary ego to come upon the stage to represent the baby. The baby is asked to kneel in such a way that the top of her head is approximately at the height of his right elbow, and the director asks the protagonist to hold her as best he can. Director: "What are you doing there, flying with her?" Patient: "I am carrying her with me through life, protecting her from harm, but I'm not very sure that I am able to do this; I seem to have trouble keeping her aloft with me." Director: "Are you afraid?" Patient: "Afraid, but also very angry." Director: "Angry at whom? The baby?" Patient: "No, at fate. Why should I be saddled with this responsibility? She is my parents' child, not mine." Director: "In the actual dream, do you speak to your baby sister?" Patient: "No." Director: "Well, here you can." (This is a psychodramatic extension of the dream.) To auxiliary ego baby: "Talk to your older brother." Baby (auxiliary ego): "I am a bit scared flying this high. Do you hold me carefully?" Patient: "I am doing by best, but you are very heavy." Baby: "You won't drop me, will you?" Patient: "I can't, though frankly, I'd like to." Baby: "Why? Are you angry at me for being here with you?" Patient: "Not at you, but after all, I'm not ready for such responsibility yet, I'm just starting college, and you're just a tiny infant." Baby: "I like you, you are my big, strong brother." Director: "What happens next in the dream?" Patient: "I clutch her and the dream just fades off." Director: "You do not see any conclusive ending? Concentrate for a moment." Patient: "No, I just wake up in a cold sweat." Director dismisses auxiliary ego, returns patient to the position of the sleeper, back in bed. Director: "You wake up in a cold sweat." Patient: "Yes, I'm thoroughly soaked."

Retraining of the Dream

Director: "Sounds like a very frightening dream. Obviously, you wish it had not ended this way." Patient: "I even wish it had never started!" Director: "Yes, of course. You see, in psychodrama, we can 'change the dream.' When you are there, at night, things happen to you which appear to be out of your control. But, after all, it is you who produced the dream, because of your fears and anxieties. We believe that if we can help you to change your dream pattern, to train your unconscious, so to speak, the next time when you are dreaming, your dreams will change in character, you will be in better control. Now, let's see how you wish to change your dream."

Patient: "I don't want to have this dream at all." Director: "Yes, I can see that, but what would you like to do instead?" Patient: "I would want to have a good talk with my parents." Director: "Fine, let's have a good talk with your parents. Get up, and pick a mother and father from the group, two auxiliary egos to represent them." Patient does so, and sets up the livingroom of their house. Patient now confronts his parents: "Gee, Mom, Dad, I know you have both been very ill in the past year, and, being the oldest son, I feel terribly burdened by the responsibility of the two younger kids, especially about Alice. Timmy is already older and not quite such a problem, but Alice is just a little infant." Director: "Tell them as brutally as possible what is on your mind; after all, these are not your 'real' parents, merely stand-ins. They will not be hurt by anything you say or feel or do." Patient (*blurts out*): "Why the devil did you have to go and have a meno-pause baby? Don't you think you have enough complications? Mother works, the housekeeper is terrible, she doesn't even speak English, is my kid sister going to learn broken English? And don't you care what she eats? That dope can't even cook, all the kid gets is cereals and mashed banana." Now mother and father respond, trying to soothe the patient, he role-reverses with them, and finally he feels more reassured that his parents still have the major responsibility for the child.

This is the unique contribution of psychodrama to dream therapy, to go into enactment over and beyond the actual dream, including actual and latent material, but, even more, to retrain the dreamer rather than to in-terpret. Interpretation is in the act itself.

12. *Therapeutic community*. This is a community in which disputes and conflicts between individuals and groups are settled under the rule of therapy instead of the rule of law. The entire population, patients and staff alike, are responsible for the welfare of every other person, participate in the therapeutic process, and have equal status.

13. *Symbolic realization*. Enactment of symbolic processes by the pro-tagonist using soliloquy, double, reversal, or mirror for their clarification.

14. *Analytic psychodrama*. An analytic hypothesis, for instance, that of the Oedipus complex, is tested out on the stage in order to verify its valid-ity. The patient takes the role of his mother in a situation with his father (coming home, fired from his job because of a heart ailment). The analyst sits in the audience and watches. Analysis of the material is made imme-diately after the scene.

15. *Auxiliary world technique*. The entire world of the patient is re-structured around him in situ with the aid of auxiliary egos. William has been classified as a dementia praecox. He calls himself Christ and has writ-ten a proclamation to the world which he wants to save. The auxiliary egos around him live in his world and are completely guided by his needs. One auxiliary ego becomes the apostle John. Christ asks him to kneel in a corner of the room with his head bowed. He does not want him to kneel

in any other room or in any other corner. Another auxiliary ego becomes the apostle Paul with whom he prays together. A third is the apostle Peter, who is the only one he permits to bathe him, once a month. He does not permit members of his family to come to visit him. The only persons he accepts are those who people the world of his psychosis, according to his instructions.

16. *Treatment at a distance.* The patient is treated in absentia, usually without his knowledge; he is replaced by an auxiliary ego who is in daily contact with him and acts as the intermediary between patient and therapist. He acts out in the clinic all crucial episodes in which the patient is involved. Other members of the immediate environment are drawn into action (for instance, the parents of the patient).

Warming-up techniques are used to induce spontaneous states:

1. *Techniques of spontaneous improvisations.* The protagonist acts out fictitious roles and tries to keep his personal character uninvolved from his fictitious characters.

2. *Mirror techniques behind your back.* Many mirror techniques are so constructed that the individual can "see" and "hear" himself through other people's perceptions of him.

In the classic mirror technique, as described above, the protagonist is physically present but psychologically absent. The auxiliary ego acts "as if" the patient were not present, so as to challenge the patient when he realizes that the person portrayed on the stage is a radically truthful exposition of himself.

Additional Techniques

1. *Behind-your-back audience technique.* The entire audience is instructed to leave the theater, but actually they are permitted to remain seated, pretending that they are not present so as to give the protagonist full freedom of expression. The patient tells each member of the group how he feels toward him; the audience members are not permitted to respond, no matter how much he provokes them. The group members are on the spot; they see themselves in the mirror of the protagonist's world. This is frequently the starting point, the warming-up period preceding a psychodrama. It is often effective if the group members *actually* turn their back.

2. *The turn-your-back technique.* Protagonists are frequently embarrassed to present a particular episode while facing the group. They are then permitted, if unavoidable for the warmup, to turn their back to the group and act as if they are alone, in their own home, or wherever the episode takes place. The director, too, may turn his back to the audience so as to

observe the protagonist or protagonists. Once the protagonists—for instance, a married couple—have reached a high degree of involvement, they become ready to face the audience.

3. *The black-out technique.* The entire theater is blacked out, although all actions continue as if there is full daylight. This is done so that the protagonist may go through a painful experience unobserved, to retain for him the experience of solitude.

Improvisation of Fantasy

Since the early days of psychodrama, improvisation of fantasies has been usefully applied in order to attain therapeutic aims. A popular technique was and still is the Magic Shop Technique. The director sets up on the stage a "Dream or Magic Shop." Either he himself, or a member of the group selected by him, plays the part of the shopkeeper. The shop is filled with imaginary items, values of a nonphysical nature. They are not for sale, but they can be obtained in barter, in exchange for other values to be surrendered by the group members, either individually or as a group. One after another, the members volunteer to come up on the stage, entering the shop in quest of an idea, a dream, a hope, an ambition. They are expected to come only if they feel a strong desire to obtain a value which they cherish or without which their life seems worthless. An illustration follows: A depressive patient, who was admitted after a suicidal attempt, came to the Magic Shop requesting "peace of mind." The shopkeeper, a sensitive young therapist, asked her, "What do you want to give in return? You know we cannot give you anything without your willingness to sacrifice something else." "What do you want?" the patient asked. "There is something for which many people long who come to this shop," he replied, "fertility, the ability and willingness to bear children. Do you want to give this up?" "No, that is too high a price to pay. Then I do not want peace of mind." With this, she walked off the stage and returned to her seat. The shopkeeper had hit on a sensitive spot. Maria, the protagonist, was engaged, but refused to get married because of a deep-seated fear of sex and childbirth. Her fantasy preoccupations involved images of violent suffering, torture, death, and so on, in the act of childbirth.

This illustration indicates the diagnostic value of the *dream shop technique*. The crux of the technique is for the shopkeeper to demand of the client what he wants to give in return, what price he is willing to pay.

Another fantasy technique is the dramatization of fairytales as described in Moreno's Theater of Spontaneity. The tale remains entirely unstructured so that the protagonists are required to fill in with their own fantasies around the theme.

Still another fantasy technique is improvisation of early childhood experiences. In the process of acting them out, the protagonists go far beyond what they actually remember.

There are several hundred psychodramatic techniques and many, no matter how odd and fantastic they may seem, can be traced back to the rituals and customs of ancient cultures and can be found in the classic writings of world literature. Moreno has merely rediscovered them and adapted them to psychotherapeutic objectives. Their real inventors are the mental patients of all times. The number of applications of the psychodramatic method is practically unlimited, although the core of the method remains unchanged (5, 6, 7, 8).

Summary

The important question which remains to be answered is the scientific evaluation of psychodrama. Does psychodrama, with or without group psychotherapy, beyond the subjective reports of therapists and their patients, produce behavior change? According to John Mann (2), forty-one studies have substantiated that fundamental changes in behavior take place.

Two studies in particular, point out the kind of change that is demonstrable, one by G. S. Harrow (3), showing the effects of psychodramatic group therapy on role behavior of schizophrenic patients. According to this study

> . . . the specific aspects of role-taking behavior which seemed to be most affected by psychodramatic treatment were found in: 1. Four areas of interaction: (a) social techniques; (b) ability to enter into relationships and develop them; (c) more mature choice of social relationships and (d) ability to share feelings. 2. Changes in reality orientation, that is, in the ability to perceive simultaneously more than one aspect of the same situation and to adapt behavior accordingly, together with greater conformity of thinking, action, and self-perception with the real situation and the accepted norms of a "normal" environment. 3. Increased emotional control, that is, in the development of adaptive defense mechanisms which prevent explosive expression of impulses, such as hostility and aggression. For some patients, emotional control was accompanied by more free and spontaneous emotional expression, while for other patients this control was accompanied by rigidity and repression.

The statistically significant Rorschach changes, together with qualitative observations of changes on all three tests, Rorschach, MAPS and Role tests, indicate that psychodramatic treatment may affect some fundamental personality process as well as overt role-taking behavior. These findings tend to support the assumption that role-taking is not a mechanical skill imposed upon personality, but an essential part of personality formation and adjustment.

M. R. Haskell, in his study of young, imprisoned drug users being considered and prepared for parole (4), found role training effective in that the results obtained were significant at the 1 percent level of confidence. He concluded that role training is a technique that can be administered by suitably trained persons and is a nonspecific influence that depends for success on a particular personality. Lasting effects can be demonstrated only after long-term follow-up studies of experimental and control groups.

Psychotherapy, of whatever kind, is still remiss in its inability to show objective findings as to its long-range effects and psychodrama is no exception. One can only hope that better measurement and evaluation procedures yet to be developed will be able to close this gap.

References

(1) MORENO, J. L. The Theater of Spontaneity. Beacon, N.Y.: Beacon House, 1947.
(2) MANN, J. Evaluation of Group Psychotherapy. In Moreno, J. L. (ed.), International Handbook of Group Psychotherapy. New York: Philosophical Library, 1965.
(3) HARROW, G. S. The Effects of Psychodrama Group Therapy on Role Behavior of Schizophrenic Patients. Group Psychotherapy, 3. Beacon, N.Y.: Beacon House, 1951.
(4) HASKELL, M. R. Psychodramatic Role Training in Preparation for Release on Parole. Group Psychotherapy, 10. Beacon, N.Y.: Beacon House, 1957.
(5) MORENO, J. L. Psychodrama, 1. Beacon, N.Y.: Beacon House, 1946.
(6) MORENO, J. L. Psychodrama, 2. Beacon, N.Y.: Beacon House, 1959.
(7) MORENO, J. L. Psychodrama, 3. Beacon, N.Y.: Beacon House, 1969.
(8) MORENO, J. L., MORENO, Z. T., and MORENO, J. D. The First Psychodramatic Family. Beacon, N.Y.: Beacon House, 1964.

19 Existential Group Psychotherapy

Hugh Mullan

*That life is worth living, is the most necessary
of assumptions, and if it were not assumed the
most impossible of conclusions.*
—George Santayana

Change

ALL SYSTEMS OF psychological treatment are predominantly concerned
with change. The proponent of each system manifests his concern differently as he sets about to *use himself* and to *use his skills* to facilitate the
process that leads to change with those he is with. In order to do this, the
existential therapist welcomes the tragic as well as the playful sequences in
the life of the patient. This focus is particularly important in the group
therapy session, that segment of the patient's life shared by the therapist
and the other members. It is here too, in the treatment group, where the
existential therapist faces his disillusionments and satisfactions.

This chapter will document what transpires in our lives together to
bring about change, those significant hours in group lived with an unusual
urgency and intensity while seeking a new direction. In our sessions we face
the passage of time and are always aware of our finiteness. Our direction
shifts as we become sensitive to our existence and question the meanings
of life. We heighten our struggle by choosing and dealing with the consequences. As we make choices and assume responsibility for these choices,
we risk. We embrace feelings of joy and sadness. We express love and hate.
It is only under this particular urgency and intensity that fundamental and
radical personality change takes place.

It is our finiteness which, when faced, demands that we seek immediate
solutions so as to change. Time's passage, an ever recurring theme, confronts the members and also the therapist, as they consider their human
condition. Olsen's statement (1, p. 89), which defines the human condition, touches upon the many elements which must be covered in this group
approach:

What man should strive to know is the human condition. And by an understanding of the human condition the existentialists do not mean knowledge of human history, of man's natural and social environment, or of the so-called laws of human behavior. An understanding of the human condition is rather a knowledge (*gained personally*) of certain general traits of human existence which remain the same in all ages: of man's contingency (his chance of being born), particularly (his absolute uniqueness), and freedom (his requirement to choose with *risk*); of man's fundamental aspirations; and of the basic ways in which the individual can relate to the world and to other human beings [all expressions in parentheses are the author's].

Change, then, is based, first, upon the patient's gradual awareness of *his* human condition and, second, upon his painful acceptance of it.

When the desired change envisioned by the patient is similar or even identical to that sought for his patient by the therapist, the therapeutic process is neither shortened nor made easier. It is only the therapist who is able to conceive the necessary investment and the difficult process required in impelling a patient to face his human condition; the long period of treatment, the arduous hours of group struggle, the intense emotional upheaval, and the despair. (I judge it essential and therefore look for patients to say, in the depths of treatment, "I wish that I had never started this damn therapy. I was in better shape before I came and submitted to all of this.")

We seek an alteration in the individual's personality so that his thinking, feeling, and acting become drastically different. Shifts in his dream life and in his fantasies are particularly sought. Illusions about his immortality, which disguise his fear of death, are to be lessened. His acceptance of himself, particularly his animal part (his odors, his feces, his sexual needs, his appetites, and so forth) is required. The patient's capacity to love is to be enhanced. His sexual gratifications are to be released from accompanying guilt while at the same time his intercourse is to become a responsible act.

The patient upon leaving is to have a different philosophy of life, or perhaps while in treatment he is to discover a theme of living which makes his life more worthwhile. In any event he is to become a more authentic person, one who realizes the preciousness of time and one who develops an urge to be free and creative. He is to be able to risk and, what is more important, to be responsible for these risks when taken and the actions that ensue.

During the course of treatment, the "therapist's" significance is to diminish. On leaving, the patient's perception of the therapist is to be much more congruent with who he (the therapist) actually *is*; the therapist's charisma along with his omniscience and omnipotence are to be things of the past. This shift in the patient's view of the therapist is most important, for it reflects an identical change in the departing patient's perceptions of authority figures, heroes, family members, and friends. Upon leaving, therefore, the patient is no longer to attribute to others characteristics and attributes which they do not possess.

Patients who initially rely upon drugs in order to cope with conflict, anxiety, depression, fear, and so forth are to lessen this reliance and, whenever possible at termination, to be free from this need. (I make it a practice not to prescribe any medication.)

Symptoms of whatever kind, including anxiety and depression, are to be markedly lessened and in some instances absent when the patient departs. Symptoms, however, are not attacked directly. Their gradual disappearance, which is a measure of group therapy validity, is dependent upon the entire process of group treatment.

Change is not easy to accomplish. Factors mitigate against upsetting the patient's rigid personality structure: the duration of the emotional illness, its early foundation in a traumatic past, the refusal to accept anxiety as one's lot, the imperative need to continue to gain neurotic satisfaction, the fear of death, and so forth.

Change comes about only in an environment—the group environment, in this instance—which is vastly different from other situations in our culture. The atmosphere of two-hour treatment sessions must rock the patient's status quo; at times he must be thoroughly disturbed, divested of his protective armor, made to face himself, required to make decisions, and encouraged first to investigate and then to accept his dreams and fantasies as indicators of who he is. In sum, all of this is to increase his consciousness, which in turn modifies his behavior (thinking, feeling, and acting).

A disruption in the status quo comes about only in a crisis where the patient's old illusions, self-concepts, and images become suspect, falter, and no longer support the self. The anxious patient frequently asks, "Hugh, what is it that you want me to do? What do you expect of me? I feel so awful!" I answer, "Change. We want you to change so that you will be with us differently." But the dissatisfied member continues, "Why is change good?" I answer, "It is only good if you will risk becoming more of who you are." In group treatment, personality change is never directed toward a restricted common denominator, the "mentally healthy woman or man," or the conflict-free woman or man. Our therapy is to bring out the unique being, confronted by his finiteness. Unamuno is clarifying in this connection because he contends that good (change) is simply "that which contributes to the preservation, perpetuation and enrichment of consciousness" (2, p. 29). This, then, is what the existential group therapist is about. He establishes the conditions for the enhancement of each member's consciousness, directing him to face his *human condition*.

The Existential Group Therapist

Existential group therapy is out of the mainstream of current therapies because this treatment so closely reflects the *lived* philosophy of the therapist. In a Guest Editorial (3, p. 1), I suggested:

> The challenge of existentialism to the psychotherapist is personal. It rests, first, in his search for new understandings about his existence and, second, in his acceptance for himself of these new perspectives. Originally, then, the curious therapist feels the impact of existential tenets. They confront him and demand that he become different.

The therapist, therefore, must be awakened by a nagging concern about his own existence so that he is challenged to become radically different.* A note from a friend describes these changes, apparent to others, that occurred in me.

> Dear Hugh,
>   On an airplane earlier this month by coincidence I sat by and talked with a colleague and (so he said) friend of yours, ———. We had a long talk and he revealed that he and others have noticed to their great concern that you seem very down, unhappy, preoccupied with morbidity and death. You can imagine how dismaying these observations were to me and how unlike the you I knew they sounded. I am concerned for you and would be greatly reassured if you could tell me they misunderstood. Hugh are you okay? . . . (a personal communication).

This personality alteration, however, is just the beginning. Treatment concepts and methods I found no longer to be germane. Dominolike, they too fell, to be replaced by ideas derived from the group members and by a way of treatment with few traditional trappings.

Individuality stands out as the essential characteristic of all existentialists. In varying degrees freedom to choose, human dignity, personal love, and creativity are traits which they extol. These qualities must first be found in the therapist if patients likewise are to discover them in themselves. The existential group therapist ignores contemporary treatment technologies and thus finds himself out of the mainstream of current approaches. Data, quantification, and verification do not appeal to him. He prefers subjectivity to objectivity, connectedness to detachment, and emotionality to intellectuality. He knows that emotion, compassion, kindness,

---

* It is my belief at this time that an existential treatment approach appeals mostly to troubled Jewish and Catholic psychotherapists who are out of phase with their own orthodoxy.

and concern cannot be parceled out by formula. He believes that to attempt to do this would at best be unreal and at worst false.

The subjective position of the existential therapist is noteworthy since it spells out the major difference between him and his colleagues. Similar to Unamuno, this therapist believes that "there is no more concrete, no more tangible person for every one of us than ourselves" (4, p. xv). Unamuno suggests also that one with an existential philosophy is obsessed with his own personality and concerned with his own life for which he exhibits a passion. The therapist, then, with this philosophy starts with his own being, with self-love and a longing for the impossible—immortality.

Should the group therapist's existential therapy be only academic—that is, learned but not actually put into practice—the therapy that results will be similar to any approach based upon intellectual understanding, except that the words used will be different. Should this be the case, the method will be highly analytical where conflict-ridden members under the direction of the would-be conflict-free therapist search for past causes of their present problems. But when the therapist *lives* his philosophical beliefs, the ambience of the entire treatment is altered. This is why in such a setting the new patient sometimes finds the group an enigma; the therapist whom he has known in preparatory sessions seems to be indistinct from the members. Their behaviors seem to blend during highly emotional periods of interaction.

In this atmosphere, where the therapist achieves great emotional intimacy with the members, he *does not* bring his past or present personal history into the group. He refrains from answering questions or offering information about his life outside the session. Through this deliberate frustration, anxiety and conflict are increased and fantasy is enhanced. Patients, in the long run, are to identify their therapist from who he *is* and how he behaves in the group.

The whole of group therapy, when practiced existentially, corrects the therapist's concept of his power and his "infinite" knowledge. When the therapist sees himself as little different from the members (all face the same paradoxes of life together); when he relies upon each group member to help him with the others; and when the therapist, while sitting in the treatment circle, is scrutinized, corrected, interpreted, admired, toyed with, made the butt of jokes, loved, hated, and so forth, all of these elements cause the therapist hopefully to reexamine himself. The result is that his magnified self-image gradually becomes less distorted. The therapist who is able to deny his expertness gains in his therapeutic acumen and, as well, in his treatment ability. No longer must he be clever, overly intellectual, and isolated. This process, therefore, of the therapist's self-inquiry points to a significant difference between the behavior and existential therapist. The behaviorist, throughout the course of treatment and afterward, maintains both an omniscience and an omnipotence while the existentialist, all through treatment for each patient and particularly at its termination, attempts to be only himself and to give up the fiction of his superiority, once and for all.

Each therapist sets the tone for his group—the traditional therapist, and particularly, the behavior therapist by *doing something;* the existential therapist by *being and becoming somebody.* The existential group leader questions his existence, and expresses an unremitting search for the meaning of life and death. More obvious to the members, he brings to the group a dedication to face therapy's (life's) paradoxes, to unravel the group's (life's) problems, and to identify the immediate meaning of being together. I have paraphrased a common example of this in the following:

(*May is an anxious, fed-up, angry woman in her mid-thirties. She is keenly disappointed.*)

MAY: I don't know why I am in this fucking group.

HUGH: Only to be with us.

MAY: I have been depressed for so long. This couldn't be the right group for me.

HUGH: May, what is wrong with simple human beings? Perhaps you need Martians.

MAY: I need more feelings from you and everyone else. I want Hugh to change.

HUGH: Hugh has changed, and you are responsible for it.

MAY: Hugh never does anything!

HUGH: You're right. There is nothing that I can do. I want to be with you. While you are so upset could we have an individual hour?

MAY: It won't do any good. I don't feel that there is any reason to live. I don't think that I can make it. I don't want to live if things don't change.

HUGH: May, you know that *things* won't change but you are changing right now.

MAY: I like you all well enough but you are not helping me.

HUGH: There is no helping you, May. But we are all staying with you through this.

MAY: At least you people respond to me. All that Hugh does is give me some double talk, some mumbo-jumbo. (*What she refers to as mumbo-jumbo is my attempt to confront her with the paradoxes in the group and in life.*)

Deep in the throes of therapy, May is where she should be. Others have been there and still others will follow her. May is neither obstructing her therapy nor that of the others.* May's dedication to the group is similar

---

* The concepts of "resistance" and "therapeutic alliance" do not seem applicable to an existential method.

to mine but, at this time of crisis, perhaps it is greater because of her struggle with life-and-death issues. What the therapist has set out to do has in part been accomplished—May is now committed to self-questioning and finds that this constant dredging up causes her distress. The point is that as May accepts the accompanying anxiety, psychic pain, and despair *as her lot,* she *is* changed and is *changing.*

In order for patients similar to May to remain in the group and to go through this essential and extreme upheaval, the group therapist cannot depend upon a *system* of treatment—to rely upon *any* system at this time with its built-in actions and responses, its role playing, and its artificialities would prevent the members and therapist from an appropriate response to May's emergency. The *real* despair of the patient must be met by an equally *real* care, warmth, responsibility, and feeling. This is doubly so when the therapist refuses to use drugs and attempts to avoid hospitalization of his patients. With May we experienced the tragedy in her life and her decision about suicide. We were close to her in the group and concerned about her well-being during the week. As we face crisis, it is obvious that therapy can neither be a learning experience nor an experience slated to correct a childhood trauma. And although our hours together prepare May for the outside world, this, too, is not our primary goal. With May each of us singly determined the purpose of our meetings. May's purpose seemed apparent—it was to face her human condition and not kill herself.

I have had to put aside the temptation to structure the group according to some system. As a result, new levels and currents in the group process and in the members' response to the group emerged. Practicing group therapy in this manner led to two significant realizations: First, for the patients, the group meeting does not simply resemble life outside, but it *is* life in all of its intensities and nuances. Second, not only is the group meeting an essential part of the patients' lives, but it is an essential part of mine as well. For two hours each week we expend our lives together!

Attitudes Leading to an Existential Therapeutic Position

The existential group therapist, as I have indicated, evolves over a period of time. Along the way he gains assumptions critical to his practice. For me the following five are noteworthy, as they crystallize my point of view: First, there is no institution, not even the therapy group, that does not threaten the person's creativity and freedom. Second, the group, when we consider group therapy, is more significant than the individual. The group includes not only seven or eight members and the therapist, but also their feelings for one another and their ties—the group environment. Third, the patient and the therapist are more alike than unalike. The basic difference between them, probably, is that the therapist has had a more fortunate early environment. Fourth, in treatment the patient's problem that must be resolved is between himself and the therapist. Fifth, anxiety is the therapist's and the patients' lot in life.

The first two assumptions require elaboration. The tenuous nature of creativity and freedom, even in the group, must be the therapist's concern. His treatment method, including his group rules, whether he articulates them or not, requires that the patients comply with them, be serious, and come to terms with the therapist's routines. Who isn't aware of the abrupt change in the patients' playful mood and light banter when the therapist enters and takes his place in the circle? Does the therapist realize, moreover, when playfulness and laughter cease, that creativity is jeopardized and perhaps lost? At the therapist's intrusion the members forgo their spontaneity, sit quietly, and await his cue. They wait expectantly, risk-free, for the "benevolent" authority to do for them or to tell them what to do. Soon, true to the Protestant ethic, they begin to substitute work for play and the session begins. Does this common occurrence enhance or retard therapy?

In a paper I indicate the importance of spontaneous behavior to the state of mental health:

> There are indications that certain activities, moderately practiced, by human beings are required for their mental well-being. Among these might be mentioned dreaming, "letting oneself go," the rough and tumble of children, spontaneous rhythmic movements as in the dance, contact sports, painting, poesy, fantasy, free association of thoughts and emotions, etc. All of these activities have certain characteristics in common, which quite specifically are included in the term nonteleological, i.e., without known future purpose (5, p. 480).

To emphasize and further indicate the central role of play in group therapy, I quote from Winnicott's *Playing and Reality*:

> I can now restate what I am trying to convey. I want to draw attention away from the sequence psychoanalysis, psychotherapy, play material, playing, and to set this up again the other way round. In other words, *it is play that is the universal*, and that belongs to health: playing facilitates growth and therefore health; playing leads into group relationships; playing can be a form of communication in psychotherapy; and lastly, psychoanalysis has been developed as a highly specialized form of playing in the service of communication with oneself and others.
>
> The natural thing is playing, and the highly sophisticated twentieth-century phenomenon is psychoanalysis. It must be of value to the analyst

to be constantly reminded not only of what is owed to Freud but also of what we owe to the natural and universal thing called playing (6. p. 41).

In group treatment the absence of play is a detriment. And similar to the constricted analysand in psychoanalysis who must be encouraged to free associate, the overly serious, intellectual group member must likewise be stimulated to let go and play.

Jason almost never engages in small, personal talk. Occasionally he will steel himself and bring up the subject of masturbation without expressing feelings and even without apparent embarrassment. As he drives to our group he gets increasingly "up-tight." He carefully rehearses what he will talk about. Ready to work, Jason ignores the seeming "trivialities" both in the waiting room and in the group room before the therapist enters. He tries to enter with the therapist. He is preoccupied until someone starts talking and then he becomes very attentive. Rarely interrupting, correcting or even agreeing, he waits for his "slice of the pie," his fifteen minutes that he discreetly takes from the two hours. His purpose for being with us is never in doubt. "I want to get from this group some sense of who I am, some feed-back about what I do to you." However, at the same time he also states, "I don't know. This group doesn't seem to be the right one for me. It's not helping." Jason's participation is always objective. He still doesn't admit to having friends or pals in the group. He doesn't distinguish members by expressing a preference for one or another. He divides our group into Hugh and "the group." During the summer vacation, for example, Jason was unwilling to attend sessions, although our group continued to meet in my absence. "What would we do together? It would not be *serious*. It would be a waste of time without Hugh."

Our first priority was to promote a playful mood in Jason. This, as it turned out, was not difficult. The group room, fitted with floor pillows, required the removal of shoes before entering. Since Jason's very first day we were all aware that Jason's socks, old as well as new, were all neatly patched with squares on the soles and heels. I began to comment upon this certainty, "I could hardly wait for the group session today. I had to see the color of Jason's patches!" Someone else joined in, "I prefer blue. It's such a light, clean color." Soon most of the members added their comments. "How come, Jason, you don't have a single pair of patchless socks?" "Is somebody playing mother?" In the same mood another asked, "Do you buy the patches before or after the socks? How do you know what color patches to put on red socks?" And still another asked, "Jason, why don't you try to match up your patches with the socks so it won't distract us so much. This is quite a trick; you getting all the attention." Soon Jason began to respond. He first defended himself, saying that he was being picked upon. Then someone said, "I have never seen these patches at Brooks Brothers. Where do you pick them up?" Jason, breaking into a laugh, responded, "I buy them when I get Billy's clothes." Everyone was laughing by this time. We all felt very close to Jason and he to us. This simple device, the focusing upon an aspect of Jason's clothing in a harmless, playful manner, making it ridiculous, brought him into the group and allowed him to relax with us. As the therapist's next vacation approached, Jason was the first to suggest that *his* group meet and meet regularly in my absence. He made the arrangements.

The second assumption, which states that the group is more significant than the single patient, must be made clear. In existential group therapy the interacting group is to become the essential agent of change, while the single patient and the therapist are of less significance. Each session, therefore, must be a full, spontaneous, and rewarding experience, not one constricted by a program of games or exercises with some immediate purpose. The therapy meeting, where intense emotional bonds are employed to facilitate personality change, must be different from all others in our culture. This point was clarified for me some years ago when I observed that many of my professional friends and particularly my group therapist colleagues eagerly followed the theater. I found (and I continue to find) most plays to be but poor reenactments of the life dramas experienced by me during arduous treatment hours. Each day I witness and participate in intense expressions of emotion, the taking of risks, the facing of the inevitable by persons intimately connected, all absolutely *real!* From this contrast, the theater and the therapy group, I developed a respect for the therapeutic possibilities inherent in the patients' meeting together. The group as an entity became an effective vehicle where, under proper conditions, hidden conflicts could emerge and crises faced with benefit to all participants. The intactness of the group, therefore, became preeminent in my thinking.

To illustrate the significance with which I view the Gestalt group, it is helpful to consider how I emphasize it when I supervise the student. Because the beginner is almost always trained in individual therapy, he is prejudiced against a group treatment. Only a forceful and direct approach will persuade him to appreciate the group's inherent curative potential. At times, for example, with heavy hand, I exhort students:

1. If there is another form of treatment, another kind of group, another system, drugs, behavior therapy, and so forth which offers a greater chance for personality change than *your group*, the one that you conduct, then by all means send your patients there!

2. A patient enters treatment. He or she is to go through a highly emotional experience—a physical and mental upheaval—and then gradually quiet down. After a long time he or she is to decide to leave, say goodbye, leave, not return to this therapist, and not go elsewhere for treatment.
3. It is our (mine and the group members) responsibility to change each member during the treatment hours.
4. No therapy occurs when the patient is absent.
5. During the first two thirds of treatment the most important engagement in the patient's life is his group meeting.
6. Patients along with the therapist are responsible for what transpires in the group.
7. Every late or absent patient is to be missed. Our response to the absent member is to be elicited immediately.
8. The patient *alone* is to make his choice to leave the group.
9. The patient who chooses to leave the group is not to be referred to another.
10. Tell patients when appropriate, "Don't leave the group. Change *your* group!"

Many issues stem directly from these points of view, all of which bear directly upon the importance of the intact therapy group.

I disagree with a group therapy supervisor who suggests that when a gifted student with an almost perfect recall carefully documents and describes each patient's history, remembers in detail the topics discussed, and remembers each patient's response to the others, that this indicates this student's high degree of competence. When the supervisor allows the student to select those elements to the exclusion of others more difficult to notice and to handle, he (the therapist) emphasizes a mere abstraction of a raw experience but overlooks the raw experience itself; he stresses the outer appearances but ignores the underlying life-and-death struggle.

Persons suffering from severe emotional problems are selected for treatment groups. But patients in groups avoid and camouflage their intrapsychic problems (7). In order, then, for the beginning therapist to elicit this inner turmoil, the supervisor must seek his open and undefended account of what *actually* occurs in his group; in his and the members' innermost thoughts and feelings; in their shifts in mood, in their feelings about self, and in their desperation. In an existential approach, therefore, the therapist's inner consciousness is most significant—his mood at the beginning and end of each session, the presence of personal problems that tend to distract him, and his dreams and fantasies.

Ralph, a thirty-seven-year-old psychiatrist in group supervision, reported in a supervisory session that a recent group meeting which he had conducted was "ideal" and "rewarding." During most of Ralph's discourse I felt that he had overlooked the major issues—that is, finiteness, intercourse, death, and so on. I said, "It seems to me the content of a group session is in some way orchestrated by the therapist. It must be a reflection of who he is and particularly his age, sex and his conflicts." Ralph thought for a minute and said, "Yes, or perhaps it is a denial of 'who he is.' " Ralph went on to tell me that his father was doing badly after a recent coronary and that his mother was barely making it. Ralph concluded by saying, "Yet in my group, we seem to ignore parents and their dying, altogether."

It is by this kind of focus that the weekly supervisory hour and indirectly the group therapy, conducted by the beginning therapist, can be made more fertile. Sensitive support from the supervisor allows the young therapist, during the training session, to express what goes on inside himself, his disillusionments, and so forth, thus insuring that his "being" is not overlooked. When the supervisor's interest includes the latent group content, as well as the manifest, the novice's reverence for his and his patients' existence is enhanced. In addition, the student therapist who had only looked for some tangible reward in that his theory seemed to work as his patients changed will now also find personal satisfaction as new meanings about *his* life emerge.

Much of the treatment environment, then, rests in the confluence of the therapist's and the patients' inner worlds. This interior field must first be discovered and then used to insure an intense and dynamic atmosphere. When this occurs, existential themes surface. For example, when the group meets for the very first time or when a new patient is admitted the therapist, sidestepping the usual rational reassurance, responds by suggesting that the meeting indeed is absurd. "Yes, John, you are right. How can a bunch of real 'weirdos' help one another?" Or again, to the question of specificity of the group, "Hugh, how come you put me into *this* group? There must be a reason." "No, Bob, none that I know. Perhaps in the future there may be a reason. Bob, you will discover the reason or maybe someone else will give you the reason." In time, the difficulties faced by randomly chosen strangers to trust each other and to reveal themselves ceases to be present. This new-found confidence signals the beginning of each person's discovery of the meaning and purpose of his group.

Later in therapy, other elements damaging to the group's integrity are noted. For example, the sensitive leader intervenes when a patient is patently wasting his time in the group and, more important, all of the members' and the therapist's time (all of our lives). (Here finiteness is the theme.) Again, the leader who has become irritated with a member who constantly exaggerates, sets him straight. (Authenticity is the theme.) And again, the frustrated group leader loses patience with the compliant, passive-aggressive member and tells him of his displeasure in no uncertain terms. (Uniqueness of each one is the theme.) Avoiding either a psychological or even a philosophical premise the elements are tackled directly. They are responded to with increasing emotion as their presence retards the group process and indicates duplicitous behavior in those involved. Those who exhibit these behaviors are intolerably egocentric, exploitative, and manipulative. At the heart, then, of the therapist's spontaneous emotional response is his desperation that his and the others' lives are being wasted by the irresponsible member.

Members are to be confronted in the existential group: their conflicts unearthed, their crises welcomed, and their new behaviors expectantly awaited. Advice and counseling are usually not given, but in their stead the group rivets its attention on the conflict-mired member, demanding that he take integrity-building risks. The purpose of these imperatives, that take myriad forms, is to upset the patient's equanimity, to disturb his passivity, and to demand his activity. "Tell your father to go to hell." "Tell your secrets here." "Why not sit differently?" "Don't try any more." "Stay in bed!" "Have intercourse." "Don't have intercourse!" "Get married!" "Get divorced!" "Be rejected, so what." "Stay still for a while." "Have a baby." "Be sick." "Be loved." "Change." "Be still." "Go away by yourself." "Don't lead with your vagina." "Be crazy for a while." "Kill your parents." "Love your parents." "Get a new hairdo." "Take a stand for once." "Tell your mother to shove it." "Take that course." "Get that degree." And so forth. These injunctions reach their mark when the member finds himself on the horns of a dilemma, anxiously debating whether to act or not. The member becomes more whole as a result of this predicament to do or not to do. The consequences which follow his making the choice are his. As individuals in the group become more complete, so too does the group. Interpretations which unify the individual member in turn unify the group, strengthening its integrity.

The therapist realizes that each patient, with little support except that gained from being with him and the other members, must face head on the paradoxical nature of his life. Faced with a difficult conflict, the upset member finds no technical help available. But he does find that the faithful and persevering members steady him and see him through the painful period. Anxiety, then, is a characteristic of the existential group, where assurance and advice are not commodities in large supply.

Robert, a twenty-six-year-old, single teacher, had been coming late to his group sessions. In talking about himself he had over the last month spoken quickly and reassuringly, implying that he was all right now and that his depression had disappeared. During this period, however, the group was not assured. Robert was pressured to face himself and his predicament. For example, members expressed their concern by asking many disturbing questions: "How come you are always late? What is wrong with us that you avoid us?" "When you visit someone, you are always doing the work. Why can't you let them take care of you for a change?" "You don't complain about anything, yet you don't seem any different to me." "No one seems to love you or to care what happens to you. Why don't you tell us about it?" And, "Who do you have besides us? Certainly not your mother and father. They couldn't care less."

The weekend before this session, feeling very alone and discouraged, Robert decided to visit his parents. Since he had been twelve his parents had required that Robert be on his own, independent, while at the same time they (the parents) became even closer, which further excluded Robert. This time he voluntarily went to their house, not waiting to be invited to come to do the usual construction or a paint job for them. He merely wanted to be with them, to sit, to complain about life, his job, his few friends, in short, to express his sadness and depression. His parents would have none of this. Pretending not to understand, they colluded to ignore his newly discovered emotions. Physically, although he was back in his childhood house, he felt stranded, excluded, and left outside on the door step. In our group, because Robert was alarmingly quiet and dejected, we encouraged him to express his feelings. He told us of a massage, with no sexual contact, that he had given a woman friend and she, two days later, had returned. He told us that if he could not touch someone or be touched he would die. The therapist and a member reached over and held him. The therapist, fearing for Robert's life, suggested that he would like to be with Robert before the next group. Robert accepted the suggested hour, much to the relief of all.

This session with Robert allows us to clarify and emphasize the difference between a behaviorist and an existential approach. The behaviorists, who are so certain that ends justify means, give as their treatment goal "the unlearning of learned neurotic symptoms." They tend to discard most of the potential humanity in the treatment meeting by overlooking what the existentialists hold to be essential to life: spontaneous participation, mutual (therapist and patient) responsibility, mutual change, the facing of life's paradoxes together, and the importance of making choices with risk. And again, it seems that the behavior patient must relinquish what the existential patient must zealously guard: his dignity, assertiveness, uniqueness, and freedom to act.

Existential treatment has few of the traditional, carefully-thought-out tactics which tend to objectify the members. But in turn, this puts the therapist's intuition and subjectivity and the use that he makes of them on the line. The therapist's dreams and fantasies, rather than being kept to himself or shared only with *his* analyst, are at times intuitively employed in the group to move through an impasse. Dreams used in this manner cause the therapist anxiety. They become part of the process of treatment and are to be responded to but not formally analyzed.

I felt put upon, overwhelmed, and sucked dry in a seven-hour extended session where female members outnumbered male, six to two, I being one of the two men. Betty made it particularly difficult for all of us. She was furious with me, but at the same time bound to me. She had tested me continuously for two years and more recently she had made repeated attempts to leave the group. Her behavior resulted in seven hours of emotional hell. Diatribes, accusations, angry silences, threats to leave, and menacing gestures to throw ashtrays and glasses left us exhausted. As the hours passed, I had a persistent fantasy which I shared: "The group was helping to bury me. The members were with my family and friends at the cemetery. As soon as the graveside ceremony was complete with my body safely in its resting place, all the group members broke away and went to a nearby bar for a drink. Betty, for the very first time, with her anger gone, was able to be with the others. She joked and played with them." Betty immediately interrupted me. "Hugh, as usual, you are right. This past weekend I enjoyed a fantasy of your dying. I wish you would! Then I could be with the others. Now I can't have you and you won't let me be with them." This clarification helped. My fantasy seemed to air what had been buried all along, that is, a felt prohibition on Betty's part against having and expressing feelings for me because the members would retaliate. Betty, now somewhat assured that this was not so, became closer to the others and less hostile to me.*

The Method of Existential Group Therapy

The method of existential group therapy appears to be a kind of non-system when it is compared to the more formal approaches of Gestalt, behavior, psychoanalysis, and transaction. It requires that the members and therapist, with great urgency and intensity, experience session after session together, as they discuss their ideas, feelings, and concerns about birth, death, and sexuality.

A sense of urgency results when the members face their finiteness. They

---

* This observation parallels Betty's basic dilemma: loyalty to father or to mother and siblings. Through the long period of treatment, Betty's alienation from her father had gradually lessened.

become "driven" as they recount missed opportunities. Intensity, on the other hand, is achieved only when the therapist abandons rigid patient selection practices and fixed rules and techniques, and when he disclaims that he alone knows the purpose of the group therapy.

The patients, especially new members unsupported by expected routines and failing to receive from the leader a clear purpose for the meeting, become anxious. When they take a second and third look at their therapist, the supposed clinical expert,* two things happen: first, the patients begin to see their therapist as a real person; second, they begin to rely more and more upon themselves and their peers.

Anxiety occurs in this setting also because little value is placed upon work and the ubiquitous "working through." The patient who "tries" is encouraged to be with us, without "trying." The academic reporting of past events is discouraged while attention is given dreams, fantasies, unfamiliar feelings, and unreal thoughts which weave in and out of the members' communications. At times the new patient is shocked by a general irreverence toward parents, children, religious figures and beliefs, and even each other. Psychological and philosophical words and phrases are rarely used as patients rely upon their vernacular, punctuated with frequent obscene and blasphemous outbursts (8).

Existential therapy is the antithesis of behavior therapy. An existential approach uses no technique. It neither forces nor commands patients to do anything. Sessions are not planned, and the interaction which occurs is neither known nor even contemplated beforehand. The therapist does not, as in behavior therapy, unfold treatment strategies at specific times.

The therapist, by being emotionally close to the members but without imposing on them rules and routines, takes support away from them— support which they eagerly need and seek early in treatment. Patients, not wanting to face themselves or their human condition, behave angrily, accusing the therapist of deliberately "doing nothing" while being paid handsomely for it. During these interchanges, the patients, particularly the newer ones, find the atmosphere so unusual as to be frightening. Painfully aware that rules and routines are lacking, they search for, but cannot find, roles to play; they examine their repertoires of usual pregroup behavior, but find none suitable for gaining a comfortable niche in the group. *And, although it is difficult, every group patient must go through a period of utter dissatisfaction (not alone with the therapist, but with the group as well). During this time he must question the purpose of the therapist and the group and his presence in the group. He must find out for himself what the purpose of the group is and, what's more, what he is doing spending his time and money with us.*

* The group therapist while *doing* therapy is not the expert. However, when teaching, consulting, administering, and so forth, the same person might be considered an expert in his specialty.

In attempting to set aside all vestiges of form and technique, patterns still do emerge. The existential group relies heavily upon its members' regular attendance at an indefinite series of weekly two-hour meetings. Members must be present and steadfast and, even through upsettingly angry at times, they must develop a deep and prevailing affection for each other. This emotional matrix over a period of time gives the group an unbroken texture and a timeless quality.

I have found only one way to encourage regular attendance. At individual sessions, I sit face to face sharing my footstool with each new patient, experiencing an indefinite number of hours together, initially achieving a first-name basis, then probing, testing, and wearing away our newness. Later, with fewer reservations about each other, we enter the group. We enter the group as a couple, brought together by a common background of weeks or months.

This major move—usually resisted by the patient—is indicated when a hard-to-identify common purpose surfaces in the private sessions: it is a jointly felt obligation to remain together even if it means being with others too.* The individual hours have left the patient inextricably involved in the process of self-inquiry, with the result that he is not only committed to his therapy but to the idea of treatment in general and particularly to the form that I might choose—that is, group, marital, or couple therapy. This mutually trusting state is marked by his realization that I am "on his side," that dreaming and dream discussion are always beneficial, that our being together is more important than what we discuss, and that the immediate moment of treatment is more significant than the end point.

The decision to enter the group, gained in this manner, proves to be preferable to the verbal promise, wrested from new patients by some therapists, to stay in the group for "at least three months." To demand such a pledge, after only one or two meetings, when the patient and therapist are practically unknown to each other, seems unreasonable. Such a promise, should the patient keep it, nullifies his right to self-determination.

As the time for group placement nears, two out of three patients will dream about the group should the therapist request it. These dreams usually reflect this difficult transition period. If intuitively used, they can assist one in determining the proper time for the patient's group entry.

Although Louis thought that it was strange that I would ask him to dream about a group that he had not met or even seen, he went home and on the ensuing nights tried to dream. At our next private hour, he told me he had had two very brief snatches of dreams but not about

---

* The possibility of sharing treatment with others, the idea of "helping" others, the development of a "co-therapeutic urge" is influenced by the referral source which indicated to the patient that I am a group therapist. Another factor is the new patient's curiosity about groups which meet before or after his private hour.

the group. In the first he was accosted by thousands upon thousands of bees, so that his entire body and even his orifices were all black. He awoke in terror. In the second dream he met a women who knew that he was bisexual. He became very frightened and again awoke.

As a result of these dreams, I reconsidered the date selected for Louis' entry into our group. I decided that Louis himself, because of his great anxiety, should have a much greater influence in determining the exact time for his (our) beginning the group experience. I left the date up to him.

The prolonged period of preparation results in the patient's dependent condition, found to be essential at the start of group, but one which must be undone before the patient's eventual departure from the group. At first his strong union to me overshadows his relations to the others and strengthens his resistance to participation. He refers to his fellow members as "they" or "the group." If for a while we continue our individual sessions, he reports his dislike for them and his uneasiness about being in the group. This is to be expected and welcomed for this patient is already experiencing and describing the central tragedy of group therapy, that is, the loss of *his* therapist. A few months before, this then helpless person sought care, warmth, love, and direction to his life. He called and came into treatment only to find that almost immediately—or so it seemed to him—his trusted therapist suggested a group. And as though this misfortune was not bad enough, the therapist completed the rejection when he proposed that the patient share the details of his intimate life with eight or nine "strangers."

The patient, in weathering this abrupt "rejection," takes a major step leading to fundamental personality change. This achievement, common to patients in group therapy, indicates not only that the newly introduced patient is *in the process of change, but also that in fact he has already changed*. In psychoanalysis, on the other hand, the patient's egocentricity is established and supported by a secret, mysterious, and precious association between himself and the analyst. The psychoanalyst and patient must await the latter's termination, two or three years or longer, in order to achieve the degree of personality modification reached by the group patient at the outset of his group experience.

It is also noteworthy that nowhere in the usual course of psychoanalysis is the therapist's and patient's mutual responsibility for their fellow man ever conceived or acted upon as it is done invariably in group psychotherapy. When the patient enters the group he accepts, at least in part, the "co-therapist's" role, and along with the therapist and the other members he becomes "his brother's keeper."

This shift from individual hours to group sessions is not only of major benefit to the patient, but it is also of singular importance to the therapist. Both grow in the rendering of the earlier relationship, the patient by beginning to split from his parents' authority and power, and the therapist by again reducing the residuum of his neurosis.

In the group, the new member, cut off from individual sessions, reevaluates me and questions my importance to him. He joins the older members who at times attack me. Similar to teenagers who examine critically and correct their parents, the members observe and complain about my imperfections and put me in proper perspective. Thus the newcomer's dependency upon the therapist is lessened while he begins to appreciate the worth of the others. Soon he becomes part of the group, discovers the timeless quality of session after session, and finds the experience to be rewarding.

Usually, however, this transition is not smooth. At first many patients vociferously complain. The group for them is a waste of time, pointless, meaningless, and so forth. This challenges the therapist to be both emotional and direct:

Ruth, a forty-year-old woman, after two months in our group, held forth one afternoon, hardly waiting for us to arrange ourselves on our pillows. Articulate and pressured, she berated me for the way that I conducted the group. She complained that I had neglected her since she came into the group, that I had failed to give her a fair share of time and attention, that I failed to help her, and that I disliked her, even hated her. She complained that I was self-centered and thought only of myself. She particularly called to our attention my refusal to help her in her relationship with her children, her husband, and on the job. (I had told her that her continuing detailing and complaining about her children, husband, and job bored me.) She went on to tell us that the group was a waste of money, for which she had a better use. As the group quieted down and while others told her they understood what she was going through, I moved over next to her. Ruth's angry complaint gradually abated. She seemed more content. At the end of the session she said, "I'll see you next time."

Ruth is painfully aware that our broken initial private relationship, established during six months of weekly individual hours, is more difficult for her than for me. The tragedy of separating from me parallels the loss of her father that she simultaneously is experiencing (his authority, control, interest, overprotection, and so on). She assumes that I hate her; otherwise, why would I put her in the group with all of the others? Every complaint that Ruth leveled at me from her perspective is accurate, with the exception that, rather than hate her, I have affection for her. I refrained from analyzing Ruth's behavior because this would put distance between us, diluting our emotions. Instead, I paid attention to Ruth, letting her accusations sink in and disturb me. The members, much more than I, told her repeatedly that they too were in the group. Someone queried, "Why after two months do you still have to get all of the 'goodies' from Hugh?" Another person impatiently reminded Ruth of a statement that she had often made to the effect that no therapist could help her anyway. And still another suggested that if none of her previous therapists had helped her, why didn't she try to get help from her group?

The ambience of the meetings which allow Ruth to change is easier to describe than are the intrapsychic dynamics involved. Faced with my own finiteness, feeling the passage of time, I have told Ruth during many previous sessions that her repetitious complaints about outside persons and situations bore, upset, and irritate me. Some members, however, taking a different tack, supported Ruth by pointing out that the solving of these problems is what the group is for. This did not dissuade me; I continued to let Ruth know that, because of her continuing complaints, I was distracted not only from the other group members, but from myself as well. Ruth, in her long diatribe, presumed either to ignore her fellow members or to allot a few minutes of her time to them, begrudgingly.

Ruth's never-ending litany of problems, repeated week after week, drives me to think only of the other members and of myself. Her accusation that I am self-centered is now more plausible. She must, I feel, stop wasting our lives!

Ruth's cry for help does not fall upon deaf ears—either mine or the group members'. In my case, that of *the group therapist*, I know that we must help her change. Ruth's conflicts are tearing her apart and the questions, then, are: What is she avoiding? What decisions is she failing to make? What is she keeping from us? How do we help her in the process of changing?

Ruth has painfully found that her pregroup behavior does not stand up in the treatment session where she is faced with her human condition. The tactics that she uses as wife, mother, and office worker, with their accompanying fantasies, are ineffectual in the group where she is faced with the fact that her birth was *only* a matter of chance, that she is unique, and that, although alive today, she *is* dying. Change in Ruth is dependent upon her continuing crisis which causes a disruption in her status quo; gradually, old self-concepts are discarded, along with old images, fantasies, and illusions. Ruth in this process is to become more of who she *is*.

In an existential group the therapist refers frequently to patients' sexuality, their chancy birth, and their certain death. For example, take the contingent nature of a member's parents' intercourse, and then the member's birth. The patient is made to face all the uncertainties connected with his birth. When he realizes that he is the result of a chance merging of a single sperm and a single egg, his egocentricities usually are reduced. Members, therefore, are encouraged and at times provoked to fantasize about their parents' intercourse, and the sexual act which produced them. In order to disrupt and involve a detached, self-centered patient, the therapist might vigorously question him in the following way: "Did you know that when your mother and father screwed that they only had you in mind?" Or, again, "Did your mother and father have intercourse for orgasm or to have you?"

Alice, a thirty-five-year-old single woman, became upset when she revealed for the first time that she was conceived just after her father ended a prolonged affair. Her parents had a tremendous blowup, followed by the real or fantasied intercourse that purportedly resulted in Alice's birth. Neither Alice's anxiety nor her tears distracted me. I said, "Alice, you could have been your half sister, not yourself, and then you wouldn't be here with us." She admitted that she had thought of this possibility, and that now she was glad she had shared her worry with us. Then she went on to tell us that a watch that Father intended to give the "other" woman became her mother's, and that her mother still wears it. To this I responded, "Yes, and when your mother dies, it will be yours."

With the other members participating, Alice was confronted with her chance presence in life (and in the group).

In this instance the group was able to start the gradual process of fantasy erosion. Alice was no longer allowed to overlook these indisputable facts as she searched for a more genuine self-esteem. Alice's total self could not be contained in some myth centering around her parent's intercourse. It must be made up of all her experiences since birth; life's meaning must be determined by herself in connection with her family, friends, associates, and peers in the group. Once again Alice's purpose for being with us week after week must be determined by herself alone. Perhaps it is to find out who she actually is.

In the same way that it is said that an entire analysis could be staged around the content of a single dream, so could an existential group therapy run its complete course centering only upon the *fear of death* (or our longing for immortality) and the methods whereby this fear is disguised. This idea is convincingly expressed by Ernest Becker in his excellent book, *Denial of Death* (9), in which he points out that the fear of death has to do with everything about ourselves: our behavior, our goals, our aspirations, our treatment of the world and of our fellow man, and our concepts concerning life after death—everything.

When the subject of death permeates the treatment environment, patients begin to conduct themselves differently; at first they are upset, aware of increased danger and conflict. Soon, however, sensing a kind of freedom, they act with verve and purpose. The death motif can be awakening and challenging and not, as some claim, morbid and nihilistic. Through its use patients are bombarded with the insignificance of their ordinary pursuits. Their usual customs, routines, conventions, and even habits all come under question. Facing the certainty of their death, many persons cease to be victims of a past dominated by their parents' irrational authority. Suddenly, they find that they must act—and with urgency.

Death as an element to be dealt with, faced, and accepted, is present always in the existential group—if it is not ignored by the therapist. Each patient, when he has chosen to leave, gives up the others, including the therapist. (This is symbolic of death and dying.) Should the patient feel, even remotely, that in the future he might need to return, treatment is not over and the termination is ill advised. Any condition other than this total and irrevocable separation, which might be entertained by the member, the other patients, or the therapist, is unacceptable because it fails to face the issue of dying and of death. The therapist who compromises on this issue of separation does a disservice to all of his group patients. It indicates that he still relies too much on his image as the all-powerful and all-knowing therapist.*

Conclusion

A resident recently asked me what is my intention, as a group therapist, when I take my place in the circle at the start of a group session. I thought for a moment and replied, "It is a time and a place for my patients and me to be together and to truly experience ourselves and each other without the usual artificialities of most meetings. A group therapist is called upon to express himself in relation to the others, and to define as well as he can who he is at that moment in the process of living with seven or eight others. He does not, however, reveal *any* of his life outside the group, except for the use of his dreams at times of an impasse. The therapist and patients attempt to be honest by expressing both joy and sadness, and both love and anger." Later, in thinking about this statement, I added the following: "The therapist and patient may not exploit each other. They are in the same boat. Therapist and patients are caught in the same struggle where their finiteness is a certainty. Both the therapist and his patients must extract *meaning* from being together in the *adventure* of therapy."

* Years ago, a weekly leaderless group of group therapists discussed what would happen to our patients if we should die. It was decided that we would make detailed arrangements for their care. We included in each patient's notes the name of the therapist to whom they were to be sent, how often they were to be seen, what their frailties were, and so forth. In retrospect, it seems we were describing our fear of dying by extending our influence, power, and knowledge over patients after our death!

The existential group therapist reviews the raison d'être of psychotherapy and finds the usual objective, "to overcome certain kinds of human suffering," limited. The reason for group treatment might be better stated if it also included "to enhance the means for humans to be together, to communicate, to grow, and to become more authentic." In this process of treatment, the existential therapist finds that suffering does occur as members and therapist face their human condition. Even though patients experience despair at first, as time goes on and therapy continues, despair, depression, and sadness give way to periods of tranquility and joy.

There must be a reordering of our goals, so that they will include not only those to be achieved at the termination of therapy, but those which will give us a fruitful and engaged life. We must develop a new kind of involved, responsible behavior by which we can use our anxiety to help others. Even though life may be absurd, our capacity to live must be enhanced.

References

(1) OLSON, R. G. An Introduction to Existentialism. New York: Dover, 1962.

(2) Unamuno, M. de. Tragic Sense of Life. New York: Dover, 1954.

(3) MULLAN, H. The Psychotherapist Is Shallenged by Existentialism. Pilgrimage, 3, No. 1 (1974), 1–10.

(4) MADARIAGA, S. DE. Introductory Essay. In Unamuno, M. de, Tragic Sense of Life. New York: Dover, 1954.

(5) MULLAN, H. The Nonteleological in Dreams. J. Hillside Hosp., 5, Nos. 3–4 (1956), 480–87.

(6) WINNICOTT, D. W. Playing and Reality. New York: Basic Books, 1971.

(7) MULLAN, H. Conflict Avoidance in Group Psychotherapy. Internat. J. Group Psychotherapy, 3, No. 3 (1953), 243–53.

(8) MULLAN, H., and SANGIULIANO, I. The Therapist's Contribution to the Treatment Process. Springfield, Ill.: Thomas, 1962.

(9) BECKER, E. Denial of Death. New York: Free Press, 1973.

Selected Reading List

Basic References

Ackerman, N. W. Treating the Troubled Family. New York: Basic Books, 1966.

Bach, G. R. Intensive Group Psychotherapy. New York: Ronald Press, 1954.

Bell, N. W., and Vogel, E. F. (eds.). A Modern Introduction to the Family. New York: Free Press, 1960.

Berne, E. Principles of Group Treatment. New York: Oxford University Press, 1966.

Bibliography in Group Psychotherapy, Parts 1, 2. Prepared by American Group Psychotherapy Association, 1790 Broadway, New York City. Also annual survey of group psychotherapy literature in the International Journal of Group Psychotherapy, official journal of the AGPA. There are also periodic surveys in Group Psychotherapy, official journal of the American Society of Group Psychotherapy and Psychodrama. B. Kotkov has prepared "A Bibliography for the Student of Group Therapy" (covering articles up to June 1949), in the Journal of Clinical Psychology, 6, No. 1 (January 1950), 77–91.

Bion, W. R. Experiences in Groups. New York: Basic Books, 1961.

Burton, A. (ed.). Encounter: Theory and Practice of Encounter Groups. San Francisco: Jossey-Bass, 1969.

Cartwright, D., and Zander, A. Group Dynamics, Research and Theory, 2nd ed. Evanston, Ill.: Row, Peterson, 1960.

Durkin, H. E. The Group in Depth. New York: International Universities Press, 1964.

Foulkes, S. H. Therapeutic Group Analysis. New York: International Universities Press, 1965.

Foulkes, S. H. Group Analytic Psychotherapy. London: Gordon and Breach, 1975.

Foulkes, S. H., and Anthony, E. J. Group Psychotherapy. London: Penguin Books, 1957.

Freud, S. Group Psychology and the Analysis of the Ego. London: Hogarth Press, 1927.

FRIEDMAN, A. S. et al. Psychotherapy for the Whole Family. New York: Springer, 1965.

GOSLING, R., MILLER, D. H., TURQUET, P., and WOODHOUSE, D. The Use of Small Groups in Training. London: Codicot Press (in conjunction with Tavistock Institute of Medical Psychology), 1967.

HARRIS, T. I'm O.K.—You're O.K.: A Practical Guide to Transactional Analysis. New York: Harper and Row, 1969.

HOBBS, N. Group-Centered Psychotherapy. In Rogers, C., Client Centered Therapy. Boston: Houghton Mifflin, 1951.

JANOV, A. The Primal Scream. Primal Therapy: The Cure for Neurosis. New York: Putnam, 1970.

JOHNSON, J. J. Group Therapy: A Practical Approach. New York: McGraw-Hill, 1963.

JONES, M. Beyond the Therapeutic Community: Social Learning and Social Psychiatry. New Haven: Yale University Press, 1968.

KAPLAN, H. I., and SADOCK, B. J. (eds.). Comprehensive Group Psychotherapy. Baltimore: William and Wilkins, 1971.

KLAPMAN, J. W. Group Psychotherapy, Theory and Practice. New York: Grune and Stratton, 1946. (2nd ed., 1959).

LOWEN, A. Bio-energetic Group Therapy. Chapter in Ruitenbeek, H. M. (ed.), Group Therapy Today. New York: Atherton Press, 1969.

MORENO, J. L. Who Shall Survive? Foundations of Sociometry, Group Psychotherapy and Sociodrama. New York: Beacon House, 1953.

MULLAN, H. Conflict Avoidance in Group Psychotherapy. Internat. J. Group Psychotherapy, 3, No. 3 (July 1953), 243–53.

MULLAN, H. Transference-countertransference: New Horizons. Internat. J. Group Psychotherapy, 5, No. 2 (April 1955), 169–80.

MULLAN, H. Group Psychotherapy in Private Practice. J. Hillside Hosp., 6, No. 1 (January 1957), 34–42.

PERLS, F. S., HEFFERLINE, R. E., and GOODMAN, P. Gestalt Therapy. New York: Julian Press, 1951.

POLSTER, E., and POLSTER, M. Gestalt Therapy Integrated: Contours of Theory and Practice. New York: Brunner-Mazel, 1973.

POWDERMAKER, F., and FRANK, J. D. Group Psychotherapy. Cambridge, Mass.: Harvard University Press, 1953.

ROSENBAUM, M. The Challenge of Group Psychoanalysis. Psychoanalysis, 1, No. 2 (1952), 42–58.

ROSENBAUM, M. Group Psychotherapy and Psychodrama. Chapter in Wolman, B. B. (ed.), Handbook of Clinical Psychology. New York: McGraw-Hill, 1965.

ROSENBAUM, M., and BERGER, M. (eds.). Group Psychotherapy and Group Function, 2nd ed. New York: Basic Books, 1975.

ROSENBAUM, M., and SNADOWSKY, A. (eds.). Intensive Group Experience. New York: Free Press, 1976.

SATIR, V. Conjoint Family Therapy. Palo Alto, Calif.: Science and Behavior Books, 1964.

SLAVSON, S. R. Analytic Group Psychotherapy with Children, Adolescents and Adults. New York: Columbia University Press, 1950.

SLAVSON, S. R. A Textbook in Analytic Group Psychotherapy. New York: International Universities Press, 1964.

WEISS, F. Group Psychoanalysis. Am. J. Psychoanal., 15, No. 1 (1955), 31–44.

WHITAKER, D. S., and LIEBERMAN, M. A. Psychotherapy Through the Group Process. New York: Atherton Press, 1964.

WOLF, A. The Psychoanalysis of Groups. Am. J. Psychotherapy, 3, No. 4 (October 1949), 525–58; 4, No. 1 (January 1950), 16–50.

WOLF, A., and SCHWARTZ, E. K. Psychoanalysis in Groups. New York: Grune and Stratton, 1962.

YALOM, I. D. The Theory and Practice of Group Psychotherapy, rev. ed. New York: Basic Books, 1975.

General and Theoretical Articles on Group Therapy

ACKERMAN, N. W. Some Theoretical Aspects of Group Therapy. In Moreno, J. L. (ed.), Group Psychotherapy. New York: Beacon House, 1945.

BACK, K. W., and TAYLOR, R. C. Self-Help Groups: Tool or Symbol? J. Applied Beh. Science, 12 (1976), 295–309.

BENNE, K. History of the T-Group in the Laboratory Setting. Chapter in Bradford, L. P., Gibb, J. R., and Benne, K. D. (eds.), T-Group Therapy and Laboratory Method: Innovation in Re-education. New York: Wiley, 1964, pp. 80–135.

BIEBER, T. B. The Emphasis on the Individual in Psychoanalytic Group Therapy. Internat. J. Social Psychiatry (1957), 275.

BURCHARD, E., MICHAELS, J., and KOTKOV, B. Criteria for the Evaluation of Group Therapy. Psychosom. Med., 10, No. 5 (September-October 1948), 257–74.

CARTWRIGHT, D. Review of Saul Scheidlinger's book, Psychoanalysis and Group Behavior. J. Abnorm. & Social Psychol., 48, No. 3 (1953), 157.

DREIKURS, R., and CORSINI, R. J. Twenty Years of Group Psychotherapy: Purposes, Methods and Mechanisms. Am. J. Psychiat., 110 (February 1954), 567–75.

GILDEA, MARGARET. The Social Function and Group Therapy. Mental Hyg., 32, No. 2 (April 1948), 203–16.

GLATZER, H. T. Working Through in Group Psychotherapy. Internat. J. Group Psychotherapy, 19 (1969), 292–306.

HADDEN, S. B. Group Psychotherapy. Am. J. Psychiat., 101 (July 1944), 68–72.

HARTLEY, E. Review of Moreno's book and Cartwright and Zander's book. J. Abnorm. & Social Psychol., 49, No. 3 (July 1954), 478–80.

KLAPMAN, J. W. The Case for Didactic Group Psychotherapy. Dis. Nerv. System, 11, No. 2 (February 1950), 35–41.

KLAPMAN, J. W. Psychoanalytic or Didactic Group Psychotherapy. Psychiat. Quart., 28 (April 1954), 279–86.

LAKIN, M. Some Ethical Issues in Sensitivity Training. Am. Psychologist, 24 (1969), 923–28.

LAZARUS, A. A. Behavior Therapy in Groups. Chapter in Gazda, G. M. (ed.), Basic Approaches to Group Psychotherapy and Group Counseling. Springfield, Ill.: Thomas, 1968, p. 149.

LIEBERMAN, R. A Behavioral Approach to Group Dynamics. Behavior Therapy, 1 (1970), 141–47.

LUCHINS, A. Methods of Studying the Progress and Outcome of a Group Psychotherapy Program. J. Consulting Psychol., 11, No. 4 (July-August 1947), 173–83.

MALAN, D., BALFOUR, F., and HOOD, V. Group Psychotherapy: A Long-Term Follow-Up Study. Arch. Gen. Psychiat., 33 (1976), 1303–1315.

MULLAN, H. Counter-transference in Groups. Am. J. Psychotherapy, 7, No. 4 (October 1953), 680–88.

MULLAN, H. The Group Patient as a Therapist. Psychiat. Quart. Suppl., 31, Part 1 (1957), 91–101.

MULLAN, H. Trends in Group Psychotherapy in the United States. Internat. J. Social Psychiatry, 3, No. 3 (Winter 1957), 224–30.

REDL, F. Psychoanalysis and Group Therapy: A Developmental Point of View. Am. J. Orthopsychiat., 33 (1963), 135.

ROSENBAUM, M. The Family under Attack in an Era of Family Therapy. Chapter in Wolberg, L., and Aronson, M. (eds.), Group Therapy, 1974. New York: Grune and Stratton, 1975.

RUEVENI, U., and SPECK, R. V. Using Encounter Group Techniques in the Treatment of the Social Network of the Schizophrenic. Internat. J. Group Psychotherapy, 19 (1969), 495–500.

SCHEIDLINGER, S. Psychoanalysis and Group Behavior. New York: Norton, 1952, chaps. 4, 6.

SCHEIDLINGER, S. Reply to Cartwright. J. Abnorm. & Social Psychol., 49, No. 3 (1953), 451.

SHASKAN, D. Must Individual and Group Psychotherapy Be Opposed? Am. J. Orthopsychiat., 17, No. 2 (April 1947), 290–92.

SHASKAN, D. Evolution and Trends in Group Psychotherapy. Am. J. Orthopsychiat., 18, No. 3 (July 1948), 447–54.

STOLLER, F. H. Accelerated Interaction—a Time-limited Approach Based on the Brief Intensive Group. Internat. J. Group Psychotherapy, 18 (1968), 220–25.

SYZ, H. Remarks on Group Analysis. Am. J. Psychiat., 8, No. 1 (July 1928), 141–48.

SYZ, H. Therapy within the Group as a Biological Entity. Am. J. Orthopsychiat., 14, No. 4 (October 1944), 603–608.

ZIFERSTEIN, I. Group Psychotherapy in the Soviet Union. Am. J. Psychiat., 129, No. 5 (1972), 595–99.

Dynamics and Process of Group Therapy

ACKERMAN, N. W. Dynamic Patterns in Group Psychotherapy. Psychiatry, 7, No. 4 (November 1944), 341–48.

Bettelheim, B., and Sylvester, E. Therapeutic Influence of the Group on the Individual. J. Orthopsychiat., 17, No. 4 (October 1947), 684–92.

Bion, W. R., and Rickman, J. Intragroup Tensions in Therapy. Lancet, 2 (November 1943), 678–81.

Bowers, M. K., Mullan, H., and Berkowitz, B. Observations on Suicide Occurring during Group Psychotherapy. Am. J. Psychotherapy, 13, No. 1 (January 1959), 93–106.

Corsini, R. J. Towards a Definition of Group Psychotherapy. Mental Hyg., 39 (October 1955), 647–56.

Corsini, R. J., and Rosenberg, B. Mechanisms of Group Psychotherapy. J. Abnorm. & Social Psychol., 51 (November 1955), 406–11.

Grotjahn, M. The Process of Maturation in Group Psychotherapy and in the Group Therapist. Psychiatry, 13, No. 1 (February 1950), 65–67.

Luchins, A. The Role of the Social Field in Psychotherapy. J. Consulting Psychol., 12, No. 8 (November-December 1948), 417–25.

Mullan, H. Status Denial in Group Psychoanalysis. J. Nerv. & Ment. Dis., 122, No. 4 (October 1952), 345–52.

Mullan, H. The Group Analyst's Creative Function. Am. J. Psychotherapy, 9, No. 2 (April 1955), 320–34.

Mullan, H. The Nonteleological in Dreams in Group Psychotherapy. J. Hillside Hosp., 5, Nos. 3, 4 (October 1956), 480–87.

Mullan, H. The Group Psychotherapeutic Experience. Am. J. Psychotherapy, 11, No. 4 (October 1957), 830–38.

Redl, F. Group Emotion and Leadership. Psychiatry, 5 (1942), 573–96.

Rosenthal P. The Death of the Leader in Group Psychotherapy. Am. J. Orthopsychiat., 17, No. 2 (April 1947), 266–77.

Shaskan, D., Flank, R., and Blum, N. H. The Function of the Group. Psychoanalyt. Rev., 36, No. 4 (October 1949), 385–88.

Sternbach, O. The Dynamics of Psychotherapy in a Group. J. Child Psychiat., 1, sec. 1 (1947), 91–112.

Wender, L. The Dynamics of Group Psychotherapy and Its Application. J. Nerv. & Ment. Dis., 84, No. 1 (July 1936), 54–60.

Technique and Organization

Baruch, D. W. Description of a Project in Group Therapy. J. Consulting Psychol., 9, No. 6 (1945), 271–80.

Borgatta, E. F. Some Research Findings on the Validity of Group Psychotherapy as a Diagnostic and Therapeutic Approach. Am. J. Psychiat., 110 (November 1953), 362–65.

Dewar, M. C. The Techniques of Group Therapy. Bull. Menninger Clin., 10, No. 3 (May 1946), 82–84.

Elmore, J. L., and Fowler, D. R. Brief Group Psychotherapy with Unwed Mothers, J. Med. Soc. N. J., 67 (1970), 19–23.

Fried, E. Benefits of Combined Therapy for the Hostile Withdrawn and the

Hostile Dependent Personality. Am. J. Orthopsychiat., 24 (July 1954), 529–37.

Hays, D. S. Problems Involved in Organizing and Operating a Group Therapy Program in the N.Y. State Parole Setting. Psychiat. Quart., 34, No. 4 (October 1960), 623–33.

Kadis, A. Re-experiencing the Family Constellation in Group Psychotherapy. Am. J. Individ. Psychol., 12, No. 1 (1956), 63–68.

Kadis, A. The Alternate Meeting in Group Psychotherapy. Am. J. Psychotherapy, 10 (April 1956), 275–91.

Kraft, I. Child and Adolescent Group Psychotherapy. Chapter in Kaplan, H. I., and Sadock, B. J. (eds.), Comprehensive Group Psychotherapy. Baltimore: William and Wilkins, 1971, pp. 534–65.

Kraus, R. F. The Use of Symbolic Technique in the Group Psychotherapy of Chronic Schizophrenia. Psychiat. Quart., 44 (1970), 143.

Lipschutz, D. M. Combined Individual and Group Psychotherapy. Am. J. Psychotherapy, 11 (April 1957), 336–44.

Locke, N. The Use of Dreams in Group Psychoanalysis. Am. J. Psychotherapy, 11 (January 1957), 98–110.

Malamud, D. I., and Machover, S. Toward Self-Understanding: Group Techniques in Self Confrontation. Springfield, Ill.: Thomas, 1965.

Merry, J. The Relative Roles of Individual Psychotherapy and Group Psychotherapy in the Industrial Neurosis. J. Ment. Sc., 99, No. 415 (April 1953), 301–307.

Merry, J. Excitatory Group Psychotherapy. J. Ment. Sc., 99, No. 416 (July 1953), 513–20.

Mullan, H. The Training of Group Psychotherapists. Am. J. Psychotherapy, 12, No. 3 (July 1958), 495–500.

Neighbor, J. E., Beach, M., Brown, D., Kevin, D., and Visher, J. S. An Approach to the Selection of Patients for Group Psychotherapy. Mental Hyg., 42, No. 2 (April 1958), 234–54.

Ormont, L. R. Acting in and the Therapeutic Contract in Group Psychoanalysis. Internat. J. Group Psychotherapy, 19 (1969), 420–32.

Rosenbaum, M. Co-Therapy. Chapter in Kaplan, H. E., and Sadock, B. J. (eds.), Comprehensive Group Psychotherapy. Baltimore: William and Wilkins, 1971, pp. 501–14.

Rosenbaum, M. Group Psychotherapy with Adolescents. Chapter in Wolman, B. B. (ed.), Manual of Child Psychopathology. New York: McGraw-Hill, 1972, pp. 951–68.

Rosenbaum, M., and Kraft, I. A. Group Psychotherapy with Children. Chapter in Wolman, B. B. (ed.), Manual of Child Psychopathology. New York: McGraw-Hill, 1972, pp. 935-50.

Sadoff, R. L., Resnick, H. L. P., and Peters, J. J. On Changing Group Therapists. Psychiat. Quart. Suppl., 43 (1968), 156–66.

Sands, R. M. Method of Group Therapy for Parents. Social Work, 1 (October 1956), 48–56.

Semrad, E., and Day, M. Group Psychotherapy with Psychotics. Chapter in Rosenbaum, M., and Berger, M. (eds.), Group Psychotherapy and Group Function, rev. ed. New York: Basic Books, 1975.

STOLLER, F. H. Accelerated Interaction—a Time Limited Approach Based on the Brief Intensive Group. Internat. J. Group Psychotherapy, 18 (1968), 220–25.

Group Therapy with Selected Cases

BARBARA, D. A., GOLDART, N., and ORAM, C. Group Psychoanalysis with Adult Stutterers. Am. J. Psychoanal., 21, No. 1 (1961), 40–57.

BARUCH, D. W. Interview Group Therapy with Allergy Patients. In The Practice of Group Therapy. New York: International Universities Press, 1947.

BARUCH, D. W., and MILLER, H. Group and Individual Psychotherapy as an Adjunct in the Treatment of Allergy. J. Consulting Psychol., 10, No. 5 (September-October 1946), 281–84.

BAUER, I., and GUREVITZ, S. Group Therapy with Parents of Schizophrenic Children. Internat. J. Group Psychotherapy, 2, No. 4 (1952), 344–57.

COHEN, R. A. Military Group Psychotherapy. Mental Hyg., 31, No. 1 (January 1947), 94–102.

DEMAREST, E. W., and TEICHER, A. Transference in Group Therapy: Its Use by Co-therapists of Opposite Sexes. Psychiatry, 17 (May 1954), 187–202.

DEUTSCH, A. L., and LIPPMAN, A. Group Psychotherapy for Patients with Psychosomatic Illness. Psychosomatics, 5 (1964), 14–20.

GALLANT, D. M., BISHOP, M. P., and STOY, B. The Value of a "First Contact" Group Intake Session in an Alcoholism Outpatient Clinic: Statistical Confirmation. Psychosomatics, 7 (1966), 349–55.

GELLER, J. J. Current Status of Group Psychotherapy Practices in the State Hospitals for Mental Disease. Group Psychotherapy, 3, Nos. 2, 3 (1950), 231–40.

GORSER, M. P. et al. Group Therapy on an Acute Service. Am. J. Psychiat., 110 (March 1954), 677–80.

HADDEN, S. B. Treatment of Homosexuality by Individual and Group Psychotherapy. Am. J. Psychiat., 114, No. 9 (March 1958), 810–15.

JACOBSON, R. J. Group Psychotherapy in the Elementary School. Psychiat. Quart., 19, No. 1 (January 1945), 3–16.

KONOPKA, G. Therapeutic Group Work with Children. Minneapolis: University of Minnesota Press, 1949.

LANDAU, M. E. Group Psychotherapy with Deaf Retardates. Internat. J. Group Psychotherapy, 18 (1968), 345–51.

LOESER, L., FURST, W., and ROSS, I. S. Group Psychotherapy in Private Practice. Am. J. Psychotherapy, 3, No. 2 (April 1949), 213–33.

McCORKLE, L. Group Therapy in Correctional Institutions. Federal Probation, 6 (1949), 34–38.

MALDANADO-SIERRA, E. D., and TRENT, R. D. The Sibling Relationship in Group Psychotherapy with Puerto Rican Schizophrenics. Am. J. Psychiat., 117, No. 3 (September 1960), 239–44.

MARKOFF, E. L. Synanon in Drug Addiction. Chapter in Masserman, J. H.

(ed.), Curent Psychiatric Therapies. New York: Grune and Stratton, 1969, pp. 261–72.

MATTHIS, J. L. Progressive Phases in the Group Therapy of Exhibitionists. Internat. J. Group Psychotherapy, 20 (1970), 163–71.

MATTHIS, J. L., and COLLINS, M. Mandatory Group Therapy for Exhibitionists. Am. J. Psychiat., 126 (1970), 1162–67.

MULLAN, H. Group Psychotherapy: A Phenomenological Response to the Physical Symptom Complainer. Presented in part at Meeting, Academy of Psychosomatic Medicine, Chicago, Ill., 1957.

MULLAN, H., and SANGIULIANO, I. Group Psychotherapy and the Alcoholic: I. Early Therapeutic Moves. Presented in part at Third World Congress of Psychiatry, Montreal, Canada, June 4–10, 1961. (Write to National Council on Alcoholism, 2 E. 103 St., New York, N.Y.)

MULLAN, H., and SANGIULIANO, I. Group Psychotherapy and the Alcoholic: II. The Phenomenology of Group Interaction with Alcoholics. Presented in part at Fifth International Congress for Psychotherapy, Vienna, Austria, August 21–26, 1961. (Write to National Council on Alcoholism, 2 E. 103 St., New York, N.Y.)

PETERSON, D. M. et al. The Federal Bureau of Prisons Treatment Program for Narcotic Addicts. Federal Probation, 33 (1969), 2, 35–40.

PFEFFER, A. Z., FRIEDLAND, P., and WORTIS, S. B. Group Psychotherapy with Alcoholics. Quart. J. Stud. Alcohol, 10, No. 2 (September 1949), 198–216.

ROSENTHAL, M. S., and BLASE, D. V. Phoenix Houses: Therapeutic Communities for Drug Addicts. Hosp. Community Psychiat., 20 (1969), 26–30.

Ross, M. Community Geriatric Group Therapies. Chapter in Rosenbaum, M., and Berger, M. (eds.), Group Psychotherapy and Group Function, rev. ed. New York: Basic Books, 1975.

Ross, W. D. Group Psychotherapy with Psychotic Patients and Their Relatives. Am. J. Psychiat., 105, No. 5 (November 1948), 383–86.

SINGER, M., and FISCHER, R. Group Psychotherapy of Male Homosexuals by a Male and Female Co-therapy Team. Internat. J. Group Psychotherapy, 17 (1967), 44–52.

SLAVSON, S. R., HULSE, W. C., and STERNBACH, O. Group Therapy in Child Care and Guidance (Report on Various Experiences in Group Therapy, Techniques in Group Therapy). Jewish Social Service Quart., 25, No. 2 (December 1948).

SMITH, C. G. Alcoholics: Their Treatment and Their Wives. Brit. J. Psychiatry, 115 (1969), 1039–42.

SNYDER, B. R., and BERMAN, L. The Use of a Psychoanalytic Group Approach with Teachers at a Junior High School. Am. J. Orthopsychiat., 30, No. 4 (October 1960), 767–79.

STONE, W. N., SCHENGBER, J., and SONGFRIED, F. S. Treatment of a Homosexual Woman in a Mixed Group. Internat. J. Group Psychotherapy, 16 (1966), 425.

VOTH, A. C. Group Therapy with Hospitalized Alcoholics: A Twelve-Year Study. Quart. J. Stud. Alcohol, 24 (1963), 289.

YALOM, I. D. Group Therapy of Incarcerated Sexual Deviants. J. Nerv. & Ment. Dis., 132, No. 2 (February 1961), 158–70.

Family Therapy

ACKERMAN, N. W. Treating the Troubled Family. New York: Basic Books, 1966.

ACKERMAN, N. W. (ed.). Family Therapy in Transition. Boston: Little, Brown, 1970.

BARD, M. Family Intervention Police Teams as a Community Mental Health Resource. J. Criminal Law, Criminal & Police Sc., 60 (1969), 247–50.

BEELS, C. C., and FERBER, A. Family Therapy: A View. Family Process, 8 (1969), 280–333.

BODIN, A. M. Family Therapy Literature: A Brief Guide. Family Process, 8 (1969), 272–79.

ERICKSON, G. D., and HOGAN, T. P. (eds.). Family Therapy: An Introduction to Theory and Technique. Monterey, Calif.: Brooks-Cole, 1972.

FERBER, A., MENDELSOHN, M., and NAPIER, A. (eds.). The Book of Family Therapy. New York: Science House, 1972.

FRAMO, J. L. (ed.). Family Interaction: A Dialogue between Family Researchers and Family Therapists. New York: Springer, 1972.

FRIEDMAN, A. S. et al. Psychotherapy for the Whole Family. New York: Springer, 1965.

HALEY, J., and HOFFMAN, L. Techniques of Family Therapy. New York: Basic Books, 1967.

HANDLON, J. H., and PARLOFF, M. B. The Treatment of Patient and Family as a Group: Is it Group Therapy? Internat. J. Group Psychotherapy, 12 (1962), 132–41.

MACGREGOR, R. et al. Multiple Impact Therapy with Families. New York: McGraw-Hill, 1964.

MINUCHIN, S., MONTALVO, B., GUERNEY, B. C., JR., ROSMAN, B. L. and SHUMER, D. Families of the Slums. New York: Basic Books, 1967.

SAGER, C. J. et al. (eds.). The Black Ghettoized Family: A Laboratory Experience. New York: Grove Press, 1970.

SATIR, V. Conjoint Family Therapy: A Guide to Theory and Technique. Palo Alto, Calif.: Science and Behavior Books, 1964.

ZUK, G. H. Family Therapy during 1964–1970. Psychotherapy: Theory, Research, & Practice, 8 (1971), 90–97.

ZUK, G. H. Family Therapy: A Triadic Based Approach. New York: Behavioral Publications, 1971.

ZUK, G. H., and BOSZORMENYI-NAGY, I. (eds.). Family Therapy and Disturbed Families. Palo Alto, Calif.: Science and Behavior Books, 1967.

Research

BORDIN, E. S. Research Strategies in Psychotherapy. New York: Wiley, 1974.

FRAMO, J. L. (ed.). Family Interaction: A Dialogue between Family Researchers and Family Therapists. New York: Springer, 1972.

HARE, A. P. Handbook of Small Group Research, 2nd ed. New York: Free Press, 1976.

ROSENBAUM, M. Obstacles to Research in Psychotherapy. Psychoanalysis & Psychoanalyt. Rev., 47, No. 1 (Spring 1960), 97–105.

STRUPP, H. H., and BERGIN, A. E. Some Empirical and Conceptual Bases. In Coordinated Research in Psychotherapy: A Critical Review of Issues, Trends, and Evidence. Internat. J. Psychiat., 7, No. 2 (1969), 18–90.

Index